OB in Action:
Cases and Exercises

Sixth Edition

Steven B. Wolff
Marist College

Janet W. Wohlberg
The Rappay Group

HOUGHTON MIFFLIN COMPANY   BOSTON   NEW YORK

Executive Editor: **George Hoffman**
Senior Development Editor: **Susan M. Kahn**
Manufacturing Manager: **Florence Cadran**
Marketing Manager: **Steve Mikels**

Printed in the U.S.A.

ISBN: 0-618-05650-5

123456789-EB-04 03 02 01 00

CONTENTS

PREFACE

In keeping with the philosophy that people achieve high levels of understanding, compliance, and commitment when given the chance to work through ideas or problems from inception to resolution, *OB in Action, Sixth Edition* gives you, the student, a chance to chart the depths of your existing knowledge, combine it with new knowledge, and to put that synthesis into practice in untangling problems and coming up with innovative ideas. This is a hands-on approach; it depends, for its success, on your being willing to get involved, to share your insights and experiences, and to take some risks.

OB in Action also introduces you to the broad range of answers and diversity of opinions that can be generated as valid responses to problems. Most of the cases and exercises in *OB in Action* have a number of possible solutions. This level of complexity and uncertainty, however, is often disconcerting to students whose lives may have been driven by what's in, what's not, and by information presented as absolute.

Many of us reach late adolescence and early adulthood believing that our ways of doing things, or those of our family and friends, are the only "right" ways. There's a right way to talk, a right way to dress, and a right way to behave. Anything that departs from our concept of "right" is wrong—or possibly even "dumb." That may work so long as we never have to go outside the small, tight community of individuals who think as we do. Such communities insulate themselves by marginalizing anyone whose ideas are different.

But the downside of such linear thinking is that there is little opportunity for change and growth. In today's global economy and worldwide communication networks, it is increasingly difficult, if not impossible, to remain aloof and apart from other people and their ideas and still succeed. Many of the problems employees and employers have with one another come from the "we–they" mentality of insular thinking. Lacking a mutual understanding of the motives, traditions, and ways of thinking each uses, employers and employees close off meaningful communication, resulting in an unwillingness to listen carefully to and respect what each believes and says. This may result in employers trying to impose their will on their "ignorant" employees, employees failing to cooperate with their "idiot bosses," and employers taking even harder lines, having concluded that their employees are "too stupid" to follow a few simple orders. Sound familiar? This kind of thinking produces rigid hierarchies, low morale, high turnover, the need to coerce workers to maintain productivity, and other workplace problems.

In *OB in Action*, you will be exposed to real workplace problems, and you will work individually and with your classmates to find solutions that would be acceptable in a wide range of workplace settings. With the increasing diversity of virtually every country's workforce, and the increasing globalization of business, this is not only a desirable approach, but may be a matter of survival.

Before beginning with the cases and exercises, it is important that you be familiar with the methods for learning about behavior in organizations, such as the case method and the various forms of experiential exercises. This information is presented in the "Methodologies and Skills" section, which also gives background on some frequently used techniques for problem solving, writing, active listening, and giving feedback. Next are icebreakers—a number of short exercises to get you started in building the kinds of relationships that will be necessary for group problem solving.

The cases and exercises in *OB in Action* are grouped into five sections. Part I, "Managing Global and Workforce Diversity," represents a new direction in the emphasis of organizational behavior. In the first four editions of *OB in Action*, global and workforce diversity management was relegated to a short section at the back of the book. Today, it is widely recognized that without a clear understanding of the diverse populations that make up our workforce, theories of leadership, motivation, change, and so forth cannot be implemented.

Part II, "Individual Processes in Organizations," deals with motivation, productivity, and job design.

Part III, "Interpersonal Processes in Organizations," will involve you in exploring leadership styles and group dynamics.

Part IV, "Enhancing Individual and Interpersonal Processes," deals with goal setting and performance appraisal and feedback. The relatively new field of peer review, particularly important in increasingly used self-managed groups, is stressed. This part encourages the use of brainstorming as a problem-solving technique.

Part V, "Organizational Processes and Characteristics," puts considerable emphasis on managing change.

A brief appendix on career management gives you the chance to evaluate interests and skills as an important first step in deciding on a career choice.

As in the "real" world, most of the cases and exercises in *OB in Action* have more than one theme. While a case or exercise may have learning about leadership as its central purpose, it will be important not to overlook secondary considerations that may be present, such as managing diversity, teamwork, ethics, sexual harassment, and so forth.

Even though each part of the book is introduced with a brief overview of the relevant topic areas and theories, we strongly recommend that this book be used in conjunction with a text and supportive readings that further develop the theories of the field of organizational behavior. These theories supply a framework within which you can begin to interpret and understand the world of organizational behavior.

Acknowledgments and Dedications

Many people have helped with this book, supplying ideas, useful critiques, and moral support. We want to thank the many managers and business executives who have supplied us with their personal stories but have asked to remain anonymous; the various contributors of ideas, cases, and exercises; Bernice Colt and Patrick Boles for their mentoring of the early editions of this book; Susan Kahn from Houghton Mifflin, who has been patient and supportive; Karen Guessford for her attention to detail and dedication in editing and laying out this book; and our families, friends, and colleagues, who either egged us on or left us alone to do what we had to do!

Finally, we want to acknowledge and dedicate this book to the following:

To Lorraine, whose love and support have made it possible for me to pursue my academic career; to my family and friends, who have cheered me through; and to Jan, who has been my mentor and staunch supporter. I appreciate your devotion to my success.
Thanks. Steve

To Morris who, for the last 25 years, has put up with all of my projects and adventures and has even joined in a few. Here's to the next 25.
Thanks. Jan

ABOUT THE CONTRIBUTORS

Aviat, Inc. is a publisher of materials designed for human resource consultants, trainers, personnel managers, and group facilitators. Located in Ann Arbor, Michigan, Aviat's product topic areas include team building, meeting effectiveness, project management, business process reengineering, workgroup redesign, group process, supervisory skills, quality improvement, and communication. In addition to the participants' materials, they provide facilitator materials and video support.

David B. Balkin received his Ph.D. in industrial relations from the University of Minnesota. Currently he is a professor of management in the College of Business and Administration at the University of Colorado, Boulder.

William S. Brown teaches at the School of Management of Marist College in Poughkeepsie, New York. He has also taught human resources management, organizational behavior, and business ethics at Babson College and the Katz Graduate School of Business at the University of Pittsburgh. In the 1996–1997 academic year, he was selected as Babson College's "Professor of the Year" for teaching excellence. Prior to entering academia, he held world headquarters human resource positions at the Prudential Insurance Company of America, Philip Morris, Inc., and Mutual of New York (MONY). In addition he was director of human resources at Barnard College, Columbia University, and Fairleigh Dickinson University.

Minnette A. Bumpus received her Ph.D. in organizational behavior from the University of South Carolina. She was an assistant professor at the University of Colorado, Boulder, and now teaches management at American University in Washington, D.C.

Ronda Roberts Callister received her Ph.D. from the University of Missouri–Columbia and is an assistant professor in the Department of Management and Human Resources at Utah State University. She has published articles in *Academy of Management Journal*, *Journal of Management*, *Journal of Conflict Resolution*, and others. Her primary research areas include conflict management, expressions of anger in organizations, and mediation in other cultures.

Sandra Deacon Carr holds a Ph.D. from Northeastern University in counseling psychology, an M.Ed. from Boston University in counseling, and a B.A. from Amherst College. She is a faculty member at Boston University's School of Management where she teaches in the undergraduate program. She is also the team consultant for the undergraduate program at Boston University's Center for Team Learning, and has been involved with several executive education programs. As team consultant, she works with faculty who use team learning across the curriculum, provides course support, and consults with student teams on a variety of team-related issues. Her research interests include team and organizational learning, knowledge management, and team dynamics. In addition to her work at Boston University, Deacon is a licensed psychologist and has several years experience in the health-care industry. As a management consultant, she provides leadership and team development training, executive coaching, and team process consultation.

Kyle E. Clough holds an MBA from Clark University in Worcester, Massachusetts.

Roland B. Cousins, professor of business administration at LaGrange College in LaGrange, Georgia, received his DBA from Indiana University and taught for 20 years in the Louisiana State University system before moving to LaGrange to serve as director of international studies. In addition to his research interests in motivation and managerial education, Professor Cousins has been involved in the USL and LaGrange College summer program in southern France.

Gail Gilmore received her BA degree in psychology from Wheaton College, her Ed.M. from Harvard University, and her Ed.D. from Boston University. She is currently assistant director at the Office of Career Services at Harvard University's Faculty of Arts and Sciences. Previously, she taught organizational behavior at the Boston University School of Management, where she also served as associate director of the undergraduate program.

Scott R. Handler received his DVM from Tufts University School of Veterinary Medicine. After four years of small animal private practice in central Massachusetts, he entered industrial veterinary medicine with a national company at which he is responsible for technical support and marketing. Scott holds an MBA at Clark University in Worcester, Massachusetts.

Alice Jacobs has taught organizational behavior at Boston University and Babson College. She is a trainer who is certified in the administration and interpretation of the Myers-Briggs Type Indicator. She holds an MA in sociology from Boston University and an MS in counseling psychology from the University of Arizona.

Ken Koziol is director of publications at the University of San Francisco's Institute for Nonprofit Organization Management.

Nancy Landrum holds an MBA from Idaho State University, MAs in psychology and clinical psychology from Marshall University, and a Ph.D. in business administration from New Mexico State University. She is an assistant professor at Morehead State University in Morehead, KY, where she teaches strategic management. She has ten years of management experience as well as teaching experience at New Mexico State University, Marshall University, and at Lower Brule Tribal Community College. She has spent a significant part of her professional career working as a therapist and an administrator in programs for abused and neglected children.

Judah Bruce Leblang is a writer and sign language interpreter. He is currently conducting educational research at Lesley College. He holds an undergraduate degree in deaf education from the University of Tennessee and an M.Ed. from Northeastern University in student personnel services. Over the last decade he has taught at the Ohio School for the Deaf, has served as a career counselor at Boston University, and has lectured in organizational behavior.

Mia Louik has an active practice as a consultant and trainer for Fortune 500 corporations seeking to improve employee time management, communication, oral presentation, and conflict resolution skills. She has taught organizational behavior at Boston University and currently teaches human management resources and organizational science at the School of Industrial Management at the Worcester Polytechnical Institute.

Mary Sue Love is currently working on her Ph.D. in management at the University of Missouri and teaching at Maryville University. Her research interests include negotiations, organizational behavior, and coworker relationships. She has had papers and articles published in *Business Horizons* and the *Journal of Applied Psychology*.

Wilfred J. Lucas is a vice president/general manager of the dealer management group of Baxter Healthcare Corporation in Deerfield, Illinois. He received his MBA from the Harvard Business School.

Paul Lyons is a professor of management at Frostburg State University of the University System of Maryland, where he teaches human and organizational performance systems, primarily in the university's MBA program. He has master's degrees in management and in counseling, baccalaureate degrees in psychology and human resources management, and holds a Ph.D. from the University of Florida. He has served as director of research, division head, dean of graduate studies, and department chair. In addition, he has experience in sales management and in human resources management with the City of Tampa, Florida, and has served as a consultant and trainer with a variety of businesses and non-profit organizations. His publications include the authoring or co-authoring of four books and more than 80 papers that have appeared in journals and the proceedings of professional conferences. He is an avid bicyclist and maintains a small stable of bicycles.

Bonnie L. McNeely, Ph.D., is an associate professor of management at Murray State University in Murray, Kentucky. She gained managerial experience with the J.C. Penney Co., Inc. Her teaching articles have appeared in *The Journal of Management Education* and *The Organizational Behavior Teaching Review*. In the 1999–2000 academic year, she received the Board of Regents Teaching Excellence Award.

Organizational Dynamics Incorporated (O.D.I.) is a management consulting and training company with offices in Massachusetts and principal cities throughout the United States, England, France, Belgium, Canada, and Australia. Founded in 1970, O.D.I.'s consultants have worked with over 500 corporations and government agencies in the areas of total quality improvement, performance management, and management education and training. O.D.I. president, George H. Labovitz, Ph.D., teaches at Boston University.

Asbjorn Osland is an associate professor of business and MBA program director at George Fox University in Oregon. He holds an MSW from the University of Washington, and an MBA and Ph.D. in organizational behavior from Case Western Reserve University. He has worked in Third World development for 11 years, beginning in the Peace Corps in Colombia and later with Plan International in Latin America and West Africa, where he specialized in founding programs. He worked for Chiquita Brands in Panama as the HR manager subsequent to completing his coursework for his doctorate. In addition, he has published articles in such journals as the *Academy of Management Journal* and the *Journal of Management Inquiry*. His primary focus is case writing, and he has served as the president of the Western Casewriters Association.

Morris Raker received his undergraduate degree from Yale and his JD from Harvard Law School. After more than 30 years in law practice, he left his partnership in the Boston law firm of Sullivan and Worcester to serve as CEO of TreeAge Software, Inc., developer and publisher of decision analysis software. In addition, he advises companies and trial counsel in applying decision analysis both to reach better settlements and to reduce the transaction costs of litigation. He has lectured on this subject at Harvard, MIT, Stanford, Boston University, and Tufts.

Fred P. Roe graduated from Boston University with degrees in advertising and finance. During his student years, he worked evenings and weekends as a hospital secretary and summers on a ferry where, he says, "I rose over the years from deck hand to purser." He is an officer with BancBoston Mortgage Corporation in Jacksonville, Florida.

Joan Bond Sax has an undergraduate degree in French from Swarthmore College, masters and doctoral degrees in Romance languages and literature from Harvard, and an MBA from Boston University. She has worked as a translator and has taught courses in languages at Harvard and Northwestern, organizational behavior at Boston University, and negotiation at American University in Armenia. Currently she is a translator and editor and heads the translation department at the French Library in Boston, Massachusetts.

Victoria Selden received her BA from Principia College and her MBA from Boston University. She is special projects manager for DMJM, an architectural engineering firm based in Los Angeles.

Shannon Gustafson Shoul is a communications advisor at PacifiCorp, a utility based in Portland, Oregon, that serves 1.5 million customers with electricity and related services. She has held positions from intern to acting director in media, government, and nonprofit arenas. Shoul holds a bachelor's degree in organizational communication from the University of Portland where she received the university's thesis award. In 1999, she accepted the Associated Church Press's "Best in Class" award for her work editing "Voice," a newsletter on ecumenism. Her skills are also utilized through service on the Community and Public Relations Committee of the local Red Cross chapter and the Citizen Budget Advisory Committee for Multnomah County.

Matthew C. Shull is developmental editor in finance at The Dryden Press, a division of Harcourt Brace College Publishers, in Fort Worth, Texas. He received his undergraduate degree in finance from Boston University's School of Management and an MBA in international business and MIS at the University of Texas, Dallas.

Tracy L. Tuten is an assistant professor of business at Randolph-Macon College. She received her Ph.D. in management from Virginia Commonwealth University. Her publications appear in the *International Journal of Service Industry Management* and *Advances in Services Marketing and Management*, as well as in many national and regional conference proceedings. Her primary research interests focus on employee responses to problems in their organizations.

Mary Anne Watson is an associate professor of management at the University of Tampa. Since joining the University of Tampa, she has been involved in the internationalization efforts of the university and has served as coordinator of the international business major since its inception in 1991. Her professional activities are focused in the development of student-centered teaching materials such as cases and experiential exercises.

Scott Weighart has undergraduate and MBA degrees from Boston University. He is on the cooperative education faculty at Northeastern University where he works with employers and students "to ensure that experiential learning is maximized." He is the author of *Dressing for the Salad Days*, published in 1988 by Mosaic Publishing, and he is currently completing a humorous book about baseball cards and the 1970s. He has taught organizational behavior at Boston University and Northeastern University and was co-author of the 3rd edition of *OB in Action*.

Maida Broadbent Williams, who serves as a facilitator to several elementary school site councils in Boston, has a BA in psychology from San Diego State University and an M.Ed. from Boston College. For almost two decades, she has worked on the planning, development, and coordination of school/university partnership programs between Boston College and a number of metropolitan school systems, including Boston.

ABOUT THE AUTHORS

Steven B. Wolff has over fifteen years of experience as an engineer in the high tech industry, seven years of which were spent as a manager, both project and line. He has conducted research in performance management of self-managed teams, peer reviews, organizational learning, and public-private partnerships for education. He has also provided training and consultation to a number of Boston School Site Councils. He holds degrees in electrical engineering from the Stevens Institute of Technology and Northeastern University, an MBA from Babson College, and a DBA in organizational behavior from Boston University. He is currently an assistant professor of management at the School of Management at Marist College in Poughkeepsie, New York.

Janet W. Wohlberg taught organizational behavior, mass communication, and andragogy at Boston University's Schools of Management and Mass Communication for more than a decade. She is currently vice president for public relations and advertising for TreeAge Software, Inc., in Williamstown, Massachusetts, and president of The Rappay Group, designers and sellers of corporate and organizational training materials. Her central area of research is in the uses and abuses of power in power-imbalanced relationships. Her recent publications have appeared in *The Bulletin of the Menninger Clinic*, *Psychoanalytic Inquiry*, *Psychiatric Services*, *The Clinical Supervisor*, and *The Journal of Sex Education and Therapy*.

METHODOLOGIES AND SKILLS

Using Cases in the Study of Organizational Behavior

Increasingly, managers are finding that their biggest problems are not balancing budgets or erecting buildings: the most complicated, the most difficult, the most time-consuming problems they face are people problems.

Every individual brings to the workplace far too many variables, many of which are never seen or only glimpsed, to allow managers to indulge in neat analyses and pat answers to these problems. Placing complex individuals in groups, setting them tasks and deadlines, and asking them to compromise much of their individuality for the sake of cooperative efforts multiplies infinitely the number of variables with which a manager must cope. The human urge to package vast numbers of variables into tidy bundles can be overwhelming. Unfortunately, doing so can also lead to answers that don't respond to the questions and problems raised.

Case studies offer you a realistic approach to the inexact science of understanding and dealing with people problems in organizational settings. Cases are microscopic cross sections of the real world in which the possibilities are seemingly endless. In analyzing cases, you will work with incomplete information from which you must extrapolate, generalize, and find meaningful answers. Because of the number of possibilities, missing information about people, and secret agendas, cases may often seem frustrating and irksome. However, in work as in life, we must make many decisions, some more critical than others, and probably never do we have all of the information needed with which to reach perfect conclusions. Instead, we make educated guesses, weigh the benefits and potential problems, and arrive, we hope, at those decisions that will bring the best possible outcomes. Cases give practice in doing just that.

What Is a Case?

A case is a story—usually a true story, but not always—that illustrates an idea, presents a problem, offers a dilemma, and leaves you hanging, wondering what to do next. Some cases give you all of the events that lead to crossroads and then ask you to decide which path to take and to project what lies ahead on each road. Other cases tell you what was done and ask you to analyze what went wrong and what could have been done better.

Cases are tightly written. Virtually every word has a meaning, a point that should be considered by those seeking to analyze the facts and issues presented. Rarely may information presented in a case be disregarded.

Case Analysis

Case analysis requires reading a case several times—with an open mind to a virtually unlimited number of possible interpretations and outcomes—and leaving enough time in between readings to consider the issues and identify the problems.[1] Often on first reading, you may identify as a problem an event or relationship that may be merely a symptom. Subsequent readings are generally helpful in sorting the symptoms from the problems, but you should not feel threatened by the possibility of confusion. The problems may be well camouflaged. For this reason, preparing a case with a case group of three to seven members may be helpful as a way to elicit the greatest number of ideas about what is really at issue.

There are many possible ways to approach case analysis, including the fairly straightforward method outlined below. Items 1 and 2 suggest ways to think about cases. They will help you put yourself into the role of a case character (or at least in the role of a fly on the wall), identify with the events taking place, and in other ways involve yourself in the case. You will find them useful in oral-case presentation, but in your ultimate write-up of the case, you should not try to describe the characters in the ways you have imagined them. This technique is meant only to give you a framework for thinking about the case.

1. *Do a stakeholder analysis.* A stakeholder is any individual or group that has an interest in your company or the ability to affect it. For example, if you work for a manufacturing company, your stakeholders include, but are not limited to, your CEO, your employees, your customers, your suppliers, your stockholders, your directors, the people who live in the area of your plant, and so forth. You may also count among your stakeholders such people as environmentalists, landlords, bankers, political groups, and a wide range of special interest groups.

   Begin by making a list of those stakeholders you believe are pertinent to the case. Be careful not to overlook the bit players, such as the secretary who is only referred to briefly and the people who are described in groups, such as the accounting team, the interdepartmental bowling league, or three friends who often get together next to the water cooler. List everything you know about each stakeholder, and then describe your mental image of each. Don't be afraid to generalize; sometimes putting faces and bodies on the case characters can help you analyze what is going on.

   Look for clues, and try to flesh out each stakeholder on the basis of those clues. Since it is likely that you will be making decisions that stem from assumptions about the characters involved, make a concerted effort to bring those assumptions into your conscious awareness. Don't just sketch the characters; draw them in full color and detail. Then, test out your perceptions of the characters against those of your study mates.

2. *Develop a chronology of events.* In this step, you can use a time-line or other method to list the events in the chronological order in which they occurred. You will quickly note that cases often do not follow a chronological order, so it is up to you to tease out the events and order them. Some events may seem minor because of the way they are presented. Don't let this fool you; they can be significant and even critical turning points, and they should be listed in your chronology.

---

1. See "Identifying and Solving Problems" later in this section.

3. *Identify and list what you believe are the basic issues.* Note especially those problems, events, acts, values, and attitudes about which decisions need to be made; for example, do government restrictions preclude certain courses of action and, if so, what can you do? Is there a mismatch of leadership styles to employee needs? Does some group of workers have norms that differ from those of the prevailing organizational culture? Using your list, arrange the items in order of priority and strength and find the relationships among them.

   In addition, draw a diagram that depicts the flow of communication in the organization. Some cases include organizational charts, but communication doesn't necessarily follow the prescribed patterns. Finding out who talks to whom can be significant in identifying both problems and solutions.

4. *List as many positions as possible that a reasonable person might take in solving the case.* The mistake most case analyzers make is to assume that there is one, and only one, reasonable solution. In fact, part of the intrigue of case discussion is finding just how many possibilities there are for solving any single problem—many workable, usually more than one with excellent results.

5. *Play out some of the possibilities.* "If I do this, will someone else do that? And if so, what will happen next?" Again, write out your results, or depict them graphically.

6. *Make a recommendation.* What do you consider the best possible solution to be? Why? This step generally presents the biggest trap. When you make a recommendation, it is far too easy to begin to believe in the singularity of your approach. For the case method to work, you must stay open to the possibilities; you must stay flexible and be willing to listen to what others have to say. Good case analysis often depends on synergy, that process in which a group of people working together can accomplish more than the same number of people working by themselves so, unless instructed otherwise, go ahead and discuss the case with your friends, family, anyone who will listen, and get everyone's input.

   You may find yourself feeling slightly inadequate after your first case discussion. "Why didn't I think of that?" is the usual question, as your peers seem to be making observations that never even occurred to you. Instead of dwelling on this question, learn to respect the power of the group, the importance of your role in the group in stimulating the ideas of others, and the role of the group in stimulating you.

Case Discussion

The presentation of a case in a classroom setting is an opportunity for peer discussion. To avoid having their opinions taken as fact, instructors act merely as facilitators, selecting the presenters and occasionally redirecting or refocusing the discussion.

Generally, the facilitator will begin the case presentation by asking one or more members of the class to state the problems and present the list of pertinent stakeholders. Sometimes writing the names of the stakeholders on a chalkboard, along with a brief description of each, can be enough to get the discussion going. Examining the differing interpretations of each stakeholder's persona most often leads into the necessary analysis of the case events. If not, move on to a presentation of the chronology, and so forth through the steps outlined above.

Case analysis can be a satisfying learning experience if you are well prepared and willing to participate. The field of organizational behavior, in which the variables seem infinite, lends itself particularly well to this method.

Writing the Case Analysis

In many courses you will be required to do a written case analysis. A thorough written analysis should include, but not necessarily be limited to, the following:

1. A clear statement of the problem(s)

2. A thorough analysis of the pertinent stakeholders and of the issues and the ways these combine to create the problem(s)

3. One or more suggested solutions, with clear explanations of the strengths and weaknesses of each solution and with each solution supported by one or more of the theories of the science of organizational behavior

4. An explanation of how the solution(s) can be implemented (by whom, etc.) and the problems that might be encountered in implementation

Occasionally, students allow themselves flights of fantasy into what "might be," adding events and other material to cases to somehow force-fit them into a selected theory. Unless such material can be solidly and logically derived from the existing case material, it has no place in a written case analysis. Even if such material is reasonably derived, it should be presented as tentative.

The quality of a written case analysis generally is judged far less on the solution(s) presented than on how well the case analyzer has supported his or her arguments with the use of case material, theory, and solid critical thinking. No statement should be included in a case analysis, whether written or oral, that is not thoroughly supportable and supported.

Writing for a Business Audience*

The best rule for business writing is KISS (Keep It Simple and Short). What does this mean?

1. Get to the point right away.

- Get your point out in the first sentence with the simplest wording possible. (My first draft of this paper had "most straightforward" instead of "simplest.")

- Next, give your detailed explanation of how you got there. Students often tend to write as if they were telling a story, preparing the ground with a long introduction and then getting to the main point about halfway through the paper. Remember that time is money in business, and it is unlikely that your boss will be willing or able to waste time

* Copyright 1994 by Joan Bond Sax, Ph.D. Used with permission.

wading through memos looking for your main point. Chances are, your boss will read your first sentence or two to get your recommendations. Later, he or she can read your explanation if further clarification is needed.

2. Use the simplest words you can.

- One way to get the most information onto a page is to be a conservationist where words and letters are concerned. "In view of the fact that" can be expressed better and faster as "because"; "eliminate the possibility of" really means "prevent"; and "at this point in time" means "then."

- Avoid redundant expressions such as "absolute guarantees"; a guarantee is a guarantee. By definition it is "absolute." Likewise, the following expressions have no need of the words in parentheses: estimated (roughly) at, (advance) planning, (already) existing, (as) for example, task (at hand), (as to) whether, (as) yet, (at a) later (date), collaborate (together), (current) trend, written (down), cancel (out), (completely) destroyed, consensus (of opinion), (first) began, first (of all), (ir)regardless, (major) breakthrough, (hard) facts, had done (previously), refer (back), (at a time) when, at (the) present (time), and (specific) example.

- Use adjectives and adverbs sparingly, asking yourself if they add any new and/or needed information. Avoid colloquial or "street" language clichés.

3. Check your vocabulary and spelling.

- Make sure you are using the word you want. For example, "affect" is a verb meaning to influence, while "effect" is usually a noun meaning outcome.

- In this age of spell-checking computer programs, there is no excuse for misspelled words. (I had three spelling errors on this page before I ran the spell check.) If you don't have a computer, be sure to have a dictionary or even a quick reference book such as *The Word Book III* (Boston: Houghton Mifflin). Use the dictionary or spell check to avoid irritating your reader (especially if that reader is your boss or professor).

4. Keep your sentence structure simple, and punctuate correctly.

- Try reading what you have written aloud to yourself or to a friend to see if he or she (and you) can understand it.

- Use commas wherever you would pause in reading the sentence, as you would have reading this sentence.

- Use commas to separate independent clauses of a sentence connected by conjunctions such as and, but, or, nor, and for.

- Commas also separate items of a list, such as the list of the conjunctions in the last sentence.

- With colons the rule is: don't use them unless you really want to announce that an important list, explanation, or example follows.

- Semicolons should be used only when two thoughts are closely tied together: "She makes all the money; he spends it." More often, semicolons should be replaced by periods.

5. Read a business publication regularly.

- One way to write better is to read more. *The Wall Street Journal* provides a particularly useful model of solid business writing.

- Reading the business section of any major newspaper, or a publication such as *Business Week*, also helps.

In addition to a dictionary and a thesaurus, the following books are useful:

The Beacon Handbook, Robert Perrin (Boston: Houghton Mifflin, 1994). Includes a special chapter with advice for students who speak English as a second language.

The New Well-Tempered Sentence, Karen E. Gordon (Boston: Houghton Mifflin, 1994). A quick and serious reference on punctuation and grammar, written with a touch of humor.

The Word Book III (Boston: Houghton Mifflin, updated regularly). A handy source for spelling and hyphenating the 40,000 most commonly used words in the English language. Includes a special "sound map" feature for poor spellers.

Using Experiential Exercises in the Study of Organizational Behavior

Experiential exercises offer ways to test out and get feedback on behavior—actions and reactions—in group situations. Management trainers have long used experiential methods for teaching personal skills, and these methods have become a standard teaching technique at many business schools. Because experiential exercises are simulations and not actual situations in which behaving in an unacceptable manner can negatively impact an individual's career path, they are reasonably safe. In fact, experiential exercises work best when participants use them to test behaviors that they might be too threatened to use in settings "where it counts."

More traditional teaching methods are what I call "filling station style." Used successfully in certain disciplines, these methods often start with the assumption that students arrive with empty tanks and that it is the instructor's role to open the cap and pour in the knowledge. According to the tenets of this methodology, students are passive recipients, and rarely do they need to interact with one another.

The responsibility for learning from experiential exercises, however, belongs to the students themselves. Exercise groups consist of two or more participants; the most common groups range in size from five to seven. The role of the instructor is to set a tone that encourages participation, interaction, and risk taking; to introduce the exercise and lead and focus the debriefing discussion; and otherwise to remain essentially neutral and on the periphery. With experiential methods, the assumption is that you, the student, have a wealth of material from which to draw, particularly when it comes to the study of human behavior. By probing this material, comparing it to the experiences and observations of others, and by being willing to accept feedback, you build on and enrich your existing base of knowledge and understanding.

6

Experiential exercises come in a number of forms. For the purposes of this book, we will look at six: role plays, decision-making and consensus-building activities, fish bowls, round robin interviews, identity group sorting, and self-assessment tools.

Role Plays

Role plays are among the most common of the experiential exercises. The exercises are structured for anywhere from two to seven participants, although occasionally they involve larger numbers. Each participant is given a description of the person he or she is to play. If role plays are to work, participants must take their roles seriously, thinking through just how, based on the description, the character to be played would behave. The purpose is to give you a chance to experience what it might be like to be in another person's situation. For example, you might be asked to take the role of a disgruntled employee who feels he or she is not being treated fairly, while one of your classmates might be asked to act the role of a manager who has to deal with you. Since good management skills often involve being able to assess how another person is feeling, role play will give you an opportunity to do so.

It is not unusual to feel awkward, or even a little silly, the first time you are asked to play a role. Having had some previous acting experience might help but, barring that, simply taking your role seriously should ensure that you play it convincingly. If you are willing to jump in, role plays can be fun as well as meaningful.

Decision-Making and Consensus-Building Activities

Many decisions, but by no means all, are best made to the mutual satisfaction of those who will need to implement the results. Decision making must be done through open discussion, since imposing a decision from the outside generally means less commitment and less compliance by those affected by the decision. Similarly, if a group resolves a problem by voting, the group members become either winners or losers; this can polarize the group and severely undermine future cooperation. Workers tend to be less motivated to carry out a decision in which they feel they had no say, and clearly this has negative implications for productivity.

Since the emphasis in business is increasingly on team approaches to problem solving, decision-making and consensus-building activities will give you a chance to refine the skills necessary for staying open to diverse viewpoints and reaching creative outcomes. These activities present a problem and require you to work with one or more of your classmates to reach a mutually acceptable resolution.

Initially you may find it difficult to let go of your own perception of just how a problem should be solved. It's not unusual to think that your answer is the best. Listening carefully to your group mates, however, will allow you to further understand the complex dimensions that a problem presents. Here the group serves to bring to light far more facets of a problem than most of us are able to recognize alone.

Fish Bowls

Fish bowls are highly structured exercises that are often used in the social sciences to explore feelings and reactions to situations. A small group of people, usually not more than five, is asked to sit in the middle of the room and discuss a topic, while everyone else sits around the outside. Those in the middle are the "fish." Fish bowls generally start with a statement such as, "Tell us about . . ."; the fish then describe the particular event, person, or thing being explored. In this book we ask students, "Tell us about a situation in which you think you had a bad leader." Other topics may include, but not be limited to, times you felt different, times you felt left out, times you think you were effective, and so forth.

It is the job of the rest of the participants, those on the outside of the fish bowl, to listen to the discussion of the fish and to try to isolate recurring and prevalent themes. Those outside of the fish bowl may not speak until the fish have completed their conversation. At that point, those outside of the fish bowl are asked to report on what stood out for them in the conversation. During the reports, fish are required to listen but may not speak.

Fish bowls tend to spark memories and reactions in those who listen carefully to the fish. They also afford opportunities to practice skills in giving and getting feedback.

Round Robin Interviews

Round robin interviews are data-gathering and consolidation experiences. A number of questions (about one per every seven to ten people participating) focusing on a particular topic area are prepared in advance and assigned to the participants. For example, if the topic is motivation, the questions might include "What role does your salary play in your life?" "How do you feel about working overtime?" "How would it impact the quality of your work to have an office in the basement?" and so forth.

Each question is identified by number, color, or some sort of visible code that participants display. Participants are then asked to conduct interviews with other participants who have a different question. In other words, if you have question one, you could interview someone with question two or three, but not someone with question one. The person you interview would, in turn, interview you with his or her assigned question. Interviews last about five to ten minutes each, with length and number of interviews depending upon available time.

At the end of the interviewing, all those with the same questions meet together to share their results and consolidate their findings into a report that is then made to the rest of the class.

These exercises help to bring out differences and similarities in responses to topical issues. They are also useful as ice breakers.

Identity Group Sorting

This type of exercise asks people to join others who identify themselves in similar ways. Categories of identification may be generated by the class or decided on in advance by the instructor. For example, if a topic is leadership, participants may be asked to sort themselves into democratic leaders, autocratic leaders, country club leaders, Theory X leaders, Theory Y leaders, and so forth. Each identity group then meets to explore such concerns as what it is like to belong to that group, how they perceive themselves and why, and how they believe others perceive them. Groups then report their findings to the rest of the class. Feedback from those outside of the group is especially important in this type of exercise, particularly since we know that the way we perceive ourselves is not necessarily the way others perceive us.

One interesting and frequently used technique with identity group sorting is to ask the group members to depict themselves graphically, using a large sheet of paper and marking pens. Each group then displays its drawing to the rest of the class, explaining the symbols used and the reasons for them.

Self-Assessment Tools

We are probably all pretty familiar with self-assessment tests: they're the ones that give us the correct answers and some feedback on why our answers are right, wrong, or have some particular meaning. We see them in magazines and newspapers fairly frequently, with the correct answers supplied by an expert. They're usually fun to do, but they should be seen only as giving limited insights and serving as jumping-off points for further self-exploration. Information from self-assessment tools is probably most useful when shared and explored with others.

Active Listening

In the workplace, it's not unusual for information, as it is passed along, from even a single sender (the person speaking) to a single receiver (the person listening), to become distorted or changed, resulting in errors, missed opportunities, frustration, and anger.

Occasional innocent misunderstandings inevitably occur, and it is virtually impossible to ensure that everyone will always receive information in exactly the spirit and meaning in which it is sent. "Active listening" can clear much of the distortion caused by "static," and help keep such misunderstandings to a minimum. "Active listening" can also help uncover new ideas and possibilities.

"Static" or "noise" is anything that distorts the information between its point of origin—the sender—and its ultimate destination—the receiver. Some theorists call these "barriers to communication." Static that is not cleared may eventually result in a general undermining of relationships and a reduction in participation.

Static may be either internal or external. Internal static may include, but is not limited to: lack of respect between the sender and the receiver, lack of a common language, and preoccupation by one of the parties with something other than the immediate message, such as time pressures and anxiety. External static generally refers to environmental factors such as a fire engine going by with screaming sirens or a room that's too hot. As the name suggests, "active listening" involves work. It is also a cooperative process. A receiver of information must regularly ask for clarification of what she or he is hearing, and both the sender and the receiver must give feedback using questions and restatements. In other words, both sender and receiver are in this together, and both must work to clear the static by actively listening to one another.

When listening actively, you should:

- Avoid distractions such as the telephone, radio or television, loud music, visitors or eating.

- Sit or stand face to face, with your body turned squarely to the other person, but avoid entering the other person's physical space. Be aware that touch can send either positive or negative messages, and use it judiciously.

- Maintain direct eye contact. This may vary from culture to culture but it is appropriate for most North Americans.

- Avoid interrupting or talking at the same time as the other person.

- Keep your voice modulated to a conversational tone and pace.

- Frequently reframe in your own words what you believe you have heard, for example, "So you are saying that we should both work together on this?" and check that you have heard accurately by asking, "Is that correct?"

- Listen with an open mind and without arguing. Avoid becoming defensive or accusing.

- Use validating verbal ("I see") or body language (nod head or lean forward) to signal that you are paying attention, but avoid signals that suggest you agree when you do not.

Learning From Experience Through Reflection*

In today's fast-changing environment the ability to learn from one's experiences is a critical skill. Learning from experience is often thought to involve a four-step cycle: experiencing, reflecting, developing new understanding, and putting that understanding into action. It is the reflection step of learning from experience that we focus on here.

* Adapted from *The Reflection Handbook: Guidelines for Leveraging Learning from Challenging Work Experiences*, copyright 1996 by Marilyn Daudelin, Ed.D. Used with permission.

When we engage in reflection, we take an experience from the outside world, bring it inside our mind, turn it over, and make connections to other experiences. Reflection is the process of stepping back from an experience to ponder, carefully and persistently, its meaning to the self through the development of inferences.

Reflection progresses through four stages. The first stage is articulation of the problem, often an insight in itself. There is often a vague sense of discomfort or perplexity that indicates the need to examine an experience more closely. The second stage is analysis of the problem, which consists of a search for possibilities. You are looking for possible cause and effect links. It may involve asking and answering a series of questions about the situation. The third stage is formulation and testing of a theory. It begins with the generation of a hypothesis. The fourth stage is action. It involves articulation of a new way of acting.

One technique for increasing the learning power of reflection is posing and answering questions. In the problem articulation stage, "what" questions allow one to fully describe the situation. Examples include: "What occurred?" "What did I see, think, feel?" "What was the most important thing?" In the problem analysis stage "why" questions are most helpful. Examples include: "Why was that important?" "Why do I think it happened?" "Why was I feeling that way?" In the hypothesis generation stage "how" questions allow an individual to begin to formulate a tentative theory. Examples include: "How is this situation similar to and different from other problems?" "How might you do things differently?" These questions help explain the problem by posing and testing possible explanations. In the action stage "what" questions become important once again: "What are the implications of all this for future action?" "What should I do now?" These questions invite the learner to take the important next step of converting insights to learning.

The results of reflection are insights that generally fall into one of four categories: self, others, task, and environment. Insights about self help us gain self-awareness. We learn our strengths and weaknesses, how we are affected by situations, how we react, and how we affect others. Insights about others help us understand and improve our relationships with them. Insights about the task help us perform better, and insights about the environment help us understand how context affects a situation. It also helps us appreciate the complexity and systemic nature of situations.

Journals

Journals are among the most powerful tools for surfacing learning from challenging experiences. They provide opportunities to explore thoughts you might never say aloud and which therefore could be lost. A journal can be a place to explore ideas and insights about an experience. A journal can help you improve your ability to take in many perspectives and develop fuller, more vivid pictures of your experiences and thinking.

The journal is not intended to contain deeply personal thoughts. Instead, use the journal to gain better understanding of your experiences and to make connections to things in your life. Explore areas that intrigue and excite you. Discuss any questions that your reflection raises. What mysteries have you uncovered that you might want to explore further? Do not use the journal simply to chronicle events, describe a situation, state your opinions, or as a forum for writing about what you already know; use it to enhance your learning and understanding by exploring events, situations, opinions, and current knowledge. The best journals are focused, reflective, personally relevant, result in new insights, and discuss how those insights can be put into action.

Although the power of writing journals comes from freely following ideas, sometimes a bit of structure helps to start the flow. Faced with a blank piece of paper and no immediate thoughts, those not familiar with the journal writing process might feel uncomfortable. This is where the basic elements of reflection can help. A provocative question, some suggested categories to consider, or a sequence to follow, can help a hesitant writer begin. This small bit of structure is often all that is needed to start a flood of ideas.

The following guidelines will help learners as they experiment with writing journals:

1. Capture insights as they occur.

2. Push beyond surface evaluation. Journals provide opportunities to question initial reactions, to explore alternative interpretations, and to probe more deeply into feelings and thoughts.

3. Adopt a spirit of inquiry. Approach the process as one of discovery, and go wherever the journey takes you. Don't try to force ideas into meaningful patterns. Let go of the need to defend a view or an idea.

4. Reread what you have written. You may discover patterns in your thinking or emotions that can be explored in new journal entries. Ideas or events recorded at one point in time may acquire new meaning when reread.

5. Learn to recognize emerging learning. If you find yourself feeling uncomfortable, angry, or reluctant to explore a topic, this may be an indication of important learning. Rather than avoiding the issue, ask yourself what the reaction means. Explore how your reactions are affecting your effectiveness and learning. Adopt a posture of inquiry, and pursue it.

6. Allow contradictions to occur. You may find that a new entry directly contradicts an earlier one. Record them both, then explore the apparent paradox from a position of "both/and" rather than "either/or."

7. Search for underlying assumptions, values, or beliefs. Journal writers often uncover new insights about basic values or beliefs that seem to govern a series of actions or reactions. Explore them and their implications.

8. Observe the process. If you find yourself thinking that this activity is silly, or that what you have just written is powerful, or that you don't feel like writing today, put it down and explore it.

9. Try to make connections between what you are learning and your life experiences. It is often helpful to think about ways that concepts and/or ideas can be applied to past experiences.

10. Use your idle time (e.g., taking a shower, commuting, waiting for the Web, etc.) to think about something you have found interesting or perplexing.

11. Trust that you will discover relevant information. If you believe this activity has value, it will.

Twelve Tips for Managing Confrontations Effectively*

A successful manager needs to develop an effective means of managing confrontation and conflict. Following are some tips to help you learn to confront others in a constructive manner:

1. Keep in mind that usually the goal of a confrontation is to change behavior and/or educate the person you are confronting.

2. Know the basic facts about the behavior you are confronting.

   - What conditions surround the behavior?

   - When did it occur?

   - What is your relationship with the person you are confronting?

   - How does the person see you?

3. Confront behaviors, not values or the individual's personality.

   - Be specific and clear about the behavior you are confronting.

   - Describe the behavior. ("You were forty-five minutes late to the group meeting today.")

   - Avoid using labeling words. ("You are a lazy and an irresponsible jerk.")

4. Be simple and direct as you speak.

   - Make one point at a time.

   - Do not rush the encounter.

5. Have the confrontation as soon after the behavior occurs as appropriately possible. Keep it private.

6. Show your concern for the individual.

   - Communicate your support.

   - Do not try to embarrass the individual.

   - Show a sincere interest in the problem.

   - Do not make a joke of the problem.

7. Frequently you will have feelings concerning the confrontation.

   - Communicate these feelings when appropriate.

* Copyright 1993 by Sandra L. Deacon Carr. Used with permission.

- If you are angry, direct your anger at the behavior rather than at the person. ("I am angry and resentful that you came forty-five minutes late to the meeting.")

8. Ask the individual how she or he views her or his behavior. Listen objectively.

9. Stick to the issues; avoid excuses, outside circumstances, or rationalizations.

10. Ask for a specific behavioral change. ("I would like you to come to all of our scheduled meetings on time.")

11. When necessary, discuss the specific and reasonable consequences should the person fail to comply with the request. ("If you are late to any more meetings, I, along with the others in the group, will enforce the firing policy and warn you of our intent to fire you from the group.")

- Do not make threats that you cannot or do not intend to keep.

12. Check to see that the individual has understood your message; ask the individual to repeat her or his understanding of it.

It is important to confront an individual with whom you have a problem to attempt to resolve the issue before you approach anyone else (for example, her or his supervisor).

Techniques for Problem Solving and Heightening Creativity

Identifying and Solving Problems*

An important part of a manager's job is problem solving. Correctly diagnosed and solved problems help an organization achieve its goals. Incorrectly diagnosed problems waste valuable resources and can create new problems. Imagine you are working as a receptionist. You have been on the job for two weeks, and there is still an unacceptable number of phone calls that get lost. Your supervisor is quick to blame you. You're doing what you have been told and don't understand why the calls are getting lost. Your supervisor tells you to read the switchboard manual and stop losing calls or you'll be fired. Only three lines have been having the problem, so you tell callers requesting to speak with those three people that they are not available. No more calls get lost. It turns out that the problem was really with the equipment, but your manager's failure to correctly diagnose the problem caused you to become demotivated and led you to avoid taking calls on the broken lines.

The first step in the problem-solving process is to define the problem. This can be more difficult than it might appear. When defining a problem, focus on visible signs of distress that are preventing the organization from reaching its goals. Avoid defining the problem in terms of solutions or causes. In the above situation, your boss defined the problem as incompetence. This is a potential cause of a problem, but it is not a visible sign of distress. The way your boss defined the problem prevented exploration of other possible reasons for lost calls. If the problem had been defined as lost calls, incompetence would be one possible cause.

* Copyright 1994 by Steven B. Wolff. Used with permission.

Another possible cause would have been broken equipment. Your boss also might have defined the problem as the need to find a new receptionist. This would be defining the problem in terms of a solution and would be equally ineffective.

It is probable that when you begin to define a problem, there will be many legitimate issues that need to be addressed and prioritized. The highest priority issues should be those which, when resolved, will help most in moving the organization toward its goals.

Once the problem is defined, gather more information to better understand the problem. If your boss had defined the problem as lost calls, she could have collected information about the calls that were lost, revealing that the calls were being lost on only three lines.

Once information has been gathered, consider possible causes. Expand the boundaries of your thinking as you generate possible causes. Often the cause of a problem is complex and involves a number of interacting issues. If you think creatively, you will be more likely to fully understand the problem. When you have a list of probable causes, again collect information to determine how much each cause contributes to the problem. Often we think we know the cause of a problem but, as the receptionist's manager would find out, we don't. After collecting information, you may find there is more than one cause of the problem. Work on correcting those causes that are contributing the most to the problem. Avoid wasting time in areas where there will be little payback.

When the major causes of the problem have been defined, you will be able to generate solutions. Again, you should be creative. Often ideas that sound implausible have seeds of a good solution. Develop a number of alternative solutions to be evaluated. Select a set of criteria, and evaluate each alternative against the criteria to choose the solution you will implement.

When implementing a solution, consider techniques for managing change. Communicate and educate employees, and allow them to participate in the planning and implementation. Provide support, and be tolerant of mistakes if the implementation requires employees to learn and use new skills.

Finally, measure and reevaluate the implementation. Without evaluation, it will be impossible to know whether your solution is really doing anything to make your organization more effective. Some solutions are easy to measure. In the above example, it would be easy to tell whether the calls are continuing to be lost, but solutions to other problems may require more elaborate measurement and evaluation. For example, you may have redesigned the structure of the organization because you believe that increased communication will reduce errors when passing work between departments. If you do not measure the errors, then you will not know if the new structure has been effective.

Brainstorming

Brainstorming is perhaps the most common group problem-solving and decision-making technique used in business today; but if you ask ten different managers to describe the process, you will probably end up with ten different responses. *The American Heritage Dictionary* defines a brainstorm as "a sudden and violent disturbance in the brain" and "a sudden clever, whimsical, or foolish idea."[©] The concept of brainstorming draws on these definitions and suggests that out of the violent disturbances and the whimsical ideas can come creative solutions to complex problems, especially when several brains storm together.

Most often, the word *brainstorming* conjures up an image of a casual process—people sitting around boxes of half-eaten pizzas and throwing out ideas as they come to mind. In fact, for brainstorming to be really effective, it should be highly structured and tightly controlled. Moreover, it should be made clear from the outset that every member of the group must participate and that, at least in the early stages, every idea generated will be deemed to have equal weight with every other idea generated.[2]

For every idea to be received and considered as being equal to all other ideas, strict rules must be followed. While an idea may seem absurd or amusing when given, laughing is generally taken personally by the idea giver and as an affirmation to all that the idea is nonsense. As a result, the idea giver feels diminished and is less likely to make additional suggestions. The idea becomes tainted and is not taken seriously. Laughing, or in any other way criticizing an idea, is sometimes called "discounting," since the value of the idea has been diminished.

The opposite is also a problem; many of us automatically believe that complimenting someone on an idea is an act of encouragement. In brainstorming, however, compliments directed at an idea during the initial stages give that idea enhanced weight and credibility. This inhibits the generation of other ideas; participants consciously or unconsciously note that since an acceptable idea has already been generated, no new ideas are really necessary and that it is unlikely they will be able to think of anything as appropriate anyway.

Stopping idea generation either by discounting or complimenting often results in premature closure and can mean diminished creativity and mediocre decisions. When this happens, it is called "satisficing."

Brainstorming tends to be most successful when carried out in groups no larger than seven nor smaller than three, not including the facilitator.

The Facilitator

It is the facilitator's job to frame the problem, set out the limits and issues, see to it that everyone's ideas are accepted equally, control the schedule, and make sure that everyone participates. The facilitator should be equipped with an easel and pad, chalkboard, overhead acetates, or other materials that will allow him or her to record, in a visible place, the suggestions generated. Ideas should be recorded, either by the facilitator or an assistant, in words as close as possible to those of the participant who suggested them.

© Copyright 1985 by Houghton Mifflin Company. Adapted by permission from *The American Heritage Dictionary, Second Edition.*

2. See A.F. Osborne, *Applied Imagination: Principles and Procedures of Creative Thinking* (New York: Scribners, 1941), for additional information about brainstorming.

Facilitators should also learn a few simple techniques:

1. When a suggestion is made that seems unclear, the facilitator may request, "Please tell me more," or ask, "Could you tell me just a bit more about what you're suggesting?" The facilitator should avoid such phrases as, "I don't understand," since they can make a participant feel defensive or uneasy.

2. The facilitator also may give clarifying feedback to participants by rephrasing a suggestion, prefacing it with, "So you are suggesting that [restatement of the suggestion in the facilitator's words]?" This allows a participant to agree or further explain the suggestion as necessary.

3. The facilitator should also check frequently with participants for affirmation that what is being recorded accurately reflects the intention. This can be done by asking, "Is this fair?" or, "Is this an acceptable/accurate depiction?"

The Process

The following six-step technique is one of many possible variations of brainstorming:

1. *Defining the problem.* In this step, the facilitator describes the problem to be solved. He or she gives the background of the problem, explains why it needs to be solved, and describes who will be affected. The definition must also include an explanation of any limits that are inherent to the problem—for example, we must be able to complete the project within six months; the product must be fire resistant; or the product must be able to be operated by one person. At this time, participants may ask for any additional clarification.

   The definition should be kept brief; too much information or too many restrictions can inhibit creativity. Step 1 is generally limited to about five minutes.

2. *Individual generation of ideas.* Each participant silently and independently generates three to four suggestions that he or she writes down without discussion with other group members.

3. *Round robin.* The facilitator begins by asking each member to give one of his or her ideas and continues to go around the room, in order, taking ideas from each of the members. After the initial round, participants continue to suggest ideas either inspired by those already raised or altogether new.

   Comments and criticisms of any kind are not allowed. Every idea is considered to have equal merit and potential. Step 3 should be time limited to twenty to thirty minutes so as to avoid boredom and frustration.

4. *Categorizing.* Sometimes called "idea structuring," this step involves examining the ideas that have been generated to find categories into which they can be sorted. Categorizing allows participants to begin to examine the distinct similarities and differences among the ideas. For example, if the problem has been to develop a vandal-proof public telephone,[3]

---

3. New York employees of NYNEX actually used brainstorming to tackle this problem.

solution categories might include telephones with limited access, telephones made of resistant materials, and telephones without moving parts. More than one set of categories may emerge; it is up to the group, with the leadership of the facilitator, to select the best ones, usually three to five.

5. *Discussing and synthesizing.* At this stage, ideas are looked at critically, and the process of eliminating the least acceptable ones is begun. In some situations, it will be possible to eliminate entire categories at once. For example, if one category of ideas is "things that require considerable research and development," and the project must be completed within a short time period, this category might be easily removed.

   During this step, it is often useful to appoint a "devil's advocate." Historically, the devil's advocate was appointed in the Roman Catholic Church to find flaws and provoke controversy in discussions over whether certain individuals would be beatified as saints. The purpose of the devil's advocate was to ensure that saints would be selected on the basis of merit and not politics. This same function works well in brainstorming. As the field of suggestions is narrowed, it is the job of the devil's advocate to raise points about possible weaknesses.

6. *Closure.* The last step in brainstorming is to do one of the following:
   a. Select the single best idea by consensus. It may also be desirable to select the top three to five ideas, and rank them to create a back-up plan.
   b. Take the best elements of several ideas, and develop a new, composite idea.
   c. Reject all of the ideas, redefine the problem based on new information gathered through the process, and start again.

Used correctly, brainstorming is a powerful tool. Remember that although it requires considerable time, brainstorming also encourages the generation of creative solutions to difficult problems.

Force Field Analysis

Force Field Analysis is a kind of accounting system for breaking down problems to clarify which parts can be dealt with meaningfully and which cannot.[4] The kind of breakdown required by a Force Field Analysis aids decision making as to the most cost-effective use of time and effort in effecting change. Force Field Analysis has an added benefit of being graphic; driving and restraining forces are laid out on a form, complete with arrows, that gives quick visual access to the problem and its component parts (Figure 1).

   Driving forces are those factors that push toward making a change. Take, for example, the change that you made in your life when you graduated from high school and decided where to go to college.[5] Driving forces may have included your having gotten good grades in high school, a desire to meet new people, your parents' desires to see you receive a top-level education, your desire for further education, college parties and social life, getting a necessary credential for a good job, and so forth.

4. K. Lewin and D. Cartwright, eds., *Field Theory in Social Science* (New York: Harper & Row, 1951).
5. Special thanks to Sandi Deacon Carr for this suggestion.

On the other side of the ledger, however, are restraining forces—those things that push away from making the decision to go away to college. These might have included the high cost of a college education, leaving friends behind, leaving family, having to have a roommate, fear of the unknown, fear of becoming "a small fish in a big pond," and so forth.

Imagine that these driving and restraining forces are pushing against one another and nothing is happening (Figure 2). The ideal situation may be to go to a college in another state, but there are many forces pushing away from that decision. Picture the driving and restraining forces as being at opposite ends of a big spring.

Pushing against the driving forces doesn't really do anything other than to increase the pressure from the restraining forces. You have to keep the pressure on at the driving end because, unless the pressure from the restraining forces is reduced, the spring will want to bounce back to its original shape.[6]

How might you go about reducing that pressure? If money is an issue, you might apply for financial aid or a scholarship. If you're concerned about missing friends and family, you might call home a lot. If you're concerned about going to the unknown, you'll probably want to visit the school, talk to students, and attend classes. The point is, doing something about the restraining forces allows the driving forces to move ahead with less resistance.

6. Special thanks to Dr. Lloyd Baird, Department of Organizational Behavior, School of Management, Boston University, for this suggestion.

Force Field Analysis

Goal:

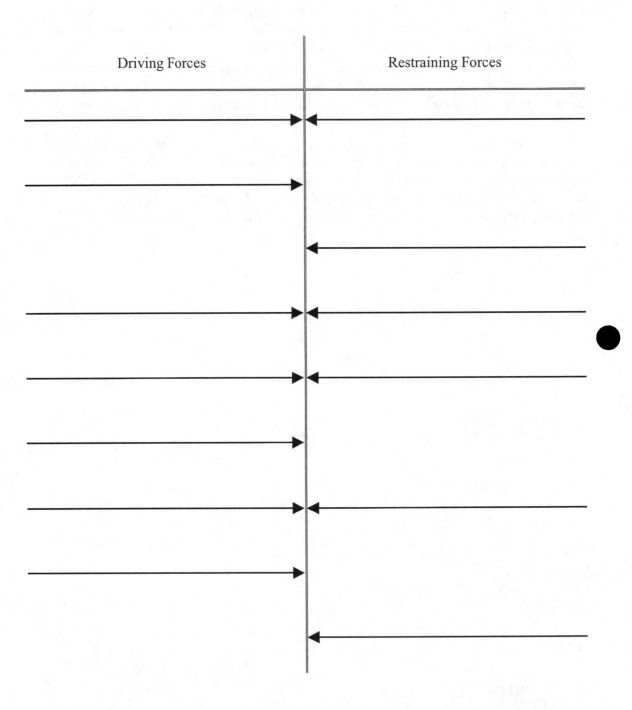

Driving Forces   Restraining Forces

Figure 1

Force Field Analysis

Goal: Going to College in Another State

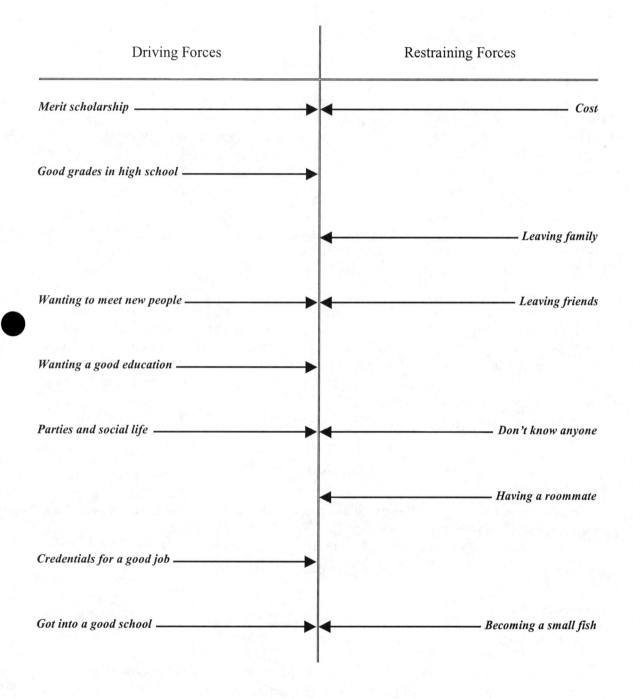

Figure 2

ICEBREAKERS

Overview

Icebreakers are used to help people get to know and feel comfortable with one another. They may offer opportunities to share only minimal background information, e.g., name, age, place of birth, and interests, or they may go more deeply into ideas and values. In either case, they serve as an important first step in helping people, who will be working and learning together, move beyond initial impressions. They begin to build a sense of community and participation.

Icebreakers that are formal and structured ensure that everyone will have a chance to participate and be heard. Informal and unstructured ice breakers, such as what might take place between two people at a social event, are selective and often omit people who might have a great deal to contribute. In a work situation, this can result in a failure to maximize all resources.

Use icebreakers to hear and be heard. Think carefully about what it is you would like others to know about you, and find a way to convey that information. Keep in mind that the impression you make during an icebreaker is likely to serve as the basis for others' opinions of you, and this image may be difficult to change once instilled. Also think carefully about what you would like to know about the others with whom you will be learning and working, and find a way to elicit that information.

Networking*

Since you'll most likely be working with one or more of your classmates over the course of the semester, it helps to learn a little about them from the outset. Following is an exercise to help you get to know some of the people with whom you will be working. This exercise will also give you an opportunity to practice your listening skills.

Instructions

Step 1 (20 minutes)

Look around the room and find someone who you do not now know but who you think would be interesting to know, or someone whose background or interests you think are the

* This exercise was written by Gail E. Gilmore.

least like yours. In about twenty minutes, learn all you can about one another. Get general information about your partner's interests, background, hobbies, plans for the future, and so forth. Find out about three things that you and your partner have in common and three things that are different. Listen carefully to what your partner tells you about himself or herself but do not take notes or write anything down.

Step 2 (20–30 minutes)

When you and your partner have finished your mutual interviews, select another pair of students to join. This time, introduce your partner to the new pair, telling them everything you have learned about him or her. Continue to go around the group until all four members have had a chance to introduce their partners.

Step 3 (open-ended)

Option 1:

When you have completed the introductions in your groups of four, join another group of four. This time, introduce a member of the new pair that you previously joined. Continue to join other groups and repeat the introductions, until you run out of time.

Option 2:

When you have completed Step 2, introduce your original partner to the rest of the class. This will give you an opportunity to practice oral presentation skills and give more people a chance to learn something about you and your partner.

Round Robin Interview

This ice breaker will help you learn about your classmates. Knowing something about each other should help facilitate working together throughout the duration of this course.

Instructions

Step 1 (30–40 minutes)

You will be assigned one of the following sets of topic areas (or others as may be selected by the instructor) about which to talk to other class members. In addition, you will be given a number, colored tag, or other item to wear that will identify you as having a specific topic area.

Possible topic areas:

1. A time when you felt uncomfortable or out of place. Explain why you felt that way and what you did about it.

2. A time when you felt really proud of something you had done. Explain why and how you reacted.

3. A time when you got very angry about something. Explain how you reacted and why.

4. A time when you really disagreed with something but went along with it anyway. Explain how you felt and why.

5. A time when someone important to you tried to get you to do something you really didn't want to do, and you said no. Explain how you felt and why.

Select a class member who has an identification other than yours, and interview that person on the topic area you have been assigned. In turn, that person should interview you on his or her topic. You may take notes. Keep your interviews brief.

Repeat the interviewing with additional people, up to four, until time runs out.

Step 2 (20–30 minutes)

Working in a group with the others who were assigned your topic area, discuss your findings and consolidate the information to develop a summary of the topic. Consider what the responses had in common and how they differed.

Step 3 (open-ended)

Report your findings to the class. Discuss.

The Realistic Job Preview*

Most people have seen the old TV commercials that promoted the army, navy, air force, and marines. Ever wonder what those did for enlistment? Not surprisingly, those images of crashing waves on exquisite beaches, Tom Cruise look-alikes flying jets while enthusiastic admirers looked on, and other "see the world" scenarios increased enlistment. But the armed services also had the equivalent of an enormous turnover problem, and re-enlistments were fairly low.[1]

Instructions

Step 1 Take a minute to note below why you believe the turnover problem existed.

_____

_____

* This exercise was written by Scott Weighart.
1. See B. Megliana, A. DeNisi, S. Youngblood, and K. Williams, "Effects of Realistic Job Previews: A Comparison Using an Enhancement and a Reduction Preview," *Journal of Applied Psychology 73,* (May 1988) 2: 259-266.

Chances are, you recognized that the actual experiences of recruits did not match their expectations and, therefore, that the recruits became disillusioned and angry. To turn this around, army recruiters started to give potential enlistees a realistic job preview. They showed them videos of what life would really be like in the service and in other ways tried to give them a balanced portrayal of military life.

Step 2 List below those positive and negative factors about military life that you think the army recruiters should have included in their realistic job preview.

Positive: _____

_____

_____

Negative: _____

_____

_____

Surprisingly, many of the enlistees found basic training to be nowhere near as bad as they had feared. However, the biggest and most unanticipated problem was homesickness. As a result of using the realistic job preview, enlistment did decrease to some extent. However, probably as a result of having given recruits an accurate picture of what to prepare themselves for, re-enlistment increased dramatically. The army gained considerable credibility and loyalty from the troops.

Realistic job previews were also used to try to decrease the turnover that airlines face with airport baggage checkers. Applicants were forewarned about the good and bad points of the job.

Step 3 List below those positive and negative factors about the job of airport baggage checker that you think the airlines should have included in their realistic job previews.

Positive: _____

_____

_____

Negative: _____

_____

_____

What impact do you believe realistic job previews had on airport baggage checker turnover?

_____ increased _____ decreased _____ stayed the same

Unfortunately, realistic job previews don't always work, because a bad job is a bad job—previews can't change that. The job is boring and stressful; impatient passengers are rude and

25

resentful. Thousands of bags must be examined, even though virtually none of them contain anything troublesome. Periodically, some handlers report, Federal Aviation Administration workers try to slip fake explosives past the checkers, and steep fines are assessed if they are caught napping. Realistic job previews can't help here.

Step 4 Try one more. If you were providing realistic job previews for applicants for the job of highway or bridge toll collector, what positives and negatives would you include?

Positive: _____

_____

_____

Negative: _____

_____

Surprisingly, jobs as highway and bridge toll collectors are very popular, despite tedium and car exhaust. Why? Toll takers get a tremendous amount of feedback. Given the nature of the equipment with which they work, toll takers generally know precisely how accurate they have been in terms of giving change. Some like being outdoors, enjoy the steady routine, and like the human interaction that comes with giving directions and otherwise helping travelers.

If you went through steps 1–4 without peeking at the answers before supplying your own, chances are you got some of the important points but missed others. The moral is that while the fields of organizational behavior and management appear to be common sense, sometimes the things that drive human behavior are either outside of our immediate experience or are counterintuitive. For example, are satisfied workers more productive workers? Sometimes, but many researchers have found that there is no great statistical correlation between job satisfaction and productivity.

Step 5 (Optional)

Hold a realistic "job preview" for the course in which you are using this book. Consider what your expectations, hopes, and fears are, then take a minute to list what you believe the positives and negatives of being in this course are likely to be.

Positive: _____

_____

_____

Negative: _____

_____

_____

When you're done, share your list with others in the class and with the instructor. Use the course syllabus as a framework for developing a realistic assessment of what the course will be like and what the job of being a student in it will be.

THE NATURE OF TODAY'S ORGANIZATIONS

Objectives

- To explore the nature of today's work environment
- To relate the characteristics of the work environment to the skills required for success

Part 1

The Situation

You are about to start a new business that will offer a wide range of products and services to clients around the globe. You are in the process of putting together your business plan and are thinking about the challenges that your business will face. The better prepared you are for the competitive challenges, the more likely your business will succeed.

You just read that organizations are open systems, which means that they are affected by the characteristics of their business environment. This makes sense to you, but you aren't quite sure with which characteristics of the environment you should be concerned.

Although your business is likely to have unique concerns, you think it would be wise to begin by gaining a broad perspective. You have decided to begin your analysis by considering those characteristics of the environment that impact most organizations.

Step 1 (2 minutes)

Working with three to five classmates, give your group a name (or one will be assigned to you).

Enter that name here: _____

Step 2 (15–20 minutes)

Discuss your perceptions of the business environment. Come to a consensus on the two environmental characteristics you believe are having the greatest impact on businesses today. If you get stuck, get started by discussing some of the areas listed below. You may want to ask yourself questions such as: How would I describe the business environment with respect to these areas? How are these areas changing? and How do these areas impact the way I need to manage the business?

a. Competition (e.g., intensity, competitors, tactics)

b. Customers (e.g., demands, needs, loyalty, location)

c. Events that affect your business (e.g., predictability, certainty, obviousness)

d. Your employees (e.g., characteristics, demands, needs, desires, abilities)

e. Knowledge (e.g., pace of obsolescence, complexity, requirements, learning)

f. Change (e.g., pace, controllability, predictability, obsolescence)

List below the two environmental characteristics that you believe will have the most impact on how you manage your business. Explain why you believe these are the most important forces affecting your business, and describe their impact on how you manage the business (e.g., structure, desired culture, leadership, processes, values, relationships, etc.).

1. Characteristic: _____

   Why chosen? _____

   _____

   _____

   Impact? _____

   _____

   _____

2. Characteristic: _____

   Why chosen? _____

   _____

   _____

   Impact? _____

   _____

   _____

Part 2

The Situation

It is one year later. You have started your business, and it is going well. Now you are looking to expand and need to hire some new employees. You know that the people you hire will make a big difference to the continued success of your organization. The skills and abilities of your employees will determine how well you can meet the challenges you have identified above.

Step 3 (20 minutes)

Discuss the demands (skills and abilities) that the two environmental characteristics chosen above place on employees. Be sure you can clearly show the connection between the particular environmental characteristic and the qualifications you will look for in your employees.

Come to a consensus on the three most important abilities that you will look for in prospective employees to ensure that your business can successfully meet the challenges posed by environmental forces. Although you will need to look for abilities unique to your business, for now, you are only interested in the more general abilities needed to successfully operate in today's business environment.

If you get stuck, you may wish to consider whether a particular environmental characteristic impacts the following areas and, if so, what types of skills and abilities will employees need to be successful under these conditions:

a. Interdependence among employees

b. Length of time that technical skills remain current

c. Flexibility required

d. Degree of uncertainty

e. Pace of change in the nature of the job

f. Degree of self-management required

g. Working relationships

h. Other

Based on your analysis of the business environment, and the demands this environment places on employees, list the three most important skills and/or abilities that you will look for in the employees you hire. Explain why these are important skills for workers in an organization operating in the environment you described above.

1. Skill/ability: _____

   Why? _____

   _____

   _____

2. Skill/ability: _____

   Why? _____

   _____

   _____

3. Skill/ability: _____

   Why? _____

_____

_____

Step 4 (5 minutes)

Using the large paper and markers distributed to you, record and post your answers for the other groups to see. Be sure your group is clearly identified by name on the poster sheet.

Step 5 (10–20 minutes)

Now, imagine that your group is the board of directors and the other groups are management teams presenting their hiring strategies to you. Your job as the board of directors is to ensure the continued success of the company. As a team, examine the answers of the management teams, and discuss in your small group the questions you have about their thinking.

   Come to a consensus on the two most important questions that you, as the board of directors, would like to ask the other management teams. As a good leadership team you should be sure that the tone of your questions is developmental and helpful rather than judgmental.

Question: _____

_____

Question: _____

_____

Step 6 (open-ended)

Each group will have the opportunity to ask questions of the other groups in an open forum.

PART I

MANAGING GLOBAL AND WORKFORCE DIVERSITY*

Overview

When it comes to explaining human behavior—whether in New Jersey, Frankfurt, Dakar, or Shanghai—there is only one universal rule and that is that there are *no* universal rules by which we can explain why humans behave the way they do. Every person carries a unique set of life experiences and genetic material which, in combination, ensures that, like snowflakes, no two of us are exactly alike.

In today's workplace, with its emphasis on global competition and its resultant demand for greater productivity, innovation, and cooperation, it is critical that we have a meaningful understanding of how to maximize every employee's output. This can only be done by first understanding what each employee, including ourselves, brings to the workplace, both strengths and weaknesses, and then finding ways to harness the strengths and diminish the weaknesses. That process requires that we be good students of the complexities of human nature, i.e., diversity.

The Study of Diversity and Its Relationship to Power

Interest in categorizing people has historically been driven by a desire for power, both productive and abusive. When categorization is used in an abusive manner, we generally refer to it as stereotyping. The most obvious abuse comes when stereotyping is used to cement hierarchical social and economic systems, thereby setting one group above another in its rights to position, ownership, political input, education, legal protection, etc. Limiting or maximizing the rights of individuals within a group to make personal choices, such as where they will live, is also a dimension of this kind of abuse. Stereotypes are often perpetuated through the use of name calling, labeling, and physical segregation.

The power that comes from categorization may also be harnessed for social and organizational benefit. This happens when categorization is used to understand and value the multiple perspectives and strengths that individuals within a category have to contribute to solving problems, implementing solutions, and enhancing overall creativity. This is done by providing the kind of environment in which everyone is able to make clear what his or her interests and needs might be. A manager who is aware of the diverse needs and interests of employees is in a far better position to provide such an environment and use it to positively influence employee behavior than one who is not.

* Special thanks to Dr. David A. Raker, Westfield State College, for his input.

The Study of Diversity

Not withstanding that the understanding of diversity is often more art than science, the study of diversity still requires a rigorous, structured approach. In the same way that science involves defining and putting into understandable order the infinite variables of the universe, art is based on the use of a set of defined and organized colors and materials set into circumscribed contexts or spaces. It is this kind of organization and definition, when applied to people, that begins to give us a clearer picture of what people do and why they do it.
Thus, organizing is one of the first steps in the study of diversity.

When diversity was first recognized as a political and management issue, the focus was almost exclusively on race, and primarily on managing race relations between whites and African-Americans. Things have changed. In order to deal successfully with diversity issues in today's environment, it is necessary to meet the demands for fairness and for equal treatment and opportunities from a wide range of interest groups. Issues of gender, religion, ethnicity, sexual preference, physical or mental abilities and disabilities, age, marital status, parenthood, personality type, and others, have been added to race on the diversity agenda. *Being able to understand and recognize the fundamental interests of each human grouping is accordingly the next step in the study of diversity.*

Having identified the various interest groups, you might think it would be easy to find ways to accommodate them. Unfortunately, these interests, sometimes presented as demands, often appear to conflict with one another and with overarching social and institutional goals. When that happens, it is important to identify underlying common interests, develop workable compromises, and find ways to implement solutions.
The next critical steps in studying diversity, therefore, are identifying common interests and finding ways to meet the needs and interests of each group in a mutually satisfactory manner.

Categorizing people as a way to anticipate and explain their behavior carries certain risks. Prominent among these is that unidimensional, concretized categories become the basis upon which we treat others and may lead us to overlook the uniqueness of individuals.
Therefore, an additional step in the study of diversity is learning to separate the individual from the category into which we have placed the individual or he or she has placed him or herself.

Who Is Responsible for Managing Diversity?

In the preface to his powerful book, *The Courageous Follower*, business executive Ira Chaleff states: "The most capable followers in the world will fail if they gripe about their leaders but don't help them improve." In managing diversity, the same holds true: Employees are responsible not just for making clear what their needs are, they are also responsible for proposing ways to help meet them. It is the role of all members of the workforce, whether leaders or followers, to identify their own needs and those of their coworkers and to encourage one another to contribute effectively to the collective effort.

When managers and employees fail to work cooperatively to recognize, understand, and appropriately manage diversity, the results, in today's litigious climate, may be devastating.

Large and even small businesses are being sued—and losing into the millions of dollars—for ignoring or mishandling employee complaints. Some judgments have been so large as to force companies and individuals into bankruptcy. And, even when the company wins, the costs of litigation are often overwhelming.

For managers and supervisors, charges by peers and employees of unfair or other inappropriate treatment and resultant lawsuits, increasingly end otherwise promising careers. And, as interest groups continue to press for recognition and fair treatment, new legislation is constantly being enacted to institutionalize rights and ensure protection.

How Will Using the Cases and Exercises in This Section Of *O.B. In Action* Enhance an Understanding of Diversity and Its Role in the Workplace?

Many of the materials that follow were initially developed for and have been extensively used by corporate trainers for teaching about the management of diversity. Because of the changing natures of the workforces of virtually every country, this kind of training has become close to a billion dollar industry as business and industrial leaders have increasingly recognized the need to harness and manage diversity.

The cases and exercises in this section are not designed to supply you with a set of rules or models for managing diversity. Instead, they have been written to stimulate ideas about how best to observe, analyze, and harness the strengths of diverse employee populations. In addition, they provide a format for inward reflection of one's own style, needs, interests, and expectations. Finally, these cases and exercises offer you opportunities to explore not only the differences that exist among people, but the similarities as well.

JWW

1

MANAGING AND VALUING DIFFERENCES: A STORY*

Pat, Chris, and Lee met during their first year in college and have been good friends ever since. They like baseball and have gone to a number of Red Sox games together. They also enjoy parties and have had their fair share during the year. They occasionally help each other with homework. Pat is very good with mathematics and is quite willing to help Chris and Lee, who generally have some trouble with courses that have a mathematical component. When it comes time to write reports, Chris finds it easy to make a coherent argument and present it eloquently in writing. Pat and Lee, on the other hand, have some difficulty with their writing, and they especially have a hard time with punctuation and grammar. They often ask Chris to edit their papers. Lee's strength is an ability to make sense out of a large amount of seemingly unrelated data. Chris and Pat often talk with Lee about the way they have analyzed a problem since Lee is able to point out important information or a problem with an argument that had not been considered by the other two.

The skills of these three friends complement each other, while their interests in baseball and parties are rather similar. This has made for a good relationship. They can help each other with their school work and have a good time together socially. They have been so busy during the semester doing school work, going to ball games and having parties, that they have never really talked much about their personal lives before college. Because they get along so well, they assumed they come from similar backgrounds.

This year Pat, Chris, and Lee are taking a course together in which they are required to work in groups. This is somewhat different than helping each other with schoolwork, because they will all be responsible for one product. The group projects will not be graded individually; each member of the group will get the same grade. They were selected to be in the same group and were pleased. Because they are good friends and get along well, the group projects, they thought, would be a breeze.

The first project that they were to do was to analyze the structure of the microcomputer industry. This seemed like an exciting project, and they were anxious to get started. They decided to begin right away rather than wait and possibly be rushed. Pat thought it would be a good idea to develop a plan of action. Feeling it would be the best way for the project to proceed smoothly, Pat wanted to determine what information would be needed, when it would be needed, and who would be responsible for each piece. Feeling uncomfortable defining things so quickly, Chris thought it would be much better if each of them went off and tried to uncover some information. Then, with some facts at hand, they could come up with a more realistic plan to finish the project. Without doing some preliminary work, Chris felt there was no way to know what the important pieces of the project would be. Lee tended to side with Chris, and so they persuaded Pat to wait before making definite plans. Pat agreed reluctantly.

* Copyright 1994 by Steven B. Wolff. Used with permission.

The three went off and began to gather data. Two weeks later, they sat down to see if they could map out a plan based on what they had collected. As they talked about the data, Pat felt it would be a good idea if each of them took some time to study it; then they could come up with a better plan of attack. Trying to come up with the plan in a couple of hours would probably not produce the best result. Lee, on the other hand, saw the data, began to feel that something was missing, and felt an important piece of the analysis would be left out. Lee suggested that they collect more data before making any plans.

Chris was getting very uncomfortable with Pat and Lee. Chris felt that what they had was good enough to get started, that they didn't need to have something that was perfect, and that if they spent much more time before developing a plan, they may not have time to finish the project.

The three friends were starting to get on each other's nerves. After a heated discussion, they finally agreed that they should start to divide the work and draw up a tentative schedule. If something needed to be changed later on, they all agreed that they would be flexible enough to do so. Pat was going to look at the financial aspects and structure of the industry, Chris would look at the competitive strategies, Lee would look at marketing aspects, and they would all attempt to predict possible future trends.

Each went off to do the research in their assigned area, wrote up a summary of what had been found, and then got together to share their findings. The meeting started out fine but eventually grew tense. As Pat was presenting the findings on the financial aspects of the industry, Lee began to feel that something was missing. Lee could not quite articulate exactly what was missing, but nevertheless expressed the concern. Pat was frustrated and remarked, "Look, if you don't like it, then do it yourself."

"I was just trying to be helpful," Lee replied, visibly upset, "but if you don't want my input, then just forget it."

Chris calmed the two of them and decided to present the competitive strategies used in the industry. As Chris was presenting, Pat recognized that Chris had neglected to consider that being a low-cost producer was also a viable strategy. Chris had focused mainly on product strategies. The incident with Lee had created an atmosphere where it did not seem comfortable to be totally open, but Pat commented anyway. Chris was no more tolerant of Pat's remark than Pat had been of Lee's. The rest of the meeting went downhill. Although the team did eventually finish the project, it was handed in late and was not done well. They got a "C," and their relationship had become strained.

The Backgrounds of the Three Friends

Before trying to understand what went wrong, we need to have some understanding of Pat, Chris, and Lee's backgrounds.

Pat comes from a wealthy family that owns a small bank. Pat would help out in the business whenever possible. The business was doing well, thanks to Pat's father who was very meticulous. He would stay late at night to check the books and go over the bank's investments to make sure the bank would remain on solid financial ground. Pat quickly learned that the way to succeed is to be very careful and methodical—take your time and do your homework before making decisions.

Chris's family is middle class. Chris's mother is a journalist and a good one at that. She had been awarded a Pulitzer prize for a story she broke on a political scandal. The story had some factual errors, but there hadn't been time to check everything out. That would have taken two more days, and by that time someone else would have come out with the story. The errors in the story were not substantial and did not detract from its essence. Chris's mother had never been able to make detailed plans about how to obtain information for a story because things would generally turn up in the most unexpected places. She had to follow leads as they came up and go with what she had when the deadline was approaching. Chris learned that to be successful you needed to make quick decisions. You could not wait for all the information or verify every detail.

Finally, Lee comes from a lower-income family. Lee's mother and father are both artists. The family lives in a small two-bedroom apartment adjacent to their art studio. Lee has learned the art of painting and took up sculpture before going to college. Art requires the ability to see an entire scene, Lee has learned, and how all of the elements of the scene come together. One must be able to change focus from the larger picture to one small element and back again. Lee has also learned that successful art is creative; it is an expression of the individual artist. This requires experimentation to find an adequate expression of the artist's inner feelings. The artist must try something, change it, try something else, over and over again before finding the expression with which the artist feels comfortable.

The Moral of the Story

Although there are many possible issues that may contribute to the story of Pat, Chris, and Lee, the one that will be focused on here is managing and valuing the diversity of the three friends. During the first year, the three friends had enough outside interests and complementary skills that they never had to manage their differences. This year when they needed to work together as a group, the differences in the way they think created problems because the friends are not aware of their differences, do not value them, and do not know how to manage them.

The three friends not only had different ways of learning and solving problems, they also had different backgrounds that gave each different areas of expertise and different ways of looking at the world. What the friends did not realize is that each could have provided leadership at different points in the project and, that by putting their perspectives together as opposed to trying to find the "right" perspective, they could come up with a much more complete view of the issues. The problem is that doing so requires work, some inevitable conflict, tense moments, and an ability to manage the process. The result, however, could have been a product more excellent than any of them could produce alone. Unfortunately they did not understand how their differences could be of benefit to them; they were not able to manage them. As a result, much energy was lost fighting and trying to convince others that their perspectives were the best ones, and an inferior product was produced.

The moral of the story is: *When differences are valued, even though doing so can be a difficult process, the result can be a superior product.*

The Advantage of Differences

As has now become evident, the three friends in our story have different ways of attacking a problem, are more comfortable with certain stages in the problem-solving process, and have different areas of expertise: Lee is good at putting ideas together to analyze a problem, is creative, enjoys hashing out new ideas, and hates the tedious work of polishing the ideas into a finished product. Pat enjoys putting the finishing details in place, is uncomfortable with the unstructured process of creating new ideas, and needs to have a plan of attack. Pat does not like schedules very much and spends so much time with details that projects tend not to be finished on time. Chris is calm in a pinch and excellent at getting things done under pressure.

One of the advantages of working in groups is that a range of skills is generally required to complete a project. There is a time when ideas need to be created. There are times when work needs to be scheduled and data meticulously put together, and there are also moments of crisis when someone needs to take the lead to get things accomplished quickly. As a project progresses, different members of a work group should come to the forefront according to the skills required at the time. If other members of the group are not skilled at or comfortable with taking a back seat when appropriate, then there will be an inevitable clash as individual group members try to control events simultaneously.

Avoiding destructive clashes is easier to say than do. It requires a conscious effort to understand and value others' skills and feel comfortable allowing them to take the lead when appropriate. If a person's ego dictates that things have to be done his or her way all the time, then that person will have difficulty. It is all the more important to recognize this and make an extra effort to explore the validity of alternate possibilities.

Another advantage of groups is in putting together the larger picture of a problem. It is like putting together a jigsaw puzzle. Each individual has a piece of the puzzle.

There are at least two ways that most people go about understanding what the larger picture is. First, if they think that they alone have the whole picture, they may try to convince others that they must be seeing their piece wrong. This generally expends a lot of energy and produces few results. Instead of trying to understand each other's view of the problem, Pat, Lee, and Chris each felt they had the best picture and tried to convince the others. This prevented them from getting a clear picture of the industry they were studying.

Second, and generally more successful, some people try to understand the perspective of others and realize that someone else's piece of the puzzle is not wrong just because it is different. When they put all of the pieces together, they get a clearer idea of the larger picture. To accomplish this, people need to make a conscious effort to listen and understand each other. If they find themselves making value judgments, such as "That's a really dumb idea," they will need to take a deep breath and make an effort to understand the other's point of view. For most people, this takes a lot of effort, but the reward is a much better outcome.

One final thing: Stereotyping may get in the way of fully understanding the perspective of another person. For example, some people may believe that all "Type X" people are not very intelligent. This leads to a tendency to discount their perspectives. Everyone stereotypes; the trick is to catch oneself reacting to a stereotype rather than to the uniqueness of individuals. Doing this allows one to make a conscious effort to understand and incorporate other perspectives.

37

Questions for Discussion

1. In reflecting on past or present group experiences, what differences have you had with other group members that have led to unproductive conflicts? In responding to this question, consider the following: Do you feel it is important to know your group mates socially? Do you feel more comfortable focusing mainly on the task? Do you need detailed facts and data to make a decision? Do you make decisions using intuition? Do you like to work alone or with others? Are you interested more in getting a grade or learning? Do change and uncertainty cause stress, or do you consider them to be challenges? Do you need to have your point of view understood before you can listen to other points of view, or do you like to listen to others first before forming an opinion?

2. How will you use the differences you have discovered to benefit any group you might work with in the future? In responding to this question, consider the following: When is each person's preferred style likely to be needed? How do the strengths and weaknesses of each group member complement each other? How will you learn from one another?

3. How will you recognize a problem that is directly related to the differences among group members before it becomes a major source of tension? In responding to this question, consider the following: How will you make sure the group becomes aware of members' concerns? How will you know when a strength is being overused or is inappropriate at the current time? How will you ensure that it is safe to express concerns in the group? How will you avoid pressuring the minority voice to conform to the majority?

2

DISCLOSING AND PREDICTING

Objectives

- To explore the accuracy of first impressions
- To examine the basis on which we form first impressions
- To practice active listening skills
- To examine how getting to know someone through an open exploration of shared and differing values helps to change first impressions and bring perceptions more into line with reality

Background

Using stereotypes, particularly stereotypes based on superficial first impressions, may sometimes help us to reach quick and efficient conclusions about people. More often, any efficiencies are severely and negatively undermined by lack of accuracy. Decisions made about people, based on first impressions or superficial observations, limit the potentials of both the observer and the observed.

Use of this exercise will help you examine the assumptions you make about others, as well as the assumptions people make about you. As you go through the exercise, you and your partner may find that your predictions about one another's attitudes and beliefs become more accurate. This generally comes about as a result of your ability to elicit more than just a minimum amount of information about your partner, thus increasing your knowledge and understanding of him or her. This means asking questions and carefully listening to the answers.

Instructions

1. (Dyads—10 minutes)

Select a partner, preferably someone you don't know very well.

Do the following:

- Tell your partner one pertinent fact about yourself. This will form one basis for your first impression.

- Rank how you feel about each of the statements on the attached list on a scale of 0 to 10, with 0 signifying total disagreement and 10 signifying total agreement. Enter your answers in the column headed "Your Ranking." Do not discuss your rankings until told to do so. Be careful not to look at your partner's rankings; this is not a contest, and there are no right or wrong answers.

2. *(Dyads—5 minutes each question)*

Using the same scale, predict the number you believe your partner will assign to statement one. Enter that ranking in the column headed "Prediction of Partner's Ranking." Remember, predict your partner's ranking for the first statement only!

When each partner has predicted his or her partner's response, do the following:

- Enter your partner's ranking in the column headed "Partner's Ranking."

- Find the numeric difference between the score you predicted and your partner's actual ranking.

- Enter that number in the column headed "Difference Between Prediction and Partner's Actual Ranking."

- Discuss why you believed your partner would respond as you predicted.

- Discuss why you ranked the statement the way you did. After five minutes, go on to the next statement. Continue through the list, one statement at a time, discussing each one before continuing.

Questions for Consideration

1. On what did you base your predictions on the earlier questions? How did this differ from the basis for your predictions on later questions? (If you and your partner got worse in predicting, or failed to improve as you went along, why do you believe that happened?)

2. Is using first impressions to judge someone inherently bad, or can there be advantages? What might these be?

3. What are the advantages and/or disadvantages of retaining first impressions? What are the advantages and/or disadvantages of moving beyond first impressions?

4. What tools do you have for reaching beyond first impressions? How can they best be used?

Work and Score Sheet

Topic	Your Ranking	Prediction of Partner's Ranking	Partner's Ranking	Difference Between Prediction and Partner's Actual Ranking
Sexual harassment is a common problem.				
Sports teach democratic values.				
A college degree is my ticket to success.				
I exercise regularly.				
I can talk to my parents about anything.				
I am politically conservative.				
I am careful about handling money.				
Dorm rules are in the best interests of students.				
Grades are important to me.				
I have a temper that shows.				
I have a hard time confronting my friends.				
I am comfortable participating in class discussions.				
I believe in life after death.				
Abortion on demand is the right of every woman.				
I consider myself to be very intelligent.				
I give money to homeless people.				
High schools should distribute condoms.				
Religion has done more harm than good.				
Sometime capital punishment is legitimate.				
Too much emphasis is placed on physical appearance.				

Total Disagreement   0   1   2   3   4   5   6   7   8   9   10   Total Disagreement

Remember, complete your discussion on each item before moving on to the next.

3

OBSERVE AND PREDICT

Objectives

- To explore the bases on which we judge other people

- To examine the way we stereotype people based on observational data

- To examine the benefits and dangers of stereotyping

- To examine how we use labeling to reinforce stereotypes

- To consider organizational issues that arise from stereotyping

Background

Most of us are unaware of the assumptions or judgments we make about one another. Applying such assumptions or judgments to whole classes of people is called stereotyping. We all do it, learning our stereotypes in early childhood from family, friends, teachers, the media, and so forth.

Various departments of the U. S. government have developed stereotyped profiles to help them decide such things as whose tax returns should be audited and who is most likely to be carrying illegal drugs through customs. In doing so, the government is making assumptions about people based on such characteristics as their jobs, their income level, or their looks. Issuers of credit cards also use stereotypes to develop profiles of people who might be poor credit risks. We use stereotypes to order our lives and make them more manageable. We use them to decide whom to believe and whom to trust.

Think for a minute about what assumptions you would make about a woman who has brightly colored dyed hair, speaks with a foreign accent, and wears oversized jewelry and micro-mini skirts? That was the description in *The Wall Street Journal* article of the woman who turned around a faltering major international consulting firm and brought it back to staggering profitability.

The late African-American actress, Ethel Waters, related in her autobiography her experience of being heckled as she admired an expensive full-length mink coat in the window of a New York furrier. To the astonishment of those who had taunted her with racial epithets, Ms. Waters walked into the store and walked out moments later—wearing the coat! Her hecklers clearly had made certain assumptions about her based on her race.

In another publicized incident, a young man went to a fancy building in the posh section of a city to inquire about renting an apartment. The rental agent gave him a brief glance, informed him that she did not rent to students, and walked away. What she saw—and probably based her judgment on—were his youthful face, his jeans, and his sweatshirt. She didn't see his $80,000 Porsche parked outside, nor did she take the time to learn that he is part owner of a multi-million dollar business, as well as being a genuinely nice guy.

In this exercise, you will have a chance to explore how you stereotype people and consider the ways in which those stereotypes affect your interactions with people.

Instructions

1. *(10 minutes—full class)*

   In class discussion, develop a list of about thirty things you first notice about people by using senses of sight, hearing, smell, and touch. Some examples might be hair color and clothing.

2. *(10 minutes—full class)*

   Draw two lines down the center of a piece of paper. Label the left column "Observations," the middle column "Generalizations," and the right column "Specific Stereotypes."

   Using the list of observations developed in Step 1, develop a list of about twenty generalizations you might make about a person based on combinations of these items. For example, you might make a generalization about a person's intelligence based on their hair color and their clothing.

   Enter the combinations of observations in the left column and the generalizations in the middle column.

3. *(10 minutes—full class)*

   Based on the list generated in response to Question 2 above, develop a list of specific stereotypes you might hold about people and the names you give to people who fit that description. (Sometimes it helps to start with the label and work backwards.) For example, you may conclude that a blond in a miniskirt has low intelligence and is thus a "bimbo."

Questions for Discussion

1. In what ways were you surprised by some of the stereotypes you and your classmates hold?

2. In what ways, if any, can stereotyping be useful?

3. In what ways, if any, can stereotyping be harmful?

4. In what ways, positive or negative, do you feel you are stereotyped? How do you feel this has affected your life? How do you think this will affect your ability to get a good job and succeed in your career?

5. Discuss the implications of stereotyping for hiring, task assignment, productivity, expectations, management methods, etc., in the workplace.

4

CROSSING THE CHICAGO HIGHWAY*

Objectives

- To explore the impact of personality on human interaction

- To examine how knowledge of another's personality aids in communicating and negotiating

- To examine how knowledge of one's own personality aids in communicating and negotiating

- To consider the usefulness of personality analysis

Background

Communicating effectively is the key to most successful interactions in the work place and beyond. Poor communication can present a serious stumbling block to working together and to managing conflict.

Too often, poor communication stems from variations on and misunderstandings of personality and personal style. If you are aggressive and outgoing, and you assume that others are as well, it may be natural to misinterpret the quiet slinking away of a coworker in the face of a disagreement. That coworker's message may be, "I am uncomfortable with confrontation, and I need time to think things over before I start to discuss the problem." Instead, you may interpret your coworker's response as an aggressive act meant to insult, and you may race after him or her, becoming angry and yelling. What is really happening is that you are failing to recognize that the two of you respond differently to the same stimulus.

By understanding your personality, and by becoming aware that others have different personalities, you may begin to understand why you and others react the various ways you do. This understanding can give you an edge in communicating, dealing with conflict, and negotiating. One personality test, the Myers Briggs Type Indicator (MBTI)$^{©}$, may help you do this. For this reason, the MBTI and similar tests are increasingly used in organizational settings.

In the following exercise, you will be given background information on the personalities of two individuals loosely based on the profiles that an MBTI test might reach. The MBTI provides you with information about four aspects of your personality: how you are energized; how you learn; how you evaluate situations; and your need for time and routine in your life.

* Copyright 1994 by Alice Jacobs. Used with permission.

How you are energized
The MBTI suggests that extroverts and introverts gain energy in two different ways—*extroverts* by the outer world of people and things, and introverts by the inner world of ideas and contemplation. *Extroverts*, according to this test, speak quickly, sometimes even before thinking, and their verbose styles often make them appear to take charge. *Introverts* prefer to study the facts before speaking, don't appreciate interruptions, and may appear to be slow to understand a situation or what they are being told.

How you learn
If you base your decisions largely on theory and instinct, the MBTI would label you as intuitive. If you rely more on data and fact, then you are characterized as *sensing*. *Intuitives* want to see the big picture: They generally view details and facts as insignificant to the main theme. *Sensing* types are likely to rely heavily on facts and tend to mistrust theoretical or imaginative ideas. Giving them lots of facts and details will earn their approval.

How you evaluate situations
If you evaluate situations objectively, with logic and rationality, then the MBTI would label you as a *thinker*. *Feelers*, on the other hand, tend to base their decisions primarily on values and on subjective evaluation of person-centered concerns. *Thinking* types look for efficient and logical resolutions. *Feeling* types are far more concerned with the results of an outcome on peoples' feelings.

Your need for time and routine in your life
According to the MBTI, people who like a planned and organized approach to life and prefer to have things settled are *judgers*. Conversely, *perceivers* like a flexible and spontaneous approach to life and keep their options open. *Judging* types keep detailed daily schedules and stick to them at all costs: Order is of absolute importance. *Perceiving* types are more concerned about the quality of a decision or an event, not its completion.

It's important to remember that we all have the capacity to use all eight preferences. Those we use most often tend to become recognized as our dominant personality type. Once you are aware of your type and the types of others, your style of communicating and approach to negotiation may become sharper and more strategic.

Instructions

1. (10 minutes)

Briefly review the background information given above to be sure you are familiar with the terminology used by the MBTI in describing personalities.

Next, read following story: Chris Jones, a manager in the Project Controls Division of the Chicago Highway Construction Authority, has just hung up from the seventh telephone call he has received in two weeks from Lee Cohen. Cohen, Ward 11 supervisor, told Jones in very loud tones that his constituents are leaning on him to say exactly when the current highway construction is going to be out of their neighborhoods. Construction has been going on in the Ward 11 neighborhoods for the last four months, and it has caused considerable noise, dirt, and irritation.

Jones estimates that the work will continue for at least nine months more, maybe longer. The truth is, he doesn't really know for sure. Unfortunately, the *Chicago Star* reported that it would be no more than five months, and Cohen keeps reminding Jones of that.

Cohen has demanded an exact answer from Jones, and he has requested a meeting in a few days to discuss the project. Jones knows that Cohen is on the Environmental Impact Statement Committee that could greatly influence his group's work schedule, possibly further delaying completion of the project or stopping parts of it altogether. In addition, Cohen is pressuring Jones to hire 20 college students from his Ward as summer interns.

Jones knows he can't afford to alienate the public, especially since there has already been some tough criticism of his project in the *Star* and around town. A number of protests and challenges by various interest groups have continued to plague the project, sometimes even bringing the work to a halt. Jones doesn't want to set a precedent of backing down in all confrontations with community groups.

Jones's several phone conversations with Cohen, plus what his friends have told him, have helped him develop a sense of Cohen's personality. From what he has learned, Jones has concluded that Cohen is extroverted, intuitive, feeling, and perceiving. This is difficult for Jones who considers himself to be introverted, sensing, thinking, and judging.

Jones has asked you to help him plan just how he should go about conducting the meeting with Cohen.

2. *(20 minutes)*

Working in a group of three to five participants, discuss the following:

a. What do you believe will be the main issues on which Cohen will focus?

b. How do you believe Cohen will present his interests and concerns?

c. Based on what you know of Jones's and Cohen's personalities, what problems do you foresee them having during their meeting?

d. What recommendations do you have for Jones on how he should conduct himself during the meeting?

Select a spokesperson to report your group's conclusions to the class.

3. *Report out and discussion (open-ended)*

5

THE DINNER PARTY

Objectives

- To reflect on the numerous dimensions of diversity

- To consider the conflicting interests and needs of diverse populations

- To explore the meaning of diversity in interpersonal relationships

- To explore the challenges and benefits of diverse work populations

Background

You have invited the following people to a small dinner party tomorrow evening at your new apartment:

1. Your uncle Jack, a cattle rancher from the big island of Hawaii, who has always given you very lavish gifts. Whenever you've visited him, he has served great steaks and roast beef.

2. Uncle Jack is bringing his nine-year-old daughter, by a second marriage, who throws temper tantrums when she has to eat vegetables.

3. A female graduate student, Gitanjali, from Madras, India. Gita lives in an elegant apartment nearby, and she wears magnificent silk saris. You believe she is Hindu.

4. Howard Ben Zadik, from Passaic, New Jersey, a classmate whom you like and want to know better. Howie always wears a small skullcap with Hebrew letters on it.

5. Linda, a school friend who spends most of her free time working for Greenpeace, Save the Whales, and other environmental causes. Linda was diagnosed with childhood diabetes at age ten and always carries insulin and a test kit.

6. Your favorite high school teacher, now retired, who you'd really like to impress. Your teacher always had boxes of Godiva chocolates and ate them constantly. Since leaving high school, you have learned that your teacher is a recovered alcoholic who is very active in A.A.

You have decided to serve a multi-course meal which will include hors d'oeuvres, entrée, at least three side dishes, and dessert, plus beverages before, with, and after the meal.

Instructions

1. *(30 minutes)*

   Working with three to five classmates, review the background information on each of your dinner guests. Come to a consensus on (a) what will you specifically avoid serving, and why; (b) what you will serve, and why?

   Use the worksheet that follows to detail your answers.

2. *(5 minutes per group)*

   Report your menu to the rest of the class, and explain the rationale for each of the food selections you will offer.

Questions for Discussion

1. In dealing with the conflicting interests and needs of your dinner guests, did you determine that the interests and needs of one or more of your guests should take precedence? Which ones, and why?

2. In determining the menu, what feelings (e.g., sympathy, impatience, etc.) did you experience towards specific guests? Why do you think you had those feelings? Were you more or less sympathetic or patient with guests whose needs and interests are similar to your own? What about those whose needs and interests are different from your own?

3. What advantages can you identify in entertaining a group having diverse needs and interests? What disadvantages? Compare this experience to dealing with diverse needs and interests in the workplace.

4. Consider that each of your invited guests represents a number of coworkers (e.g., a group of recovered alcoholics, a group of first-generation immigrants, etc.) instead of friends and relatives, and your task is to plan the company's annual outing. What will you do differently? Why?

The Dinner Party — Worksheet

What to avoid serving	Why avoid serving it?

The Dinner Menu

Course	What will be served?	Why?
Hors d'oeuvres		
Entrée(s)		

Continued on the following page

The Dinner Party — Worksheet (Cont'd)

Course	What will be served?	Why?
Side dishes		
Dessert(s)		
Beverages		
before dinner		
with dinner		
with dessert		

6

MERCURY'S WINGS*

The Perfect Fit

Sarah Shapiro has been working for Mercury's Wings, a relatively new athletic shoe company, for exactly two months. As assistant to the director of overseas marketing, she is excited about finally being able to put her marketing skills to good use.

This is Sarah's second job since graduating from college two years ago with a degree in marketing. Her previous position, as an interviewer at a marketing research firm, had been fun, and she had learned a lot. She had enjoyed the collegial and relaxed atmosphere of the small company, and their flexible policies had been particularly important for her. As an Orthodox Jew, Sarah observed many religious holidays throughout the year. At the research firm, her taking the various holidays off from work had never been a problem. As time went on, however, Sarah found the work at the marketing firm to be less and less challenging, and she saw no real opportunities for upward movement. After two years, she knew it was time to move on.

During her senior year in college, Sarah had worked as an intern at Mercury's Wings. Thinking about where to look for a new job, she decided to give her former supervisor, Victoria White, a call. There had been no openings at Mercury's Wings when Sarah had graduated, but maybe there would be something available now.

Victoria had been pleased to hear from Sarah and had encouraged her to submit her résumé for a new position that was being created. As Victoria had explained, the position would involve assisting the director of overseas marketing with marketing campaigns targeted at international markets, particularly in Europe. The job would require long hours and frequent travel, but the pay was good and the experience invaluable. It had sounded like a perfect fit to Sarah and, so far, it had been.

A Very Big Deal

Sarah and her boss, Erin McCarthy, were in the process of planning a major product show in London. This was the first product show that Mercury's Wings had presented abroad and, as such, the company was charting new territory. Peter Smith, president of Mercury's Wings, constantly referred to the product show as a "very big deal!" Peter made clear that he expected everyone in the company to assist Erin and Sarah with the planning of the show, and this assistance had certainly made the project less daunting. However, since there were still a lot of last-minute details to wrap up, Sarah and Erin would be working overtime and then some for the next few weeks.

* This case was written by Gail E. Gilmore.

51

The long hours didn't matter to Sarah. She had obtained her first passport, arranged for a friend to take care of her cat, and was looking forward to what promised to be an incredible learning experience. She also knew that if the event was successful, it would pave the way for her future growth within the company. Sarah agreed with Peter Smith—the product show definitely was a very big deal!

The Bombshell

In the weeks before Sarah and Erin were to leave for London, they had worked many hours going over and over the intricate details of planning a major product show. They often had lunch and dinner together, and Sarah grew increasingly to like her boss. She particularly appreciated Erin's willingness to ask her opinion—and to take it seriously. Erin had also used many of Sarah's ideas in developing the overall marketing strategy of the product show. They had worked together as a team and, Sarah thought, a very productive one at that.

Things were going along smoothly until Peter came in one afternoon and dropped "the bombshell." Due to a last-minute scheduling conflict involving the convention center in which the product show was to be held, the show had been moved up a week, from June 13 to June 6. This was just two weeks away. Because Peter had needed to rebook Sarah's and Erin's flight on such short notice, the only flight he had been able to book was one leaving on June 4.

"Oh, no," Erin groaned. "I don't know how we're ever going to get everything done by then!"

"I'll make sure you get all the help you need," Peter assured her. He looked over at Sarah, who had said nothing since his announcement but who seemed suddenly quite distressed. Even his assurances of increased help did not seem to help whatever was bothering her.

"What's the matter?" he asked her.

Sarah cleared her throat. "Actually, Mr. Smith, I have a problem. June 4 is an important religious holiday for me. I'm an Orthodox Jew, and I observe Shavuoth. I can't ride on that day, which means I can't travel on that day. I'm sorry."

London Bound?

"Sarah, I really need you there to help with everything. You have to go!" Erin said, panic rising in her voice.

"Can't we get another flight?" Sarah asked.

"Look," Peter responded, "I was lucky to be able to rebook the flight at all. I can't believe what a disaster you're turning this into! We need you there. This is a pretty obscure holiday. I've never even heard of it, and I can't imagine that it's more important than your obligation to make sure this product show runs smoothly. You'll be letting Erin down if you don't go, not to mention all the other people in this company who've put in extra hours on this project. I'm sure you can make an exception this one time." It was clear to Sarah that Peter Smith did not understand how important her religion was to her. She didn't think that Erin understood either.

"My religious beliefs are very important to me," she explained. "But my professional responsibilities are also very important. I wish there was some alternative so I wouldn't be forced to choose between them."

"I'm afraid you're going to have to make a choice. As far as I'm concerned, I'll expect to see you in London."

With that, Peter Smith walked out the door. "Well, I guess you have some serious thinking to do," Erin said coldly. "I hope you make the *right* choice."

Erin left, leaving Sarah to ponder her decision. Whatever choice she made, she lost. In spite of Erin's parting words, Sarah felt there was no right choice. It was a question of what would be the lesser loss—her religious beliefs or her career with Mercury's Wings. Sarah pondered the irony of the name; if only she had Mercury's wings, she could fly to London without having to ride in anything. That would certainly solve her problems!

Unfortunately, she did not. She would have to make a decision.

Questions for Discussion

1. When the needs of an organization and the needs of an individual employee conflict, whose needs take precedence? Why?

2. What do you see as the consequences for Sarah if she decides to go to London? If she decides not to?

3. What is Mercury's Wings' obligation to Sarah? What is Sarah's obligation to Mercury's Wings?

4. Thinking about Sarah's dilemma, as well as other dilemmas faced by members of today's workforce, e.g., work-family issues, ethical issues, etc., in what ways is it possible for organizations to meet the diverse needs of their workforce? How do you view the role of lawmakers in requiring organizations to meet these needs?

7

THE CULTURE QUIZ

Objectives

- To stimulate awareness of cultural differences
- To promote consideration of the impact of cultural differences in a global economy
- To stimulate dialogue between domestic and international students
- To explore issues raised by culturally diverse workforces

Background

Few, if any, traditions and values are universally held. Many business dealings have succeeded or failed because of a manager's awareness or lack of understanding of the traditions and values of his or her foreign counterparts. With the world business community so closely intertwined and interdependent, it is critical that managers today become increasingly aware of the differences that exist.

How culturally aware are you? Try the questions below.

Instructions

Working alone or with a small group, answer the questions (without peeking at the answers). When you do look at the answers, be sure to read the explanations. If you are taking the quiz with students from other countries than your own, explore what the answer might be in your country and theirs.

1. In Japan, loudly slurping your soup is considered to be
   a. rude and obnoxious.
   b. a sign that you like the soup.
   c. okay at home but not in public.
   d. something only foreigners do.

2. In Korea, business leaders tend to
   a. encourage strong commitment to teamwork and cooperation.
   b. encourage competition among subordinates.
   c. discourage subordinates from reporting directly, preferring information to come through well-defined channels.
   d. encourage close relationships with their subordinates.

3. In Japan, virtually every kind of drink is sold in public vending machines except for
   a. beer.
   b. diet drinks with saccharin.
   c. already sweetened coffee.
   d. soft drinks from U.S. companies.

4. In Latin America, managers
   a. are most likely to hire members of their own families.
   b. consider hiring members of their own families to be inappropriate.
   c. stress the importance of hiring members of minority groups.
   d. usually hire more people than are actually needed to do a job.

5. In Ethiopia, when a woman opens the front door of her home, it means
   a. she is ready to receive guests for a meal.
   b. only family members may enter.
   c. religious spirits may move freely in and out of the home.
   d. she has agreed to have sex with any man who enters.

6. In Latin America, businesspeople
   a. consider it impolite to make eye contact while talking to one another.
   b. always wait until the other person is finished speaking before starting to speak.
   c. touch each other more than North Americans do under similar circumstances.
   d. avoid touching one another as it is considered an invasion of privacy.

7. The principal religion in Malaysia is
   a. Buddhism.
   b. Judaism.
   c. Christianity.
   d. Islam.

8. In Thailand
   a. it is common to see men walking along holding hands.
   b. it is common to see a man and a woman holding hands in public.
   c. it is rude for men and women to walk together.
   d. men and women traditionally kiss each other on meeting in the street.

9. When eating in India, it is appropriate to
   a. take food with your right hand and eat with your left.
   b. take food with your left hand and eat with your right.
   c. take food and eat it with your left hand.
   d. take food and eat it with your right hand.

10. Pointing your toes at someone in Thailand is
    a. a symbol of respect, much like the Japanese bow.
    b. considered rude even if it is done by accident.
    c. an invitation to dance.
    d. the standard public greeting.

11. American managers tend to base the performance appraisals of their subordinates on performance, while in Iran, managers are more likely to base their performance appraisals on
    a.   religion.
    b.   seniority.
    c.   friendship.
    d.   ability.

12. In China, the status of every business negotiation is
    a.   reported daily in the press.
    b.   private, and details are not discussed publicly.
    c.   subjected to scrutiny by a public tribunal on a regular basis.
    d.   directed by the elders of every commune.

13. When rewarding an Hispanic worker for a job well done, it is best not to
    a.   praise him or her publicly.
    b.   say "thank you."
    c.   offer a raise.
    d.   offer a promotion.

14. In some South American countries, it is considered normal and acceptable to show up for a social appointment
    a.   ten to fifteen minutes early.
    b.   ten to fifteen minutes late.
    c.   fifteen minutes to an hour late.
    d.   one to two hours late.

15. In France, when friends talk to one another
    a.   they generally stand about three feet apart.
    b.   it is typical to shout.
    c.   they stand closer to one another than Americans do.
    d.   it is always with a third party present.

16. When giving flowers as gifts in Western Europe, be careful not to give
    a.   tulips and jonquils.
    b.   daisies and lilacs.
    c.   chrysanthemums and calla lilies.
    d.   lilacs and apple blossoms.

17. The appropriate gift-giving protocol for a male executive doing business in Saudi Arabia is to
    a.   give a man a gift from you to his wife.
    b.   present gifts to the wife or wives in person.
    c.   give gifts only to the eldest wife.
    d.   not give a gift to the wife at all.

18. If you want to give a necktie or a scarf to a Latin American, it is best to avoid the color
    a. red.
    b. purple.
    c. green.
    d. black.

19. The doors in German offices and homes are generally kept
    a. wide open to symbolize an acceptance and welcome of friends and strangers.
    b. slightly ajar to suggest that people should knock before entering.
    c. half-opened suggesting that some people are welcome and others are not.
    d. tightly shut to preserve privacy and personal space.

20. In the area that was formerly West Germany, leaders who display charisma are
    a. not among the most desired.
    b. the ones most respected and sought after.
    c. invited frequently to serve on boards of cultural organizations.
    d. pushed to get involved in political activities.

21. American managers running businesses in Mexico have found that by increasing the salaries of Mexican workers, they
    a. increased the numbers of hours the workers were willing to work.
    b. enticed more workers to work night shifts.
    c. decreased the number of hours workers would agree to work.
    d. decreased production rates.

22. Chinese culture teaches people
    a. to seek psychiatric help for personal problems.
    b. to avoid conflict and internalize personal problems.
    c. to deal with conflict with immediate confrontation.
    d. to seek help from authorities whenever conflict arises.

23. One wedding gift that should not be given to a Chinese couple would be
    a. a jade bowl.
    b. a clock.
    c. a basket of oranges.
    d. shirts embroidered with dragon patterns.

24. In Venezuela, New Year's Eve is generally spent
    a. in quiet family gatherings.
    b. at wild neighborhood street parties.
    c. in restaurants with horns, hats, and live music and dancing.
    d. at pig roasts on the beach.

25. If you order "bubble and squeak" in a London pub, you will get
    a. two goldfish fried in olive oil.
    b. a very cold beer in a chilled glass, rather than the usual warm beer.
    c. Alka Seltzer® and a glass of water.
    d. chopped cabbage and mashed potatoes fried together.

26. When a stranger in India wants to know what you do for a living and how much you earn, he will
    a. ask your guide.
    b. invite you to his home and, after getting to know you, will ask.
    c. come over and ask you directly, without introduction.
    d. respect your privacy above all.

27. When you feel you are being taken advantage of in a business exchange in Vietnam, it is important to
    a. let the anger show in your face but not in your words.
    b. say that you are angry, but keep your facial expression neutral.
    c. not show any anger in any way.
    d. end the business dealings immediately, and walk away.

28. When a taxi driver in India shakes his head from side to side, it probably means
    a. he thinks your price is too high.
    b. he isn't going in your direction.
    c. he will take you where you want to go.
    d. he doesn't understand what you're asking.

29. In England, holding your index and middle fingers up in a vee with the back of your hand facing another person is seen as
    a. a gesture of peace.
    b. a gesture of victory.
    c. a signal that you want two of something.
    d. a vulgar gesture.

Answers to "The Culture Quiz"

1. b. Slurping your soup or noodles in Japan is good manners in both public and private. It indicates enjoyment and appreciation of the quality. (source: Eiji Kanno and Constance O'Keefe, *New Japan Solo,* Japan National Tourist Organization: Tokyo, 1990, p. 20.)

2. b. Korean managers use a "divide-and rule" method of leadership that encourages competition among subordinates. They do this to insure that they can exercise maximum control. In addition, they stay informed by having individuals report directly to them. This way, they can know more than anyone else. (source: Richard M. Castaldi and Tjipyanto Soerjanto, "Contrasts in East Asian Management Practices." *The Journal of Management in Practice*, 2:1, 1990, pp. 25–27.)

3. b. Saccharin-sweetened drinks may not be sold in Japan by law. On the other hand, beer, a wide variety of Japanese and international soft drinks, and so forth, are widely available from vending machines along the streets and in buildings. You're supposed to be at least 18 to buy the alcoholic ones, however. (source: Eiji Kanno and Constance O'Keefe, *New Japan Solo,* Japan National Tourist Organization: Tokyo, 1990, p. 20.)

4. a. Family is considered to be very important in Latin America, so managers are likely to hire their relatives more quickly than hiring strangers. (source: Nancy J. Adler, *International Dimensions of Organizational Behavior*, 2nd ed., PWS-Kent: Boston, 1991.)

5. d. The act, by a woman, of opening the front door, signifies that she has agreed to have sex with any man who enters. (source: Adam Pertman, "Wandering No More," *Boston Globe Magazine*, June 30, 1991, p. 10 ff.)

6. c. Touching one another during business negotiations is common practice. (source: Nancy J. Adler, *International Dimensions of Organizational Behavior*, 2nd ed., PWS-Kent: Boston, 1991.)

7. d. Approximately 45 percent of the people in Malaysia follow Islam, the country's "official" religion. (source: Hans Johannes Hoefer, ed., *Malaysia,* Prentice-Hall: Englewood Cliffs, N.J., 1984.)

8. a. Men holding hands is considered a sign of friendship. Public displays of affection between men and women, however, are unacceptable. (source: William Warren, Star Black, and M.R. Priya Rangsit, eds., *Thailand,* Prentice-Hall: Englewood Cliffs, N.J., 1985.)

9. d. In India, as in many Asian countries, toilet paper is not used. Instead, water and the left hand are used, after which the left hand is thoroughly cleaned. Still, the left hand is considered to be polluted and therefore inappropriate for use during eating or touching another person. (source: Gitanjali Kolanad, *Culture Shock! India,* Graphic Arts Center Publishing Company: Portland, Oregon, 1996, p. 117.)

10. b. This is especially an insult if it is done deliberately, since the feet are the lowest part of the body. (source: William Warren, Star Black, and M.R. Priya Rangsit, eds., *Thailand,* Prentice-Hall: Englewood Cliffs, N.J., 1985.)

11. c. Adler suggests that friendship is valued over task competence in Iran. (source: Nancy J. Adler, *International Dimensions of Organizational Behavior,* 2nd ed., PWS-Kent: Boston, 1991.)

12. b. Public discussion of business dealings is considered inappropriate. Kaplan, et al. report that, "the Chinese may even have used a premature announcement to extract better terms from executives," who were too embarrassed to admit that there was never really a contract. (source: Frederic Kaplan, Julian Sobin, Arne de Keijzer, *The China Guidebook,* Houghton Mifflin: Boston, 1987.)

13. a. Public praise for Hispanics and Asians is generally embarrassing because modesty is an important cultural value. (source: Jim Braham, "No, You Don't Manage Everyone the Same," *Industry Week*, February 6, 1989). In Japan, being singled out for praise is also an embarrassment. A common saying in that country is, "The nail that sticks up gets hammered down."

14. d. Though being late is frowned upon in the United States, being late is not only accepted but expected in some South American countries. (source: Lloyd S. Baird, James E. Post, and John F. Mahon, *Management: Functions and Responsibilities,* Harper & Row: New York, 1990.)

15. c.   Personal space in most European countries is much smaller than in the United States. Americans generally like at least two feet of space around themselves, while it is not unusual for Europeans to be virtually touching. (source: Lloyd S. Baird, James E. Post, and John F. Mahon, *Management: Functions and Responsibilities,* Harper & Row: New York, 1990.)

16. c.   Chrysanthemums and calla lilies are both associated with funerals. (source: Theodore Fischer, *Pinnacle: International Issue,* March–April 1991, p. 4.)

17. d.   In Arab cultures, it is considered inappropriate for wives to accept gifts or even attention from other men. (source: Theodore Fischer, *Pinnacle: International Issue,* March–April 1991, p. 4.)

18. b.   In Argentina and other Latin American countries, purple is associated with the serious fasting period of Lent. (source: Theodore Fischer, *Pinnacle: International Issue,* March–April 1991, p. 4.)

19. d.   Private space is considered so important in Germany that partitions are erected to separate people from one another. Privacy screens and walled gardens are the norm. (source: Julius Fast, *Subtext: Making Body Language Work,* Viking Penguin Books: New York, 1991, p. 207.)

20. a.   Though political leaders in the United States are increasingly selected on their ability to inspire, charisma is a suspect trait in what was West Germany, where Hitler's charisma is still associated with evil intent and harmful outcomes. (source: Nancy J. Adler, *International Dimensions of Organizational Behavior,* 2nd ed., PWS-Kent: Boston, 1991, p. 149.)

21. c.   Paying Mexican workers more means, in the eyes of the workers, that they can make the same amount of money in fewer hours and thus have more time for enjoying life. (source: Nancy J. Adler, *International Dimensions of Organizational Behavior,* 2nd ed., PWS-Kent: Boston, 1991, pp. 30 and 159.)

22. b.   Psychological therapy is not an accepted concept in China. In addition, communism has kept most Chinese from expressing opinions openly. (source: James McGregor, "Burma Road Heroin Breeds Addicts, AIDS Along China's Border," *The Wall Street Journal*, September 29, 1992, p. 1.)

23. b.   The Chinese regard a clock as a bad omen because the word for clock, pronounced *zhong*, is phonetically similar to another Chinese word that means the end. Jade is highly valued as symbolizing superior virtues, and oranges and dragon patterns are also auspicious symbols. (source: Dr. Evelyn Lip, "Culture and Customs." *Silver Kris*, February 1994, p. 84.)

24. a.   Venezuelans do the reverse of what most people in other countries do on Christmas and New Years. On Christmas, they socialize. While fire works are shot off on both nights, most restaurants are closed, and the streets are quiet. (source: Tony Perrottet, ed., *Venezuela,* Houghton Mifflin: Boston, 1994, p. 97.)

25. d. Other popular pub food includes Bangers and Mash (sausages and mashed potatoes), Ploughman's lunch (bread, cheese, and pickled onions), and Cottage pie (baked minced meat with onions and topped with mashed potatoes). (source: Ravi Desai, ed., *Let's Go: The Budget Guide to Britain and Ireland,* Pan Books: London, 1990, p. 83.)

26. c. Indians are generally uninhibited about staring at strangers and asking them about personal details in their lives. Social distance and personal privacy are not common social conventions in India. (source: Frank Kusy, *India,* The Globe Pequot Press: Chester, Conn., 1989, p. 27.)

27. c. Vernon Weitzel of the Australian National University advises never to show anger when dealing with Vietnamese officials or business people. Showing anger causes you to lose face and is considered rude. Weitzel also recommends always smiling, not complaining or criticizing anyone, and not being inquisitive about personal matters. (source: Daniel Robinson and Joe Cummings, *Vietnam, Laos & Cambodia,* Lonely Planet Publications: Australia, 1991, p. 96.)

28. c. What looks to Westerners like a refusal is really an Indian way of saying "yes." It can also express general agreement with what you're saying or suggest that an individual is interested in what you have to say. (source: Gitanjali Kolanad, *Culture Shock! India,* Graphic Arts Center Publishing Company: Portland, Oregon, 1996, p. 114.)

29. d. In England, this simple hand gesture is considered vulgar and obscene. In a report to *The Boston Globe*, an American who had been working in London wrote, "I wish someone had told me before I emphatically explained to one of the draftsmen at work why I needed two complete sets of drawings." (source: "Finger Gestures Can Spell Trouble," *The Berkshire Eagle,* January 26, 1997, p. E5.)

8

"WHEN IN BOGOTÁ..."*

As Jim Reynolds looked out the small window of the Boeing 757, he saw the glimmer of lights in the distance. After a five hour flight, he arrived in Bogotá, Colombia, at 9:35 p.m. on a clear Friday evening. It had been nearly five years since Jim had seen his best friend, Rodrigo Cardozo. The two had met in college and kept in touch over the years. During their school years, Rodrigo would often accompany Jim when he went home to Chicago for the holidays.

Entering the main terminal, Jim found himself in what looked like a recently bombed building. Piles of debris were everywhere. Lights hung from the ceiling by exposed electrical wires, and the walls and floors were rough, unfinished concrete. "Certainly, aesthetics are not a major concern at the Bogotá International Airport," Jim thought.

As he came to the end of the long, dimly lit corridor, an expressionless customs official reached out his hand and gestured for Jim's travel documents.

"Passaporte, por favor. Bienvenidos a Bogotá, Señor Reynolds. Estás en vacacciones?"

"Sí," Jim replied.

After a few routine questions, Jim was allowed to pass through customs feeling relatively unscathed.

"Loquillo! Loquillo! Estamos aquí! Jim, Jim," a voice shouted.

Trying to find the origin of the voice among the dense crowd, Jim finally spotted Rodrigo. "Hey, man. How've you been? You look great!"

"Jim, it's so good to see you. How've you been? I would like you to meet my wife, Eva. Eva, this is my best friend, Jim. He's the one in all those pictures I've shown you."

Late Night Begins the Day

Close to an hour later, Jim, Rodrigo, and Eva arrived at Rodrigo's parents' house on the other side of Bogotá from the airport. As Jim was aware, it is customary for couples to live with their parents for a number of years after their marriage, and Rodrigo and Eva were part of that custom.

Darío, Rodrigo's father, owned an import/export business in Bogotá. He was a knowledgeable and educated man and, from what Jim knew, a master of business negotiations. Over the years, Darío had conducted business with people in nearly every country in Central and South America, the United States, Europe, Hong Kong, and some parts of Africa. Jim had first met Darío with Rodrigo in Boston in 1989.

* Copyright 1994 by Matthew B. Shull. Used with permission.

"Jim, welcome to my house," Darío boomed effusively as the group walked in. "I am so pleased that you're finally in Bogotá. Would you like something to drink—whiskey, bourbon, Aguardiente?"

"Aguardiente!" Rodrigo urged.

"Yes, Jim would like some Aguardiente. I understand you're going to Bahía tonight," Darío added.

"Where?" Jim asked, looking around. "I didn't know we were going anywhere tonight."

"Don't worry, Jim, todo bien, todo bien," Rodrigo assured him. "We're going dancing, so get dressed. Let's go."

The reality of being in Colombia hit Jim at about 11:15 that night when he and his friends entered Bahía, a Bogotá nightclub. The rhythms of salsa and merangue filled the club. Jim's mind flashed back to the Latin dance parties he and Rodrigo had had in Boston with their friends from Central and South America.

"Jim, this is my cousin, Diana. She'll be your partner tonight," Rodrigo said. "You'll get to practice your Spanish too; she doesn't speak a word of English. Have fun."

For the next six hours, they danced and drank. This is the Colombian way. At 5:30 the next morning, Rodrigo decided it was time to leave to get something to eat. On the drive home, they stopped at an outdoor grill in the mountains where many people had congregated for the same reason. Everyone was eating arepas con queso and mazorca, and drinking Aguardiente.

Next, they continued to an outdoor party just down the street. Here, they danced and drank until the sun crested over the mountains of Bogotá. It was about 7:00 a.m. when they decided to conclude the celebration—for now.

Saturday was spent recovering from the previous evening and also touring some local spots in the country. However, Saturday night was a repeat of Friday. After being in Colombia for three days, Jim had slept a total of about four hours. Fortunately, Monday was a national holiday.

Business Before Pleasure Before Business?

Although Jim was having a great time, he had also scheduled a series of business meetings with directors of business schools at various Bogotá universities for the week to come. Jim worked as an acquisitions editor for Academia Press, a major publisher of college-level business textbooks. The purpose of the meetings was to establish business contacts in the Colombian market. It was hoped that these initial contacts would lead to others in Latin America.

At Academia Press headquarters in New York, Jim and Caroline Evans, his boss, had discussed the opportunities in Latin America. Although Academia Press routinely published international editions of its texts, total international sales never represented more than 15 percent of their gross. Consequently, international markets had never been pursued aggressively. Caroline, however, saw the Latin American markets as having a lot of potential within the next three to five years. She envisioned this market alone could, in time, represent 15 to 20 percent of gross sales. Moreover, she felt that within the next ten years, international sales could reach 40 percent if developed properly. With numbers like that, it was evident to Jim that this deal was important not only to the company but to his career as well. If Jim was able to open these markets, he might receive a promotion and be able to continue to work in Central and South America.

Jim's first meeting was scheduled for 11:00 a.m. on Tuesday, the second on Wednesday at 11:00 a.m., and the third on Friday at 3:00 p.m. At precisely 11:00 a.m. on Tuesday, Jim arrived at Javeriana University where he was to meet with Professors Emilio Muñoz, Diana Espitia, and Enrique Ronderos. When he arrived, Professor Muñoz was waiting for him in the conference room.

"Señor Reynolds, I am delighted to meet you. How was your flight?"

"Wonderful," Jim replied.

"And how do you like Bogotá so far? Have you been able to sightsee?"

"No, I haven't had the chance to get around the city yet. I hope to see some things later in the week."

"Well, before you leave, you must visit *El Museo de Oro*. It is the finest collection of gold artifacts from the various indigenous Indian tribes in Colombia. Although much of the gold was stolen by the Spanish, many pieces have survived." For the next thirty minutes, Professor Muñoz spoke of everything from the upcoming presidential elections to world cup soccer.

Jim looked at his watch, concerned about the other professors who had not yet arrived and about the meeting for which he had prepared.

"Is there something wrong, Señor Reynolds?"

"No, no, I was just wondering about the others; it's 11:30."

"Don't worry. They'll be here shortly. Traffic in Bogotá at this hour is terrible. They're probably caught in a traffic jam."

Just then, Professors Espitia and Ronderos walked in.

"Muy buenas, Señor Reynolds," Professor Espitia said warmly. "Please forgive us for the delay. Traffic is simply awful at this time of day."

"Oh, that's not necessary. I understand. Traffic in New York can be absolutely horrendous as well," Jim replied. "Sometimes it takes two hours to get from one end of the city to the other."

"Have you had lunch yet, Señor Reynolds?" asked Professor Ronderos. Jim shook his head.

"Why don't we go to lunch, and we can talk there?" Professor Ronderos suggested.

After discussing the restaurants in the area, the professors decided on El Club Ejecutivo. It was nearly 12:30 p.m. when they arrived.

"It's been an hour and a half, and we haven't discussed anything," Jim thought. He was concerned that the Colombians were not very interested in what he had to offer. Throughout lunch, Jim grew increasingly concerned that the professors were more interested in his trying typical Colombian dishes and visiting the sights in Bogotá than in Academia's textbooks.

64

They were fascinated that Jim knew how to dance salsa and merangue and impressed that he spoke Spanish with a slight Colombian accent; Señorita Espitia said she found it amusing. That seemed much more important than his knowledge of business textbooks and publishing in general.

By the end of lunch, Jim was nearly beside himself. It was now after 2:30 p.m., and nothing had been accomplished.

"Why don't we all go to Monserate tomorrow? It's absolutely beautiful up there, Señor Reynolds," Professor Ronderos suggested, going on to describe the mountain that overlooks Bogotá and the myths and traditions that surround it.

"That's a wonderful idea," Professor Espitia added.

"Monserate it is then. Jim, it has been a pleasure. I look forward to our meeting tomorrow," Professor Ronderos said with a slight bow.

"Señor Reynolds, would you like a ride home?" Professor Muñoz asked.

"Yes, if it's not too much trouble."

On the way home, Jim was relatively quiet. "Do you feel okay?"

"It must be jet lag catching up to me. I'm sure it's nothing," Jim responded. Concerned about the way the meeting had gone, Jim realized that he had never even had a chance to mention Academia Press's various titles and how these texts could be used to create a new curriculum or supplement an existing curriculum at the professors' business school.

When in Bogotá

On arriving at the house, Jim went upstairs and sat in the living room glumly sipping a cup of aguapanela. "I just don't get it," he thought. "The Colombians couldn't have been happier with the way the meeting turned out, but we didn't do anything. We didn't even talk about one book. I just don't understand what went wrong."

In a short time, Darío arrived. "Muy buenas, Jim. How did your meetings go today with the directors?" he asked.

"I don't know. I don't know what to think. We didn't do anything. We didn't talk about business at all. We talked more about the sights I should see and the places I should visit before I leave Colombia. I'm supposed to call my boss this afternoon and tell her how the initial meeting went. What am I going to tell her? 'Sorry, we just decided to plan my vacation in Colombia instead of discussing business.' I can't afford to have this deal fall through." Darío laughed.

"Señor, I'm serious."

"Jim, I understand. Believe me. Tell me about your meeting today."

Jim recounted every detail of the meeting to Darío, who smiled and nodded his head as he listened.

"Jim, you have to understand one thing before you continue negotiating with the directors."

"What's that?"

"You're in Colombia now," Darío said simply.

Jim stared at him with a puzzled look. "And?" "

And what, Jim?"

"Is there something else I should know?"

"That's were you need to start. You let the directors set the tone of the meeting. It's obvious they felt very comfortable with you, or they wouldn't have invited you to Monserate. Here in Colombia, Jim, we do business differently. Right now, you're building friendship. You're building their trust in you. This is very important in doing business in all of Latin America."

"Jim," Darío continued, "would you rather do business with a friend or someone you hardly know?"

As Darío went on to analyze the meeting, Jim realized that his perception of the situation had been formed by his experiences in the United States. "When in Bogotá," he thought, "I guess I had better think like the Colombians."

"Jim, you've gained the respect and the trust of the directors. In my opinion, your first meeting was a complete success."

"What should I expect in the meetings to come?" Jim asked.

"Don't worry," he responded. "Just let the directors worry about that. You'll come to an agreement before the end of the week. I guarantee it."

Questions for Discussion

1. What differences does Jim notice between life in the United States and life in Colombia? How might these same factors differ in other countries?

2. What differences does Jim notice between doing business in the United States and doing business in Colombia? How might these same factors differ in other countries?

3. What advice would you give Jim for closing his deals? Why?

9

WHO TO HIRE?

Objectives

- To explore participants' cultural biases and expectations
- To examine cultural differences
- To consider the impact culture has on hiring decisions

Instructions

Step 1 (10–15 minutes)

Read the background information and descriptions of each of the applicants. Consider the job and the cultures within which the individual to be hired will be operating. Rank the candidates from 1 to 5, with 1 being your first choice, and enter your rankings on the ranking sheet in the column marked "My Ranking." Briefly list the reasons for each of your rankings.

Do not discuss your rankings with your classmates until told to do so.

Step 2 (30–40 minutes)

Working with three to four of your classmates, discuss the applicants, and rank them in the order of group preference. Do not vote.

Rank the candidates from 1 to 5, with 1 being the group's first choice, and enter your group's rankings on the ranking sheet in the column marked "Group Ranking." Briefly list the reasons for each of the group's rankings.

If your group represents more than one culture, explore the ways in which each person's cultural background may have influenced his or her individual decisions.

Step 3 (open-ended)

Report your rankings to the class, and discuss the areas of difference that emerged within your group while you were trying to reach consensus.

Questions for Discussion

1. Was your group able to explore openly any culturally-based biases that came up—for example, feelings about homosexuality, religion, personality traits, politics?

2. Did you make any comments or observations that you feel would have been fully acceptable in your own culture but were not accepted by the group? Explain.

3. If the answer to Question 2 was yes, how did the reaction of the group make you feel about your membership in it? How did you handle the situation?

4. What implications do you believe these cultural differences would have in business dealings?

Background

You are a member of the management committee of a multinational company that does business in twenty-three countries. While your company's headquarters are in Holland, your offices are scattered fairly evenly throughout the four hemispheres. Primary markets have been in Europe and North America; the strongest emerging market is the Pacific Rim. Company executives would like to develop what they see as a powerful potential market in the Middle East. Sales in all areas except the Pacific Rim have shown slow growth over the past two years.

At present, your company is seeking to restructure and revitalize its worldwide marketing efforts. To accomplish this, you have determined that you need to hire a key marketing person to introduce fresh ideas and a new perspective. There is no one currently in your company who is qualified to do this, and so you have decided to look outside. The job title is "vice-president for international marketing"; it carries with it a salary well into six figures (US$), plus elaborate benefits, an unlimited expense account, a car, and the use of the corporate jet. The person you hire will be based at the company's headquarters and will travel frequently.

A lengthy search has turned up five people with good potential. It is now up to you to decide whom to hire. Although all the applicants have expressed a sincere interest in the position, it is possible that they may change their minds once the job is offered. Therefore, you must rank them in order of preference so that if your first choice declines the position, you can go on to the second, and so on.

Applicants

Park L., age 41, married with three children

Park L. is currently senior vice-president for marketing at a major Korean high technology firm. You have been told by the head of your Seoul office that his reputation as an expert in international marketing is outstanding. The market share of his company's products has consistently increased since he joined the company just over fifteen years ago. His company's market share is now well ahead of that of competing producers in the Pacific Rim.

Mr. Park started with his present company immediately after his graduation from the University of Seoul and has worked his way up through the ranks. He does not have a graduate degree. You sense that Mr. Park has a keen understanding of organizational politics and knows how to play them. He recognizes that because the company he works for now is family controlled, it is unlikely that he will ever move much higher than his present situation. Mr. Park has told you that he is interested in the growth potential offered at your company.

In addition to his native tongue, Mr. Park is able to carry on a reasonably fluent conversation in English and has a minimal working knowledge of German and French. His wife appears quiet and quite traditional, and his children speak only Korean.

Kiran K., age 50, widow with one adult child

Kiran K. is a Sikh woman living in Malaysia. She began her teaching career while finishing her DBA (doctorate in business administration) at the Harvard Business School and published her first book on international marketing ten months after graduation. Her doctoral dissertation was based on the international marketing of pharmaceuticals, but she has also done research and published on other areas of international marketing.

Two months after the publication of her book, Kiran went to work in the international marketing department of a Fortune 500 company, where she stayed for the next ten years. She returned to teaching when Maura University offered her a full professorship with tenure, and she has been there since that time. Her academic position has allowed her to pursue a number of research interests and to write authoritative books and papers in her field. At present, she is well published and internationally recognized as an expert on international marketing. In addition, she has an active consulting practice throughout Southeast Asia.

You have learned through your office in Kuala Lumpur that Kiran's only child, a twenty-three-year-old son, is severely mentally and physically disabled. You sense that part of her interest in the job with your company is to have the income to guarantee his care should anything happen to her. Her son would go with her to Holland, should she be given the job, where he will need to be enrolled in special support programs.

In addition to fluency in Malay, English, and Hindi, Kiran speaks and writes German and Spanish and is able to converse in Japanese and Mandarin.

Peter V., age 44, single

Peter is a white South African. He had worked in a key position in the international marketing division of an American Fortune 100 company until the company pulled out of his country eight months ago. While the company wanted to keep him on, offering to move him from Johannesburg to its New York headquarters, Peter decided that it was time to look elsewhere. He had begun to feel somewhat dead-ended in his position and apparently sees the position at your company as an opportunity to try out new territory. Like your other candidates for the position, Peter has a long list of accomplishments and is widely recognized as outstanding in his field. People in your company who have had contacts with him say that Peter is creative, hard working, and loyal. In addition, you have been told that Peter is a top-flight manager of people who is able to push his employees to the highest levels of performance. And, you are told, he is very organized.

Peter has a Ph.D. in computer science from a leading South African university and an MBA from Purdue's Krannert School of Business.

Peter had been a vehement opponent of apartheid and is still very much a social activist. His high political visibility within South Africa had made his life there difficult, and even now, with the end of apartheid, he would like to get out. His constant male companion, P.K. Kaahn, would be coming with him to Holland, and Peter would like your personnel office to help P.K. find an appropriate position.

Peter speaks and reads English, Dutch, Afrikaans, and Swahili and can converse in German.

Tex P., age 36, divorced with one child

Tex is currently job hunting. His former job as head of marketing for a single-product high technology firm—highly specialized workstations for sophisticated artificial intelligence applications—ended when the company was bought out by Texas Instruments. Tex had been with his previous company virtually from the time the company was started six years earlier. Having to leave his job was an irony to Tex as it was largely due to the success of his efforts that the company was bought out. You sense that he is a little bitter, and he tells you that jobs offered to him by TI were beneath him and not worthy of consideration.

Tex has both his undergraduate and MBA degrees from Stanford University. In addition, he was a Rhodes Scholar and won a Fulbright scholarship, which he used to support himself while he undertook a two-year research project on the marketing of high-technology equipment to Third World countries.

You have learned through your New York office that Tex has a reputation for being aggressive and hard driving. Apparently he is a workaholic who has been known to work eighteen to twenty hours a day, seven days a week. He seems to have little time for his personal life.

In addition to his native English, Tex has a minimal command of French—which he admits he hasn't used since his college days.

Zvi C., age 40, married with five children

Zvi began his career after receiving his MBA from the Sloan School of Management at the Massachusetts Institute of Technology (MIT). His first job was as marketing manager for a German company doing business in Israel.

Zvi's phenomenal success with this company led to his being hired away by an international office equipment company in England. Again, he proved to be outstanding, boosting the company's market share beyond all expectations within two years. After five years, Zvi was offered a chance to go back to Israel, this time to oversee and coordinate all the international marketing programs for an industrial park of fourteen companies run as an adjunct to Israel's leading scientific research institution. It has been his responsibility to interface the research component with product development and sales as well as to manage the vast marketing department. Again, he has shown himself to be a master.

You have learned through your Haifa office that Zvi is highly respected and has extensive contacts in the scientific and high-tech worlds. He is exceptionally creative in his approach to marketing, often trying bold strategies that most of his peers would dismiss as too risky. Zvi, however, has made them work and work well.

Zvi is a religious man who must leave work by noon on Friday. He will not work Saturdays nor any of his religion's major and minor holidays—about eighteen a year. He will, however, work on Sundays. In addition to his native language, Dutch (Zvi and his family moved to Israel from Holland when Zvi was six), he speaks and writes fluent Hebrew, English, German, and Arabic.

Ranking Sheet

Rank candidates from one to five with one as your first choice.

Applicant	*My Ranking*	*Reasons*	*Group Ranking*	*Reasons*
Park L.				
Kiran K.				
Peter V.				
Tex P.				
Zvi C.				

10

FREDERICK INTERNATIONAL*

In July of 1979, Gordon Frederick and Lewis Naehring, president and vice-president, respectively, of Frederick Engineering in Brookfield, Connecticut, decided to form a new division of their safety products company. The goal of the new division, Frederick International, would be to broaden the market for the company's main product, the Proxagard, a high-tech safety device, beyond the borders of the United States.

The Proxagard is used in such manufacturing equipment as punch presses. Punch presses are extremely dangerous. Around the world, many punch press operators have lost parts of fingers and hands when they have become careless and have allowed their hands to get in the path of the powerful machines. As a result, the punch press industry, and operators of hazardous equipment as well, were getting slapped with lawsuits when employees lost fingers or suffered other damage to their hands. In addition, OSHA, which regulates occupational safety and health in the United States, has the power to fine a company if an inspection or complaint reveals that the organization is jeopardizing the well-being of employees.

By electromagnetically sensing fingers when they come dangerously close to a press, the Proxagard provides customers with a fail-safe method of preventing injuries and does so at a competitive price. Another plus for the Proxagard is that help with installing and servicing this device is just a phone call away for customers in the United States. As companies have begun to see the rising costs of workers' compensation and costs associated with defending themselves against liability claims, they have started to weigh the bottom-line costs and benefits of safety equipment such as the Proxagard. In the United States, Frederick had been selling seven hundred to nine hundred of the safety devices per year.

Frederick's first sale to a foreign customer had been in September of 1976. Lapin Industrielle, a large company that specialized in importing American equipment, had seemed like a promising sales representative for the fledgling company. Frederick and Naehring were surprised and delighted when Lapin bought thirty Proxagards, which, at that time, cost about $450 each. All were installed in a company that used dozens of punch presses.

In addition to buying thirty Proxagards, Lapin Industrielle helped Frederick's cause by beginning the process of obtaining the necessary federal approval for the product in France. Without government approval, a product was supposedly not allowed to be sold in France. The early model of the Proxagard—the PG 101—that Lapin had purchased, had not received approval. Unlike OSHA in the United States, French federal inspectors have the authority to shut down a plant if equipment is considered unsafe. Lapin had installed the thirty Proxagards at the punch press company without telling anyone, so it was especially important that they keep up their efforts to gain federal approval. At this point, however, Lapin had lost

* This case was written by Scott Weighart.

interest in continuing to seek approval. As Frederick's engineers refined and improved a new PG 110 model of the Proxagard—that did eventually receive approval—Lapin did very little.

"We told Lapin that they had to get one salesman completely committed to the Proxagard," Frederick's sales people contended, "but they told us that they didn't have the resources to send one man out to sell and install the Proxagards to ensure they would pass inspection."

In early 1979, Rick Knackert, a navigator for Fresh Airlines and a personal friend of Frederick's, met salesman Pierre Vachon during a trip to Brussels. Upon hearing Knackert describe Frederick Engineering's Proxagard, Vachon was intrigued and extremely confident that he could sell a high volume of the devices.

Then came a curious turn of events: Vachon injured his back and was ordered to bed by his doctors for six weeks of rest. As Vachon was a workaholic, this was something he wouldn't take lying down—even if he was flat on his back. Vachon had his wife set up a Proxagard and its sensing antenna at the foot of his bed. For weeks, he experimented with the device by wiggling his toes around to determine the size of the sensing field. He also read every piece of sales literature and other information that Frederick could provide for him.

After spending six weeks in bed with the product, Vachon had fallen in love. Back on his feet, he began new negotiations for getting the French government's approval, and he was successful. Then in 1985, Vachon met Jean-Claude Laperrière, who, on seeing the Proxagard in action, also became a devotee of the product. Laperrière was a tinkerer who loved to build gadgets and toy with new ideas. He had recently separated from his wife and was more than happy to go around the countryside installing Proxagards and building antennas that were perfectly tailored to each customer's needs.

Meanwhile, a French federal inspector discovered the thirty Proxagards that Lapin had quietly installed seven years earlier.

"What is this thing?" the inspector had demanded to know. "Who sells this?" After learning that the machines had been working for years without failures or accidents, he became fascinated by the device. He eventually traced the product to Frederick Engineering and to Laperrière and Vachon.

Suddenly all the pieces began to come together for Frederick International. When the French inspector found unsafe equipment, he would threaten to close down the plant and recommend a call to Pierre Vachon. By now, Frederick was charging $700 for the Proxagard, but Vachon and Laperrière could sell it for the equivalent of $2,500 to French companies, plus a charge for Laperrière's meticulous installations. This was steep compared with the American price, but consistent with prices charged by companies that made optical scanners or light curtains, which perform roughly the same function as the Proxagard but with different technology.

Laperrière installed between 125 and 150 Proxagards; he had made a great deal of money doing what he liked. Likewise, Vachon had earned substantial commissions, while Frederick had profited as well.

Since Frederick International's first venture was so successful, Lewis Naehring was very excited when the possibility for a similar arrangement in Japan arose. Mitsui Products, a maker of safety equipment in Japan, expressed serious interest in the Proxagard. Mitsui made palm buttons and light curtains for protecting punch presses: Palm buttons force the machine operator to keep both hands away from the path of the press; light curtains are similar to electric eyes. However, some of Mitsui's applications could only be carried out with something like the Proxagard.

Unlike Europe—where worker safety is a reasonable priority—some observers believe that Japanese claims of placing a high priority on safety are weakly supported by barely enforced standards. In comparison with the United States, Japan has far fewer lawyers per capita, and employee lawsuits are extremely rare.

"If an accident occurs, the individual is considered stupid for letting it happen," Naehring says. "Also, unions are not powerful because Japan is still largely a caste society and the socialized medical system covers any costs from injuries."

As was the case with France, government approval of the Proxagard had to be obtained, and while the approval processes were similar, it soon became clear that the Japanese government disapproved of imports unless it was proved that no comparable product could be built domestically.

When Naehring went to Japan's Department of Labor to secure approval, the official he spoke with got right to the point: "In selling your Proxagard in our country, are you attempting to replace light curtains?"

"No," Naehring replied. "This is for other applications."

"Good," the official replied. "Now the meeting can continue."

As he had once done with Lapin Industrielle, Naehring told Mitsui's executives that it would be crucial to find a person who could be an antenna design expert and who would make a full commitment to the project. The Mitsui president and engineers consistently said yes to whatever Naehring raised.

"Would you send your antenna expert to the United States for training?" Naehring asked. His question was met with vigorous nods of agreement. Naehring was led to believe that twenty to twenty-five Proxagard orders per month would be possible.

A few months later, a Mitsui official came to Connecticut and expressed much enthusiasm for the project. That was in 1988. Since then, however, the Mitsui connection has resulted in very few orders for Proxagards, an average of fewer than fifty per year.

Through correspondence and occasional phone calls, Naehring tried to figure out what was going wrong.

"Are you really making an effort to sell these things?" he asked.

"Oh, yes," was the reply. "But we have not sold many yet, although we remain hopeful."

When he tried to determine if they had really followed through by assigning a person to travel the country, Naehring received a vague and roundabout letter in return, stating that Mitsui officials were taking appropriate action to ensure success in their mutual endeavors.

Today, Naehring remains unclear as to why the product is so successful in America and France but has failed to meet expectations in Japan. Was it really Mitsui's fault? Should Frederick sink some money into advertising in Japan? Would Frederick International be successful in Japan with a different partner? In the maze of government regulation, cultural

74

differences, workers' compensation, and competition, Naehring couldn't be sure exactly where Frederick International had gone down the wrong path. He assumed that companies across the world would want to protect their workers from accidents with the best available technology, so it must be something else that went wrong.

Questions for Discussion

1. What has kept Frederick International from being as successful in Japan as it has been in the United States and France? Would finding a different Japanese representative be a good idea?

2. Do you believe it is possible to make Frederick International more successful and profitable in Japan? How?

3. What overall advice would you give Frederick and Naehring for making Frederick International more successful?

Force Field Analysis

Add arrows as necessary.

Goal: Successful Sales of Proxagards in the United States

Driving Forces	Restraining Forces

Force Field Analysis

Add arrows as necessary.

Goal: Successful Sales of Proxagards in Japan

Driving Forces	Restraining Forces

Force Field Analysis

Add arrows as necessary.

Goal: Successful Sales of Proxagards in the France

Driving Forces	Restraining Forces

11

TUCKERMAN-SAWYER ADVERTISING*

Background

Bill Tuckerman, Jr., vice president of Tuckerman-Sawyer Advertising and son of one of the founders, frowned as he looked out his twelfth-floor window onto the tops of some straggly Florida palms. Most any other phone call from Andres Martinez, one of his top young account executives, would have been business as usual, but this time Andres insisted that they meet immediately, said the matter was urgent, and refused to tell Bill what it was about before they met. Bill certainly hoped that Andres, one of the few minorities in the firm and the only Latino, wasn't going to tell him he was leaving. He was doing a terrific job with all the Latino accounts, and Bill didn't want to lose him, not just because there would be no one in the agency to replace him, but also because Bill really liked Andres and saw a bright future for him with the agency.

Bill Tuckerman

"I got advertising in my pabulum," Bill often joked. "And as hard as I tried to spit it out, it just became a part of me." Bill had been a month or so under two years old when his father, fed up with the pace of life in Chicago, packed the family and moved south to Miami. With his strong educational background and six years of experience in the Chicago office of a national advertising firm, Bill Sr. had quickly landed a job with a small but prestigious agency whose owner was nearing retirement. In less than ten years, Bill Sr. had bought the agency, having convinced his brother-in-law, Tom, to put up part of the money and join him as managing partner. Over the next thirty years, they grew the business to more than ten times the revenues than when they began.

While all five of the Tuckerman and Sawyer children had worked summers in the firm from about junior high school on, only Bill Jr. really wanted to be in the field. Of Bill Jr.'s sister and cousins, one went to medical school, two to law school, and the other to Los Angeles to work in the film industry, happily leaving Bill Jr. to work the eighteen-hour days, seven-day weeks that advertising often demanded.

In 1985, Bill Sr. died of a massive coronary while working on a campaign he had planned to pitch to the Tobacco Growers Association. With his father gone, Bill Jr. took over the bulk of the business responsibilities, with his Uncle Tom increasingly playing only a token role as president of Tuckerman-Sawyer Advertising. For all practical purposes, Bill Jr. was in charge.

* This case was written by Gail E. Gilmore.

Copyright © Houghton Mifflin Company. All rights reserved.

79

Bill Jr. was not just respected but also genuinely liked by the Tuckerman-Sawyer employees. While he worked hard and expected no less from those who worked for him, he was also considered to be eminently fair and honest in his business dealings. He insisted on quality work from his employees, but he was also willing to invest the time, energy, and money in them to teach them what they needed to know. As a result, Tuckerman-Sawyer's highly trained people were often head-hunted by the competition, and it was largely a sense of loyalty to Bill Jr. that kept them in the firm.

Andres Martinez

Andres Martinez had been hired by Tuckerman-Sawyer right out of graduate school. Having known since his freshman year in college what he wanted to do for a career, he had systematically and aggressively sought out and found opportunities to learn about the advertising business. The top student in his very competitive graduate program, Andres had managed to acquire an impressive amount of professional experience through a variety of evening jobs during the school year and challenging summer internships. Some of the internships Andres took paid and some didn't, but to Andres the money was irrelevant; what mattered was the experience.

When he was hired by Tuckerman-Sawyer, Andres knew his hard work had finally paid off. He was additionally pleased to be able to stay in the area in which three generations of his family had been born and raised. Working in Miami meant being around lifelong friends and spending time with his large and close family—his parents, brothers, sisters, and vast numbers of aunts, uncles, and cousins who lived in and around the area.

Andres began his position as a junior account executive with much enthusiasm, pleased and excited to have been assigned to three accounts, all small companies owned and operated by Latinos. He enjoyed the opportunity to work with other Latinos and felt that until he was familiar with the way things were done at Tuckerman-Sawyer, three accounts would be all he could handle. In addition, he was excited to have the opportunity to work directly for Bill Tuckerman on one of the accounts, a women's clothing manufacturer located in Miami's Little Havana.

At the end of his first year, Andres was still working with the same three accounts. Despite feeling that he was now ready to take on additional clients, none were assigned to him. He began to wonder if his work was not up to Tuckerman-Sawyer's standards, but his end-of-the-year performance evaluation dispelled his doubts. He received excellent ratings in all categories.

Shortly after he received his written performance evaluation, Andres had a meeting with his supervisor, Peter Martin. Peter told him that both the clients and the agency were very pleased with the quality of his work and that if he could keep it up, his future with the agency would be assured. Comfortable that he now had some credibility, Andres explained that although he enjoyed working with the accounts he had, they were small and didn't offer much opportunity to stretch, grow, or even really put his current talents and skills to full use. What he really wanted, he told Peter, was one big account or some other small accounts with real growth potential, something he didn't see much of in the clients he was presently handling. Peter assured him that he would be assigned other, more extensive accounts in the coming months.

Four months later, Andres was finally assigned to another account. Although the new client's company was a bit larger than those of his current clients, it was also Latino-owned. This essentially meant that advertising strategies would be targeted towards the same population as his other accounts, providing little in the way of variety or challenge, and offering no real opportunity for Andres to improve his skills. In addition, the small Latino-owned companies did not result in the substantial revenues attributable to most of the agency's other accounts. In time, he knew, his low revenues would probably work against his chances for moving up in the company or even for getting hired by other agencies.

Although Andres was becoming increasingly frustrated, he continued to do the best job he could do with his accounts. His advertising campaigns were consistently effective, and he derived a real sense of achievement from his clients' satisfaction. Through word of mouth, he brought a number of other small Latino accounts into the firm, but these were generally assigned to interns or new hires because of their small size.

As he approached the end of his second year without being assigned to any of the types of accounts for which he continued to ask, Andres realized that his clients' satisfaction was no longer enough to motivate him. He felt that he was not being provided with the same opportunities to develop the range of experience and skills as his colleagues, and the sense that he was being discriminated against by Peter Martin grew from a faint gnawing to a daily and prominent concern and source of anger. When Nancy Harrigan, who had come to the firm almost a year after Andres, was assigned a major food brokerage account, he finally let his anger take over. While he really felt like yelling and throwing things, Andres decided that the most appropriate thing would be to request an immediate meeting with Bill Tuckerman to discuss his concerns.

Mumbling to himself, Andres rehearsed what he was going to say to Bill Tuckerman as he wove his way through the maze of cubicles on the way to Bill's office. "Most of all," he said, half aloud, "stay cool. Tuckerman's a good guy, and he probably just doesn't realize what's been going on."

The Meeting

Bill Tuckerman greeted Andres with a warm handshake and ushered him into the office.

"So, what can I do for you?" he asked.

Clearing his throat, Andres began to explain his concerns.

"Mr. Tuckerman, I don't feel that the accounts that I'm being assigned to work with provide the kind of diversity and challenge that I feel I'm ready for. I am not being given the opportunity to develop my skills, and I'm afraid that this will result in my being passed over for promotion. I also realize that the amount of money an account brings in can be a factor in promotions and raises, and I feel that my accounts put me at a disadvantage in this area as well."

"I enjoy working with fellow Latinos," Andres continued, "but I feel like I'm being stereotyped and pigeonholed. To just keep working with Latino accounts exclusively doesn't give me a chance to develop advertising strategies for other populations."

Andres stood up and walked to the window. He felt nervous and wondered whether he had done the right thing by insisting on seeing Bill Tuckerman right away. But here he was, and it didn't make much sense not to go ahead and tell Tuckerman what was on his mind.

"The way things are going now," Andres said, sucking in his breath, "I don't feel that I'm learning anything new or growing professionally in any way. I discussed my concerns with Peter, but all he did was assign me another Latino account. He just doesn't get it—or maybe he does."

Bill Tuckerman felt so relieved that he let Andres' last vague suggestion float by unnoticed. This wasn't nearly as bad as he'd imagined. He could relieve these concerns easily.

"Well, I really have to say that you've been worrying needlessly," he told Andres. "Since you have a substantially different client base than your colleagues, we obviously won't be using the same standards of promotion for you as we would for them. After all, we hired you to work with our Latino accounts; we figured you'd have a much better understanding of your own people than of our people, and vice versa. Within another five years or so, if you keep going the way you've been going so far, we figure you'll have the reputation and stature to bring a lot of Latino business into this firm. You're a real go-getter, and there's hundreds of thousands, probably millions of dollars in Latino business here in Florida just waiting to be plucked."

"As far as I'm concerned," Bill Tuckerman said, swiveling in his chair, "you're a long-term investment for Tuckerman-Sawyer, and this is a great opportunity for you and for us. So we're certainly not going to punish you for doing what we hired you to do!"

Andres couldn't believe what he was hearing. Walking back to the desk, he put his hands on its edge and leaned forward, facing Bill Tuckerman. If he had been able to control his anger when he walked in, it was getting away from him now.

"Mr. Tuckerman," Andres said, feeling his jaw tighten and his back teeth grind together. "First of all, let me say that I was under the impression that I had been hired based on my experience and qualifications, rather than my ethnicity. Secondly, although you are obviously unaware of it, you are punishing me. By not giving me the same opportunities or holding me to the same standards as the other account executives, you're limiting my possibilities. That's what the people in power in this country have always done to keep their power and keep us in our place. I thought you were different. I thought you could see me as a person, and I was clearly wrong."

Pushing away from the desk, Andres glared at Bill Tuckerman. "Well, I'm afraid you're going to have to find yourself another token Latino," he hissed. "I'm resigning—effective immediately."

Questions for Discussion

1. Andres makes a number of arguments that suggests he is being discriminated against. Do you agree? Why or why not?

2. Bill Tuckerman will soon be hiring a replacement for Andres. What would you suggest to ensure that he doesn't make the same mistakes again?

12

JUST-IN-TIME FOR TEMPORARY EMPLOYEES*

Part 1

Just-In-Time Distribution

Approximately five years ago, Medical Supplies Corporation (MSC) decided to expand its organization through forward integration. This approach to organizational growth involved MSC's shifting many of the materials management functions from stocking facilities at client hospitals to its own Just-in-Time (JIT) distribution center. The center provides a "just-in-time," or stockless method of supply procurement and distribution.

The JIT distribution center is located in a large urban area near the hospitals it serves. In its most recent twelve months, it has experienced rapid growth, doubling its annual revenues from $15 to $30 million. The number of employees also doubled—from thirty to sixty—in this same time period.

The very nature of a JIT program involves tailoring services to each customer's needs. The just-in-time procurement and distribution of hospital supplies, which includes medical/surgical supplies, laboratory supplies, dietary products, x-ray supplies, linens, and intravenous solutions, is a unique service that most medical supply companies are not able to provide. Close coordination between the hospital staff and the employees of the JIT unit is essential.

What had been started as a just-in-time service by MSC has now become a stockless inventory service for its two hospital clients. That is, the just-in-time service has developed into a low unit-of-measure departmental delivery system which operates around the clock, 365 days a year, with two shifts working in the JIT distribution center daily and three shifts at each of the hospitals. This service includes five scheduled deliveries to each of the hospital clients, daily bulk delivery, emergency back-up, consolidated shipping, consolidated billing, patient-charge stickering, automated order-entry, system linkages, guaranteed fill rates, and twenty-four-hour availability. The hospitals benefit by being able to control and even reduce the costs of purchasing and storing excess inventory, assure product standardization and quality, and save on labor.

A fully integrated logistics system provides the JIT distribution center's employees who work in the hospitals, in positions such as inventory technicians, with the ability to constantly monitor inventories and replenish supply bins on a twelve-hour cycle. The inventory technicians use hand-held computer terminals to track information on the average daily use of medical supplies. Orders for additional supplies to the unit can be made on the computer

* Copyright 1997 by David B. Balkin and Minnette A. Bumpus, University of Colorado, Boulder, and Wilfred J. Lucas, Baxter Healthcare Corporation, Deerfield, Illinois.

network so that materials handlers at the warehouse can quickly fill the order and send it to the hospital. By systematically tracking product usage and monitoring demand by the patient care unit of the hospital, the just-in-time process ensures that the right product is at the right place at the right time.

Jobs in the warehouse consist of four categories: There are pickers who fill the clients' orders by locating the requested supplies by stock number in the storage area, removing the items from the shelves, and placing them into the clients' carts. Next, there are fork-lift operators who move boxes of supplies to different locations where they are needed. Third, stockers unload the supplies and place them onto the designated shelves by stock numbers. Finally, loaders load supplies onto and off the trucks and onto the fork lifts. Employees in the warehouse work in cross-discipline teams composed of pickers, stockers, fork-lift operators, and loaders.

Sam Kellogg, a fifteen-year employee with MSC, was placed in charge of the four employees whose task is to operate the JIT distribution center. Sam says he views the difference between managing the JIT distribution center and other units at MSC as analogous to the difference between racing a high-performance sports car and driving the family station wagon. Managing a just-in-time operation is demanding on both managers and employees. A mistake in hospital inventory can have serious consequences for patients who require the medical products; hence management places a very high priority on satisfying the needs of its client hospitals.

Staffing

The workforce of the JIT distribution center is racially diverse. About 30 percent of the employees are African-American, 10 percent are Hispanic, and the remaining 60 percent are white. However, all four of the managers, including Jessica Jordan, the material services manager, are white.

The numbers of full-time positions approved by corporate headquarters have not been sufficient to meet customer needs, particularly since those needs have doubled over the previous twelve months. In an effort to solve the warehouse labor shortage, at least for the short term, as well as the shortage in the hospitals, the JIT distribution center staff is supplemented with temporary employees.

Temporary employees presently comprise 40 percent of the workforce at the JIT distribution center. All non-management workers start out as temporary employees. Permanent employees are then selected from the pool of temporary employees based on the quality of their performance. Since temps are given the opportunity to apply for full-time positions that become vacant, it is not unusual for several temps to view themselves as being in competition for a permanent job opening.

The process for requesting permanent positions from corporate headquarters requires the submission of a detailed long-range human resources demand forecast. Additional full-time employees are only hired upon position approval from corporate headquarters. Top management has traditionally allocated funds to hire full-time staff only after stable growth has been seen.

Because of the need for a large number of temporary employees, Sam Kellogg uses two different sources—Murphy Temps and Speedy Personnel Services. Speedy Personnel Services is located in a largely African-American section of the city, not far from the JIT distribution center.

Whenever there is a need to supplement the JIT distribution center, either the team leader, the operations manager, or the regional program manager makes a request to one of the temp agencies for light industrial workers to fill long-term but indefinite temporary assignments. The JIT distribution center might also obtain a temp through the "payrolling system." That is, the JIT distribution center gives a job applicant the names and addresses of the two temp agencies, asks the applicant to select one, and instructs the agency to hire the applicant. The agency then sends the applicant to the JIT distribution center for a temporary position.

The Telephone Call

When Sam Kellogg arrived at work yesterday, he had a voice-mail message waiting for him from MSC's corporate Director of Human Resources. Calling him back, Sam was dismayed to learn that an African-American temporary employee in the JIT distribution center had called the company's Vice President of Diversity Management to complain about discriminatory pay practices. The Vice President of Diversity Management had then telephoned the Director of Human Resources to inquire about the accusation. The employee had charged that some temporary employees were receiving higher pay for the same work.

The last thing Sam wanted was to have to deal with litigation over a pay-law violation, since the time necessary to settle such a problem could be substantial. Sam was already working sixty-hour weeks tending to the demands of a rapidly growing entrepreneurial business operating within a corporate bureaucracy that was not always nurturing to entrepreneurship.

Questions for Discussion

1. Based on what you know about MSC and the JIT distribution center, what do you see as the strengths and weaknesses of its personnel practices?

2. What problems, if any, do you feel might arise from the present system? Why?

3. Given the problem Sam now faces, what would you advise him to do?

Part 2a

The Investigation

Sam's first response was to call Jessica Jordan into his office, ask her to investigate the situation, and request that she report back to him with her recommendations. One of the reasons Sam wanted Jessica to look into this problem was that she had been hired only two weeks earlier—from outside the company—to fill the newly created material services manager position. His reasoning was that she could more objectively assess the situation than an employee who had been at the company longer.

This was Jessica's first supervisory position. Since receiving her B.S. in marketing three years earlier, she had worked as a marketing representative in the computer industry. Hiring Jessica had taken some of the pressure of day-to-day operations management off of Sam and put him in a better position to devote more time to human resources matters. While he recognized that the pay discrepancy issue was a matter that needed immediate attention, he also asked Jessica Jordan to do a more thorough investigation and provide him with some recommendations for dealing with the management and compensation challenges present in a workforce that consists of a significant portion of temporary employees.

Questions for Discussion

1. How do you feel about Sam's selection of Jessica to do the investigation of the pay discrepancy? Why?

2. If you were Jessica, how would you proceed?

Part 2b

The Investigation

Jessica Jordan's first step was to undertake an audit of the pay records for both temporary agencies. This revealed that, in fact, all temps were not being paid at the same hourly rate and that there were inconsistent pay practices between the two agencies.

Jessica next contacted the temporary agencies to learn why temps were being paid at different rates. She learned that Murphy Temps had a policy of paying a standard wage of $8.50 per hour for working at the JIT distribution center. Speedy Personnel Services paid between $7.25 and $9.00 per hour, depending on experience level and the individual's skill at negotiating a favorable wage rate.

Wages for a temp, along with agency fees, were directly paid by the JIT distribution center to the temporary agency that employed the temporary worker. Both temporary agencies agreed with the JIT distribution center to pay a higher wage to a temp who worked a night shift or was trained to operate fork-lift equipment. Upon completion of fork-lift equipment training, either the team leader, the operations manager, or the regional program manager would pass this information on to the appropriate temporary agency. Training dates were contingent upon customer demands and staffing levels.

While gathering the data to assess the fairness of the JIT distribution center's pay practices, Jessica came to believe that the differences in pay were based on factors other than race.

Questions for Discussion

1. Do you agree or disagree with Jessica's conclusion? Why?

2. What other factors do you see as the possible reasons for the differences in pay? Why?

3. Why do you think the temporary employee reported the pay discrepancy to the corporate officer rather than the managers at the JIT distribution center?

Part 3

Jessica Probes Further

After hearing what the two temp agencies had to say, Jessica next decided to gather the information she would need to make recommendations to Sam with regard to the overall management and compensation of the workforce. In doing so, it quickly became clear to her that the JIT distribution center did not have many established administrative procedures. Because of this, many administrative matters fell through the cracks.

Jessica also became aware that temporary employees were not always well informed about company policies. Some misinformation, such as that temps were under a 90-day probationary employment period, was widely believed. Temps felt that, in order to avoid assignment termination, they should keep their mouths shut and not voice opinions during this period.

In reality, there was no such thing as a probationary employment period for temps. Management could end an assignment for a temp at any time. However, in the past, no temp's assignment had been arbitrarily ended. During such rapid growth, management was keenly aware that it would be a hardship to find and train a replacement. In most cases, temps were given many opportunities to correct their mistakes.

In addition to lack of information on company policies, Jessica learned that temps were also given only a cursory explanation of the mission and values of MSC and its JIT distribution center. Some had only a vague idea of what management expected from them. Even though both full-time and part-time employees worked closely together in teams to provide service to the customer hospitals, management spent far less time orienting temps than permanent employees.

The formal meetings between management and team leaders that were held once a month consisted of one-way communication, from management to the employees, and were used only to disseminate relevant corporate-wide or JIT distribution center information.

Questions for Discussion

1. Given this new information, do you agree or disagree with your prior assumptions as to why the temporary employee reported the pay discrepancy to the corporate officer rather than the managers at the JIT distribution center? Why?

2. Based on what you now know about MSC's policies and the JIT distribution center, what recommendations should Jessica make to Sam with regard to the management of the temporary employees? With regard to the full-time employees? Provide the rationale for each of the recommendations.

13

THE LOCH NESS COTTON COMPANY:
SEXUAL HARASSMENT? YOU BE THE JUDGE!

The Task

You are the committee of workers and managers that has been assembled to consider and act on a complaint by Dana Tibbetts, who claims to have been sexually harassed by coworker and supervisor, Alex Lehmann.

You have met with each of the parties separately and now have a transcript of each one's statement. You have also talked with a couple of Alex's and Dana's coworkers and have gotten statements from them.

You have also done some research into what sexual harassment is all about and have learned that it is a form of sex discrimination that violates Title VII of the Civil Rights Act of 1964.

According to Title VII, "unwelcome sexual advances, requests for sexual favors, and other verbal or physical conduct of a sexual nature constitute sexual harassment when submission to or rejection of this conduct explicitly or implicitly affects an individual's employment, unreasonably interferes with an individual's work performance, or creates an intimidating, hostile, or offensive work environment."

Sexual harassment can occur in a variety of circumstances, including but not limited to the following:
- The victim as well as the harasser may be a woman or a man. The victim does not have to be of the opposite sex.
- The harasser can be the victim's supervisor, an agent of the employer, a supervisor in another area, a coworker, or a non-employee.
- The victim does not have to be the person harassed but could be anyone affected by the offensive conduct.
- Unlawful sexual harassment may occur without economic injury to or discharge of the victim.
- The harasser's conduct must be "unwelcome."

Based on what you now know,

1. Take a position on whether you believe there is or is not sexual harassment; or whether the facts given are inconclusive, and why?
2. Whether or not you believe sexual harassment has taken place, it is clear the situation must be defused. Develop a proposal for handling the situation.

Back up your conclusions and recommendations.

Background

The Loch Ness Cotton Company, manufacturers and importers of cotton dry goods, was founded in 1897 by Scottish immigrant Ian Mactavish. In the early days of the company, Mactavish employed a handful of his countrymen as supervisors for the lines of young immigrant women who worked as knitting machine operators and stitchers in his plant on the Lower East Side of New York. Despite the founding of the International Ladies Garment Workers' Union in New York in 1900, Loch Ness was never organized, and the women at Loch Ness continued to work long hours in poorly lighted and dismal surroundings for more than four decades into the twentieth century.

In 1942, Mactavish sold his interests in Loch Ness to a large conglomerate. The new owners moved the manufacturing facilities to a modern plant in North Carolina where manufacturing outputs ebbed and flowed according to demand. This resulted in multiple lay-off periods interspersed with significant increases in hiring.

By the late 1970s, the parent company had increasingly turned its interests to less expensive imports from such countries as Egypt and Bangladesh, and more than 60 percent of the workforce was cut over a ten year period. In 1987, faced with the inevitable closing of the plant, the 262 remaining employees at Loch Ness took control of the company in an unusual leveraged buy-out by the employees. Within eighteen months of the LBO, Loch Ness had become profitable, and morale was at a new high.

As part of the arrangements with their local lenders, the employees agreed to leave the existing management structure in place for a period of six years after the buy-out. However, while there were few women in management positions and few men on the line, there was an ongoing attempt to build a "we're all in this together" atmosphere: a profit-sharing plan was put into place, quality circles were implemented and, in an effort to give employees more job satisfaction and a greater sense of ownership and responsibility, decision making was systematically pushed down to those who were doing the day-to-day work. In addition, a performance appraisal and feedback system was developed and instituted by a committee of managers and workers, and it was agreed that this system would serve as the basis for awarding bonuses and promotions.

Loch Ness President and CEO Henry MacDougall prided himself on the enlightened management that he, freed from the constraints previously imposed by the parent company, had rushed to implement. He credited much of the company's turnaround to this progressive management approach and was pleased at the spirit of cooperation that now pervaded Loch Ness. Thus, he was surprised and distressed to learn that one of his front office employees had complained to the company's human resources director about being sexually harassed on the job by a veteran employee and supervisor, Alex Lehmann. Worse yet, MacDougall was told, the employee, Dana Tibbetts, was threatening to file a law suit against the company unless something was done about Lehmann's behavior. Tibbetts was also making it clear that little short of firing was likely to be satisfactory.

Loch Ness had never had a sexual harassment claim against it before. MacDougall, in keeping to his commitment to employee empowerment, decided to appoint a committee of workers and managers to consider the situation and propose resolutions.

Dana Tibbett's Statement

"This is the beginning of my fifth year at Loch Ness. I spent the first almost four and a half years in the stock room, and I worked hard to finally land a front-office job. That was a big step for me because I only have a high school diploma, and most of the others went to college. Unfortunately, my supervisor, Alex Lehmann, has made my new job unbearable and also made it impossible for me to do good work. It's not fair; I worked hard for this job, and I want to keep it."

"The sexual harassment didn't just happen once. It happens over and over, and Alex's attitude towards me seems to have made the others in the office think it's okay for them to bug me as well. Probably the worst part of it is that everyone in the office seems to think it's okay to make comments about my looks and my clothes, and I think that's because Alex thinks it's okay. Sometimes they whistle or say things that are really crude. They've even left porno pictures in my desk drawer. I told Alex that it upsets me, but Alex hasn't done or said anything to make them stop, and besides, Alex is the worst. Alex has really been coming on to me, staring at me and always making comments about the way I look."

"I dress really well most of the time, not like the rest of the people in the office who usually look like they're going to a funeral; and I work out a lot, so I'm in good shape. I'm also one of the few single people in the office, so maybe Alex and the others think that what they're doing is okay. I think Alex is pretty angry that I'm not interested, and that got taken out on me on the quarterly performance appraisals. I read the comments, and they just weren't fair. Alex wrote that I always come late for work and that I make a lot of mistakes."

"I didn't start coming late until a couple of months ago. I haven't wanted to tell anyone why because I'm afraid it will only make things worse. When I first started in the front office, I was always on time, if not early. But Alex and the others always start making their comments to me first thing in the morning when I walk in, so I started coming in a little late to try to avoid them. I even come in a side door so they won't see me, but sometimes I just have too much work to do, and besides, when I come in late, no matter what I tell Alex about why, Alex just yells."

"For a long time, I was afraid to complain about what Alex does to me. I don't want to get fired. But what's going on has made me so nervous that I'm making a lot of mistakes, and Alex is already using that against me. Besides, I'm having trouble sleeping at night because I'm so worried about my job, and I even went back to smoking, something I told myself I would never do again after I stopped three years ago."

"While I don't want to get fired, if this keeps up I might as well quit. But it isn't fair, because I'm not to blame. Alex is. When I heard that Alex is up for promotion to office manager, I really got upset, and I'll bet some of the others in the office aren't too thrilled either; but I don't know. When I told my friends in the stockroom what was happening, they told me it was sexual harassment and that I should complain and probably sue. You can ask any of them and they'll tell you that I work hard."

"I'm not sure what I want to do. Even though my stockroom friends told me I can't get fired for complaining, this is really hard. Anyway, Alex shouldn't be working here. If anyone gets fired, it should be Alex, and I finally decided that I have nothing to lose by doing something about what has been going on."

Alex Lehmann's Statement

"In no way have I been anything but supportive of Dana Tibbetts, and I'm really angry about the charges that have been brought against me. Since I first came to work for Loch Ness, almost 18 years ago, I have proven myself to be reliable, honest, and dependable. I've always gotten along with my coworkers, I've played on the company softball team, and I've co-chaired the annual Christmas party for the past six years."

"Since becoming a supervisor, I've gone out of my way to help my employees, including Dana Tibbetts. Dana and I both came from the same place, right out of high school and into the Loch Ness stockroom. That's pretty much a minimum wage position, but I worked hard, and I also went to school nights to get my associate's degree and then my bachelor's in psychology. That's how I got to be a supervisor in the stockroom, and that's how I got moved up to the position I'm in now. Right now I'm in line for the office manager's job that should be opening up sometime in the next six months when Freida Allenby retires."

"One of the things that really concerns me is that these charges of sexual harassment might get in the way of my promotion, and I can't help but wonder if Dana doesn't know that and is trying to get back at me for what I wrote at the time of the last quarterly performance appraisal reports. For months, Dana has been showing up late for work at least two days out of every five. There always seems to be a different excuse—"I missed the bus," "my alarm clock didn't go off," "the phone rang just as I was leaving"—and nothing I have said seems to have gotten the point across that showing up on time is important. I've tried to gently hint, and I've tried yelling. Now I don't even get an excuse; all I get is a sarcastic crack of some sort or a dirty look."

"Dana has also been responsible for an awful lot of the mistakes made in our office. If something is missing, there's a good chance that Dana was supposed to have filed it. If numbers don't add up, there's a good chance Dana was supposed to have handled the math. I couldn't just let all that go by, so I wrote the problems up as things to be worked on. And, I've made a real effort to help Dana improve."

"I know that at least part of the harassment complaint is that I've frequently commented on Dana's clothing, and this I freely admit. I'll also admit that Dana is really good looking, and I'm not surprised by what some of my people tell me about Dana's social life. But this is business. When you work in the stockroom, it's okay to dress casually, but in the front office, with buyers and other businesspeople going in and out, you have to dress more professionally."

"I've tried to help Dana understand things like how to dress in the front office by making a point of saying something complimentary when Dana dresses appropriately. When Dana wears clothes that are too tight or too flashy, I don't say anything. I do this because I learned in my college psychology classes that if you reinforce appropriate behavior, it will be repeated and that inappropriate behavior will go away after a while if it is not reinforced. In Dana's case, it doesn't seem to be working, and sometimes it gets really bad. About a week ago, Dana's pants were so tight that you could see everything, and some of the other people in the office whistled and made comments. Frankly, I didn't blame them, but I was careful not to say anything."

"At no time have I harassed Dana Tibbetts, sexually or otherwise. I'm convinced that Dana's complaint is not about sexual harassment but rather because Dana is angry about my comments on the performance appraisal and doesn't understand that I'm trying to help. While I haven't talked about the accusations against me with any of the others who work for me in the front office, I am sure that everyone of them will tell you that I haven't done what I've been accused of doing."

Chris Alton's Statement

"Dana and I started out in the stockroom together and got to be really good friends. When anything needed to be done, we all knew we could count on Dana to do it and do it right. There were times when Dana came in on weekends, even without being asked, because something needed to get finished by a deadline. That's why we were all really happy when the promotion to the front office came through. Dana wanted it and worked hard to get it."

"I'm pretty upset by what Dana is going through now. Frankly, I think the people in the front office are just a bunch of snobs and that they treat Dana the way they do as kind of a put-down. I also think that Alex Lehmann is mad because Dana isn't interested in, you know, a social relationship, if you know what I mean."

Lee Moriarity's Statement

"I've been at Loch Ness for a long time. I've worked at the machines, in shipping, in purchasing, and I've been in the front office for three years longer than Alex Lehmann. I can tell you that Alex is the best supervisor I've ever had. Alex has a sense of humor and knows when to let us fool around to break the tension, but Alex also knows how to get us to work hard. If it weren't for Alex and all the help Alex has given me, I wouldn't be up for the supervisor's position when Alex's promotion to manager comes through. When there's a problem, Alex is always supportive and is really interested in pushing us ahead and making us look good. Alex puts time into everyone, even that loser, Dana Tibbetts."

14

NATURE OR NURTURE?*

The Announcement

It was 5 p.m. on Friday, and Diana Houghton, who worked as a writer in the corporate communications department of a large bank, had just finished gathering up her purse, her planner, and a folder of work to do over the weekend. She was halfway out the door when her phone rang. Diana had been playing phone tag all day with a colleague in the corporate giving department with whom she really needed to speak, and she hoped that the caller was he. If not, a substantial portion of the work she was bringing home would have to wait until Monday.

"Hello," Diana said. "Oh, Maggie. Hi!"

"Hi!"

Diana could tell immediately from Maggie's voice that she was excited about something.

"I couldn't wait 'til you got home to tell you," Maggie went on. "I just got back from the doctor. I'm pregnant!"

"Maggie, that's wonderful! I'll be home in about twenty minutes; let's go out to dinner to celebrate!"

"Okay, see you in a bit," Maggie replied.

Making Plans

Diana hung up the phone and raced out of her office. She couldn't wait to get home. She and Maggie had wanted to have a child for a long time, but until now it had seemed that this was a dream that would go unfulfilled. Diana was in her early forties, and Maggie was in her late thirties—hardly optimal years for childbearing. But finally, the dream was real. Diana knew she and Maggie would make terrific parents. They both had so much to give a child; love, warmth, a strong sense of self, and an economically secure environment. This was going to be a very lucky child.

Diana and Maggie spent the weekend talking about plans for the baby's arrival. Maggie was due to deliver at the end of April, which was just over six months away. They needed to buy baby furniture and clothing, paint the nursery, and find a day-care provider for the two to three days a week that Maggie would need to be physically at her law firm; the rest of the week, she could work from home. Diana thought that she herself would be able to work from home one of the days, as the bank had arranged such schedules for other working mothers,

---

* This case was written by Gail E. Gilmore.

93

and for a few fathers as well. This way, the baby would have to be with a day-care provider only one day a week.

Maggie would be taking two months of maternity leave, and Diana also planned to ask the bank for the same. After all, this was her child too. She felt it particularly important to be there during the first two months, both to develop a bond with the baby and to support Maggie. Realistically, there was no one else available to provide postpartum support: Maggie was an only child whose parents had died quite some time ago, and Diana's parents were elderly and lived on the other side of the country. Diana and Maggie were essentially on their own.

All Mothers Are Not Created Equal

Diana went to see her boss, Susan Fitch, first thing on Monday morning. She told Susan that her partner was pregnant and that her delivery date was near the end of April. She also told Susan that she would like a two-month maternity leave from the last week in April through the last week in June, and that she wanted to discuss a schedule that would enable her to work from home one day a week. She was not prepared for Susan's response.

"I'm happy for you and Maggie," Susan told her, "but I'm not going to be able to grant your request for a four-day work schedule. Since you're not the actual mother, it wouldn't be equitable. It would basically open the door for anyone to make a request for a special work schedule."

"As for the maternity leave," Susan continued, "you'll need to speak with personnel about it. But I'm not very hopeful that it will be approved."

"Susan," Diana protested, "just because I'm not the biological mother doesn't mean that the child isn't mine. Maggie and I will be raising the child together, as a couple. Our child will have two parents, and I'll be one of them. Why doesn't that entitle me to the same considerations that other people in this organization have been given?"

"Because you're not the one having the child," Susan insisted.

"But that doesn't make any sense. What about some of the men who have been allowed to arrange their work schedules around day-care issues? They didn't actually have the child either, so why is it a problem in my case?"

"Well, a father is also a biological parent," Susan replied. "You aren't. And that, in a nutshell, is the problem. The company's policies don't provide any child-related benefits for employees in your situation, only for biological parents. I'm not saying that I necessarily agree with these policies, but I am saying that I can't change them."

Diana stood up. "I guess this bank hasn't dragged itself into the twentieth century yet," she said to Susan as she walked out the door. "But I don't think it's fair that my partner and I and our child should have to pay for corporate ignorance."

To Litigate or Not to Litigate

By the end of the day, Diana was fuming. A discussion with the Office of Personnel had been, as Susan had predicted, unproductive. Citing the same rhetoric and policies, the personnel officer had refused to grant Diana maternity leave. After her meeting with Susan, Diana had expected as much, but this fact made her no less angry. She had worked for the bank for ten years, and by all accounts was a highly valued employee. She had received consistently solid performance reviews, regular salary increases and bonuses, and several promotions.

Diana looked out her office window and thought about her options. The way she saw it, she had three—stay, leave, or sue. She weighed each option in her mind. She believed the bank was discriminating against her and that she probably had grounds on which to sue. She wondered, however, whether the cost of this action might be too great. She knew, for example, that she could lose and even be blacklisted and find it impossible to get another job. Even if she won the lawsuit and remained at the bank, it was highly possible that her career would come to a virtual standstill. And she wondered whether any other bank would be any more enlightened.

Diana concluded that the decision was difficult—and she didn't want to make it in the heat of anger. Instead, she thought she would wait a day or two and then decide.

Questions for Discussion

1. What do you see as the positives and negatives of the bank's policies? Why?

2. What do you think about Diana's request? What arguments do you think she might use to convince the bank to see things her way?

3. In what ways does an organization benefit from enabling employees to successfully balance work and family needs and/or responsibilities?

4. If you were Diana, what would you do, and why?

PART II

INDIVIDUAL PROCESSES IN ORGANIZATIONS

Overview

The central areas of focus in this section are perception and motivation and their relationship to one another. In working through the various cases and exercises in this section, you will test the theory that the way we perceive people is the way we treat them—and the way we treat people has a great deal to do with just how motivated they will be to carry out their assigned tasks. If we believe, for example, that all members of a certain religious faith are high achievers, chances are we will expect and demand more from them than we might expect or demand from someone not of that faith. If we're lucky, they will be motivated to meet our expectations, but they might also consider that they are being treated unfairly because we are making demands on them that we are not making on others. Here perception plays a slightly different role: people are likely to be motivated by the way they *perceive* they are being treated—which may be very different from the way we *believe* we are treating them. In addition, they are more likely to be motivated by their perceived rather than their actual needs.

Perception

Consider that you've been a reasonably successful student and are able to land a management position with a prestigious company. Three months after you've started your dream job, the national economy collapses. Suddenly you're called into your boss's office. She concedes that you have been an excellent performer—one of the best she's got—but times are hard. She reminds you that you have the least seniority on the job. She then informs you that you're being laid off, shakes your hand, and shows you to the door.

Although you are upset, you are confident that you can find another desirable and professional job. Unfortunately, you are wrong; nobody is hiring young business graduates. In the seven months that you have been job hunting, the only job offer you've received has been from a local branch of a national chain of grocery stores. They want you to be a grocery bagger. You see no alternative and accept.

What would be going on in your mind during this situation? Would you perceive it as unfair? How motivated would you be about bagging groceries if this really happened to you? The answer to that is probably obvious. What would someone else think about it? Answering that is not nearly as simple as it might seem.

Perception is the way we make sense of what we experience. The fundamental rule of individual processes is that we all differ in the way we perceive events and in how we are motivated. Our perceptions and motives are driven by what we have learned through our experiences.

Although two individuals may see the same reality or experience the same event, their perceptions of what they have seen or experienced may differ greatly. For example, two people may experience their college graduation in completely differently ways. Whereas one person may see it as a beginning, the other may see it as an ending. Most likely, their previous experiences have caused them to react in contrasting ways.

Another example is that of two people who work for the same exacting and demanding manager. While one person considers the manager to be an inspiring leader, the other finds the manager to be overbearing and intimidating. The manager is the same person; the two employees simply differ in the way they perceive the manager.

Motivation

What drives us to do the things we choose to do each day? Lynn, a marketing manager for a shoe company, can't understand why her office manager, Jack, doesn't go to graduate school and get a better job. She persuades Jack to take the GRE test; Jack scores at the 98th percentile on all three subtests. Lynn is thrilled for him, but Jack asks her not to tell anyone else in the office about it, fearing that it might affect his friendships with his coworkers. Nothing Lynn says convinces Jack to make the most of his intellectual ability. Lynn is completely puzzled.

Why are there such dramatic differences in what motivates people? Many social scientists have determined that we all have our own motivational needs: we try to act in ways that will fulfill our individual needs, but our needs may change frequently, depending on our life situations. If a professional couple decides to have a child, perhaps the husband will feel less inclined to strive for great achievements at work and want to stay at home to fulfill more basic affiliation needs. As a successful businessperson approaches retirement, he or she may stop devoting large amounts of energy to job achievements or personal friendships. Instead, he or she may concentrate on taking all the right steps to ensure that personal finances are invested properly, perhaps to make sure that there will be enough money available to survive retirement.

On a more personal level, think about the bosses you've had on summer or part-time jobs during high school. Did your bosses treat you as if you were a responsible adult, or did they act as if you were lazy and had to be forced to do your work? Did they assume that you would want to do the best work possible, or did they act as if you were a lazy kid who had to be forced to do anything and everything? Managers are no different from employees; they perceive things based on their experiences and may or may not have treated you in the way that you deserved.

Now reconsider our first example: how do you think a skilled and educated individual would respond to being laid off during a bad economy? How would he or she perceive it? How would this event affect this person's motivation? This kind of layoff actually happened

97

to a Scottish immigrant back in the 1930s. The man had an engineering degree and was earning a better-than-average salary after moving to the United States, getting married, and having two children. Suddenly he no longer had a job and, indeed, the only work he managed to get was as a grocery bagger at a local supermarket.

How did he respond to this disappointing blow? The night before he began work as a grocery bagger, he asked his wife and children to empty all of the groceries from the cabinets. He proceeded to practice bagging the groceries as fast as he could. Due to the discouraging economic environment and the responsibilities of providing for a family, he perceived the grocery store job to be a good one; it would help him fulfill what had become his most crucial motivational need—making enough money to survive and to have some sense of security.

When the Great Depression ended, he was again able to find work as an engineering draftsman and earned the respect of his colleagues for his professionalism and high level of motivation.

What You'll Need to Know Before Tackling the Cases and Exercises

Before reading the cases or exercises included in this section, you will need to have an understanding of perceptual processes and how they affect attitudes and motivation.

Douglas McGregor's Theories X and Y are useful ways to describe the philosophies and preconceived notions of the managers illustrated in the cases and exercises. Remember that it is not worker behavior that McGregor describes, but rather managerial perceptions of workers—for example, workers are lazy and won't work unless pushed, or workers will work hard if given a chance.

You should be familiar with attitudes and the concept of cognitive dissonance. An individual experiences cognitive dissonance when he or she has contradicting thoughts, such as "I love smoking cigarettes" and "I don't want to have emphysema at the age of thirty-five." The theory suggests that when people have these conflicting thoughts, they strive to reduce the conflict by changing their thoughts or behaviors. The person could either quit smoking or could start thinking, "Well, the air is so polluted that I'm no better off if I give up the cigarettes."

Review of Theories of Motivation

The following is a brief review of some theories of motivation. You should understand that behavior is complex, and these theories cannot possibly explain all behaviors. Nor is it likely that the variables described by any one theory are the sole causes of a given behavior. It is best to think of the theories as a set of tools that will aid you in understanding why people behave as they do at work. They are ways of looking at the world, not the definitive answers to why the world is as it is.

Once you have some tools to understand why people behave as they do, you can develop strategies for motivating them. Following are summaries of various motivation theories. You will need to do further reading to understand these theories fully.

Needs Theories

Maslow's Hierarchy of Needs[1]

Maslow suggested that there are five hierarchical levels of need: physiological, safety, social, esteem, and self-actualization. A person will be motivated to fulfill the lowest need in the hierarchy that remains unfulfilled. The theory is hierarchical because Maslow believed that to be motivated to fulfill needs at a given level in the hierarchy, the needs at all lower levels must be fulfilled. Do not make the mistake of assuming that a person with needs at a higher level in the hierarchy is somehow better than a person with lower-level needs. Everyone moves up and down the hierarchy depending upon their current situation; however, only one need is dominant at a given time. Thus, a person who has met physiological and safety needs would be motivated by social needs. If that person is in a situation where safety needs are threatened, say for example the person is laid off, then the person will move down the hierarchy. Safety needs will dominate, and social needs will become secondary.

Maslow's Needs Defined

The most basic needs, physiological needs, are the things that keep you alive, i.e., air, water, food, etc. Once you have the basic physiological needs met so that you can stay alive, you then begin to look for things that will keep you safe, i.e., safety needs. These may include housing, a good working environment, and a secure job. When physiological and safety needs have been satisfied, a person will look to fulfill their social needs, that is, to interact with people, be accepted by others, and avoid loneliness. Ego/esteem needs, the next step on the hierarchy, involve looking for recognition and achievement. This includes looking for a sense of accomplishment and a feeling of self-respect. Few people reach the self-actualization stage for other than short periods of time. A self-actualized person is motivated from within to reach his/her full potential and does not require external rewards or recognition.

Alderfer's ERG Theory[2]

Alderfer proposed three general categories of need: existence, relatedness, and growth. These needs overlap with the five needs defined by Maslow. The major difference between Alderfer and Maslow is that Alderfer does not assume a hierarchy of needs. More than one need can be active simultaneously. Thus, if a person appears to have more than one dominant need, her or his motivation is better explained using Alderfer's theory than Maslow's theory.

Herzberg's Two-Factor Theory[3]

Herzberg studied thousands of people at work. He asked them what contributed to their satisfaction and what contributed to their dissatisfaction at work. He found that workers responded with two different sets of conditions: Those that are associated with satisfaction he calls motivators (e.g., responsibility, opportunity for achievement, recognition, etc.), and those that are associated with preventing dissatisfaction he calls hygiene factors (e.g., pay, working conditions, rewards, relationships, etc.).

The two lists are independent: This implies that a person can be satisfied and dissatisfied at the same time. In other words, the presence of motivators may lead to satisfaction, but if hygiene factors are absent there will also be dissatisfaction. Similarly, the presence of hygiene factors will not produce satisfaction. What it will produce is the absence of dissatisfaction. This theory is useful when analyzing the work environment.

Although Herzberg does agree that there are personal factors that affect an individual's motivation, his theory focuses on characteristics of the work environment which he believes have similar effects on all people.

McClelland's Three-Needs Theory[4]

McClelland proposes the following three needs in the workplace: power, affiliation, and achievement. The need for achievement is the drive to excel and compare oneself against a set of standards. People with a high need to achieve want jobs with personal responsibility, feedback, and a moderate degree of risk. The need for affiliation is the desire for satisfying relationships. People high in affiliation prefer cooperative relationships and mutual understanding. The need for power is the need to exert influence and be in control. Power can be personalized or socialized. People with a need for personalized power like situations where they can be in charge, and they prefer competition over cooperation. People with socialized power needs operate from a strong set of social values and exercise their power for the benefit of others. They derive satisfaction from the success of those they lead.

Process Theories

Goal-Setting Theory[5]

When goals are specific and challenging, they lead to higher levels of performance than general goals. Acceptance of the goals, however, is harder to achieve with more difficult goals. Including people in developing a goal will lead to a greater acceptance of the goal.

Expectancy Theory[6]

Expectancy theory states that people's efforts are a function of what people expect their efforts will achieve. If a person believes a given effort will result in a particular desired outcome, she or he will be motivated to put forth the necessary effort to achieve it. The theory states that a person must believe all of the following: First, the person must believe that her or his effort will lead to the necessary level of performance. Secondly, she or he must believe that achieving the appropriate level of performance will lead to the desired outcome or reward. Finally, the person must value the expected outcome or reward if she or he is to be motivated to put forth the effort required to achieve it. A person's past performance will affect her or his expectations of what is possible to achieve. This will, in turn, affect that person's future motivation to accomplish the task.

Equity Theory[7]

Equity theory states that people will compare the rewards they receive from their job, given their level of input, with the rewards received by others given their inputs. When people are putting in more than others but receiving similar rewards, they will reduce their input to achieve equity. If they are putting in less for similar rewards, they will increase their input. In either case, they will be dissatisfied because an inequity exists, even in the case where they are receiving more for less input. Only when equity is achieved will people be satisfied. Inputs include factors such as knowledge, effort, education, experience, and seniority. Outcomes [i.e., rewards] include factors such as pay, promotions, raises, recognition, and a sense of accomplishment.

Reinforcement Theories

Reinforcement theories state that behavior is a function of the rewards and punishments that a person receives.

The Law of Effect[8]

Behavior is motivated by its consequences. Behaviors that produce desired outcomes will be reinforced, while behaviors that produce undesired outcomes will be extinguished.

Operant Conditioning

This term is most notably associated with the work of B.F. Skinner.[9] It is based on the law of effect and refers to the process of influencing behavior through its consequences. There are four strategies a manager can use to influence behavior based on the application or removal of positive or negative consequences: *positive reinforcement* is providing a positive consequence for a desired behavior; *avoidance* is removing a negative consequence when a desired behavior occurs; *punishment* is introducing a negative condition or removing a positive condition when an undesired behavior occurs; and *extinction* is ignoring undesired behaviors.

Experience with operant conditioning in organizations suggests that managers must remember that a lack of response to a given behavior has consequences. Employees must understand what behaviors are being reinforced. They must be given feedback, and reprimands should be done in private.

Theory X and Theory Y[10] Are Not Motivation Theories

Do not confuse Theory X and Theory Y with theories of motivation. They are a label for a set of beliefs that a manager holds about employees. The beliefs that managers hold will most likely result in certain leadership styles that can affect motivation. The actions of the manager in a particular situation, not the beliefs they hold, ultimately motivate or demotivate employees. Thus, a manager whose beliefs can be categorized by Theory X could have a motivated workforce, and similarly a manager with Theory Y beliefs could have a demotivated workforce.

When using Theory X/Y, you can say that the set of beliefs leads to certain actions that affect motivation. You cannot say someone is motivated by Theory X/Y, or a manager uses Theory X/Y to motivate employees, or a person's motivation can be understood using Theory X/Y. Theory X/Y is not a theory of motivation.

101

Implications for Managers

Stephen Robbins[11] makes the following suggestions when applying the theories of motivation: Recognize that different people have different needs; match people to their jobs; use specific and challenging goals that employees will believe are attainable. Recognizing differences in people's needs means that you should tailor rewards to the individual. Be sure rewards are linked to performance and that they are given equitably.

Job Design[12]

Research done by Hackman and colleagues identified core job dimensions that affect worker outcomes. The core job dimensions are skill variety, task identity, task significance, autonomy, and feedback. *Skill variety* refers to the degree to which the job requires the worker to use a variety of skills and bring the full self into the performance of the job. This is in contrast to tasks that are repetitive and use only a small number of worker skills over and over. *Task identity* is the degree to which the job involves completing an identifiable piece of work. For example, workers responsible for assembly of an entire television have greater task identity than workers on an assembly line responsible for installing individual components. *Task significance* refers to the degree to which the job has an impact on others. *Autonomy* is the degree to which the worker is free to determine how the task will be performed and scheduled. *Feedback* is the degree to which the worker can tell upon completion of the task how well it was performed. Thus, workers assembling an entire television know how well they did because they can plug it in and determine whether it works. Workers installing components do not know the results of their work unless they are told.

The core dimensions of the job lead to three psychological states: experienced meaningfulness, experienced responsibility, and knowledge of results. The core dimensions of skill variety, task identity, and task significance contribute to a feeling that the work is meaningful. Autonomy contributes to a feeling that one is accountable for one's work, and feedback contributes to an understanding of how satisfactorily one has performed. The three psychological states then lead to four outcomes: internal work motivation, quality performance, satisfaction, and low absenteeism and turnover.

Since individual processes are the most fundamental components of organizational behavior, be sure to devote ample time to mastering these theories. When we consider broader organizational issues and more complicated cases later in this book, a solid understanding of these concepts will greatly enrich your understanding and analytical base.

Courageous Followership[13]

Motivation theories generally take the manager's perspective of an organization. Ira Chaleff, in his book, *The Courageous Follower*, argues that motivation is a shared responsibility. Certainly, leaders have a responsibility to create a motivating environment, but followers have a responsibility to help their leaders achieve a common purpose. Ultimately, motivation is a choice. We can choose to let circumstances serve as an excuse for the level of energy we put into our jobs, or we can choose to empower ourselves to make a difference. Courageous followers assume responsibility for themselves and the organization. It takes courage to make a difference, and we may feel that we do not have the power to do so. What can we possibly do if our boss is a tyrant? The answer is "plenty"—if we decide to be courageous and channel our energy in positive ways.

The foundation for being a courageous follower is a common purpose pursued with a set of values. It is the common purpose that binds the leaders and followers together and the set of values that prevents unethical or immoral actions in pursuit of that purpose. If the common purpose is not clear, then people will likely pursue their self interest. Your first job as a courageous follower is to commit to the common purpose. If the common purpose is not clear, then you must help the leader clarify it.

Courageous followers recognize that leaders are human and that they must be continually learning if they are to remain effective. Instead of complaining and griping about leaders, courageous followers respect their leaders and help them learn to use their power effectively in pursuit of the common purpose. Courageous followers are able to understand the pressures on their leaders and help them avoid potential pitfalls. Chaleff points out that the mark of a good follower is the growth of leaders.

There are five dimensions of courageous followership. The first dimension is the courage to assume responsibility for oneself and the organization. Courageous followers manage themselves and take action when needed. The power to act comes from a commitment to the common purpose. The second dimension is the courage to serve. Courageous followers believe in the common purpose and work passionately with their leaders to achieve that purpose. The third dimension is the courage to challenge. When a leader's actions are impeding progress toward achieving the common purpose, courageous followers speak up. They have the courage to take risk and to deal with potential emotional tensions that may arise. The fourth dimension is the courage to participate in transformation. Courageous followers champion the need for change when current practices inhibit achievement of the common purpose. They do not bail out when the going gets rough. They are also self-reflective, recognize the need for personal change, and work on their own development. The fifth dimension is the courage to leave. When leaders are not open to change, and their actions are harmful to the common purpose or morally and ethically questionable, a courageous follower must be ready to withdraw his or her support.

Chaleff offers many specific and practical suggestions for carrying through on each of the dimensions of courageous followership. We will not address these here. However, it is important to recognize that being a courageous follower requires planning, developing a strategy, providing recommendations, understanding your personal motives, and being sincere in your effort to be helpful. Courageous followers do not simply go to their leaders and provide evaluations of their behaviors. This is likely to be career suicide—not courageous followership.

A courageous follower is sensitive to a leader's pressures, self image, preferred forms of interaction, goals, aspirations, needs, and hot buttons. A courageous follower also understands organizational politics, outside pressures, and other factors that constrain what can be done. The courageous follower then acts in a sensitive, caring, and helpful manner that takes these factors into consideration as he or she helps the leader and the organization to achieve the common purpose. The courageous follower has the courage to take risks, the persistence to stay with it, the ability to understand why a particular strategy may have been ineffective—

and to learn from it and devise a new one. The courageous follower has empathy and compassion for the leader and patience, because he or she knows that changing old habits takes time.

Sources

1. Maslow, Abraham, *Motivation and Personality*, New York: Harper & Row, 1954.

2. Alderfer, Clayton P., *Existence, Relatedness, and Growth*, New York: Free Press, 1972.

3. Herzberg, Frederick, "One More Time: How Do You Motivate Employees?" *Harvard Business Review* 46, pp.109–120, 1987.

4. McClelland, David C., *The Achieving Society*, New York: Van Nostrand Reinhold, 1961.

5. Tubbs, Mark E., "Goal-Setting: A Meta-Analysis Examination of the Empirical Evidence," *Journal of Applied Psychology*, August 1986, pp. 474–483.

6. Vroom, Victor H., *Work and Motivation*, New York: John Wiley and Sons, 1964.

7. Adams, J. Stacey, "Toward an Understanding of Inequity," *Journal of Abnormal and Social Psychology*, 67, 1963, pp. 422–436.

8. Thorndike, Edward L., *Animal Intelligence: Experimental Studies*, New York: Hafner, 1965, p. 244.

9. Skinner, B. F., *Science and Human Behavior*, New York: MacMillan, 1953.

10. McGregor, Douglas, *The Human Side of Enterprise*, New York: McGraw-Hill, 1960.

11. Robbins, Stephen P., *The Essentials of Organizational Behavior* (3rd ed.), Englewood Cliffs, NJ: Prentice-Hall, 1992.

12. Hackman, Oldham, Janson, and Purdy, "A New Strategy for Job Enrichment," *California Management Review*, Summer 1975, pp. 57–71.

13. Chaleff, Ira, *The Courageous Follower: Standing Up To and For Our Leaders*, San Francisco: Berrett-Koehler, 1995.

15

WHAT YOU SEE ISN'T NECESSARILY WHAT YOU GET

Objectives

- To examine the relationship of perception to attribution
- To explore the impact of selective perception
- To examine the link between perception and behavior

Background

You have just checked into a hospital room in anticipation of having minor surgery tomorrow. When you get to your room, you are told that the following people will be coming to speak with you within the next several hours:

1. The surgeon who will do the operation
2. A nurse
3. The secretary for the department of surgery
4. A representative of the company that supplies televisions to the hospital rooms
5. A technician who does laboratory tests
6. A hospital business manager
7. The dietician

You have never met any of these people before and don't know what to expect.

About half an hour after your arrival, a woman who seems to be of Asian ancestry appears at your door dressed in a straight red wool skirt, a pink and white striped polyester blouse with a bow at the neck, and red medium-high-heel shoes that match the skirt. She is wearing gold earrings, a gold chain necklace, a gold wedding band, and a white hospital laboratory coat. She is carrying a clipboard.

Questions for Discussion

1. Of the seven people listed, which of them is standing at your door? How did you reach this conclusion?

2. If the woman had not been wearing a white hospital laboratory coat, how might your perceptions of her have differed? Why?

3. If you find out that she is the surgeon who will be operating on you in the morning, and you initially thought she was someone different, how confident do you now feel in her ability as a surgeon? Why?

Instructions

Step 1 (individually: 5–10 minutes)

Read the situation to yourself, and decide who it is that is standing at your door and why you believe it to be that person. Make some notes as to your rationale for eliminating the other possibilities and selecting the one that you did.

Step 2 (small groups: 10–20 minutes)

Working in small groups or with the class as a whole, discuss who might be standing at your door and why you believe it to be that person.

In a place visible to all, reproduce the grid found with this exercise, and use it to record the responses of class members.

Step 3 (open-ended)

In class discussion, consider the stereotypes used to reach a decision, and consider the following:

1. How hard was it to let go of your original beliefs about each individual?

2. What implications do perceptions of people have about how you treat them and the expectations you have of them?

3. What implications do your responses to the above questions have to the way you, as a manager, might treat a new employee? What will the impact be on that employee?

4. What are the implications for yourself in terms of job hunting, relationships to peers, subordinates, and superiors in the workplace?

What You See Isn't Necessarily What You Get
Decision Grid

On the grid below, list the reasons that the woman standing before you
is or is not each of the following individuals.

Take a class vote, and list the number of people who select each possibility.

Possibilities	Why the woman is/is not this person	# who believe this to be the case
Surgeon		
Nurse		
Secretary		
Television Representative		
Laboratory Technician		
Business Manager		
Dietician		

16

OPERATION TRANSPLANT
Part 1

Objectives

- To explore decision making under conditions of uncertainty and complexity

- To practice the skills of group decision making by consensus

- To help participants explore the values and beliefs they hold that impact their interactions with others

Background

You are a member of the Ethics and Policy Committee of a medium-size urban hospital and teaching facility. Your committee is charged with making decisions about research proposals and innovative medical procedures. When resources are short, the committee must also decide which patients will receive special services. This last responsibility usually leaves you with the uncomfortable feeling that you are being asked "to play God." You are painfully aware that many patients who are not selected for special services face almost certain death.

This is exactly the case before you now. Five patients in your hospital have been recommended by your hospital's surgical transplant team as having the physical and psychological stamina necessary for a liver transplant operation. Without liver transplants, *all* of them will die within three to six months. With a transplant, their individual chances for survival range from about 80 to 85 percent. Under the best possible circumstances, that is, if five matching livers become available fairly rapidly, you might be able to save all five patients. The greatest likelihood is, however, that you will save up to three at most.

It is impossible to know just when a liver will become available. When one does, it will be on such short notice that it is important to have decided in advance in what order the patients are to be considered for the operation. Because all the patients are critically ill, it is conceivable that one or more could die before a liver becomes available, or that one or more could develop complications from their diseases that could render them unacceptable as transplant candidates. If either of these possibilities comes about for the individual who is Number One on the priority list, your transplant team needs to know immediately which patient will be moved in to take his or her place. Because any number of the patients could become unacceptable, you need to establish the order in which you will consider the five patients for transplant.

The transplant team has given you histories on each of the patients, including their personal and family backgrounds. You must consider the information and make your decisions. Your committee should discuss each candidate and reach a consensus (based on discussion rather than voting) as to who will be first, second, third, fourth, and fifth in line for this life-saving operation.

Instructions

1. *(5 minutes)*

   Before rank ordering the candidates, do the following:

   a. List three to five personal values you feel are important in making this decision (for example, "Children's lives are more important than adults.").

   _____

   _____

   _____

   _____

   b. List three to five responsibilities you feel you have been charged with fulfilling (for example, "To be fair").

   _____

   _____

   _____

   _____

2. *(15 minutes)*

   When you have finished, carefully read the descriptions of each of the transplant candidates; then enter your personal rankings in the column headed "My Ranking" on the grid found at the end of the exercise.

Candidates

Sandra T., age 34, Asian, Methodist

Sandra is a registered nurse with three children, all under nine. She had worked the 11 p.m. to 7 a.m. shift at your hospital for six years until four months ago when her illness became too severe. The money she had been earning, and her willingness to work the night-to-morning shift, allowed her husband, Charles, a full-time paralegal in a major law firm, to pursue a law degree at a local night law school. Over the past four months, Charles has had to stop his law school classes (in which he was consistently earning top grades) to care for Sandra and the children. During the day, home health aides assist Sandra. Charles drops the youngest child off at day care and drives the two older children to school on his way to work. He leaves work at lunch time to pick the older children up and take them to the day care provider; in the evening, he picks them up. There are few community support services available to the couple. Sandra is an only child whose parents had her rather late in life; both have been dead for over ten years. Charles has one married brother, but he lives in another city 700 miles away, as do his parents who, themselves, are not well.

When Sandra and Charles were married almost a dozen years ago, they were full of high hopes. Charles had just graduated from a major university with a degree in business and had taken his job with the law firm, initially in their bookkeeping department. Sandra had graduated from the nursing school of the same university. They have both been active in their church, and Sandra organized a support group for young mothers in their community.

Now Sandra is scared and depressed. She is increasingly upset with the realization that her illness has drained their young family both financially and emotionally, and she worries about her children and the impact her illness is having on them. Sandra prays that she will be considered to be a viable candidate for a liver transplant so that she and Charles can continue to raise their family and share the love they feel so deeply for one another.

Sara Y., age 42, white, Jewish

Sara, an English professor at a local university, is popular with students, has won the school's award for excellence in teaching, and consistently receives highest evaluations for her courses. She is a member of the Democratic Women's Caucus and The League of Women Voters, and she is an abortion rights activist.

Last April, Sara received both good news and bad news on the same day: Her first book won a national writers' award, and she was diagnosed as having sclerosing cholengitis of the liver. She is currently on leave from teaching, as her illness has left her physically exhausted, unable to concentrate, and in need of almost constant hospitalization.

Sara grew up in a middle-class family in the Midwest. She received her undergraduate degree from an eastern women's college, a master's degree in English from Stanford and, just after she turned 24, she settled into the role of housewife, having married her high school sweetheart. At age 29, she became a widow when her husband died in a plane crash. She was left with three young children. A substantial settlement from the airline allowed her to live comfortably, care for her children, and return to school for a Ph.D. in English literature, which she completed in five years. During her Ph.D. program, Sara met and married a history professor fifteen years her senior. A widower, he had four children, two of whom are now students at the university, a sophomore and a senior respectively. The oldest child has completed college and works in Vermont on an experimental farm; the youngest is still in high school. Sara's children are also still in high school. The couple adopted one another's children, creating what Sara calls "sort of a Jewish Brady Bunch." Sara's second husband died suddenly two years ago when he had a heart attack during his tenure hearings.

"My work isn't over," says Sara. "I know I'm not the only one in the world who can teach English and write books. That's something I do for me, something I feel good about. But I am the only one left for seven terrific kids, and they just don't deserve this."

Peter V., age 27, white, no religion stated

Peter is a college drop-out who has never held a steady job. His father, a board member of your hospital, has been particularly useful in helping the hospital weave its way through local red tape and politics. Peter's father has also been a major donor and an invaluable fundraiser. His efforts have been critical to the continued operation of the surgical transplant unit which year after year incurs an enormous operating deficit, with costs for care of liver transplant patients, for example, ranging up to $250,000 per case. Even now, the unit operates under the constant threat of being closed for lack of funds.

Unlike his very generous father, Peter is arrogant, demanding, and entitled. During his multiple admissions to your hospital over the past four months, he has angered much of your staff. His nurse call button always seems to be on, but the nurses complain that when they respond, his demands are for channel changes on his television, pillow adjustments, and other petty requests. In addition, many staff members say they're uncomfortable with the steady stream of questionable characters who visit Peter's room night and day.

You have known Peter since he was a small child, when he was sweet, bright, fair-haired and lively. All that changed as Peter entered adolescence, and you're aware that Peter was suspended several times from the posh private school he attended for coming to classes drunk. Each time, his father pressured the school to take him back. Ultimately he graduated, although you suspect he was given "social passes" to get him through without alienating his parents. Peter went on to a local two-year college, and for a time things looked better. However, he flunked out mid-way through the second year and has neither gone back nor gotten any sort of job. His parents, who continue to be his sole support, tell you that they will never abandon their son and that they believe their love will ultimately bring him around. Between his admissions to the hospital, Peter lives in his parents' home.

Peter's father appears dispirited by Peter's medical condition. Peter's mother, however, is angry and seems to hold the hospital responsible for every ache and pain her son is suffering. She has stated openly to members of her various clubs that if Peter does not receive a liver, she and her husband will "stop all financial support and see to it that the hospital is made to pay for its negligence."

Chris J., age 37, white, Methodist

Chris holds a Ph.D. in biology and worked on a research team at a biotech firm until two months ago when health complications made further work impossible. Scientists at the biotech firm believe that, thanks in large part to a major breakthrough by Chris, they are close to developing a drug intervention for use when AIDS is diagnosed at an early stage. The profits from such a drug potentially would be enormous. Largely on the strength of Chris's work, the firm has been able to raise considerable capital and two government grants to continue the investigation and drug development.

You've had a recent visit from the CEO of the biotech firm, a personal friend and former member of your hospital's staff, who came to plead on Chris's behalf. "Without Chris," the CEO told you, "we would not be as close to a cure for AIDS as we are. We're on the edge here of being able to save thousands of lives, and Chris is important to us."

Chris has been in a stable, same-sex "marriage" for thirteen years with Pat, a social worker for a local "safe house" for battered women. Chris and Pat have established a home in the suburbs, and Chris's elderly mother lives with them. (Chris's father was an alcoholic who disappeared when Chris was nine.) They have been active in their community where they are socially popular and accepted by most, although by no means all, of their neighbors. A year ago Chris and Pat co-chaired their community's successful Red Feather charity drive.

As a scientist, Chris is philosophical about the likelihood of a liver transplant. "Life is so fragile and uncertain," says Chris. "I see that everyday in the laboratory. I desperately want to live because I think I have a lot to contribute, but I also know that I could walk across the street and get hit by a car. Who ever knows?"

Jean-Paul D., age 34, Haitian, Catholic

Jean-Paul arrived in the United States in 1994 on an overcrowded boat from Haiti. Reaching shore sick and exhausted after seventeen days at sea without adequate food or water, he asked for and received political asylum.

Although he was an engineer in his native country, after receiving his green card, Jean-Paul took the first job he could find, as a mechanic's assistant. Until he was hospitalized, he had been scrupulously saving every possible penny in the hope of one day bringing his wife and four young children to the United States and to safety.

While in Haiti, Jean-Paul had been arrested and imprisoned for political agitation. Although he admits to occasionally criticizing the current regime in private discussions with his friends, he contends that he made a point of being apolitical in public to avoid trouble for himself and his family. Daily beatings while in prison left him with both emotional and physical scars.

Before his hospitalization, Jean-Paul had been living in a two-bedroom apartment with nine other Haitian men, all of whom had left families behind. Jean-Paul is especially concerned about his fourteen-year-old son, who will likely be a target for military conscription, or worse, for arrest and torture. Without help from Jean-Paul, his wife and children have little possibility of getting out of Haiti, where conditions are worsening daily. "I have to live," he says, in his limited and heavily accented English. "I am their only hope."

OPERATION TRANSPLANT
Part 2

Once you have completed your individual ranking of the candidates for the liver transplant, you will be asked to join with a group of your classmates to arrive at a group ranking.

Instructions

1. (5–10 minutes)

Before rank ordering the candidates, do the following:

a. Using the personal lists that you developed in Part 1, Step 1a, list below the three values that were most listed by group members.

_____

_____

_____

b. Using the personal lists that you developed in Part 1, Step 1b, list below the three responsibilities that were most listed by group members.

_____

_____

_____

2. (40–45 minutes)

Working in your group, discuss the candidates and rank order them. Enter your rankings on the grid in the column labeled "Group Ranking." Do not vote. Instead, reach consensus through discussion.

3. Select a group spokesperson to report your decisions to the class.

Questions for Discussion

1. Were members of your group able to work cooperatively to arrive at a decision?

   a. How did the individuals in the group deal with disagreement and conflict?

   b. When someone in the group disagreed with you, how did you handle the disagreement?

   c. Did you feel others listened to you?

   d. Did you listen to others?

2. What criteria were used to arrive at a determination?

   a. Were the criteria uniformly applied?

   b. If not, what do you see as the implications of not using uniform criteria here and in the workplace?

3. In what ways were your values and belief systems similar to and different from those of your classmates? To what do you attribute this?

   a. In what ways did your agreed-upon values and responsibilities influence your decision making?

   b. In what ways do you believe your values and belief systems will impact how you treat people in the workplace?

Scoring Grid

Patient	My Ranking	Group Ranking	Comments/Reasons
Sandra T.			
Sara Y.			
Peter V.			
Chris J.			
Jean-Paul D.			

FAMILY VALUES*

Brandi Rice-Christiansen

It was January of Brandi Rice-Christiansen's junior year of college. She had spent the fall semester concentrating on her course work and had worked particularly hard on the requirements for her accounting major. She would be completing her Bachelor of Science in Business Administration the following May and, if all continued to go well, she hoped to graduate *magna cum laude*.

It was now time for Brandi to begin the process of securing a full-time summer internship with a major accounting firm. If she performed well, she would be almost assured of a job offer. Early job offers were part of the beauty of being an accounting major. Since it was very likely that Brandi would be working for the firm at which she did her internship, it was of utmost importance that she choose the right firm. Although she was sure that every other student in her position felt the same way, Brandi believed that her needs were very different from those of her peers. At age twenty-five, Brandi had three children and a husband to fit into her professional life.

A Crooked Path

Brandi Rice-Christiansen had definitely not followed a straight and narrow path from high school to college. At age fourteen she had given birth to her first child. The child's father had provided Brandi with no support, and Brandi had struggled to raise her daughter alone. Brandi's mother, a single parent herself, worked three jobs and was unable to provide much assistance.

Despite daunting circumstances, Brandi was determined to finish high school and attend a good college. For three years following her daughter's birth, Brandi either left the child with relatives or brought her along to classes. It was a struggle, but Brandi managed to finish high school with grades that were good enough to earn her a full scholarship to a highly regarded local university. Brandi knew that going to college was her way out—her ticket to a better life for her daughter and herself. What she didn't anticipate was getting pregnant again.

Brandi began her freshman year at Stuart University motivated to succeed in the challenging management curriculum. Her first semester went well. However, by the second semester she had begun to experience some difficulties. Two of her courses required extensive teamwork, and Brandi's child care problems made it impossible to participate fully with her teams. This resulted in two barely passing grades, although she did well in her other

* This case was written by Gail E. Gilmore.

courses. The two low grades caused her cumulative average to fall just below the 3.0 required to maintain her scholarship, and she was put on probation for the following semester.

Shortly after the end of her freshman year, Brandi gave birth to her second child, a factor that increasingly complicated her life. She spent most of the summer trying to find suitable and affordable day care for her children so that she could return to school in September. Unfortunately, she was only able to find morning coverage. She tried to rearrange her class schedule so she could take all her classes in the morning, but she was unable to do so. By the time Brandi's sophomore year began, she felt frazzled and much less confident in her ability to succeed in her academic program.

By the middle of the first semester of her sophomore year, Brandi was forced to withdraw from all courses but one, in which she received a failing grade. Her life was just too complicated, and juggling all her responsibilities seemed impossible. She was given one more semester in which to pull up her grades or her scholarship would be revoked. Unfortunately, the second semester of her sophomore year was no more successful than the first, and Brandi withdrew from all her courses. At the end of the year, she was informed by the Office of Financial Assistance that her scholarship had been canceled.

Picking Up the Pieces

The next two years were hectic for Brandi, but ultimately fulfilling. She got a job in the accounting department of a community health center where she was given increasing levels of responsibility. She met and married a man who encouraged her to return to school and finish her degree, and she had her third child. This time she felt much more in control of her life, as she had a husband who was supportive and an enormous help with child care responsibilities. By the time the baby was a year old, she felt she was prepared to return to Stuart University. This time, things would be different.

The Right Fit

And things *were* different. Brandi took a full course load each semester, as well as during each summer session. She made the Dean's list every semester, and because of her remarkable academic turnaround, she qualified for a generous financial-aid package.

With the support of her husband, Brandi was able to successfully juggle her family responsibilities and her academic responsibilities. Now she had to find an internship that would lead to the kind of job that would make the sacrifices of the past years worthwhile. It had to be with the right firm, one with an organizational culture that enabled working mothers to balance family and work obligations, and where women with families were respected and not passed over for promotions.

Thinking about finding the right internship, Brandi realized that she didn't know how to determine whether a firm possessed the qualities she needed to succeed. She knew she could ask outright, but she wasn't sure she would get an honest answer. She also feared that such an approach could prejudice a prospective employer against her from the start. Brandi now had to make a decision—her first interview was in three days.

Questions for Discussion

1. What would you advise Brandi to do? Create a list of the ways Brandi might obtain information regarding the firm's track record on work-life linkages.

2. If you were in charge of hiring interns for your company, given what you know about Brandi, how would you view her as a candidate? Why?

3. In what ways, if any, do you believe organizations benefit from being sensitive to the work-life concerns of their employees? Why?

4. What values would you like to see in your own company (either one you work for or one you own) with regard to work-life concerns? Why?

WAITING TABLES FOR GODOT*

Instead of spending her summer vacation at her parents' house in King of Prussia, Pennsylvania, college student Diane Almeida decided to stay in Boston and take a job waiting on tables at La Maison d'Essence, a fancy French restaurant near the upscale Faneuil Hall Market Place. Diane felt fortunate to get such a job: The pay was $2.35 per hour, plus tips. Considering that the average dinner for two, with wine, ran about $90, Diane thought that she could make big money if she worked hard enough to earn 15 to 20 percent tips.

When Jean-Pierre Godot, owner of La Maison d'Essence, hired Diane, he emphasized that he expected excellence from his staff. He spoke about his vision for his restaurant and the importance of working as a team. She decided right then that she would really give it her all to prove just how good she could be.

Godot seemed dedicated and industrious, but he was also prone to emotional outbursts. When the restaurant got crowded, and people got restless waiting for their dinners to be served, Godot would stomp into the kitchen and shout at the chef in French: "Dépêche-toi! Tu es un escargot paresseux; ma grand-mère peut faire la cuisine plus vite que toi!" (Hurry up! You are a lazy snail; my grandmother can cook faster than you!)

Godot essentially ignored Diane during her first several weeks on the job. Hearing how he spoke to the cook, she was actually a little relieved. Still, she was surprised that he hadn't said anything to her. As far as she could tell, she was doing a good job, and she was averaging close to 20 percent in tips. Customers complimented her on her efficient service— from previous experience, she had learned to balance several plates on her arms, so she didn't have to waste time making extra trips to the kitchen. She also knew that giving really good service meant doing a lot of little extras.

Diane was sure, as well, that she was helping La Maison d'Essence make more money from each customer. She had a knack for recommending the right wines to complement meals, she frequently walked by to see if people needed to have drinks refreshed, and she tempted her customers into buying lavish desserts by describing them in sensuous detail.

Diane spoke French well enough to use it when the occasional French or French-Canadian diner ate at the restaurant. She displayed her excellent memory by always remembering who ordered what and handing out the entrées accordingly, and she remembered repeat customers and greeted them with "Welcome back."

Despite all of this, Godot took little notice of her, merely grunting at her when she said hello or goodbye each day. Then, one night, he finally spoke to her. More precisely, he yelled at her when she dropped a bowl of bouillabaisse appetizer on the carpet. Diane was very apologetic and hurried to get a sponge, but Godot shouted at her in rapid-fire French and

* This case was written by Scott Weighart.

told her that he would be deducting $8.95 from her pay—the price of the bouillabaisse—plus $5 for the cost of cleaning the stain in the rug.

Walking home that night, Diane felt angry and confused. Sure, maybe she shouldn't have tried to carry out four appetizers at once, but it was just a small mistake. What about the things she did to give the customers great service? Godot never seemed to notice those things. Waiting for Godot to give a compliment was like waiting for a million dollars to fall from the sky.

Diane decided to slow down a little on the next night, not wanting to inspire another outburst from her boss. It was a Friday night, and the place was packed. Diane brought out no more than two dishes at a time, and her tips went down to under 15 percent, much less than her one-night high of 23 percent.

Although she didn't break anything, Godot still got irritated with her and the rest of his staff. As the wait staff almost ran in and out of the kitchen, Godot kept saying to them, "Vite! Vite! Avez-vous plomb dans vos souliers?" (Quick! Quick! Do you have lead in your shoes?)

By the end of the night, Diane was really sick of his griping, and she slowed down considerably. Unfortunately, this made her tips sag. Really needing to make money so she could afford to eat something other than rice or spaghetti during her next college semester, Diane forced herself to go back to her original fast pace, praying that she wouldn't drop anything. She could hardly wait for September. Waiting for Godot had turned out to be all work and no play.

Questions for Discussion

1. Consider this case in terms of operant conditioning: What positive and negative reinforcements are used by Godot, if any?

2. What impact does punishment have on behavior, and on Diane's behavior specifically?

3. Using the concept of cognitive dissonance, explain what you believe are Diane's perceptions of the events at La Maison d'Essence.

19

NUDE DANCING COMES TO WESLEYVILLE—OR DOES IT?*

Only a month ago, John Thompson was absolutely certain he was making a sound business move. Now, he was having second thoughts. Reverend Beach had certainly touched a nerve, and even though it had been hours since the Reverend's departure, Thompson still couldn't seem to shake his parting question. It conjured up a mental image that was abhorrent and unthinkable.

Background

Earlier this year, Thompson had noticed that the number of nude dancing establishments in a large nearby city was rapidly increasing, and he began to watch their growth with keen interest. They seemed to be doing well there; so well, in fact, that he began wondering how successful such an establishment might be in Wesleyville, the small town in which he lived. The more he thought about it, the more feasible the prospect of success seemed to be. It wasn't long before visions of a lucrative new business opportunity began filling his head.

Thompson decided to follow up on this idea by visiting nine clubs and gathering information about their operations: number of patrons, liquor sales, cover charges, etc. He personally talked to bartenders, bouncers, disk jockeys, dancers, and shift managers. Their descriptions and accounts strongly reinforced his original impression—this was, indeed, a very lucrative business. On the basis of these investigations, Thompson decided to introduce nude dancing to Wesleyville, and he immediately set to work developing a business plan. He didn't want to waste any time getting his project off the ground.

Exactly one month ago, Thompson had put the first phase of his business plan into action when he signed a lease and took possession of the building soon to house his county's first nude dance club. The building, formerly a restaurant, had been vacant for almost a year. It was on Smithton Road, a location he thought ideal. There were no houses or churches in the immediate vicinity, the nearest neighbors were an automobile salvage yard, a petroleum bulk plant, and a veterinary hospital. Surely, he thought, these neighbors would not be adversely affected. In addition, while the location was beyond the city limits, it was near enough to town to draw a large crowd.

Acutely aware of Wesleyville's heart-of-the-Bible-belt location, Thompson intentionally kept his plans quiet, reasoning that the people of Wesleyville would find out about the club soon enough. He thought that the likelihood of any organized opposition, or even of any competition, would be greatly reduced if it was a *fait accompli* when word got out. He insisted that his contractors instruct their workmen to keep quiet about the remodeling; the people of Wesleyville did not need to know about the lighting system, runways, mirrors, or

* Copyright 1994 by Roland B. Cousins. Used with permission.

even the liberal use of red velvet. They already knew that a nightclub was about to open, and that was all they needed to know.

In the interest of secrecy, Thompson was also less than forthcoming on the application for his liquor license. He wrote only the words "live entertainment" and "music" in the appropriate places on the form. The required public notices were placed, followed by the compulsory public hearing. Much to Thompson's delight, the liquor license acquisition process was "clear sailing." Not a soul showed up at the hearing to speak in opposition to his application, and the license was granted with virtually no discussion. A major hurdle had been cleared.

The Meeting

Everything seemed to be running smoothly until last night when Reverend Beach came calling. After introducing himself, he announced that he had just come from an emergency meeting of the ministerial alliance where the imminent opening of a nightclub featuring nude dancing was the topic for consideration. As Reverend Beach uttered the words "nude dancing," Thompson felt his teeth and fists involuntarily clench. He had a terrible feeling that this could become a very unpleasant and volatile encounter.

During their ensuing discussion, Reverend Beach mentioned that he had been contacted by a fellow minister from Selby, a small town thirty miles to the west of Wesleyville, who told him that Thompson had been there recruiting dancers for a club in Wesleyville that would feature nude dancing. Beach had also heard that Thompson had been very successful in his recruiting efforts, presumably because of the high unemployment rate in the county and the existence of a regional university in the town. There had been no public outcry in Selby, Reverend Beach had said, apparently because the establishment would not be located in that community.

The longer Reverend Beach spoke, the more obvious it became that Thompson's initial concern about this meeting was right. Beach's voice became louder and higher pitched. His face was beet-red as he wagged his index finger at Thompson and declared that the good people of Wesleyville would run him and his entire family out of town if he followed through with his plans.

As Beach slowed to catch his breath, Thompson asked, "Reverend, exactly what do you have against the opening of this club? I will run a clean and decent place; there will be no touching allowed, and certainly no solicitation for prostitution or any other illegal activity."

Reverend Beach, angry and shaking, screamed, "I'll tell you what we don't like! How can you possibly say you will run a decent place when you're going to have wanton women running around buck naked, stimulating evil thoughts in the minds of the sinners who would patronize such a place? It's ungodly, decadent, and a threat to everything the good people of this community stand for. You say there'll be no prostitution, but that's exactly what your so-called dancers will be doing—prostituting themselves for the almighty dollar. Surely drug use and organized crime will soon flourish in our very midst if this house of Beelzebub is allowed to open."

"You just wait, Thompson," he added in a low and threatening tone. "We are going to organize a protest like you have never seen. Your club, home, and even your used car lot will be picketed around the clock."

"If you get so far as to open the doors, we will be videotaping the cars coming and going, maybe even calling some of your customers' homes to let their wives know what their husbands are up to. Sheriff Peterson is a member of my congregation, and he assures me that he will personally see to it that not one car leaves your establishment driven by a person who might be under the influence of alcohol. Your activities will be denounced from every pulpit in town. And, while I certainly wouldn't condone it, we may not be able to stop an outbreak of violence should you continue with this scheme."

"There is going to be a deafening public outcry against this decadent establishment," he went on, his voice rising again. "You, sir, are clearly in league with the devil."

As Reverend Beach finally slowed to catch his breath, Thompson jumped in.

"Reverend," he said firmly, "I certainly respect the right of you and your flock to stay out of my establishment, if that's what you choose. However, you must respect my right to open and run my business as long as I operate within the letter of the law. I have done nothing illegal so far and fully intend to see to it that absolutely no illegal activities take place on my property in the future.

"If you and your followers have all of this time and energy and want to work for the public good, why don't you donate your time to help our community solve some real problems? You mentioned that somehow my club was going to introduce illegal drug use to Wesleyville. Maybe you didn't read the *Wesleyville Patriot* last week. An eleven-year-old boy was arrested at the elementary school for selling pills to his playmates. And that certainly wasn't the first such incident reported in this town—only the most recent.

"Hardly a week goes by," Thompson continued, "without some tragedy involving our kids appearing in the local paper. Why don't you organize your followers to combat illiteracy, teenage pregnancy, school drop-outs, drug use, gang activity, or a myriad of other problems that our town faces? You could really make a contribution to our community if you chose to address those problems instead of spending your time harassing honest business people."

Reverend Beach jumped in as Thompson paused. "We've always played an active role in improving all facets of life in Wesleyville," he insisted. He agreed that the problems Thompson mentioned did deserve some attention, but he also repeated that nude dancing was the work of the devil and needed to be purged immediately. As a parting shot, Reverend Beach asked Thompson if he had ever thought of this business as degrading to women.

Bristling at this suggestion, Thompson responded.

"Reverend," he said, "I'll tell you what's degrading to women—a society that offers no support for unskilled single mothers, apparently expecting them to successfully raise children with a job that pays minimum wage and offers virtually no benefits. That's degradation. My dancers will probably earn about a thousand dollars a week just dancing for tips. This position will offer a sense of independence and security. It's the fast food restaurants and other similar employers that demean women, not me."

Ready to end the discussion, and on his terms, Reverend Beach retorted, "We'll be meeting again on this matter very soon, but let me leave you with one thought. I understand you have one daughter who is about eighteen and another about fifteen. I hear they're both fine young ladies. How would you like it if your eighteen-year-old was dancing naked in front of a group of leering, drunken men in your "decent" establishment? You just think about it, Mr. Thompson."

With that, Reverend Beach turned, walked to his dark gray Oldsmobile, got in, and drove away.

For the rest of the afternoon, Thompson was plagued by Reverend Beach's final question; he could not get it out of his mind. Before this, he had been absolutely certain that what he was doing was right. Now, however, he kept imagining his little Cathy dancing on the runway. The image made him shudder.

Questions for Discussion

1. Should John Thompson reconsider opening the nude dancing club? Why? Justify your conclusion.

2. If you were advising John Thompson, would you be influenced by the public outcry? Why?

3. Discuss the following: "Any business which is legal is both moral and ethical."

4. What is the responsibility of business owners and operators to their host communities?

20

PICKING THE PROJECT TEAM AT THE OZARK RIVER BANK

Objectives

- To examine the human resources needs, including personalities and expertise, to successfully undertake and complete a project

- To consider the impact of personal values and group norms on group functioning

- To consider other relevant factors in assembling a high functioning team

Instructions

1. (Individually: 15 minutes)

As you read the background information on each candidate, highlight or underline the job requirements you believe should be considered in selecting the three team members. Develop a list of the qualities and expertise the candidates should have, individually and collectively, to be part of the team.

As you read the profiles on each of the candidates, similarly mark the information, positive and negative, that will lead you to decide to use or not use that candidate for your team.

2. (Small group: 30 minutes)

Discuss the project, the team requirements, and the candidates' strengths and weaknesses. Select the three team members.

3. (15 minutes minimum)

Report your decisions and the reasons for them to the class. Discussion to follow.

Background

Two years ago, the Ozark River Bank, the largest commercial bank in a six-state area, became a major lender in a worker-led leveraged buyout. To finance the buyout, the workers pledged the assets of the company as collateral for their loans. Now it has become clear that the business plan on which the buyout was based is not meeting projections. Although the new owners have been able to turn the company around from a losing situation to one that is marginally profitable, it is unlikely that cash flow will be sufficient to meet debt-service requirements when a large issue of zero-coupon bonds matures in about eighteen months.

The original worker buyout was a highly publicized event in which more than a thousand jobs were saved, financial disaster for a community was averted, and the bank was hailed for its assistance and support. To let the company go under because it is unable to meet its financial obligations on the loans would throw the community into a severe recession, increase joblessness, and put the bank in a bad light. Therefore, the bank needs to explore a creative plan for the workout in which the various lenders, including a group of other financial institutions that hold unsecured debt (debentures), and the stockholders (both management and the workers) arrange a restructuring that would reduce debt-service requirements consistent with current cash-flow projections. This could involve a variety of techniques, including the conversion of some debt into equity, salary reductions for management, and efficiency cuts in the workforce.

Dealing with this kind of situation is sensitive, high in stress, and severely time constrained. You have found that the most successful approach to doing this kind of work is to assign it to a project team. The job of the team will be to put together a restructuring plan that meets the needs of the bank and the other lenders and that can be put into place quickly at the time of default.

Five people in your department have the knowledge and ability to do the kind of work necessary. It is important that the three people you select for this team be high-functioning and successful. They must be able to work well together to accomplish the task accurately, quickly, and without delay. Your job is to decide which three will work best together to accomplish the stated objectives. The success of this team will be important to its members' career paths and to yours.

The following people in your department are available:

Harold, age 52

Harold has been a loyal employee of the bank for twenty-six years. He is respected by his peers and his superiors, and he has a solid understanding of the industry involved. In addition, he has worked successfully on smaller but similar projects. Harold sets careful timelines for work in projects and pushes the members of his teams to be fastidious about meeting deadlines. Over the years, he has proven himself to be both a leader and a team player. Recently, Harold returned to the bank after a six-month medical leave of absence because of a heart attack. He is eager to get back into work and is actively looking for something to do.

Joan, age 41

Joan is a detail person. She understands the fine points of leveraged buyouts and reorganizations better than anyone in your department and, when she is on a team, it is rare for there to be any loopholes or glitches in the results. Through hard work and determination, Joan has risen in the company fairly quickly. She is an outspoken feminist whose sexual harassment case against the bank, brought seven months ago as a reaction to a situation with a prior project team, has still not been resolved. Apparently, the two men with whom she had been working used a great deal of locker-room language, persisting in this practice despite her objections. The previous manager of your department, your immediate predecessor, failed to take her complaints seriously.

Cynthia, age 31

Cynthia is married and has two young children. She came to work in your department five and a half months ago, just after receiving her MBA, and is still learning the ropes. Her job before and during her MBA program was as a project manager with the company that is now the object of the workout. She was there throughout the leveraged buyout proceedings and had been part of the group that developed the original business plan. You had hired Cynthia to replace Harold, who you hadn't expected to return; however, some people also believe that she was hired specifically to undercut the credibility of Joan's case. For the last three months, Cynthia and Joan have been working together on a plan for an on-site day care program at the bank.

Jack, age 35

Jack is a bachelor who likes to spend his free time at sporting events or at a local bar with his friends. Of all the people in your department, Jack is probably the most knowledgeable about workouts on complex loan defaults. He has an excellent reputation for being innovative, but he is also known to be a procrastinator—one of those people who likes to push deadlines, waiting until the last minute before he really gets going. Then, Jack works virtually round the clock, pushing his coworkers to do the same. In the end, he always seems to come through.

Joshua, age 62

Joshua has an air of Old World chivalry and is very conservative about women. He has been outspoken in his belief that women belong at home taking care of their husbands and children, but he makes his comments with such charm that most people don't take offense. Having been at the bank for more than thirty years, and being an active member in the local community, Joshua knows just about everyone and has ready access to a wide range of resources. He knows how to work the system to get what he needs when he needs it. This kind of networking ability could prove to be an important factor in the ultimate success of this project.

Questions for Discussion

1. In what ways would the various people described work well together? In what ways might they have problems?

2. Given the answers to Question 1, which three people will you select, and why?

21

MANAGING PERFORMANCE BY SETTING GOALS

Objectives

- To examine the use of goal setting in performance management
- To practice the techniques of performance management

Part A
Background

You are the parents of a teenager who, despite having above-normal intelligence, is doing poorly in high school. At present her grade point average is 1.3 on a four-point scale, and she is failing English and Social Studies. She has been getting into trouble in and out of school because of antisocial behavior. Her bedroom is a mess, and she is often late for school because she can't find clothes, books, etc. She has also lost her much-needed job for being late once too often. Your teen admits that she doesn't feel very good about herself and would like to change—but she feels overwhelmed.

You know from your college course in organizational behavior that setting clear and realistic goals is an important aspect of helping a person improve performance. You think you'll try this with your teen, starting with a performance evaluation.

Procedure

1. (15 minutes)

Working in a group of three to four classmates, decide what long- and short-term goals you should set with your teen to help her improve. Consider what you think would be a realistic schedule, and create a time-line along which you chart at least seven goals.

2. (20 minutes)

As a group, decide what you will do to help your teen achieve her goals, what you will do if she fails to achieve a goal, and what you will do when your daughter achieves a goal.

3. (Optional 5–10 minutes each round)

Select two people to role play the goal-setting conversation between parent and teen. After the role play, discuss how effective the conversation was and what could have been done better.

Next, select two people to role play the conversation between parent and teen when the teen fails to meet a goal. Discuss the effectiveness of this conversation.

Finally, select two people to role play the conversation between parent and teen when the teen has met a goal. Discuss this conversation as well.

4. (10 minutes)

As a group, explore what you see as the strengths of the goal-setting approach and how effective you think this approach would be with you. Consider what you see as the parallels between the use of goal setting with a family member and goal setting in the workplace.

5. (5–10 minutes each group)

Report your findings to the class beginning with showing your time-line. Share your reflections on the questions in #4.

Part B

1. (10–20 minutes)

Working in the same group, have each group member briefly describe a situation in which they or someone they know needed to improve work performance. As a group, select one of the situations and discuss how the supervisor or manager could have used goal setting to help that individual.

2. (5–10 minutes each round)

Role play the situation, this time role playing the conversations between employee and manager, beginning with a performance evaluation and then following the instructions in Part A, Question 3 above.

Questions for Discussion

1. Why do you feel goal setting would be a successful (or not so successful) technique to use in the workplace?

2. What do you see as management's responsibilities for helping employees set and meet goals? Why?

3. As you role played or observed the role plays of the stages of performance management, how comfortable were you with the conversations that took place? What might have been done to make the conversations more comfortable?

22

ANOTHER SALES CONTEST AT PATTERSON DEPARTMENT STORES*

"How on earth did they arrive at *this* number?" Kathy asked. She looked up dismayed from the letter her store manager had just handed her. It was from the district office stating the store's goal of $38,000 for the second Easter Dress Event contest, a goal that to Kathy sounded high. When she went to her office to calculate the change, she found that it was a whopping 46 percent increase over the previous year. Kathy's heart sank. She recalled how diligently she and her staff had worked the year before, during Kathy's first dress contest, to produce only a 30 percent increase over the previous year. She thought, "How will we ever reach this impossible goal?"

Kathy Joins the Patterson Company

Kathy Lewis graduated from the University of Tennessee at age twenty-two, got married, and moved with her husband to a medium-sized community in Alabama where her husband started a sales career with a pharmaceutical company. After a year of working odd jobs and hunting for a position that would allow her to use her college education, Kathy landed a position with the Patterson Department Store as a management trainee. She was excited about facing the challenges of her first professional job, and she was sure that her degree in home economics would help her in buying clothing for the women's ready-to-wear department. Although she was a fast and eager learner, Kathy also knew she had a lot to learn about business.

After completing Patterson's year-long intensive training program, Kathy was made merchandising manager of the women's ready-to-wear department. She loved her job and hoped to turn it into a long and successful career. In addition, she and her husband had just bought their first house, and the raise that came with the promotion would help to furnish it.

Not long after starting her new position, planning began at the store for the annual Easter Dress Event. Two weeks prior to Easter, the Patterson Department Store chain holds a dress contest among the merchandisers in their twenty or so stores. The merchandiser who has the highest percent increase in sales of women's dresses from the previous year is awarded a trophy and is recognized by the district manager. Categories include junior, misses, and half-size dresses.

Kathy was determined to win the contest. She felt that if she could prove herself in her new position by winning this first contest, it would increase her chances for future promotions. Since she was still paying off college loans, as well as furnishing her new house, the potential salary increases that would accompany promotions were highly motivating to her.

* Copyright 2000 by Bonnie L. McNeely, Ph.D., Murray State University, and Mary Anne Watson, Ph.D., University of Tampa. Used with permission.

Setting Sales Goals for Kathy's First Contest

Kathy's enthusiasm for the contest was shared by her sales force. She and her dress department staff knew that if they were to win the contest, they would first need to know the previous year's sales figures. This information would help them determine how many dresses they needed to sell and in what price range. Looking at the approximately $20,000 sales figure from the previous year, they felt that with hard work and luck they might be able to generate $27,000 in sales. This was a 35 percent increase from the year before and a goal they believed would win the trophy and the recognition.

Kathy and her sales staff brainstormed and came up with several ideas for increasing their sales during the contest. Because this was her first contest, Kathy was particularly opened to the advice of her experienced sales staff.

Together, they decided to get every employee in the store involved in promoting the event. First, every employee was asked to wear a special tag announcing the Easter Dress Event attached to his or her regular employee name badge. Second, employees were asked to mention the Easter Dress Event to every customer they served during the two weeks, inform customers of a drawing for gift certificates in the women's dress department, and give them an entry form. Customers had to visit the dress department to deposit their entry forms in a special drawing box located only in that department. The name of the employee who had encouraged the customer to participate appeared at the bottom of each form. When the drawings for the gift certificates were held on the last day of the contest, the employee named on the winning certificate received a cash award. This encouraged many sales associates to give out gift-certificate entry forms freely while informing the customer of the dress event.

To promote the contest, the sales team decided to have its first ever in-store fashion show for the public. On Friday night of the first week of the contest, the show was held in the dress department during store hours. The top of the long sales counter was temporarily converted into a show runway, store employees served as models, and Kathy announced and described the fashions. The show was well attended, and at the end the cash register rang.

In addition to the drawings for gift certificates and the fashion show, Kathy's sales team agreed to dress in a similar theme each day of the contest, wearing store merchandise to model it for the customers. Kathy purchased extra stock, and inventory was strong. Store window displays and the in-department merchandise displays were changed every two days during the event, three times more often than normal. Everything possible was done to keep the inventory looking fresh and to maintain excitement about the contest.

A huge chart showing daily sales figures hung in the employee section of the store; it could be seen by employees each time they reported to work or took a break. The results of each day's sales were posted, and the accumulated sales were totaled to see what progress was being made toward the goal. The increase in sales was excellent, and the enthusiasm about winning the district contest grew stronger each day.

When the contest was over, the sales increase was 30 percent with about $26,000 in sales. While the department did not reach the goal they had set, the increase in sales was impressive. The sales team members believed they had a good chance of winning. The results were turned into the district office, and they waited for word on the winning store.

Sales Contest Results: Kathy's First Year

Two weeks after the contest results were turned in, Kathy arrived at the store at her usual reporting time of 8:30 a.m. The receptionist greeted her with the news that her department had come in second. While Kathy was disappointed that they had not won, she was still very pleased with the results. She looked forward to sharing the news with her sales staff. While doing some paperwork at her desk prior to the store opening, Kathy looked up to see the store manager approaching. She sat up straight in her chair and smiled thinking she was about to be congratulated for the effort put into the contest, the 30 percent increase in sales, and coming in second in the competition.

When the manager, not smiling, arrived beside Kathy's desk, he said, "Have you heard that the dress contest results are in?"

"Yes, sir," Kathy replied smiling, anticipating a compliment.

"Do you know what they say about people who come in second?" he growled.

Kathy looked confused. "No, sir," she said.

"They say nothing about people who come in second," the manager barked. At that, he turned and walked away.

The Following Year

It was hard to believe that a whole year had passed, and it was time again for the annual Easter Dress Contest. As in years past, the winning store would be the one that had the highest percent increase from the previous year. This year, however, instead of each store setting its own goal, the district manager sent a letter to each store with an assigned goal derived in the following way: Management at corporate headquarters in New York decided on the overall company goal. This company goal was divided into five regional goals. Regional managers, in turn, determined the goals for each of their districts, and finally, district managers assigned the goals for individual stores. For Kathy's department, the goal had been set at a 46 percent increase.

Kathy felt a sense of rising resentment. She and her staff had made super efforts the previous year, had had a 30 percent increase, placed second in the contest, and had received zero recognition for their efforts.

Later that day, dreading how the news would be received, Kathy told her sales staff of the assigned goal set by the district manager. Every staff member shook her head, frowned, and asked, "What could we possibly do that we didn't already try last year?" The goal of $38,000 was viewed not only as too high but also out of the range of possibilities.

"With all of the work we did last year, we still didn't win or come anything close to this new figure," they groused. They agreed to think about how they might compete in the upcoming contest and to meet again the following week to discuss their plans.

Epilogue

Forced to accept the assigned goal, Kathy and her staff went through the motions of trying to promote dress sales. Daily sales were again posted, but the figures were weak. After the contest, total sales for Kathy's department for the Easter Dress Event were $25,500, a 2 percent decrease from the previous year.

Questions for Discussion

1. What motivated Kathy to want to win her first dress contest?

2. How was Kathy's goal determined for the first contest? What impact did that have on her behavior?

3. What other motivators did you see in action?

4. How has the motivational situation changed in the second contest?

5. Is there anything the store manager could have said after the first year's results that might possibly have changed the second year's results?

6. What could Kathy do to motivate her sales staff to work toward the assigned goal the second year?

23

LINDA SIFUENTES

Chris Chuang continued to chew on an already well gnawed-on rollerball pen and to think back over the seven years since Linda Sifuentes had joined the accounting office of Maven Development. It was clear that Linda, who had just left Chris's office, was angry about her semiannual performance-appraisal discussion and the news that her salary increase was to be just 4 percent. Attempts to assure Linda that she was being treated "just like everyone else," to encourage her, and to offer support for any problems she might be having at home had obviously not helped. Chris feared that Linda was going to continue in the less-than-optimal performance pattern she had begun just over five months ago and had tried to warn her that her work had to improve. Linda's reaction had been defensive and somewhat accusing.

Maven Development

Maven Development is one of New England's largest commercial real estate developers. The company had been started in 1968 by Dersh Maven. Originally from Brooklyn, Maven had stayed on in Boston after his graduation from Boston University's School of Management in 1964. His summer internship with Cabot, Cabot & Forbes had turned into a challenging and interesting full-time job and proved to be a good training ground for learning about the politics and finances of real estate development. But Maven had always wanted to be his own boss, so, less than four years after graduation, he left CC&F and started Maven Development.

During the building boom of the late seventies and eighties, Dersh Maven had grown his company from what was, by that time, a mid-sized firm developing largely in the outlying suburbs, to a giant. From 1983 to 1988, Maven developed three of the new office buildings in Boston and had created similar projects in Providence, Hartford, and Nashua, New Hampshire. Consistent with the practice of many of the developers doing business at this level, outside architects and general contractors were hired for design and construction. It was Maven's job to assess the financial feasibility of a project, assemble the parcel of land, get clearance to build from local authorities, get zoning and environmental clearances, arrange for construction financing with a major bank, arrange long-term financing, and then market and ultimately manage the new building.

With the onset of the current real estate downturn, Maven began to face financial setbacks for the first time. While the company stretched to complete ongoing projects, rental of the new space began to fall well behind projections. Dersh Maven was reasonably sure that if he could hold on, he would do well when the market again turned around. In the meantime, the drain on cash flow was significant. The fall-off in the real estate market was severe in the Northeast. Along with problems with renting new space, leases on existing buildings were having to be renegotiated at substantially reduced prices to hold tenants. This further eroded the cash flow situation. Without a doubt, Maven was being financially squeezed.

Dersh Maven was a hands-on company president who was loyal to his employees and made a point of knowing them by their first names. When his company's profits began to sag, he imposed a wage freeze on upper management while trying to keep salary increases for lower-level employees at around 7.5 percent. Bonuses, tied to profitability, were eliminated. In addition, he had instituted a hiring freeze that was now in its second year. While most of his industry competitors had laid off up to 25 percent of their employees, Dersh Maven was determined not to follow suit. In order not to lay off, however, Maven realized that this year's salary increases for lower-level employees were going to have to be not much more than 4 percent for top performers and that mediocre performers would probably get a lot less. *The Wall Street Journal* had only recently reported that average salary increases nationwide had dropped to 5.6 percent, with increases in the Northeast averaging 4.4 percent.

Linda Sifuentes

Linda was one of those success stories about whom newspaper columnists love to write. She had grown up in Lynn, Massachusetts, a depressed manufacturing town just outside of Boston. She was the eldest of four children, three girls and a boy, whose parents seemed perpetually out of work.

In her sophomore year, Linda became pregnant and dropped out of high school, despite attempts by her guidance counselor to help her complete her education. Two years later, Linda had a second child. She lived in a subsidized housing unit in Boston with her children, not really making it on welfare.

At age twenty-two, Linda decided that she had to have a better life for herself and her children. With considerable effort, she finished high school, receiving top grades and a scholarship to study at Boston University. While it took her six years of attending night classes to complete her college program, working during the days to support her family and studying on weekends, Linda did well. She met Dersh Maven when he came as a guest speaker to one of her classes in her senior year, and he had been impressed enough to offer her a job after graduation.

In May of that year, Linda went to work in the accounting office of Maven Development at a starting salary of $19,785. From the beginning, Linda had loved working at Maven. She had quickly become friendly with the other nine people in her department with whom she often went out after work and on weekends. Several of the others had children around the same ages as Linda's, and family outings with them became the norm. For the first five years, Linda had enjoyed a close relationship with her supervisor, Pat James, who had been supportive and who Linda felt she could always count on to be fair in the treatment of workers in the accounting department. Linda believed that her hard work and diligence at Maven would allow her to move ahead in the company, her next step being into a position like Pat's.

Linda's work record had been impeccable. Except for having taken two days off at the time of her mother's death, Linda showed up regularly, always on time, worked late, and would often come in on weekends to finish important projects. Her work was accurate and well above average. At the end of her seventh year with Maven, she was earning $32,225 and had moved from her dismal, subsidized apartment to a small but comfortable one in a pleasant section of Quincy. Her children were doing well. During the previous summer, she had begun to date a real estate broker with whom she was now making wedding plans.

The Accounting Department

Five years after Linda had begun her job, Pat James had left Maven for a middle management job with Beacon Construction. Around the same time, Lee Elsworth, who had joined the accounting team about a year after Linda, was promoted to a management position in another department. Two other employees, close friends of Linda's, left for jobs in other companies, one following a spouse to the west coast.

Chris Chuang, Pat James's replacement as supervisor of the accounting department at Maven, was brought in just before the hiring freeze went into effect. Chris had an MBA from Boston University's Graduate School of Management and three years of accounting experience. Single, and younger than most members of the accounting department, Chris liked to spend summer weekends sailing and winter weekends skiing. Notwithstanding some sense that commercial real estate development was a troubled industry, Chris had been satisfied that the supervisory job at Maven was, at least for the time, a satisfactory rung on the climb up the corporate ladder.

Other than Chris, no one else had come into the accounting department to replace those who had left. The department was unquestionably short-staffed, and work had begun to pile up. There was considerable pressure from upper management to produce the figures needed for reports to the banks, insurance companies, and other lenders, all of which were getting nervous over the downturn in the market. As each of the department's workers began to show strains from the increasing work load, the once-supportive environment became noticeably tense. Still, Dersh Maven was adamant about the hiring freeze. "Until we can return to profitability," he had written in a company memo, "no new workers will be hired. We must work together, support one another, and preserve Maven Development for the brighter future that lies ahead."

Chris's Problem

With added pressure from above, Chris thought this was no time for a reliable employee like Linda Sifuentes to become unreliable—but unreliable she was. Over the past five months, Linda had begun to come in late, take long lunch breaks, and call in sick, particularly on Mondays and Fridays. Chris had tried everything—threats, promises, you name it, but Linda's difficult behavior continued. "If I could only understand what's going on here," Chris thought, "maybe I could turn this around."

Questions for Discussion

1. Using at least two—but not more than three—theories of motivation, analyze and explain Chris's problem.

2. If you were Chris, given your analysis of the situation, what would you do?

24

SPANGLEMAKER PUBLISHING*

For nearly 25 years, Marty Callahan had been the executive editor at Spanglemaker Publishing, a small company that specialized in children's books. Although Marty had had a long and happy career at Spanglemaker, he was headed for semi-retirement.

The president of Spanglemaker, Lawrence Guthrie, had recently announced that the company planned a much more aggressive marketing strategy. Noting that a successful children's book—such as Chris Van Allsburg's *The Polar Express*—could be on the best-seller lists for years, whereas adult literature had a much shorter life span for high-volume sales, Guthrie had decided to produce more innovative children's books in the hopes of discovering an occasional long-term "cash cow."[1]

While Marty understood Guthrie's rationale, he decided that the new goals and directions of the company were not consistent with his interests and that it was time to leave. Marty had always enjoyed the friendly atmosphere of Spanglemaker—how people would clip cartoons for him and how he and some of his colleagues would have long lunches in a nearby park, swapping book tips and jokes. As a sixty-two-year-old widower whose children had moved out of state, these get-togethers had become important to him.

Although Guthrie had said nothing directly, Marty realized that his boss's new expectations for the executive editor would mean a faster pace that would leave little time for friendly chats. Guthrie had hinted that Marty could step down and again become a copy editor, a move that would allow him to continue his long lunches and coffee breaks. But, in view of his age, Marty decided to do freelance work at home for a variety of large and small publishing companies. It wouldn't be hard to get enough business; over the years, Marty had made many connections, and he was well liked and respected in the industry.

In a short meeting, Marty told Guthrie of his decision to take early retirement. Guthrie wished him luck and asked him if, before leaving, he would recommend someone to take his place. Three Spanglemaker copy editors had expressed an interest in the job. It would be a sensitive decision: each candidate had a great deal of experience and was confident that he or she would be the best choice.

Initially, Marty eliminated Charles Langley from the list of candidates. Though they were good friends, Marty was sure that Charles would be obsessed with being in charge of his workers. Although he had more experience and seniority than the other two candidates, Charles would certainly be a big "rule maker" who might alienate the workers. He was bright and one of the better copy editors, and his people had the reputation of being highly productive. Charles was known to be hard-working and to expect nothing less from those who worked under him.

* This case was written by Scott Weighart.
1. A "cash cow" is a product that, after initial costs, continues to generate a high rate of income with only minimal additional expense.

The maximum stay at Spanglemaker for most people who worked for Charles seemed to be about two years, considerably less than the company average. After getting some really good training from him, the people who worked for Charles generally left to take higher-paying jobs with competitors. When Spanglemaker executives offered to match what competitors were offering, as an enticement to stay, few accepted. Having a fairly constant string of new employees meant a lot of fresh and new ideas, although Charles insisted that his people master the basics before getting involved in innovation.

Of the other two candidates, Marty decided first to interview Dominique Bernays, who had been with the company for more than ten years. In the past, Marty had been a reluctant admirer of Dominique's. She had shown a knack for discovering new authors and working with them. Many of her projects were unconventional but successful. For example, she had done well in helping an author develop a book for young children—a story about a little girl who had a single mother. Dominique believed that Spanglemaker should publish books geared toward the children of single parents, house-husbands, and even gay parents. Marty wasn't sure that the world was ready for such things.

Marty was also concerned that Dominique's personality would be problematic. He found her to be—well—"pushy." She was always deadly serious about her job and never seemed to have time for a friendly word. At work, she mostly stayed in her office, just wryly chuckling and continuing to work even when someone told her she needed a breather.

"Tell me why you should get the job," Marty said during the interview.

"I think my record shows that I thrive on responsibility," Dominique replied, staring into Marty's eyes so hard that it made him uncomfortable. "As you know, most of the books that I've been involved with have been recognized by the critics as real breakthroughs in children's literature, such as the bilingual books for Hispanic families. Given my performance over the last several years at Spanglemaker, I feel I deserve an opportunity to grow while the company grows."

"Your individual performance has been outstanding," Marty admitted. "But how would you manage the copy editors?"

Dominique gave him a hard glance, and Marty wondered if he had sounded more skeptical than he had intended. But why not? He had legitimate doubts about her interpersonal skills.

"As executive editor, I would do several things differently," she began. "First, rather than just assigning people to an author, I would let them choose the projects that they would find most interesting. If a copy editor prefers to do primarily realistic fiction, or fantasy, or whatever, I'd let them do it whenever possible. At the same time, I would work closely with the copy editors so that I would always know what they are working on. If someone did a particularly good job, I would reward him or her—you know, a plaque for the office, his or her name displayed somewhere—or maybe just an occasional day off for anyone who doesn't seem comfortable about being publicly congratulated. Most importantly, though, I would emphasize that Spanglemaker should produce the best books possible—whatever it takes, I'll make sure that we publish the most dynamic books."

"As you know, sometimes the executive editor has to deal with support staff—temporary secretaries, receptionists, and various others—people who tend to be unmotivated. How would you deal with that?" Marty asked.

"It would really depend on the situation," she replied. "I think some people work fine without much input from a boss, while others are basically lazy and have to be ordered around if you want anything to get done."

Would Dominique be a tough, single-minded slave driver if she became boss? Marty couldn't be sure.

Next, Marty interviewed Lou Healy, another veteran employee of Spanglemaker. For twelve years, Lou had done more than work for Marty. He had frequently joined him for lunch, and they had even attended poetry readings and wine-and-cheese book signings together. Nonetheless, Marty was determined to be all business in this interview. He wanted to be fair and make the best possible decision for the company.

"Why should you become executive editor?" Marty asked.

Lou spoke in his usual relaxed and confident voice. "I believe that, above all, a manager of workers should be a "people person," much the way you, Marty, have been over the years. I get along with almost everyone here, as you know. I don't think I've had a single argument in all the years that I've been here."

Marty knew this was true, and this sentiment was even reflected in the kind of children's books with which Lou preferred to work. He liked books that were traditional, even nostalgic—warm stories about girls who owned horses, or realistic novels that supported the idea of family togetherness.

"What kind of manager would you be?" Marty asked.

"I would supervise everyone closely," Lou responded, "but in a friendly way. I believe that a close relationship between a boss and his workers is what motivates those workers to be the best that they can be. Under no circumstances would I yell at an employee or lower the boom on anyone. People basically want to do a good job. A manager should be a positive thinker and be supportive to help them do that kind of job."

Marty and Lou shook hands, and Lou left. Sitting alone amid the bookshelves in his office, Marty pondered the decision. He had to admit that Dominique had some interesting ideas that might prove to be effective—letting people choose their own book assignments, for example. But he still had serious concerns about her ability to get along with others. It seemed as if work was the only thing that mattered to her: wouldn't the other copy editors find her to be too "gung ho?" He knew that Lou wouldn't like her as a boss. And what would Charles Langley think about taking orders from a woman?

On the other hand, what would happen if he chose Lou? Would Dominique be able to accept that?

"Hell, I don't have a crystal ball," Marty said to himself at last. He didn't want to spend too much time making a decision. Already the pace had been picking up at Spanglemaker; the number of books in production had increased by 25 percent in the last two months. Soon the little publishing company he had loved would become a fast-paced marketing machine that would leave him in the dust.

The next morning, Marty called Dominique into his office. "I'm sorry," he said, "but I'm going to recommend Lou Healy for the job."

"It figures," she snapped.

Uncomfortable, Marty tried to explain the importance of having a people-person as a manager and how his decision in no way was meant to diminish the excellence of her performance. Her dark brown eyes stared at him in silent anger, making him stutter as he finished his explanation.

"Don't think that I believe any of that," she said. "We women have had to deal with this kind of treatment for centuries."

"That has nothing to do with it!" Marty insisted. "Charles has more experience and seniority than you do, and I still put you ahead of him in making my decision." With a sense of frustration, Marty realized that the last chapter of a successful career in publishing had revealed an unpleasant twist in the plot.

Questions for Discussion

1. Using the various theories of motivation, explain how the characters in the case differ both in the way they themselves are motivated and the methods they would use to motivate others.

2. Why do you believe Marty made the decision that he did?

3. Consider that you are Lawrence Guthrie. Would you accept Marty's recommendation? Why? If not, who would you select, and why?

QUEENS VETERINARY HOSPITAL: KEVIN'S STORY*

A Dog's Life?

As I walked around the office, I realized there was nothing I was supposed to be doing. This would be fine if it was the end of a day and I had finished all my tasks. Unfortunately, it was over an hour before lunch.

Everyone else seemed to be involved in what they were doing. The veterinarians and technicians were seeing patients; the front office staff was taking calls, making appointments, filing, pulling records, ordering supplies, and stocking the shelves with the various pet supplies that were sold through the hospital; even the boarding kennel staff was busy walking the dogs and cleaning the runs and cages. Hanna Picard, the hospital manager, was bent over her desk trying to figure out a discrepancy in the month's income statement.

I had been working as the assistant manager of Queens Veterinary Hospital (QVH) for six months, but nobody seemed to need my help. I wondered whether I had done such a great job that everything was now running like clockwork, or whether something else was going on.

Walking down the hall, I ran into Lyla Moy, owner and president of QVH, who had come flying out of her office carrying a stack of papers.

"What are you doing?" she asked.

"Nothing."

"Well, what are you supposed to be doing?" she demanded.

I shrugged my shoulders.

"Nothing."

"Then why don't you go prune the hedge out front?"

I watched as Dr. Moy disappeared down the hall, and I wondered if she really cared what I was doing as long as I was doing something. I felt like one of those dogs you see walking along looking like it's on a mission when really it's not going anywhere important at all.

Queens Veterinary Hospital

Queens Veterinary Hospital, in Queens, New York, a borough of New York City, has a busy veterinary practice as well as boarding and grooming facilities. There are two full-time veterinarians in addition to Dr. Moy who devotes a large part of her time to operations. In addition, the hospital employs two full- and three part-time technicians, three full- and two part-

* Copyright 1997 by Kyle E. Clough, DVM. Used with permission.

time clerical assistants, a boarding and grooming staff of two full- and three to five part-time staff, a kennel manager, an assistant kennel manager, and Hanna.

QVH serves primarily Queens with some additional patients coming in from Flushing. Being a city practice, the patients are mainly dogs and cats, although there are also birds, small rodents such as Guinea pigs and gerbils, and an occasional exotic pet like a ferret or boa constrictor.

Veterinary care provides the majority of QVH's annual revenues of about $750,000. Boarding is a growing revenue source that now accounts for about 20 percent of the total, while grooming accounts for less than 5 percent.

Since competition is rapidly increasing, veterinary practices must show consistent growth if they are to survive in the current business climate. In addition, while veterinary practices must be cost conscious, they must also keep up with technological innovation so as to provide comprehensive care. Pet owners who have to be referred elsewhere for specialty care generally become lost to the specialty care providers who also provide a full range of services.

QVH has grown steadily since its founding, and its business practices are now much more complex. As hospital manager, Hanna, who started with Dr. Moy in 1982, has just kept taking on more and more responsibilities. She deals with client relations, bookkeeping, scheduling, setting the agenda for and running staff meetings, virtually all personnel management, purchasing of major equipment, and other issues as they arise. As the hospital has grown, Hanna's responsibilities have grown far beyond what is humanly possible for a single individual. Finally, so much was falling through the cracks that Dr. Moy suggested hiring an assistant manager, and I got the job.

My Background

I have always been interested in business and thought about making it my college major. I found, however, that doing so would have made it impossible for me to take many of the psychology and sociology courses in which I was interested. Instead, I majored in social sciences and took a handful of business courses.

I've been "officially" working since I turned 16, although before that I earned money by doing yard work, snow shoveling, dog walking, and so forth. Just before I moved to New York and took the QVH job, I worked in a consignment art gallery in Breckenridge, Colorado. I wasn't given much responsibility, and I didn't really learn much of anything about managing. I wanted to learn more, so I was excited to land the position at QVH. I thought it would give me valuable experience and perhaps be a stepping stone to even more challenging jobs. "Maybe," I thought, "this will be a great thing, and I will have found my place in the working environment."

For the first several weeks at QVH, I spent time in all of the various positions—except veterinarian, of course—to get a feeling for what everyone was supposed to be doing. I learned a lot, and it was actually fun some of the time. I was aware, however, that I wasn't getting much satisfaction from the process. Most of the time, people were just working around me while I was observing. Much of what I saw seemed inefficient, like things could take less time if processes were changed here and there.

What I really wanted was to learn the business aspects, and when I finally got to do so, I found them fascinating. Among other things, I learned the bookkeeping system, came to understand how inventory was handled, and was able to solve the various problems presented by the quirky computer system that was forever breaking down and driving people crazy.

The more tasks assigned to me, the happier I was. I mastered the material as quickly as possible and passed on to Hanna what I had learned. She did the same for me, when she had time.

The one part of my job that seems the most difficult has been assigning others to tasks. I've never really done this before, and I feel uncomfortable when I have to do so. I want people to like me, and I'm really concerned that asking people to take on work will make them angry or make them feel that I'm being bossy.

Often, when I've had work to assign to another person, I've ended up doing it myself even though my time could have been spent more productively elsewhere. At this point, I've begun to feel a division between myself and the other employees, since I'm torn between wanting to be their friends and telling them to get to work.

I think if I could have been more harsh, and if I hadn't tolerated any fooling around, maybe they would have worked harder. After all, you have to push people to work at jobs that aren't so exciting—like walking dogs, feeding them, and cleaning up after them. But, I find myself feeling sorry for the employees. They're young, and they seem to be stuck in dead-end jobs.

Sometimes I've had to push the technicians to get to work and not just stand around. They have more exciting work than the dog walkers, but they're also older than me. It's hard to tell people who are older and have been on the job longer what to do. My thoughts are of losing friendship and creating a hostile place to work when that could be seen as my flexing of "authoritative muscle."

From time to time, Dr. Moy has made new rules or changed processes. Generally these new ideas don't get off the ground because the staff likes things the way they are. After a while, nearly every new idea gets overlooked "by accident." Or sometimes, there's just no follow-up, and the changes are never implemented.

As time has gone on, I've had less and less to do. I've never been given any long-term goals or tasks, and everyone else is always too busy to even think of something for me to do or suggest ways that I could benefit the organization. I've thought about going to veterinary school, but that clearly isn't for me. I like the business end of things, but I'm not really that crazy for animals!

Having mastered all of the original tasks, and with nothing new going on, my job seems aimless. As I thought about trimming the hedge, as Dr. Moy had suggested, I decided my time would be better spent polishing my résumé.

Questions for Discussion

1. Whose responsibility is it to keep Kevin busy and motivated in his job? Why?

2. Using Alderfer's ERG Theory, how would you describe what motivates Kevin? If you were Kevin's boss, what would you do to help him be more productive?

3. Using the Hersey-Blanchard Life Cycle Theory, how would you describe Kevin and the management style he requires?

4. What would you advise Kevin to do at this point?

MOTIVATION AT BALD EAGLE SOFTWARE*

Martin Blanchard, vice president for research and development at Bald Eagle Software, sat in his office staring at an urgent memo from his boss. Although the memo had been sent to all five of the company's vice presidents, Blanchard assumed that there was something personal in it that had been directed to him.

The message was simple but intense; orders were skyrocketing, but there was also a short-age of personnel to handle the demands of the high-tech company's rapid growth. "In short," the note said, "productivity has to improve."

For several minutes, Martin thought about his workers: Was there a bad apple who wasn't pulling his or her weight? Before long, he thought he knew who it was in his department who had inspired the memo.

Eager to take steps towards pleasing his boss, Martin buzzed his secretary. "Tell Hank Seaver I want to see him right away," he said. When Hank arrived, Martin told his secretary to hold all calls during their meeting.

"There are some important things we need to discuss," Martin began, drumming his fin-gers on his oak desk as Hank took a seat across from him. "First of all, I want to tell you that I'm giving the team leader position to Olga Richardson."

"Really?" Hank replied, smiling. "That's great! I'll be sure to congratulate her."

Martin raised his eyebrows.

"Do you understand what I'm saying, Hank? Olga has only been working here for six months, and she's getting a raise and a promotion. You could have had that promotion if you had pushed yourself to earn it."

"Oh well," Hank replied, shrugging in his easy-going way. "I really wouldn't have wanted that job. If I got a promotion, I'd be stuck in an office with a pile of papers. I'd hate that. The best thing about my job is that I get to work with people. The guys in marketing—they're the best; they really make me happy to come in every morning."

Martin glared at Hank. "That's another thing I want to talk to you about, Hank," Martin continued. "It seems like you spend about an hour every morning chatting with the produc-tion workers, joking around with the marketing team . . . ."

Hank's smile faded, and he leaned forward in his chair.

"Well, sure . . . ," Hank replied, "but I get the work done, don't I? Have I ever let you down by not getting something done?"

* This case was written by Scott Weighart.

"No," Martin admitted. "In terms of output—both quality and quantity—you're one of the best in the department . . . but that's not the point."

"Then, what is the point?" Hank asked, looking confused.

Martin slammed his fists on the desk.

"You're undermining my authority—that's the point!" Martin blurted out. "I'm in charge of this department! How do you think it makes me look when the president of the company walks through the production line and sees you sitting around having coffee? I want him to respect the control I have over my department. I want to be recognized as one of the strongest managers here! It makes me look bad when one of my most experienced software designers spends the whole morning making the rounds like a neighborhood gossip. You must become more productive."

"But, Martin," Hank objected, "I am productive—you said yourself that I'm one of the best in the department! Sure I like to chat with my buddies . . . but I also stay here past seven almost every night. I put in my hours just like everyone else."

"No, Hank," Martin replied, looking his subordinate straight in the eye. "From now on you'll put in your hours like everyone else. You're going to have to play the game by my rules."

Hank's face turned white. He loosened his tie before he spoke.

"What does that mean?" he stammered.

"First," Martin began, "it means you will work here from nine to five with a half hour break for lunch. That's it—no other breaks. Second, you can't go around visiting other departments unless you have my permission beforehand. I'll let you go—but only when a matter of company business is involved. Third, if you don't shape up, don't come crying to me next December when you don't get a bonus."

Hank was visibly shaken. "But, Martin," he pleaded, "you know I don't care about the money . . . It's just . . . " His voice trailed off, and he stared at the carpet.

"Look," Martin said stiffly, "I'm just trying to be fair to everyone who works here. I can't let personalities and relationships get in the way of these kinds of decisions. I'm even fair with Olga Richardson. Hey, I was skeptical when they hired a woman as a software designer, but she knows who the boss is, and she did what she had to do to get ahead. She's growing with this company, Hank. You're at a standstill. I hope that what I've said today will help you turn yourself around. We need everyone here to be as productive as possible."

Again, Hank looked confused. As he opened his mouth to reply, Martin stood up, clearly indicating that the meeting was over. Hank mumbled something about getting back to work and quickly left the room.

Alone, Martin strolled over to the bay window of his office. Clasping his hands together behind his back, he watched a group of Bald Eagle Software's second-shift production workers walk towards the building's entrance.

"Workers are like horses," he said to himself. "Leave them alone, and they'll wander aimlessly. If you expect to get any work out of them," he thought, "you have to keep them on a tight rein."

146

Questions for Discussion

1. Based on what you know about how people are motivated, what would you say motivates Hank? What about Martin?

2. Will Martin's efforts to make Hank more productive be successful? Why or why not? Explain what you believe will happen to Hank.

3. If you were Martin, what would you have done differently, if anything?

THE SALES CONTEST THAT NEVER GOT OFF THE GROUND*

Background

Mr. Boyle, store manager of the B.B. Patterson Department Store in Bowling Green, Kentucky, one of 1500 in a national retail chain, returned to the store from a district management meeting in Nashville. While at the district meeting, another store manager had shared his success using a unique employee sales contest to increase sales. The district manager then encouraged all of the other store managers to run the contest.

During his next weekly management meeting, Mr. Boyle told his five departmental managers about the new and exciting employee contest that was virtually guaranteed to generate higher sales and happier employees.

Listening intently to the details of the contest, the departmental managers had some serious reservations about its potential for success in their particular store. They quickly pointed out that their store was on three levels, with several departments on each level, while the store that had first tried the contest was very small and on one level.

The department managers' second reservation about the contest was that their sales associates were assigned to a single department on one level, while the other stores' sales staffs had the freedom—and were encouraged—to sell in all departments. The department managers noted that on each of their store's three levels, there were multiple departments, each with merchandise of different value. For example, on the first floor there was the men's department. This department sold mainly expensive suits and coats. Immediately next to it, the costume jewelry department carried merchandise of low value. Similarly, the women's department on the second floor carried high-value coats and suits, while the nearby infants' and children's departments carried merchandise of lower value. Rarely did salespeople enter other departments. Product knowledge and sales floor coverage generally kept salespeople in their own departments.

Despite their reservations, Mr. Boyle insisted that he wanted to try the contest. It was clear to the department managers that no objective evaluation of the contest was going to change his mind.

The Contest

The sales contest was to run for a three-week period and would work as follows: The employee with the biggest single sale each day on each level would receive a ten dollar bonus at the end of that working day. Add-on sales and multiple sales were the goal.

---

* Copyright 1997 by Bonnie L. McNeely, Ph.D., Murray State University, Murray, Kentucky.

To keep track of sales, the employee on each level who made the first sale of the day would be given a ribbon to wear in a place that would be clearly visible from a distance. When another sale on the floor was made, the employee making the new sale was to check with the employee wearing the ribbon to see if the new sale was higher. If so, the employee with the new and higher sale would pin it on him or herself. This procedure would be repeated with each new sale made throughout the day. The employee wearing the ribbon at the end of the day would thus be the obvious winner of the ten dollar bonus.

When the department managers announced the contest to their sales associates, they received mixed reactions. Employees in the low-value item departments immediately recognized that they had no chance of winning, and they quickly lost interest. Employees in the other departments were willing to give it a try until some of them saw the ribbons. They came right from the gift wrap department—very, very big and very, very gaudy!

The Results

By the end of the first five days, it was clear that the contest was not having the intended results. While Mr. Boyle was too removed from the sales staff to see what was happening, the department managers were quite aware of the lack of enthusiasm for the contest. Some employees complained that they had no chance of winning because of the value of goods they were assigned to sell. Others decided that wearing a gaudy ribbon during the sales day, a ribbon that was the constant target of curiosity by customers, especially regular ones, was not worth the ten additional dollars.

In chatting among themselves, some of the employees decided to let a particular sales person, who they perceived as an "eager beaver" or "gung-ho," win every day. Most also said they intensely disliked the idea of approaching a fellow sales associate to take something away from him or her, essentially "the lousy ten bucks." Rather than do that, they simply did not actively participate in the contest.

What Mr. Boyle thought would be a fun way to create healthy competition turned out to be a disaster, leaving many employees feeling uncomfortable and resentful.

The contest ran its three-week course with the same winners on most days. The department mangers had to bite their tongues to prevent "I told you so" from slipping from their mouths in front of Mr. Boyle.

Questions for Discussion

1. Using the expectancy theory, explain some of the reasons why the majority of the sales employees refused to put energy into the contest.

2. In what ways would you modify or change the contest to bring about the results desired by management?

149

DR. WATSON GETS PUBLISHED*

Steiner Willhelm, president of the Regional University of the South, hit the buttons on his phone as if they were mini-punching bags.

"Bill," he shouted, when the phone on the other end was picked up, "you had better read the letter to the editor on page thirty-one of the *Tribune*, and then get on over here. We have to figure out who wrote it and how to deal with it."

In less than half an hour, Bill Bolles, dean of the Regional University's College of Business, and Henry Lessing, the university's academic vice-president, were sitting in President Willhelm's office, each with a copy of the *Tribune* in his hand.

"I knew," Bolles moaned, "that there was going to be some backlash when we instituted the new performance appraisal and reward system for the faculty. I never expected it to be open warfare."

"Whoever wrote this obviously is angry and wants to cause trouble," he added.

"If the economy had held up, it wouldn't have had to be this way," said Lessing. "But when we changed the emphasis of our goals, and money started to dry up at the same time, some of our best classroom teachers, particularly at the College of Business, actually had their salaries frozen. We have a real problem here, and we had better figure out how to handle it before the phone starts to ring."

The Letter

To the Editor:

I am writing this letter to inform the local taxpaying public concerning adverse changes that are taking place within the College of Business at the Regional University of the South. Because I am a professor at this college, I feel it would not be prudent to sign this letter.

As you are well aware, our state is experiencing a severe economic recession because of our overdependence on one declining industry. As this decline has severely reduced our tax base, the state legislature has been forced to make drastic cuts in funding for all state services, including higher education. At the same time that the Regional University of the South is experiencing another in the series of annual reductions in funding, this time 13 percent, the current university administration is changing the mission of our

* Copyright 1992 by Roland B. Cousins. Used with permission.

College of Business. For over fifty years, we have been viewed as a regional teaching institution in the second tier of universities within our state.

We have attempted to provide excellence in classroom teaching as our primary goal. University and community-service objectives were secondary, as was research. The dominant (first tier) state university is the one with doctoral programs and a corresponding emphasis on research.

Suddenly, the rules have changed. Research has become our primary objective. Over 50 percent of the salaries paid to some faculty members is compensation for research productivity. These faculty, who are the highest paid in the college, are teaching fewer courses and students. This is a gross misuse of what are already very limited state funds. You, the taxpayer, are supporting this institution for the purpose of providing an excellent under-graduate education for your sons and daughters. You are receiving zero return on your investment when your money is spent on the generation of articles that are published in obscure journals having very small circulations. The local and regional business community will never see any benefit from the esoteric kind of article being bought and paid for by you. At the same time, the cost of educating each undergraduate student is escalating because of this misuse of your hard-earned dollars.

I ask that you contact your legislator and/or President Willhelm of the Regional University of the South, and tell him/them what you want from your university. Do you want the best education for your children, or do you want articles generated just for the purpose of article generation?

Name and Address Withheld by Request

Questions for Discussion

1. Was it appropriate for Dr. Watson (the letter writer) to write this letter? Why?

2. Do you agree with Dr. Watson? Why?

3. What distinctions would you draw between the acceptable goals and purposes of a state college or university as opposed to a private college or university, if any?

4. What do you think the administrators should do now that this letter has been published?

29

THE ISSUE OF EQUITY*

Objectives

- To understand the relationship of inputs to outcomes in organizational settings

- To explore the role of perception in employee motivation and satisfaction

- To reach a better understanding of equity theory and its application

Background

An organization's reward system plays a critical role in the recruitment, satisfaction, and motivation of its employees. This exercise asks you to test that concept.

In doing this exercise, be sure to complete "Section 1" before looking at "Section 2."

Section 1

The Situation

Five and a half years ago, when you received your BS in management, you were lucky to get a job in the Chicago office of a major consulting firm. Your starting salary was $42,000 plus 100 percent health coverage and additional benefits with a value of about $12,000. You have worked hard and well and have received outstanding performance evaluations. You have also received regular raises of 3 to 5 percent a year. Six months ago, you were promoted to junior consultant at a base salary of $62,000 plus benefits. In addition, you will receive a bonus of 6 percent of your base salary for being 80 percent or more billable, and you are now eligible for the employee stock option plan.

Procedure

Part A (10 minutes)

Working alone, record your answers to the following questions:

1. How do you feel about your job and your career path so far?
2. How do you feel about your salary package?
3. How do you feel about the way your company has treated you?

---

* Adapted from Wendell French, *Human Resources Management*, 4th ed., Houghton Mifflin Co., Boston, 1998. This exercise was prepared by Janet W. Wohlberg, The Rappay Group, 1075 Main Street, Williamstown, MA 01276 and used with permission.

Part B

1. (20–30 minutes)

Working with a group of three to four classmates, discuss your answers to the three questions above. Record your answers.

2. (3–5 minutes each group plus open-ended discussion)

Report your answers to the class for brief class discussion.

Section 2

The Situation

Today you inadvertently saw the salary and benefits information for employees in your office. You learned the following: Your department secretary, eleven years on the job, earns $38,000 a year plus benefits; a junior consultant with an MBA was hired seven months ago at a base salary of $87,000 plus full benefits and a 6 percent signing bonus; your manager earns $102,000 per year, full benefits, and a 10 percent bonus package; the senior manager earns $123,000 per year, full benefits, and a 15 percent bonus package. In addition, you read in *The Wall Street Journal* that the CEO of your company had a salary and bonus package last year of just under $12M.

Procedure

1. *(20-30 minutes)*

Working with your group, and based on this new information, answer the following questions:

1. How do you now feel about your job and your career path?
2. How do you now feel about your salary package?
3. How do you now feel about the way your company has treated you?

Explore why you feel differently or the same as you did before having this information.

2. *Class discussion (open-ended)*

Explore what you see as the reasons for the differences in your feelings between Sections 1 and 2. Consider whether it is better for employees to know or not know what others in their companies are earning, and what would have to be in place for such an open system?

30

THE WORKSTATION BONUS

Objectives

- To consider the relationship of performance appraisal, feedback, and reward to motivation
- To consider the interdependency of team members
- To explore the difference between bonus rewards and salary

Background

You are the manager of the high-technology department in an industrial design firm. Several months ago, your company decided to bid on a project to design the housing for a new generation of computer workstations to be based on the latest RISC technology. Realizing that this could ultimately turn into a million-dollar contract, you carefully selected two three-member teams and set them to work to design the prototype, giving each team the customer's specifications and the following clear instructions: the housing had to be designed quickly; it had to be high in quality and durability; it had to be aesthetically distinctive; and it had to be modular, cost-effective, easy to assemble and service, and easy to ship.

Yesterday, you were excited to learn that your company got the job. Your very happy CEO has authorized $35,000 in bonus money for you to divide among your employees in any way you deem fair. You know that the way you give out the bonuses can have a serious impact on the morale and motivation of your employees and can affect their participation on future projects.

Knowing something about equity, expectancy, and other theories of motivation, and understanding the basic tenets of performance appraisal and feedback, you know that you have to have a clear basis for apportioning the bonuses. In addition, you know that this project would never have gotten done well and on time without a team approach.

The way you give out the bonuses may affect how well your employees work together in the future.

Instructions

Step 1 (20–30 minutes)

Read the background information and the profiles of each of the team members as they appear below. Using the individual decision worksheet, list the amount of the bonus you would give to each and the reasons for your decision.

154

Step 2 (40–60 minutes)

Working in groups of five to seven students, discuss the problem and come to a group consensus on how the bonus money should be divided and why. It is useful to discuss the philosophy on which you will base your decision before making it.

Step 3 (15–30 minutes)

Report to the class how your group divided the bonus money and why. The instructor should record each group's response in a visible place.

Step 4 (open-ended)

Class discussion.

Team A

You had assigned the following people to Team A:

Jennifer

Jennifer had worked off and on for you on a part-time basis for five years. A divorced mother with two young children, it had been impossible for her to come on full-time until both of her children were in school. Jennifer began full-time this past September. You were pleased to hire her, because she is an unparalleled designer with a sense of the practical. Indeed, you weren't let down by her abilities on this project. Her initial sketches served as an excellent starting point and as the basis upon which the housing was ultimately designed. What did cause some problems, however, was that her children both came down with the chicken pox in the middle of the project, causing her to miss almost a full week at work. During that time, she came in nights, weekends, and whenever else she could find child care.

Abdul

Abdul is a true workaholic. Whenever you have assigned him to a project, he has worked virtually seven days a week, twenty-four hours a day, until completion. This project was no different. Abdul is pretty much of a loner, and you're aware that he frequently made his teammates angry when he made changes to their design plans without consulting them. When confronted, Abdul always acted disgusted as he pointed out just why the changes were necessary; more often than not, his teammates grudgingly went along with him. Unfortunately, you ended up spending a lot of time putting out the emotional fires that Abdul regularly seemed to start. Abdul is a job hopper; he has been looking for another job since he started with your company just eight months ago.

Hank

Quiet, competent, and self-assured, Hank goes about his business as business. You wanted Hank on this team because he is stable and reliable. He isn't, however, particularly creative and innovative. What he does best is to take other people's ideas, refine them, and execute them. He is also an excellent model builder, and the models he produced for this project are meticulous. Hank rarely stays late or works overtime, unless absolutely pushed. Instead, he prefers to spend nights and weekends with his family and in community activities. He is very active in his church and occasionally gets calls during working hours from church members who have pressing questions. In the past, you have asked Hank to limit his nonbusiness telephone time. Over the course of this project, you have noticed that he has had few calls, and those he has had have been brief. Hank has been very understanding about Jennifer's problems and has done everything he can to help her out and cover for her.

Team B

You had assigned the following people to Team B:

David

When David first came to the company, you were concerned that he wouldn't work out. He had been fired from his previous job. You were told by a friend that it was for frequent absences; however, David tells you it was because his boss didn't like him. While he hasn't been absent very often since joining your department, he has come to work late on a regular basis. David never did very much actual work on this project, and he couldn't be counted on to meet deadlines; but he is the only person other than Jennifer who has the design expertise and an understanding of aesthetics necessary to do this job. He is a brilliant innovator, and he came up with some terrific ideas, a couple of which were incorporated into the final design. They may have been the reason that your company got the contract.

Mei-Ling

Mei-Ling is your most reliable materials expert, but she knows little about design. She selected the materials for the project's prototype, and Hank tells you that her ideas were brilliant. Thanks to Mei-Ling, the workstation is durable, lightweight, and can be broken down into modules for easy assembling, servicing, and shipping. You're not sure whether it is out of modesty or loyalty to her team that she tells you that she selected the materials based on David's suggestions and that she couldn't have chosen the correct materials without him. Mei-Ling has been excited about her project and about her team. She has asked that the three members be allowed to work together again on any upcoming projects.

Maida

Maida is one of those people who organizes things, gets after people to do their jobs, and picks up the pieces for others when they don't follow through. She generally does this without complaining, and she constantly praises those around her as knowing more and being more able than she is. On this latter point, she may be right—she isn't particularly brilliant or creative, but she is a plodder. So long as Maida is around, things get done and generally on time. When projects bog down or team members become upset with one another, Maida is there with support, homemade brownies, and occasionally a joke—she's a real team player. You put Maida on this team because you thought she would be able to offset some of David's irregularities, and that is exactly what she did. Maida, Mei-Ling, and David generally eat lunch together, and you have overheard them making weekend plans with one another on a number of occasions.

The Results

Team A finished their project in seven weeks. It was largely their design, combined with a few of Team B's innovations, that resulted in the company's winning bid. Team B had actually finished ten days earlier than Team A, but there were a number of small flaws in their design that resulted in its being rejected. The $35,000 in bonus money is ready to be distributed. You suspect that giving everyone who worked on the project the same amount might be perceived as rewarding some questionable behaviors and failing to reward some other positive behaviors adequately.

Questions for Discussion

1. How much, if any, of the $35,000 will you award to Team A? How will you divide the amount among Team A's members? Why?

2. How much, if any, of the $35,000 will you award to Team B? How will you divide the amount among Team B's members? Why?

3. What do you believe the positive and negative effects on employee behavior and productivity, as individuals and as team members, will be as a result of the way you have allocated the bonus money?

4. Would it be possible and advisable to bring the team members into the decision-making process? How?

Worksheet for Use in Individual Decisions

1. List the general criteria on which you will base the bonus awards.

   _____

   _____

   _____

   _____

   _____

   _____

2. How much will you give to each employee?

   Abdul $_____ or ____ % of $35,000 _____

   David $_____ or ____ % of $35,000 _____

   Hank $_____ or ____ % of $35,000 _____

   Jennifer $_____ or ____ % of $35,000 _____

   Maida $_____ or ____ % of $35,000 _____

   Mei-Ling $_____ or ____ % of $35,000 _____

3. Why?

   _____

   _____

   _____

   _____

   _____

   _____

Worksheet for Use in Group Decisions

1. List the general criteria on which you will base the bonus awards.

_____

_____

_____

_____

_____

2. How much will you give to each employee?

Abdul $_____ or ____ % of $35,000 _____

David $_____ or ____ % of $35,000 _____

Hank $_____ or ____ % of $35,000 _____

Jennifer $_____ or ____ % of $35,000 _____

Maida $_____ or ____ % of $35,000 _____

Mei-Ling $_____ or ____ % of $35,000 _____

3. Why?

_____

_____

_____

_____

_____

31

DISHONORABLE INTENTIONS*

"I've told those people in design that if they can't move things along, they probably ought to start looking for other jobs," Sean Lavelle, Director of Product Design and Development at Artemis Software, said to his boss, Andrea Marx. "I told them that we get ten résumés a day from people who want to work here and that we can't afford to keep people on who aren't being productive.

"The real problem, though, is Dale Carini," Sean continued. "We better do something about that and fast."

As Sean walked out the door, Andrea, Vice President for Production of Artemis Software, Inc., picked up the phone and asked her secretary to get Dale Carini into her office as quickly as possible.

Within minutes, Dale appeared at her door.

"Look," Andrea said. "We've got a problem. Over the past three or four months, your design group has gone downhill. Customers are complaining that their upgrades are crashing, and several projects are overdue. Upper management is on my back, sales are down, and we're losing customers to the competition."

"Sean tells me that you're a major cause of all this. He says you're holding the group back, that you're coming in late, leaving early, refusing to work overtime, and that morale is at an all-time low. The design group is the backbone of this company. What's going on?"

Haltingly, Dale described the events that had taken place over the previous year, including Sean's having used Dale's ideas without giving credit.

"Look, I'm sorry," Dale told her. "I really used to look forward to coming to work everyday. I really like the people, and I liked the work even more. I was creative, I really felt good about what I was doing, and I loved going into the big book and computer stores to see people buying the software that I helped design."

"It just isn't the same anymore," Dale lamented. "We used to have a good time in the unit, and I liked being able to help people out. We'd work hard all week and go out for pizza and beer together on Fridays after work. When things got hectic, there wasn't anyone who wouldn't agree to stay late and come in weekends."

"When you were our boss," Dale told Andrea, "things were different. Now, with Sean in your old position, he just gives orders and locks himself in his office to 'create'—at least that's what he tells us he's doing. About the only thing he ever talks about, besides how great he is, is when he tells us about all the parties he throws. He never invites anyone from the unit, and I'm really fed up with having to listen to that stuff."

* Copyright 1992 by Matthew B. Shull. Used with permission.

"Besides," Dale grumbled, "the way he got that job really infuriates me. Maybe I ought to just get my résumé together and start looking around."

Andrea could feel herself turn cold. For more than a dozen years, Dale Carini, supervisor of the software design group, had increasingly served as the motivational catalyst who had inspired the group to work longer, harder, and better. At the same time, Dale had been able to draw upon some fifteen years of software development experience to provide superior guidance on tasks.

Andrea knew from her previous position as Director of Product Design and Development, that Dale used a hands-on approach to supervising the most important projects and delegated the work on minor projects to other group members. Even when authority and responsibility were delegated to others, however, Dale maintained close contact in order to oversee the progress and to provide additional support when and if necessary. The other members of the group considered Dale to be a real team player. "Dale doesn't just tell us what to do," one of the designers once told her. "Dale's in there, with rolled-up sleeves, all the way through a project. When something goes wrong, Dale's the first one to shoulder the blame. When things are right, Dale tells us what great jobs we did!"

Sean Lavelle

Sean had been a relative newcomer to the software design field when he arrived at Artemis, just over two years earlier. He had an undergraduate business degree from a solid midwestern university, had worked for a year as a waiter between his undergraduate and graduate programs, during which time he had lived at home with his parents, and he had a newly-earned master's in MIS. While he had never worked at a software company, at age sixteen, Sean had written a program for his father, a psychiatrist, for use in keeping patient records and for billing. He managed to package and sell enough of the programs to other psychiatrists to earn his college tuition for his freshman year.

It had quickly become apparent to Dale that Sean preferred to work alone, or with one other person, rather than on any sort of task force or team production. Dale had personally identified with this headstrong young man. "I was like that, too," Dale had once told Andrea, a few months after Sean had joined Artemis. "My idea of software development was to hole up in a room somewhere by myself, kick off my shoes, have a few beers and 'create.' While we can't afford to have a whole department full of Seans, there is still a place in the software world for his kind of eccentricity."

If the workload of the group became bogged down by multiple projects, Dale often assigned one of the projects to Sean to do by himself, thus allowing Dale to concentrate energy and efforts on supporting the other members of the group. This was fine as far as Sean was concerned, but some of the other group members didn't share Dale's enthusiasm for Sean's talents. Says Martha, a programmer, "Sean is arrogant and thinks he knows it all. When glitches become a problem in a program, Sean makes it clear that it's our problem, not his, and he acts disgusted, as if we're holding him back."

Andrea Marx

While Andrea was Director of Product Design and Development, Dale reported directly to her. Andrea's job was to submit the project parameters to the design team as they came from the various clients. As the products were designed, Andrea would then work with the customers to determine the kinds of adjustments and refinements that would have to be made, and she served as liaison between the design and development teams. Beyond this, she had little, if anything, to do with actual design, relying instead on Dale to keep the group running smoothly. She knew that Dale would see to it that jobs were done well and in a timely manner.

The Krane Project

During an especially busy time at Artemis, the design team had two major projects to complete, Krane and Serex, in addition to the usual array of upgrades and small programs based on standard formats. These two projects alone were expected to generate close to 20 percent of the year's income and would require considerable overtime efforts for the team. Both Krane and Serex had unique requirements that were unlike anything Artemis had done before. This meant using every bit of creativity the team could muster, but it also meant working people in ways that generally discouraged rather than inspired creativity—long, exhausting days and seven-day weeks.

Dale assigned most of the team to the Serex project, the bigger of the two undertakings, and worked on Krane with Sean. However, the Serex group ran into unexpected problems, and Dale told Sean that he would have to work alone until the problems with Serex could be resolved. At this time, Sean had been at Artemis for less than a year. "No problem," he had assured Dale. "I'll let you know how I'm doing."

After just two weeks, Sean had told an amazed Dale that Krane was just about finished. Thanks to Sean's ability to work without much supervision, both projects were completed on time, and Andrea and the CEO praised Dale and the group for their outstanding work. Dale invited the group members to a home barbecue as a special thank-you and presented each with a sweatshirt and a coffee mug on which were written, "I'm an Artemis star!" They all came except Sean, who said he had other plans.

The Night in Question

Several months later, Dale and Sean sat chatting over a take-out pizza. They had stayed late to do some minor reworking of the Krane project after the customer had complained of several bugs. Unfortunately, when the score on the self-scoring part of the program went over a certain total, the program crashed. In a few spots, the wrong answers came up on the screen, and occasionally, no answer came up at all.

Dale was philosophical about the problems. "These things happen all the time," Dale thought. "Besides, it was probably my fault. We were busy, and I probably didn't give Sean enough supervision. I have to hand it to him, though; he really gave it an honest try."

Toward the end of dinner, Dale began to tell Sean about an idea for a new format for software for children. "I think," Dale said, "that at very young ages, the keyboard may be a barrier. I have an idea that would allow a computer to process a child's verbal commands. I've been working on this off and on for a couple of years now, and the prototype is looking good." Dale went on to describe the idea in considerable detail, talking about the partially completed prototype.

"Well, I don't know," Sean had responded. "There are probably all sorts of problems with voice tones, and without a market study, how can we really know whether something like that will sell?"

"Oh well," Dale sighed. "It was just an idea. Truth is, I don't have time to work on it anymore anyway. I'm pretty busy with the department, so this is going to have to sit on a back burner. Who knows if I'll ever get to it? Maybe it's just a dream."

Neither Dale nor Sean raised the idea again.

Talking It Up

It was just after New Year's when Sean Lavelle walked into Andrea's new office to tell her about the software he had designed and developed. Andrea, now a vice president, quickly realized the potential of what Sean was showing her. As he demonstrated his prototype, Andrea became excited. The software responded to verbal commands and, Sean explained, the program could be adjusted to react to different voice tones for use by the adult market as well as by children.

"Amazing," Andrea told him. "You really are creative! Let's get a presentation together, and I'll see if I can get it on the agenda for next week's Board meeting. This is something I think we'll really want to run with. I can think of several publishers who'll probably go nuts for this concept."

The Board members confirmed Andrea's belief that the idea was terrific, as did reviewers and customers when the technology was later announced and released. Orders for programs based on Sean's prototype came flooding in, company profits grew, and Sean was promoted to Andrea's former job, which had been left vacant after Dale had turned it down. Sean also received a sizeable lump-sum payment from Artemis for the rights to the program.

As often happens in the software field, rival companies quickly came out with more advanced product lines, and Artemis seemed unusually slow at producing the upgrades on Sean's software that were needed to stay competitive. With his new job, Sean had told Andrea that he was kept far too busy to work on it himself.

Epilogue

News that things weren't right in the design team had been drifting up to Andrea's office for quite some time. "I'm sure Dale and Sean will work things out," she had reassured herself. "This must just be some temporary downturn." But pressure from the CEO had forced her to demand an explanation from Sean, and Sean's explanation had led her to Dale.

After listening to Dale's story, she knew that the problem was more serious than she had wanted to believe, and she also knew that Dale wasn't about to forgive Sean for what had happened.

"Look," Andrea told Dale. "You're too important to this company for me to let you go just like that. You tell me what would turn this around for you, and I'll do the best I can to see that you get it."

Questions for Discussion

1. Using one or two theories of motivation, compare and contrast the motivational needs of Dale and Sean. Give examples.

2. Using one or two theories of motivation, compare and contrast the ways with which Dale and Sean motivate their workers. Give examples.

3. What do you think could be done to help Dale become productive again? Why?

4. Using one or two theories of motivation, describe your own motivational needs and how, if you were in Dale's position, your solution for Andrea relates to those needs.

5. Is there an ethical issue here? What is it? How do you feel about it? What do you think ought to be done about it, if anything, and why?

THE MUSIC TEACHER FROM HELL*

Joe Swanson, principal of the Cornelius Mercker Elementary School in Dacron, Ohio, was not a happy man on the first day of the school year. He had just learned that Martha Vandeberg had been assigned to the Mercker as a music teacher. Vandeberg was notorious throughout the school system; every principal who had supervised her told horror stories about faked illness and injuries, unexcused absences, and remarkably persistent attempts to do as little as possible without getting fired.

When she showed up for the first day at Mercker, Vandeberg told Swanson that she could not teach on the second floor due to a fractured toe. When he asked for a doctor's note, she became angry. "Fine then," she said, making a spectacle of hobbling up and down the stairs. On the third day of school, she called in sick due to a "bruised tooth root" resulting from excessive flossing.

When Vandeberg did work, she went from classroom to classroom, spraying Lysol on her hands and in the air before playing records at maximum volume. The children sang with their hands on their ears. She opened the windows as wide as possible—even in subfreezing temperatures, and the children either would have to put their coats on to avoid catching cold or sit shivering and with teeth chattering.

Unfortunately, the Dacron Teachers' Union was very powerful; Swanson did not have the authority to fire her. Even giving her an unsatisfactory rating would have no effect on her salary. He had no ability to influence her, and she treated him, as she treated all principals with whom she had come in contact, as the enemy from day one.

About all Swanson could do was make life as miserable as possible for Vandeberg. If she had not signed in by 8:30, he wrote "LATE" where her signature would go. Instead of getting her own mailbox like most teachers, she had to share one with the custodian.

When it was time for the annual school Christmas concert, Swanson asked the school's substitute teacher to lead the chorus, while Vandeberg was given meaningless paperwork to fill out. She didn't dare defy him by refusing to comply. Although Swanson realized this was all very childish, twenty years as a school principal had taught him that this was the only way to get rid of someone who was incompetent. He had seen other principals try to be nice to her, and she had responded by getting away with as much as possible. He made sure to keep a file of every rule infraction that she made, in case she tried to sue him for any reason.

Vandeberg lasted the entire school year, taking every sick day available to her and giving the students the same records to listen to and sing along with week after week. Fortunately for Swanson, she didn't choose to return to Mercker the following year. Still, the year had been stressful and sickening. Due to the pay scale, based on seniority, the city of Dacron would be increasing her pay from $36,300 to $37,100 the following year. Many younger

* This case was written by Scott Weighart.

teachers—who earned just over half that amount—were angry to see that their hard work did nothing to narrow the vast difference between their salaries and those of the music teacher.

Questions for Discussion

1. What sources of power does Joe Swanson have in his dealings with Martha Vandeberg? Give examples of each. What sources does he lack? Why?

2. Consider what you know about motivation. What connections can you make between the sources of power and the impact they have on an individual's motivational profile?

33

UNITED DYNAMICS: DOWNSIZING—FIRING BY ANY OTHER NAME

Objectives

- To examine the responsibilities that go with managerial power
- To examine short-term effects of layoffs on group cohesiveness, morale, and productivity
- To examine long-term effects of layoffs

Background

Within an hour of the announcement, the news had spread throughout the workforce at United Dynamics (UD)—the government had selected a competitor to develop a new generation of jet engines for the military. It was no secret that UD had been counting on this contract, and that without it massive cutbacks would have to be made throughout the organization. This would, by necessity, include laying off not only many of the people who had been brought in to work on the development of the engine prototype, but cutting many who had been with the company for longer periods and in different capacities as well.

Your unit is composed of ten engineers specializing in cooling and heating systems; you have been instructed to lay off three immediately. You have also been told that further layoffs are likely should other contracts not come through.

Over the past several years, you have been able to build an almost perfectly functioning team. Your unit is highly cohesive. The engineers cooperate with one another's efforts and act as sparks for one another's creativity. In addition, their friendly and supportive relationships go beyond the limits of the workplace.

You have heard from other managers about how difficult it is to lay off employees, especially when they are as good as those in your unit, but you never really believed you would have to wield the axe. You know that the negative effects on morale will be devastating, and you realize that the layoffs are also going to cause work overloads for those who remain.

Following are the names of the engineers in your unit and the things that come to mind about each of them as you contemplate your task. Who will you lay off, and why?

In making your decision, consider the following:

1. How your choices of layoffs will impact the group's ability to function effectively both in the near and long terms.
2. What the impact will be on diversity, creativity, and socialization.
3. What the effects will be on the group's cohesion. Other issues to consider are short- and long-term costs, ethics, politics, seniority, corporate image, social responsibility, legal issues, and the ability to meet organizational goals.

Instructions

1. (30 minutes)

Read the background information and the profiles on each of the engineers. Make careful notes on the pros and cons of keeping or laying off each engineer.

2. (5 minutes)

On the main score sheet on the last page of this exercise, note who you will lay off, who you will retain, and why.

3. (40 minutes)

Working in a small group, discuss the characters and come to a group consensus as to who you will retain and who you will lay off. Select a spokesperson for your group who will report to the class who your group agreed to lay off and why.

4. (15–30 minutes, depending on the number of groups)

Report-in and discussion.

Engineers

Wei Tan

Tan has been at UD and with your unit just over two years. He came to the United States as a political refugee from China, not having been able to readjust to China's social system when he went home after receiving his engineering degree from an American university. Tan left China with his wife, who speaks no English, and two young children, with three suitcases of clothing and little else. It took him nearly a year, while living at virtually poverty level, to find the job with UD after arriving here. Tan and his family just recently moved out of the tiny apartment they had been sharing with another family.

Tan is an excellent engineer, and he has always been willing to work nights and weekends as project deadlines approached. Occasionally Tan's English has led to some communication problems within the department; once the wrong equipment was ordered because someone misunderstood what he was saying. However, the other engineers like Tan and feel protective toward him. Several have made concerted efforts to help him and his family. Eugene, particularly, passes his own children's outgrown clothing on to Tan's children.

Eugene Stapleton

Eugene is a single father whose wife died of lupus seven years ago and left him with three children, then ages two, three, and six. At that time, Eugene took four months of leave from

UD, some of it in accumulated vacation days, to get himself and his young family settled into their new way of life. You know that child care costs still take a large part of Eugene's salary and that he has put a fair percentage of his flexible benefits package into the company's voucher system for helping to cover those costs.

Eugene is another genuinely good engineer and your only real expert in the design of cooling systems for boats, a steady 20 percent of your business. His efforts have been major factors in winning several large-sized contracts.

Because of his child care responsibilities, Eugene is rarely able to stay at work after five or to come in on weekends. However, he does have a computer at home on which he often works nights and weekends.

Zelda Karas

Zelda is a star performer and one of only two women in your department. When she first came to UD, almost fifteen years ago, she was the first woman employee in the company above the clerical level. She has consistently turned down managerial level jobs, preferring hands-on engineering instead. She has been the leader on a number of successful projects and is seen by the younger engineers as a mentor; when they have a problem, they generally turn to Zelda for help. She is also frequently consulted by engineers from other units.

Zelda is married to a successful ophthalmologist, her children are grown and off on their own, and she and her husband travel frequently. About every three or four years, Zelda takes an extra month of vacation—without pay—to go to Europe or Southeast Asia with her husband. She has always been careful to delay this until after the completion of whatever project she has been working on.

Murray Mangino

Murray has solid engineering skills. Over the past twenty-two years, he has been in a number of departments throughout UD, having originally started as a draftsman with an associate's degree from a nearby community college. Murray was the first one in his family to go to college. In his early years at UD, he continued with his education by going nights and weekends, ultimately getting both undergraduate and graduate degrees in engineering.

Because of his career path at UD, he knows the company well and can sometimes perform what no one else can for your unit. When your unit has needed special items or people, it is Murray who gets them even when you have been told that it is impossible. It never ceases to amaze you just how many people Murray knows who are willing to do favors for him.

While Murray is generally well liked by the others in the unit, he often gets tense and edgy when time is short and deadlines are tight. Murray and his wife have two children in college and one about to graduate from high school. Murray's wife, Cynthia, has a full-time job as the manager of a small dental office, and her income helps to pay the bills. Not long ago, Murray confided to you that he also took out a second mortgage on his house to help pay his children's tuition.

Matt Peebles

Matt is one of the UD engineers who has been closely mentored by Zelda. Under her tutelage, he has become a first-rate engineer with an eye for detail. On a number of occasions, Matt has picked up design problems that the others in the unit have overlooked, and when problems arise, he is a valuable and reliable troubleshooter. He is also the best on-site person in the unit, overseeing the installation and start-up of systems. In this area, Matt has been able to develop good working relationships with a number of major clients.

Matt recently tested HIV-positive—something you think the others in the unit probably don't yet know. Being laid off will mean that he will lose his health benefits and will not get the support he is probably going to need during the critical stages of the AIDS disease.

Matt lives with his mother and is her sole source of support.

Jane Calloway

Jane is the sister-in-law of the UD vice president within whose span of control your unit falls. She is an average engineer and is well liked by the others in the unit. In many ways, Jane sets the tone for the group. She is virtually always upbeat and ready with a joke or a story. When something goes wrong or the stress of deadlines starts to get to people, it is Jane who helps the others find the humor in the situation and who helps the group get back on track.

Jane and Matt are good friends and often go out socially. She has also been very helpful to Eugene and has volunteered from time to time to take care of his kids to give him some time off. Just recently, Jane spent her long holiday weekend with Eugene's kids while he went fishing with a friend.

Jane is the one in the unit who volunteers to chair the annual Red Feather and other charity drives, and she also organized the unit's recycling program.

Harold Aldrich

Harold has the most seniority at UD, having been with the company for over thirty years. He joined the company right out of the armed services, where he had received his education and had been a member of the Army Corps of Engineers. Harold still maintains contact with some of his old buddies from the military, most of whom are now retired from the service and working in private industry. One of his army friends is now a congressman and another is on the staff of a cabinet secretary in the present administration.

Harold's history of employment at UD has been solid. While never a star like Zelda or some of the others, he has been reliable and loyal. On any number of occasions, he has taken voluntary pay cuts and worked extra hours, always expressing concern for the "good of the company." Harold is a real team player.

The social activities in the office revolve around Harold. He and his wife always hold the annual unit outings at their house as well as numerous barbecues, birthday celebrations, and special events.

Harold is scheduled to retire in four years. Being laid off now will result in a significant loss of retirement benefits. It is also unlikely that he will be able to find other employment in his field, if at all.

Robert Anderson Selkirk

Robert is the newest member of your engineering team and the only black. He is an excellent engineer—a member of the "star" category—although young and not as fully acquainted with some of the ongoing projects as some of the other, more seasoned engineers. Nonetheless, he has fit right into the group.

Robert was specifically recruited to fill the government mandate for racial diversity in companies that receive government contracts. You are aware that this is closely monitored.

At present, Robert, Harold, and Zelda are in the middle of an important project for the air force. Zelda keeps telling you how impressed she is with Robert's skills and that the success of the project is largely going to be the result of his efforts.

Robert's wife is a lawyer; she is pregnant with their first child.

Adam Twersky

Adam was hired away from a competing company with promises of more money and a brighter future with UD. He came in just a few months before Robert and at a higher salary. At the time he was brought in, a note from the executive vice president of UD made clear that Adam was being groomed for a higher position. You have no idea of just what that position is to be.

Adam is far from your most talented performer. As an engineer, he is little better than adequate. He does seem to be hard-working, however, and the others in the unit often request him for their project teams because of his strengths during planning stages.

Adam is unmarried. Last Friday, he let you borrow his new sports car so you could take a friend for a ride.

Lloyd Hunt

Lloyd is an average engineer who is somewhat on the fringes of the group. He has the second most years in service of anyone in the unit.

Lloyd is litigious. It seems that every time you turn around, Lloyd is suing someone for something. The amazing thing is that he very often ends up settling his cases for substantial amounts.

In the early 1980s, while working as an engineer in another unit at UD, Lloyd found a defect in a product that was being built for the U.S. Navy. His supervisor, who no longer works for UD, told Lloyd that the product was fine and that Lloyd should mind his own business. Lloyd's response was to write a letter to his congressman detailing the problem and expressing his opinion that the defect could put the lives of navy personnel in danger. During the investigation of UD that followed, Lloyd's supervisor fired him, ostensibly for constant lateness and absenteeism from work.

Lloyd successfully sued UD for wrongful dismissal; he was awarded punitive damages and his lost wages, and the court ordered that he be reinstated. Since assuming your position as manager of the heating and cooling engineering unit, Lloyd has regularly reminded you of his triumph.

Main Score Sheet

Engineer	Keep	Lay Off	Reasons to Keep	Reasons to Lay Off
Harold Aldrich				
Jane Calloway				
Lloyd Hunt				
Zelda Karas				
Murray Mangino				
Matt Peebles				
Robert A. Selkirk				
Eugene Stapleton				
Wei Tan				
Adam Twersky				

34

GIVING NEGATIVE FEEDBACK POSITIVELY*

Objectives

- To explore the managerial task of giving performance feedback to employees
- To consider how to make feedback useful
- To practice the skills of giving helpful feedback

The Situation

This year your company, after careful consideration, has instituted a 360-degree feedback performance evaluation system. It was agreed that one of your jobs as a manager would be to meet with each employee individually to go over his or her results.

You are about to meet with Chris Damone, a line supervisor who has been with the company for seven years. A review of Chris's past performance evaluations indicates an employee who has been reliable and has had above-average productivity. Results from Chris's 360, however, have a definitely negative consistency, i.e., avoids trying new ideas, uses coercion with peers and subordinates, doesn't listen well, ignores feedback, often fails to return phone calls or other inquiries, blames mistakes on others or tries to cover them up, and is often unavailable when questions arise. In addition to this feedback, you are aware that Chris has been an outspoken opponent of the company's affirmative action policy and was particularly angry to have been passed over for a recent promotion in favor of a minority employee.

The Task—Part A

1. Role play (full class: 10 minutes)

Two people will be selected to role play the situation detailed above in front of the class. One should take the role of manager and the other of Chris.

2. Discussion (full class: 5-10 minutes)

After the role play, discuss what each of the role players could have done to make the interview more effective.

* Adapted from Wendell French, *Human Resources Management* (Houghton Mifflin Co., Boston, 1998). This exercise was prepared and adapted by Janet W. Wohlberg, The Rappay Group, 1075 Main Street, Williamstown, MA 01267. Used with permission.

3. (20-25 minutes)

Repeat #'s 1 and 2 above with new role players.

The Task—Part B

1. Preparing an action plan (small groups: 20-30 minutes)

Working in groups of three to five, prepare an action plan to help Chris improve. It might be useful to assign a group member to the role of Chris. Select a spokesperson to report your plan to the class.

2. Report out (5 minutes each group)

Present your plan to the class.

3. Class discussion (open-ended)

Questions for Discussion

1. What could the manager have done differently, if anything, to clearly present the problems with Chris's behavior? Did the manager check frequently with Chris to be sure that the message being sent was the one being received?

2. Were Chris and the manager able to listen to one another without becoming confrontational or defensive?

3. Are the goals of the action plan clear and helpful?

4. How should the manager proceed as the goals set with Chris are met or fail to be met?

PART III

INTERPERSONAL PROCESSES IN ORGANIZATIONS

Overview

In this section, we will consider what happens when individuals, each with their own perceptions and ways of being motivated, are put into situations in which they must interact with managers and fellow workers. We will focus on leadership roles in groups, power, political behavior, communication, and the match—or mismatch—between leadership styles and the needs of workers.

Group Dynamics

Wouldn't it be logical to assume that a manager would be fortunate to be always in charge of cohesive groups, groups in which individuals have shared goals and work hard together to achieve them? Not necessarily. Some groups may have goals that have nothing to do with organizational success and everything to do with self-serving or undermining and destructive objectives.

Imagine a department of maintenance engineers working for a nuclear power plant. They are a relaxed, fun-loving group. Instead of monitoring their computer screens to make sure the nuclear reactor is a glowing success, they take turns playing video games while one group member is assigned to watch out for the boss. When the boss approaches, the lookout person gives a quick whistle. The group has worked very hard in developing a system for not getting caught goofing off. They have designed a remarkable computer program that allows the user to simply touch a specific key to make the video game disappear and to be replaced with a screen of nuclear facility data.

People who live near the nuclear plant wonder why the incidence of certain types of cancers is increasing in their neighborhood, but no one can deny that the engineering group is very successful and productive in working toward its goals.

Leaders of organizations have control over some group dynamics. Typically, managers create formal groups of people who must work together temporarily or permanently on some designated task. When management assigns people to formal groups, they must make crucial decisions about size and composition. However, informal groups still develop at organizations, and managers can't easily control their size, composition, or purpose for existence. Likewise, group norms, those mutually agreed-upon and accepted ways of behaving, may fall outside management's jurisdiction. Some group norms can be beneficial for the organization;

for example, there are several religious cults in which members are expected to devote most of their time to making money or recruiting new members.

Every time you walk into a classroom, sit down, listen, take notes, and ask questions, you are displaying several norms of student behavior. Likewise, the professor comes in and speaks, writes key points on the blackboard, and asks questions. All of these behaviors are norms, that is, patterns of behavior that we have come to accept without question.

Sometimes students make the mistake of believing that norms are rules that a group openly and consciously chooses. For example, if an organizational behavior teacher assigns students to groups and requires the members of each group to work together to create a firing policy before beginning a group project, the group will write a list of rules that could be considered norms. However, many norms represent unwritten and undiscussed rules for behavior: If an individual is late for a group meeting, the other members may joke about firing the person but quickly drop the issue. If the person continues having problems in meeting the expectations of the group, the joking may become bitter sarcasm. The other group members might retaliate for the breech of norms by assigning the most boring jobs to their problem member. Often there is no official decision to treat the person this way; this is an unspoken norm that has developed as part of the group's process.

If you have ever been required to complete a group project, you might have noticed that group development goes through several stages—sometimes referred to as forming, storming, norming, and performing.[1] In the first stage, people try to find out about one another and form tentative alliances. Second, some issues must be resolved: Personality clashes must be dealt with; the authority hierarchy must be established; and the roles of each of the group members must be determined. In the third stage, norming, groups are consciously or unconsciously developing ways of getting things done, and they create their unwritten rules of conduct. An unsuccessful group may fail to get through a stage and never reach the point at which everything is in place and the group is performing adequately.

Intergroup Dynamics

In intergroup dynamics, groups from different divisions or functions may recognize their interdependence and collaborate to advance the best interests of their organization. Sometimes, however, they may see other groups in their own organizations as their enemies or competitors, perhaps vying for limited funds or supplies, and avoid contact whenever possible.

In 1987, a plant manager at a large company spent a great deal of time studying a revolutionary "Just-in-Time" manufacturing system. Because the manager appreciated the role of another functional group—the finance department—he liked the idea that the "Just-in-Time" system would save his company millions of dollars in inventory costs while freeing valuable warehouse space. This made the company's product much more accessible for the trucks in the distribution department. Collaborating with other functional groups, the plant manager made the best of intergroup dynamics.

1. See B. W. Tuckman, "Development Sequence in Small Groups," *Psychological Bulletin* 63, 1965, pp. 384–399.

177

However, some of his superiors in production were unhappy. His innovative process made production's efficiency numbers worse in the short run. The superiors pressured the manager to abandon his plan, fearing that the efficiency figures would upset the company's executives; the most important thing to them was that production not look worse than the other divisions. That the system would greatly benefit the company's overall functioning was of little importance.

Communication

How has the communication process functioned in organizations in which you have been employed? Did the boss have countless meetings with an inner circle of employees while ignoring all others? Did the boss bark out orders and instructions, or did he or she ask for your feedback or input? Or, did the boss stay closed up in an office and dictate a steady stream of memos?

In some organizations, communication can be a one-way process in which managers are simply order givers; they function to tell people what to do and have no interest in what employees think of their management style. A July 6, 1994, article in *The Wall Street Journal* describes the rise and fall of Richard Snyder, the former chairman of Simon and Schuster, as someone who "reigned by intimidation and fear over the publishing empire he built…. Whenever something went wrong or a goal wasn't achieved," reported one of Snyder's colleagues, "Dick had to make it personal and blame someone…. As a result, people wouldn't come forward with problems…."

Since we know from studying motivation that workers are more willing to commit to tasks and decisions in which they have had a say, it should be easy to imagine the negative effect that one-way communication can ultimately have on an organization's bottom line.

While two-way communication tends to produce better results overall, there are times when one-way communication is the most appropriate form of communication to use. A cardiologist summoned to the emergency room to save a patient who is in cardiac arrest, for example, is not likely to spend time discussing the patient's history and asking for suggestions from the assembled medical team. There is neither the time nor the need for such an interaction. It is important, therefore, that you as a manager assess a given situation to determine the best form of communication to use.

Review of Leadership Theories and Sources of Social Power

Leadership Theories

Leadership theories can be categorized as trait, behavior, or contingency theories. Trait theories of leadership attempt to find a set of personal characteristics that distinguish highly effective leaders from others. However, researchers have not found a generally accepted set of traits that all highly effective leaders possess. Inability to find a set of leadership traits led researchers to examine how leaders behave. Behavioral theories focus on what leaders do rather than the traits they possess. There are two important behavioral studies:

- University of Michigan Studies identified two dimensions of leadership behavior: task-centered and employee-centered. Task-centered leaders are mainly concerned with getting the job done. They focus on the technical aspects of the job and are likely to closely supervise their employees. Employee-centered leaders focus on building relationships. They are concerned with employee needs and professional development.

- Ohio State Studies also identified two dimensions of leadership behavior: consideration and initiating structure. Consideration refers to the degree to which leadership relations are characterized by trust and respect for employees. Initiating structure is the tendency of the manager to structure tasks and clearly define working relationships. These are not mutually exclusive dimensions. A manager can be high or low on either dimension.

Research found that in many cases leaders high on both behavioral dimensions were more effective; however, this was not always true. Researchers began to realize that the most appropriate leadership style is dependent upon the situation. As a result, the following three contingency theories were developed:

Fiedler's Contingency Model[1] suggests that a leader's effectiveness is determined by how well his or her style fits a situation. The situation is defined by three dimensions: leader-member relations, task structure, and position power.

Leader-member relations refers to the degree of trust and respect that subordinates have for the leader. Task structure is the degree to which tasks and procedures for carrying out the tasks are defined. Position power refers to the extent to which the leader controls variables likely to influence subordinates, e.g., salary, bonuses, and discipline.

The leader's style may be task or relationship oriented. The most effective style depends on the situation. In the most favorable or least favorable situations, a task-oriented style works best. A relationship-oriented style works best in a moderately favorable situation. Fiedler states that a leader cannot easily modify his or her style. Thus, the fit between situation and leadership style should be maintained by either seeking suitable situations for the leader's style or altering the situation so it is compatible with one's style.

House's Path-Goal Model[2] is based on expectancy theory. House suggests that leaders support followers by providing a clear path for attaining goals. This involves appropriate coaching, support, and reduction of obstacles, as well as setting appropriate goals and rewards. Managers can best help clarify the path by adopting one of four leadership styles depending on the situation, i.e., directive, supportive, participative, and achievement-oriented. Two situational factors that affect the choice of style are worker characteristics and work environment. Unlike Fiedler, House believes that leaders can change their style to fit the situation.

Hersey and Blanchard's Life-Cycle Model[3] suggests that an effective leader adjusts his or her style based on worker maturity. Maturity includes ability to set high but attainable goals, willingness to accept responsibility, and possession of knowledge and experience needed to complete the task. The four leadership styles are 1) telling, which is used when employees need to be trained to perform required tasks; 2) selling, which is used after employees learn the basics and need reassurance; 3) participating, used when employees are increasingly proficient, can be given more autonomy, and can work with others; and 4) delegating, used

179

when workers can manage themselves, resolve conflicts, effectively work in groups, and are proficient at the task. The leader should use different styles as employees advance or regress in their maturity level. Regression may occur when a job changes or new tasks are required.

Recent thinking in leadership has begun to examine the way we conceptualize the work of a leader. Manz and Sims[4] have identified four perspectives on leadership that have emerged over the years: the strong man, the transactor, the visionary hero, and the superleader.

The strong man is the person who knows the best direction, solves problems, tells people what to do, and metes out punishment for not toeing the line. The transactor is focused on goals and rewards. This type of leader gets people to follow by providing rewards for what she or he wants them to do.

The visionary hero is popular today. This is a person who can motivate people through communication of a compelling vision. The leader is still the source of direction.

The final type of leader, the superleader, "becomes super—that is, possesses the strength and wisdom of many persons—by helping to unleash the abilities of the followers (self-leaders) that surround them." Superleadership is important today because world competition, the changing workforce, and the fast pace of change have all put pressures on today's businesses. To cope with these pressures, businesses are increasingly using work-place designs that involve worker participation. This presents new challenges for leaders, challenges that superleadership is designed to meet.

Power

The first three perspectives on leadership identified by Manz and Sims assume that the leader holds some form of power over followers. This power allows the leader to influence the follower to do something he or she would not have otherwise done. French and Raven[5] identified the following sources of social power:

Legitimate Power comes from the position one holds. People will be influenced because of the formal authority that they believe you possess. Thus, an employee may listen to a manager simply because the manager is defined by the organization as the person in charge.

Reward Power results from the ability to give or withhold rewards valued by the person you are trying to influence.

Coercive Power is the power to influence others through the ability to mete out punishments or threats of punishment. This source of power is based primarily on fear. A person may be influenced if she or he wishes to avoid the consequences of not complying.

Expert Power is the ability to influence others because you possess expertise. This may be some special skills, knowledge, or information. The person being influenced must value the expertise you possess.

Referent Power is based on admiration. This is sometimes called charismatic power because influence is often based on interpersonal attraction.

Having power is not by itself either good or bad. It is the manner in which the power is used that determines a leader's effectiveness over the long term. Power can be used for personal gain at the expense of others, or it can be used to promote common goals; it can be held by the leader or shared with others. Leaders effective over the long term have been found to have a high need for power. However, this need is for socialized power, not personalized power.[6] Social power is exercised for the benefit of others rather than for personal gain. Effective leaders exercise their power under the guidance of a strong set of social values and gain satisfaction from the success of those they lead rather than from their own personal gain.

Superleadership is based on a fundamental fact of power not recognized by the other forms of leadership, i.e., one's ability to use power to influence another is ultimately the choice of the follower. For example, a manager may hold the threat of dismissal as a source of power. However, it will only influence the follower as long as he or she chooses to remain in the organization. The superleader recognizes that his or her strength and power ultimately come from loyal and committed followers who own and support goals compatible with the organization's effectiveness. The superleader, therefore, shares power and empowers others to be self-leaders. It is a paradox that the superleader becomes more powerful by giving up power. As power circulates among followers, they become stronger, more effective, and more committed to their leaders. This, in turn, makes leaders more effective and ultimately more influential.

Sources

1. Fiedler, Fred E., *A Theory of Leadership Effectiveness*, New York: McGraw-Hill, 1967.

2. House, Robert J., "A Path-Goal Theory of Leader Effectiveness," *Administrative Science Quarterly*, September, 1971, pp. 321–338.

3. Hersey, Paul, & Blanchard, Kenneth H., *Management of Organizational Behavior: Utilizing Human Resources*, 3rd ed., Englewood Cliffs, N.J.: Prentice-Hall, 1977.

4. Manz, Charles C., and Sims, Henry P. Jr., "Superleadership: Beyond the Myth of Heroic Leadership," *Organizational Dynamics*, Spring, 1991.

5. French, John R. P. Jr., and Raven, Bertram, "The Bases of Social Power," In Dorwin Cartwright (Ed.), *Group Dynamics: Research and Theory*, Evanston, Illinois: Row, Peterson, 1962, pp. 607–623.

6. Kelly, Charles M., "The Interrelationship of Ethics and Power in Today's Organizations," *Organizational Dynamics*, Summer, 1987, p. 5.

35

THE EYES HAVE IT

Objectives

- To examine the value of face-to-face communication
- To consider the benefits of two-way versus one-way communication
- To examine the cues and information that body language provides

Background

While e-mail, voice-mail, and memos to distribution lists can certainly make complicated work lives more manageable, the value of face-to-face communication should not be underestimated.

Face-to-face communication provides important clues to the ways in which a receiver, i.e., the person to whom you are addressing your words, is encoding, i.e., interpreting, your message. It also provides information as to the way a person feels about a conversation's content, about herself or himself, and about the sender.

Likewise, two-way communication affords opportunities to explore whether or not both parties have the same understanding of the information being conveyed.

As you work through the following exercise, pay particular attention to what is missing from a conversation in which the parties do not see each other (remote communication) and the communication is one-way to what is not missing when the parties are face-to-face and the communication is two-way.

Instructions

1. Remote communication (10 minutes)

Choose a partner whom you do not know well, and sit back-to-back with him or her. Begin by having one partner, the sender, describe either a positive or negative work experience. The second partner, the receiver, should listen without comment. After five minutes, reverse roles, and repeat the process.

2. Face-to-face communication (20 minutes)

Turn to face your partner. Begin by having one partner describe the same work experience she or he described in Step 1. This time, the receiver should feel free to ask questions. When the first partner is finished, reverse the roles, and repeat the process.

3. Identifying the differences (15 minutes)

Working with your partner, explore what you have learned about each other and the experiences each of you described when communicating face-to-face and two-way, as opposed to communicating back-to-back and one-way.

4. Report out and discussion (open-ended)

Questions for Discussion

1. What were you able to learn about your partner and her or his experience when it was re-counted back-to-back and one-way? What do you see as the benefits and drawbacks of this kind of communication?

2. What were you able to learn when the experience was recounted face-to-face and two-way? What do you see as the benefits and drawbacks of this kind of communication?

3. What role did body language play in providing clues regarding your partner's feelings about her or his experience?

4. In what workplace situations would you consider remote, one-way communication to be appropriate? What workplace situations might require face-to-face, two-way communication?

5. What do you see as the implications of this exercise in the use of today's communication technology, e.g., e-mail, video-conferencing, etc.?

36

KAREN CARLIN*

Karen Carlin graduated from Plympton University's School of Management in 1995. Though she was a top student and planned someday to get an MBA, she wanted for the moment to work in Manhattan. Karen grew up in the small town of Mechanicsburg, Pennsylvania, and she was excited at the idea of living in the big city. She figured New York was the next logical step after going to school in Pittsburgh.

Having heard many horror stories about the cost of living in Manhattan, Karen wasted no time trying to find a job. While working at the *Daily Free Press*, Plympton's student newspaper, Karen had learned a great deal about word processing. Accordingly, she went to Temployee Specialists and applied for a job.

The interview was high pressured. The woman in charge of Temployee Specialists, Jane Thorley, gave her four consecutive timed typing tests, followed by a Dictaphone test. She asked Karen unusually specific questions about her education and work background. Finally, Thorley brought her to an Apple Macintosh computer with Microsoft Word and Pagemaker software.

"Have you ever used one of these?" she asked. Karen reluctantly admitted that she hadn't.

"Well, you seem bright enough," Thorley told her. "Sit down, and give it a try."

Although Karen felt a little intimidated, she tried calling up files and doing simple commands. It was different from the Free Press's Varityper system, but she managed to figure out the basics.

Fifteen minutes later, Jane Thorley came in and watched over her shoulder.

Although it was hard to tell from her all-business expression, Thorley was apparently pleased. She told Karen that she had a long-term assignment for her at Hepplewhite & Boyce, a large accounting firm in a huge office building near Canal Street. Karen was shocked and thrilled to have gotten a job so easily. However, there was a catch.

"If they ask you if you've used the DataLogic computer, just tell them that you have," Thorley said. "You're a quick study; you'll pick it up right away. If you get stuck, just ask if you can take a look at the manual. Tell them you need to refresh your memory. If you could photocopy the manual for us, that would be even better."

Karen felt uneasy about deceiving her first client, but she also felt she couldn't afford to pass up a job offer. In Manhattan, who could tell how long she might have to wait for another one? She had found a great apartment in the West Village through a Matching Roommates agency. Her room was claustrophobically small, and her rent was $575 a month, but she wanted to be in the heart of the city. She decided she couldn't afford to pass up this opportunity.

* This case was written by Scott Weighart.

By the time she was sitting behind her computer at Hepplewhite & Boyce, Karen was a nervous wreck. She typed frantically, certain that someone would find her out. She had been assigned to the schedule typists' office, where there were three other women, all sitting at desks with computers and all studying her out of the corner of their eyes. Their job was to update lengthy tax schedules for the fifteen accountants who worked in their department.

After half an hour of typing as fast as possible, Karen was interrupted by Pauline, a thirtyish woman sitting across from her, who walked over to her with an annoyed expression on her face. For ten long seconds she stood and watched Karen work. Finally, she spoke: "What in the world do you think you're doing?"

Karen turned bright red. She was sure her charade had been discovered. Instead, she was amazed as Pauline scolded her for working too hard. "Would you please slow down?" she said. Then she shook her head, and as she walked back to her desk, Karen could hear Pauline mutter, "Can you believe these eager-beaver temps?"

Before long, Karen was almost fascinated by how little work was done in the office. The system was almost ingenious. When the accountants needed work to be done, they sent it to the schedule typists through the internal mail system or dropped it by personally. Either way, the work piled up in the office in-basket. The office supervisor, Keith Frazier, would stop by every day or two. If there was only a small pile of work in the in-basket, Frazier would get extra work from another floor to keep them busy. If there was a large pile of work in the in-basket, he would take some of it to another floor to be done. Sometimes, instead of taking the extra work elsewhere, he would hire an additional temporary employee to deal with it.

Karen realized that this was why she had been hired. Two of the women in the office, Pauline and Pat, had purposely been doing the least possible amount of work for the last few weeks. They had correctly realized that the more of the tedious work they did, the more they would have to do. On the other hand, if they spent all morning getting coffee, chatting about their weekends, and so on, Frazier would take the work elsewhere. It was unbelievable.

The third woman in the office, Myra, was different. While Pauline and Pat were white and from England, Myra was an Indian immigrant who commuted from the Stuyvesant area of the Bronx. Although she laughed at Pat's off-color jokes, Myra kept working away while the others dawdled. She never criticized them for fooling around even though their lack of effort generally meant that she was the one who did most of the schedule preparation.

When Karen started working in their office, the others were polite to her but not very friendly. Slowly, Pauline began asking her questions. What did she think about Manhattan? Where was she living? And so on. The others eventually joined in.

After a while, Karen started to enjoy working in this group. Pauline and Pat, who lived in Brooklyn, were very quick-witted and entertaining. In particular, things seemed to revolve around Pauline, who was the ringleader behind most of the mischief-making. When Pauline started coming to work at 10 a.m., Pat did the same. After a week, even Myra and Karen were coming in late, around 9:15. Myra was shy and quiet, but sometimes Karen had good conversations with her when the others took one of their ninety-minute to two-hour lunches at a nearby café.

Even though the four of them were very different in race, nationality, and background, Karen was intrigued to find that they each stuck up for one another. If Frazier stopped by while Pauline and Pat were taking an extra long lunch, Myra would tell him that they were checking on work with an accountant on another floor or that they were getting supplies from the stationery center. Karen learned that Pat had occasionally taken a whole day off to go shopping uptown—and been paid for it—while Frazier thought she was up in the schedule typists' office, working away.

Karen believed that the Hepplewhite & Boyce employees in other departments didn't like her or anyone else in the office. If she sat down in the cafeteria at lunch and told someone where she worked, she felt she was treated like a nobody. When she asked Pauline about it, Pauline just chuckled. "We're what you might call the Black Sheep Office. No one wants to have anything to do with us because they know what we do is just busywork, something any moron can do."

As Karen listened, she glanced out the window of the office, which overlooked an ugly jumble of back alleys and construction projects. Pauline went on to explain that they had initially pushed Frazier to give them a little more free rein in how they did their work.

Karen was confused. "Don't you have free rein already?" she asked. "Frazier only checks on us about twice a week."

"Yeah, right," Pauline said. "But he still tells us we have to do things his way." The current procedures were rigid and monotonous. Pat had suggested that the schedule typists should be able to fix obvious mathematical errors without sending them back to an accountant, and Pauline herself had asked if they could each be responsible for working with three or four specific accountants so that the schedule typists could get used to the style and handwriting of each one. Doing that, Pauline had told Karen, might save time.

Pauline was certain that they could have come up with many more ideas, but Frazier had assured them that his way of getting the work done was the most efficient. Using his system, for example, it wouldn't matter if one person was absent, because someone else would just do her work. Since absenteeism was high, he felt this was an important consideration.

"After a while, we stopped complaining," Pat said, "because, number one, he wouldn't listen, and, number two, it's easier to do less work his way."

Pauline nodded. "Why should we knock ourselves out? This way we have a lot more time to chat and have long lunches. The day goes by just as fast either way."

Within a few weeks, the typists began having increasingly serious conflicts with Frazier. He had started to receive some complaints from the accountants about the delays in getting tax schedules updated. Then he succeeded in tracking down a bunch of international phone calls that were being made from the schedule typists' office. Pat had a sister who was married to an Air Force colonel in Keflavic, Iceland, and she had been calling her regularly. Frazier's solution was to change the phone system so that it was impossible to make anything but an internal phone call from the schedule typists' office.

Pauline, angered about this development, took it as a personal challenge to beat the system. Within twenty-four hours, she discovered that it was possible to make international calls from the emergency telephone in the office elevator. She and Pat commandeered the elevator for a half hour, while Pat called her sister. By now, Karen, also annoyed because she couldn't even call her temp agency without using a pay phone on another floor, was fully willing to cover for her new friends.

186

One Monday morning, Frazier called Karen to his office, a spacious corner room with a beautiful view of the southern tip of Manhattan and the Hudson River. When Frazier asked about whether everyone was pulling their weight in schedule typing, Karen said they were.

During the conversation, it became clear to Karen that Frazier had found out about the elevator episode and that he intended to take action. Still, Karen was astonished by his plan.

"Some people around here need to learn a few lessons," he said. "Since you've been here, Karen, you've worked hard, and you're certainly qualified." Karen blushed, knowing how untrue that was.

"Frankly, Karen, I don't have time to baby-sit certain individuals in certain departments. So, I'm putting you in charge of the schedule typists. You can do whatever you want, be as tough as you like. Just don't fire anyone. As you probably know from your management background, that's an expensive alternative, a last resort."

Frazier added that he was responsible for over thirty workers so he hadn't been able to give the schedule typists the iron hand of discipline he felt they needed. "Still, I've always spelled out for them everything they have to do. They just don't want to listen. They need someone like you to slap their hands as soon as they get out of line."

Karen accepted the position, figuring it would be a good opportunity to find out if she could apply what she'd learned in her management courses at Plympton. Nonetheless, she had many doubts and anxieties. Regardless of what Frazier had said, she knew that he wasn't making her leader because of her ability. He was probably more interested in embarrassing Pat and Pauline by appointing someone who was much younger and much less experienced than they, and someone who came in from a temp agency to boot. It was clear that it would surely be fine with Frazier if Karen made their lives miserable.

What could she do to make the group productive? Frazier would probably laugh in her face if she suggested raises and bonuses for the "black sheep" group. Besides, the salaries were already more than reasonable, given the nature of the work. After all, the women would have probably quit long ago if money was the issue.

Another worry was that Pauline was unquestionably the informal leader of the group. She had been there the longest and knew the most about the computer system, and she was well liked. Karen liked Pauline and couldn't really blame her for most of what she had done. Still, how could she keep Pauline from being a problem?

There was another dilemma. After work, Karen took the subway to the midtown office of Temployee Specialists so she could tell Jane Thorley about her promotion. Thorley thought it was a wonderful thing. "Now we can deal with you directly when Hepplewhite & Boyce needs another temp!" she said.

Karen smiled weakly, knowing that Temployee Specialists would probably continue to send inexperienced but eager college graduates who would cheerfully lie about their computer ability to make it past the personnel department. When tax season arrived, Karen knew she would probably need to hire one or two temporaries, regardless of how successful she was in managing Pauline, Pat, and Myra. If she did use Temployee Specialists, she would be encouraging more lying, which didn't seem right.

Karen had made a regrettable decision at a time when she felt desperate for money. Now that she was a manager in a position of responsibility, she felt she should be a good role model and earn the respect of her business associates. At the same time, she would feel like a hypocrite if she told Jane Thorley that she wouldn't go along with the scheme. It would mean that she had been willing to lie when her own selfish interests were at stake, but not when someone else was involved. Admittedly, Thorley had put her through a tough selection procedure, Karen thought. Maybe Thorley was actually able to identify workers who could do good work, even if they weren't technically qualified. Still, did the end justify the means?

Karen now believed that she shouldn't have jumped at her first job offer, but at the same time there was no way to make that decision again. She realized that she had been naive. Now, in many ways, she had to grow up in a hurry.

Questions for Discussion

1. Using what you have learned from your readings about organizational behavior theories and principles, analyze and explain the situation in the schedule typists' office of Hepplewhite & Boyce.

2. What is the central problem here?

3. Pretend that you are Karen Carlin, and write a specific and comprehensive action plan that you would use to correct the problem.

4. Regarding Karen's ethical dilemma with Jane Thorley and Temployee Specialists, what should she do?

37

A STRAW IS A STRAW IS A STRAW—
EXCEPT IN THE HANDS OF A HIGH-PERFORMANCE TEAM©

Objectives

- To provide hands-on experience in the use of leadership to create a high-performance team

- To provide an opportunity to examine how a leader, formal or informal, conveys a clear vision and the ways that vision drives the execution of a task

- To provide an opportunity to examine the role of followers in achieving a leader's vision

Background

A leader who is able to convey a strong and clear vision of the goals and purposes of an organization has the best chance of developing groups of individuals into high-performing teams. It is the leader's role to provide a clear framework within which work is to be carried out and to build an environment in which individuals become committed to supporting one another and the organization's goals.

This exercise provides a hands-on experience that will allow you to study leadership in action. The learning from the exercise comes largely from your role as an observer, not just of the leader's behavior, but of the leader's impact on you and your motivation and commitment. To get the most out of this exercise, first read the "Questions for Consideration" and "What to Look For" below.

Instructions

A valued customer has asked you to design and build a model for the tallest, sturdiest, and most attractive office building possible. The building is to be built in a city where land is expensive and parking is a problem. Eventually a microwave tower will be erected on the roof, and you must provide for it.

Your customer has let you know that a number of other companies will be vying for the contract to build the actual building.

There are certain customer preferences and restrictions:

- At least 95 percent of the model must be constructed out of drinking straws.

- The model must be delivered by _____ (ending time will be given to you by the facilitator).

- The model must stand for at least one full minute after delivery.

- The customer dislikes triangles.

1. *(25 minutes)*

Select a leader. Once the leader has been selected, it is up to him or her to provide the subsequent instructions for how to continue.

When your model has been completed or time is called, whichever comes first, take a few minutes to jot down some answers to the "Questions for Consideration."

2. *(15 minutes)*

Select someone other than the exercise leader to facilitate a discussion of the process you followed in building the model. Use the "Questions for Consideration" and "What to Look For" as a guide.

Select two spokespeople to communicate your observations to the class. Assign one the task of presenting your building and its features. The other should describe your process.

3. *(open-ended)*

There will be a report out and a class discussion when you have completed the exercise. During the report out you will have approximately four minutes to:

- Present your model.

- Briefly describe what your goal was as defined by your leader.

- Briefly describe how you went about carrying out your leader's missions.

- Briefly describe one leadership behavior that worked well and one that didn't.

Questions for Consideration

1. In what ways did the leader convey a vision and facilitate a shared understanding of the assigned task and approach?

_____

_____

_____

_____

2. If you had been (or were) the leader, what would you have done differently, what would you have done the same, and why?

_____

_____

_____

_____

3. For the followers, what worked, what didn't work, and why?

_____

_____

_____

_____

What to Look For

- How the leader encouraged or discouraged input and participation

- How the leader determined and used the skills of each team member

- The emergence of an informal leader (someone other than the appointed leader) who set the goals and brought the group together

- Power struggles in which more than one person tried to take a leadership role, and the impact of that on the efficiency of the team

- Whether you felt valued, motivated, and part of the team

38

TWO LEADERSHIP FISHBOWLS

Fishbowl #1

Objectives

- To examine the elements of good and poor leadership
- To examine the participants' experiences with good and poor leadership
- To practice the important leadership skill of active listening

Procedure

1. (20 minutes)

Five students will be selected randomly or by volunteering to be the "fish." Sitting together in the middle of the class (or in a central place where they can be seen and heard by the other members of the class), the fish should tell the stories of their experiences with bad or good leaders, and then discuss them with the other members of the fish group only.

Students on the outside of the fishbowl are not to speak while the fish are speaking. Their job is to observe, listening for common threads as well as differences in what they are hearing. Those outside of the fishbowl should listen carefully but not take notes.

If there is a lag in the conversation, it is important for everyone, including the facilitator, to resist the temptation to jump in and help. It is not unusual for such lags to occur at the very beginning of the exercise and again before the onset of the general discussion that takes place among the fish after each has told his or her story.

Option 1: *Think about people for or with whom you have worked and who you felt were good leaders.*

Option 2: *Think about people for or with whom you have worked and who you felt were poor leaders.*

2. (15–20 minutes, depending on size of group)

Going around the class, every student on the outside of the fishbowl should report on one thing that he or she has heard about the elements of leadership discussed by the fish. During this phase, the fish are not allowed to talk. These common elements should be listed in a visible place.

3. *(Full class: 10–15 minutes)*

When the observation list has been completed, exchange and general discussion between the fish and the observers may take place.

4. *(Small groups: 10–15 minutes)*

When the first four steps have been completed, the class should be divided into groups of five or six. If possible, there should be at least one fish in each group.

Working in these small groups, do one of the following:

Option 1: *Develop a twenty-five to fifty word definition of leadership that begins with the phrase "A good leader is..." and incorporates at least three to five elements of good leadership.*

Option 2: *Develop a list of the personal and interpersonal traits, skills, and abilities you would like to see in a leader.*

5. *(open-ended)*

Report your results to the class. Discussion should follow.

Option 1: *Drawing on what you have learned about leadership from personal experiences, readings, lectures, and the fishbowl exercise, discuss your ideas with the other members of your group, and together develop a definition of leadership in twenty-five to fifty words.*

　Step a. *List the elements of good leadership you believe should be included in your definition.*

　Step b. *Write a definition of leadership beginning with the words "A good leader is...."*

Option 2: *Drawing on what you have learned about leadership from personal experiences, readings, lectures, and the fishbowl exercise, discuss your ideas with the other members of your group, and together develop a list of the personal and interpersonal traits, skills, and abilities that you and your fellow group members would like to see in a leader.*

Briefly describe each item on your list, and explain why each is important personally and interpersonally.

Fishbowl #2*

Objectives

- To observe the process of leadership as it emerges in a group discussion
- To examine the elements of poor and good leadership
- To practice the important leadership skill of active listening
- To explore cultural differences in how effective leadership is perceived

Procedure

1. Set-up and debate (20 minutes: 5 minutes for set-up; 15 minutes for debate)

You will be given a topic to debate for fifteen minutes. Six students will then be selected, either at random, or from volunteers, to debate each side of the issue (three on each side). These students will be the "fish" and will sit in a small circle in the center of the class (or in a central place where they can be seen and heard by the other members of the class). The fish will have fifteen minutes to debate the assigned topic, and they may only speak with the other fish.

Students on the outside of the fishbowl are not to speak while the fish are speaking. If you are one of these students, your job will be to observe the debate. You will be asked to comment on what you have observed regarding leadership, so listen carefully—but do not take notes.

Note: If there is a lag in the conversation, it is important for everyone, including the facilitator, to resist the temptation to jump in to help. It is not unusual for such lags to occur at the very beginning of the exercise and again before the onset of the general discussion that takes place among the fish after each has voiced his or her opinion.

2. Observations (15–20 minutes, depending on the size of the group)

Going around the class, every student on the outside of the fishbowl should comment on one thing that he or she has observed with regard to leadership. During this part of the fishbowl exercise, the fish are not allowed to talk.

List the observations in a visible place.

3. Discussion of observations (5–10 minutes)

When the observation list has been completed, exchange and general discussion between the fish and the observers may take place. The discussion should focus on the comments and observations made, not on renewing the debate.

* Copyright 1997 by Sandi Deacon Carr. Used with permission.

4. *Class discussion of leadership observations (open-ended)*

Drawing from the comments made, a focused discussion of the elements of leadership should take place. Discussion points might include:

- Examining the issues of power and influence in the group as they relate to leadership.
  Who had the most influence? Why?
  Who talked the most?
  Who sounded most like an expert? Did that person have more or less influence? Why?
  Was anyone able to change or sway your opinion on the issue? Why

- Examining cultural differences.

- Examining the importance of active listening and its role in leadership.

- Examining the process of the discussion:
  Who started the discussion?
  How, or by whom was it determined who would speak and when?
  Did the fish listen to one another, talk over one another, or interrupt one another?

5. *Small group exercise (10–15 minutes)*

When the first four steps have been completed, the class will be divided into groups of five or six. If possible, there should be at least one fish in each group.

Working in these small groups, do one of the following:

Option 1: *Develop a twenty-five to fifty word definition of leadership that begins with the phrase "A good leader is..." and incorporates at least three to five elements of good leadership.*

Option 2: *Develop a list of the personal and interpersonal traits, skills, and abilities you would like to see in a leader.*

6. *Report out and discussion (open-ended)*

Report your results to the class. Discussion should follow.

THE GREAT POST-IT® MASSACRE*

The yellow Post-It® slipped off the lapel of Beverly Sadowsky's silk suit and fluttered to the floor. Beverly, chief operating officer (COO) of Adventures Plus, had been taken aback when Bob Scanlan burst into her office and slapped the note on her, but not half so shaken as she was about to be. Reaching down, Beverly picked up the note and inhaled hard as she read, "RS…Follow the instructions I give you. When I want your input, I'll ask for it. G. Fishman, 1st V.P."

"I can't take much more of this," Bob fumed. "I've been asking around about other jobs, and if it weren't for how hard I've worked to get to corporate, I'd probably be out of here. Ever since Fishman was promoted to first vice president, it has been one of these demeaning, obnoxious notes after another. He writes me notes about things I've already done, notes about things we've already talked about, and notes that simply nitpick. I get constant reminder notes—do this, do that, notes that tell me how wide the margins should be on department memos, and notes about notes. It doesn't matter how high- or low-priority the project might be, the notes are the same. And it's always 'I'm the boss; you're working for me.' He never says 'thank you' or 'good job'; it's just more notes about something I forgot to do, or a typo in a fifteen-page document my people produced."

Background

Beverly Sadowsky had been first vice president of Adventures Plus, a rapidly-growing discount travel agency with fifty offices throughout the United States and Canada, for about a year when Bob Scanlan was promoted to small business accounts and assigned to the head office in Dallas. Since joining the company right after college, Bob's assignments had been mostly in sales and customer service in several offices around the country. He had found the other jobs he had previously held at Adventures Plus generally high-pressure but lacking in challenge. However, he had remained interested in the travel industry and saw a future in it. With his promotion to the head office, he reported to Beverly Sadowsky's immediate subordinate. An older woman, Gertrude Tocco had been in the position for sixteen years. Gertrude was planning to retire within the year, and she made it clear that she wanted to do as little as possible until that time.

Bob had been happy to find that his new job situation, while still not particularly exciting, was at least more relaxed, and people seemed to appreciate his efforts. He worked hard and did his best, but he rarely went beyond the service side of the job, since in the discount travel business one rarely knew just how long he or she would be staying in any one place. Consistent with that, Bob didn't become too involved with supervising the large and somewhat

* Copyright 1992 by Victoria Selden. Used with permission.

unreliable part-time workforce who, though many were in sales and on commission, seemed to spend a lot of time fooling around; nor did he try to make any changes to the haphazard office systems. Instead, he concentrated his efforts on quick turnaround of business travel arrangements, especially booking and ticketing, and soon he was getting lots of positive comments about his work and the wonderful service.

After watching him for about a month, Beverly realized that Bob took his responsibilities seriously, and she also realized that he had far more potential than was being tapped. This was the result, she thought, of Bob's not "belonging" to the department, having been moved from place to place over the eight years since he had joined Adventures Plus. When Beverly first asked Bob if he would be willing to step into the department supervisor's position that was soon to become vacant, he had turned her down flat. Having a degree in management science, he was looking for more responsibility and challenge, and he was concerned that becoming department supervisor would be little more than a dead-end job full of routine tasks. Finally, after several months of asking in various ways if he would take the job, Beverly asked Bob what she needed to do to get him to take it. Not really wanting the position, Bob decided to really "ask for the moon." To his surprise, Beverly told him that same day that all his requests would be filled, including more money and a fairly comprehensive benefits package that included up to $5,000 a year for further education and training.

This was the beginning of a great relationship. Beverly's hands-off attitude and delegation of many of the responsibilities of her job to Bob made the job challenging. Bob quickly learned how to find his way around the company's bureaucracy at even the highest levels, and he prided himself on making his boss and the department "look good." He took virtually complete charge of the office, and even supervised the cleaning and updating of files. He and Beverly conferred from time to time on things they thought would make the department and the company function better, like new computers and a company-wide voice-mail system, suggestions they were then able to sell to senior management. Beverly always found the funding for Bob's innovations in the small-business office, but she left the research and selection of items up to him. In time, she also delegated to Bob projects like budgeting; financial tracking; hiring, training and supervising of the part-time sales and clerical force; scheduling; and making important presentations. Generally, she would work with him at doing a particular task at the outset, but as soon as she was comfortable that he could do it, she would give him the task and leave him alone.

While it was never talked about, Bob and Beverly seemed to have an understanding that Bob could use his initiative and judgment on day-to-day administration, which included signing Beverly's name on routine forms. Bob always knew that he could call on Beverly when he had a question, and Beverly was happy to have someone on whom she could rely to carry out the supervisory duties of the business sales department. From her point of view, Bob was a resource—she didn't want to be bothered writing things down or knowing anything she could count on Bob to know. Nor was Beverly interested in enforcing strict workday hours on Bob.

"Take courses," she encouraged him. "If you need to take a course during the day, get one of your employees to cover the office while you're not here; if that isn't possible, shift your calls over to our voice-mail system, and leave a message that people can talk to me if there's an emergency. Really, there aren't many calls that are that critical that they can't wait an hour or two for a call back."

Seeing this as an opportunity he would not otherwise be able to afford, Bob enrolled in an intensive twelve-week management training program at a nearby university. The program ran from 7 to 10 a.m. two mornings a week, all day on Saturdays, and from noon until 5 p.m. on Sundays. As a result, Bob often stayed late on the days he had classes to be sure that work was done and done right.

Two years later, when Beverly Sadowsky was promoted to COO, the small business accounts office was considered to be a model for how things should be done in the discount travel business. Even administrators and staff of other, bigger departments, like convention planning, knew they could turn to Bob to get quick and efficient service on their requests and answers to their questions.

While many other departments had trouble getting enough qualified people to fill full- and part-time clerical and sales slots, Bob always had about five times more applicants than he could use. He interviewed and hired students, retirees, and homemakers, and he trained and supported them. Once they seemed to understand their jobs, Bob left them alone to do them, rarely looking over their shoulders unless he had a sense that there might be a problem. When a problem arose or an employee was asked to do something new and different, Bob would work with him or her, sometimes shifting the workload until it made sense, given a particular worker's capabilities and time availability. Joe Sutcliffe, for example, a retiree from a commercial airline, had been working in the office for almost two years and could do just about everything, with the exception of budgeting, that Bob could do. When a job came up, Bob would tell Joe what had to be done, and Joe would do it. Adrienne Hsu, on the other hand, had just started. Her job consisted mainly of photocopying and typing travel orders and itineraries. With Adrienne, Bob would tell her what needed to be done, explain how it was to be done, and then check in with her from time to time to answer any questions and give whatever additional instructions were needed. Although Fred Claxton had been around for almost two years, some of the routine jobs still seemed to throw him. Bob, not by nature a particularly patient person, nonetheless took extra time to go over a job or assignment with Fred, constantly encouraging him to try to do the work on his own before coming to him.

"I know you can do this," Bob would tell him, "but if you get stuck, I'll be happy to help you work out any problems." With Bob running the office, morale was high, and the full-timers and part-timers worked hard and did their best. With the exception of George Fishman, then supervisor of the auditing department, everyone seemed comfortable that Bob was running a solid and efficient department.

George Fishman

When Beverly Sadowsky was promoted to COO, George Fishman, having some seniority, an MBA, and a solid track record in auditing, was promoted into Beverly's position as first vice president. George was a detail-oriented person and a self-professed perfectionist. In addition to the long hours of his professional life, George was active in his church where he served as treasurer and chaired several committees. This included what seemed to be a perpetually functioning search committee necessitated by an unusually high incidence of turnover among pastors.

From virtually the first minute that Bob had started at corporate, George would spell out even the tiniest details of how work should be done. Checking his voice-mail early in the morning, Bob would generally find two or three terse messages from George, apparently left while the office was closed. Often coming into the small-business accounts office personally to repeat his instructions, George would leave behind a trail of pastel-colored Post-It® notes on Bob's desk and the desks of others in the office.

Despite what Bob considered his proven competence to do the work, George's behavior continued. Even more frustrating to Bob was the fact that when he asked George why he didn't seem to trust him to figure out what needed to be done, George seemed surprised and claimed that everything was fine.

As time went along, Bob began increasingly to dread work interactions with George. When the notes and stream of instructions became unbearable, Bob would beg Beverly to get George "off his case." He was never sure just what Beverly did, but a week or ten days of relative peace usually followed. Beverly also helped Bob see that this was George's way of supervising, and little was likely to change.

After George took on the position of first vice president, things between Bob and George got steadily worse. George demanded that the office be "covered" from nine to five everyday, telling Bob that having callers get an answering machine or a lower-level employee was unacceptable. One of the main messages Bob received from George, both implicitly and explicitly was, "I'm the boss—you're not." In addition, George's new position brought the two into far greater and more regular contact than had previously been the case. Now instead of having a job situation that involved George once or twice a week, Bob had ten or twelve situations a day, ranging from routine to moderately complex. Virtually none, Bob thought, were too difficult for him to handle alone; but no matter what the task, George emphasized perfection and seemed to give every job equal weight.

Wanting to be informed about and involved in even the most mundane decisions, at one point George had become furious on learning that Bob had signed his name to a routine document. "Look," he told Bob, "this is my responsibility. I have to know what's going on in this job or I'm not going to be able to do it the way it ought to be done. If you make a mistake, I'm going to get blamed for it, and I don't want that."

Scanlan's Last Stand

This latest incident seemed like just too much. George had asked Bob to write up a two-page report for the meeting of the executive officers to explain a new system that the department was considering implementing. Realizing that the report went two lines over onto a third page, Bob, now afraid to make the decision on his own, had left George a note suggesting that a minor adjustment to the margins would allow him to get the entire memo on just two pages. It was in response to this that the yellow Post-It® Bob had just slapped on Beverly Sadowsky's lapel had been written.

Questions for Discussion

1. Using one or two theories of leadership, compare and contrast the leadership styles of Beverly Sadowsky, George Fishman, and Bob Scanlan.

2. Knowing what you do about motivation, explain the connection between the motivational needs of Beverly, George, and Bob to their respective styles of leadership, that is, in what ways does the leadership style of each of the three impact positively or negatively on the needs of each one's followers? What should be changed, and why?

3. If you were Beverly Sadowsky, what advice would you give to Bob and George?

4. Assuming George isn't going to change, if you were Bob and wanted to make things better at your job, what would you do differently?

40

WHO WORKS SATURDAY NIGHT?

Objectives

- To explore leadership styles—autocratic, democratic, and laissez-faire
- To examine the effectiveness of the different styles in decision-making situations
- To examine the impact of leadership styles on subordinates

Background

Autocratic leaders generally impose their decisions without considering the input of their subordinates. Laissez-faire leaders may relinquish their decision-making powers to their subordinates. Democratic leaders clarify the goals to be met by a decision and work with subordinates to find the decision that best meets those goals.

As you do this exercise, consider the leadership style being used by your group's manager and the ways in which you believe that style to be appropriate or not.

The Story

Your small company, Turnem, Inc., a manufacturer of valves that have a wide variety of uses, including use in several aspects of the aerospace industry, is on a tight deadline to complete a project. The prototype product is due to be demonstrated to the leaders of the aerospace industry the following Monday.

To finish on schedule, it will be necessary for one member of your team to work on some of the highly technical parts of the project this Saturday evening, probably having to stay until at least midnight. The entire team will have to work at its most productive and cooperative level for the full day on Sunday. The budget allows for only one member of the team to be paid to work Saturday night.

The contract for this project, although not your company's only source of revenue, is important.

Instructions

1. (10 minutes)

Read the background information above, and the role that has been assigned to you in class. In addition, read the questions on the "Observer Sheet" and the "Questions for Discussion."

Review and plan your role thoroughly. Think about how you will justify the position you will need to take with regard to working Saturday night. Do not discuss your role with any of your classmates until you have been told to do so.

2. (30 minutes)

In your work group, decide who will work Saturday night and why.

Select a spokesperson for your group to report to the rest of the class how your group solved the problem. Your spokesperson should also be prepared to describe the efficacy of the manager. Use the "Observer Sheet" and the "Questions for Discussion" as a guide.

3. (10 minutes)

Read the instructions on the "Score Sheet," and rate your manager and your satisfaction with the decision according to the directions given.

4. (30 minutes)

Report out and discussion.

Questions for Discussion

1. Given the problem presented, did the manager of your group use an appropriate leadership style? Why or why not? (If you were the manager in your group, how did you feel about the effectiveness of the leadership style you used?)

2. What do you think the manager should have done differently?

3. Did the manager listen to and consider each employee's arguments?

4. How was the decision made? Did the manager elicit input from the employees?

5. What are the implications of the decision for each member? For the effectiveness of the team on Sunday? For the ultimate success and quality of the project?

Observer Sheet

1. Briefly describe the manager's dilemma.

   _____

   _____

   _____

2. Were the employees given a fair chance to explain their concerns?

   _____

   _____

   _____

3. How would you rate the manager's overall listening skills and why?

   _____

   _____

   _____

4. What factors do you think the manager failed to consider in making a decision?

   _____

   _____

   _____

5. What factors did the manager appear to use in reaching a decision?

   _____

   _____

   _____

6. How did the employees react to the manager's leadership style, and why?

   _____

   _____

   _____

Score Sheet

1. Working alone, rate your group manager on the following scale:

10	5	1
Autocratic	Laissez-Faire	Democratic

Calculate the average rating in your group (not counting the manager's opinion!) by adding all ratings and dividing by the number of workers in the group.

Group rating: _____

2. Working alone, rate your satisfaction with the decision on the following scale:

10	5	1
Very Dissatisfied		Very Satisfied

Calculate the average rating of satisfaction in your group by adding all the ratings and dividing by the number of workers.

Group rating: _____

Generally, groups that perceive their leaders to be autocratic will be more dissatisfied with decisions made about who works Saturday night. Laissez-faire managers can also be frustrating to groups. Keep in mind that this may vary depending on the composition of the group: Some people actually like to be told what to do. In some cultures, managers who involve workers in decision-making processes, such as those represented by this exercise, are considered to be ineffective; in other cultures, managers are expected to seek input from subordinates regularly. The occurrence of and acceptance of laissez-faire styles of management, however, tend to be rare compared to that of more autocratic styles.

Questions for Discussion

1. How did your group feel about the style of your manager, and why?

2. In what situations would you consider autocratic leadership to be both appropriate and acceptable, and why?

3. In what situations would you consider laissez-faire leadership to be both appropriate and acceptable, and why?

TROUBLE WITH THE TEAM PROJECT*

Objectives

- To develop skills in team problem solving

- To explore methods and styles of conflict resolution

- To examine the ways in which leaders influence group processes

Background

The paper for your management class's team project is due early tomorrow morning. You and your teammates have been working on it for the past month, and you have spent many hours together over the past several days trying to agree on the final form and content.

Each of you has come to this meeting with the rough drafts of your individual parts of the paper. As you have come to expect from team projects in other classes, some parts are much "rougher" than others—some even fail to meet the agreed-upon two-page requirement. In addition, and despite your prior agreement that all work was to be typed, most of the drafts are hand-written.

It is now 2 p.m. on the day before the project is due. Several tasks need to be finished if you are going to hand in a high-quality paper, i.e., the paper needs to be written in a coherent form, integrated, typed, proofread, edited, polished, and the exhibits need to be created and added. You are now all present for the team meeting at which you must resolve how you will complete the paper by the time it is due tomorrow morning.

Keep in mind that your team will need to work closely together again next week to put together a class presentation on the project.

Instructions

1. (5 minutes)

Read the background information above, as well as the role that has been assigned to you, and carefully prepare what you will say to your group.

* Copyright 1997 by Sandi Deacon Carr. Used with permission.

2. (20–25 minutes)

Begin the role play by explaining to your team who you are and what you think your role should be in getting this paper done. After twenty-five minutes, stop the role play whether or not your team has reached a resolution.

3. (20 minutes)

Read the "Questions for Discussion" (below), and discuss the answers with your group. If your team failed to resolve the problem, use the questions as a guide to explore why this may have been your result.

Questions for Discussion

Problem Solving

1. On a step-by-step basis, describe how your team went about solving this problem.

2. Explain the process by which the paper will be completed. How did the team arrive at this decision?

3. Given this plan, what grade is the paper likely to get? Why?

4. Did the team focus on their common goals in trying to resolve the problem?

Conflict

5. How are the relationships among the team members? Does anyone feel angry, insulted, or upset with the team and/or the decision? Why?

6. Did the team arrive at a win/win decision? Win/lose? Lose/lose? Why?

7. What impact do you think the conflict is likely to have on future team performance, particularly preparing and delivering the final presentation?

Leadership Style

8. What style of leadership did your team leader demonstrate?

9. How did this style influence the team's decision-making process?

10. Did anyone else on the team emerge as a leader? When? What impact did this have on the team's ability to solve the problem?

Observer Sheet

1. Describe the team leader's leadership style. Was it appropriate?

   _____

   _____

   _____

   _____

2. What impact did it have on team interactions and motivation of team members?

   _____

   _____

   _____

   _____

3. Who emerged as (an) informal leader(s)? When? Why?

   _____

   _____

   _____

   _____

4. Was the team able to focus on common goals?

   _____

   _____

   _____

   _____

5. What conflict-management strategies did you observe?

   _____

   _____

   _____

   _____

6. What happened as those strategies were utilized? Did conflict subside or escalate?

_____

_____

_____

_____

7. What conflict-management strategies might have been more helpful?

_____

_____

_____

_____

8. Do you feel that the team was successful in resolving this problem? Why?

_____

_____

_____

_____

9. Describe any other significant observations you made regarding leadership and conflict.

_____

_____

_____

_____

42

MEADOWBROOK GARDEN CENTER*

Located in Raleigh, North Carolina, Meadowbrook Garden Center, a top level greenhouse/ nursery in the floriculture industry, offers literally hundreds of high-quality and unique varieties of plants, trees, and shrubs to its retail and wholesale clients. Christmas holiday shoppers find poinsettias in basic colors, as well as rare varieties like Peppermint, Monet, Jinglebells, and Freedom Red—a classic variety of poinsettia plant with dark red blooms and dark green leaves. In 1996, Meadowbrook Garden Center sold out its entire crop of 30,000 chrysanthemums, including more than thirteen color varieties, many of which were not available from other local retailers. Meadowbrook even sells plants to competing firms that are unable to produce comparable quality, quantity, or variety.

Jack Ward, general manager of Meadowbrook, prides himself on running a business that provides the highest quality floriculture products in the greater Raleigh area. However, Jack has also begun to recognize his limitations in improving operations. Despite the seventy-hour-plus work weeks he devotes to the operation, understaffing and low performance have directed Jack's attention away from the management of Meadowbrook, and problems are increasing.

A key concern for Jack is that Meadowbrook Garden Center has operated at less than capacity for quite some time. Meadowbrook Garden Center is currently selling all it produces and doing so with minimal advertising. Despite competition from other small operations and garden centers in Lowe's, Walmart, and other large retailers, demand for Meadowbrook's plants is sufficient to allow for an increase in production by as much as 25 percent without acquiring surplus stock.

Problems exist at other levels of the organization as well. For example, for several years Meadowbrook Garden Center participated in a local annual flower and garden exhibition, a trade show in which area floriculture concerns exhibit and sell. All of Meadowbrook Garden Center's competition participates in this show. Jack says that Meadowbrook will no longer participate in the show because the show was "too much trouble and too demanding on manpower."

Even the condition of the Center's property is suffering. Despite the fact that Meadowbrook Garden Center's greenhouses are enclosed, one of them contains a huge mud puddle. This condition is created by poor drainage which has been unattended primarily due to a "shortage of time and manpower."

Jack now wonders what should be done to overcome these issues, provide him with more time to plan for the future of the business, and give him opportunities to pursue other personal goals.

* Copyright 1997 by Tracy L. Tuten, Ph.D., Randolph-Macon College, Ashland, Virginia. Used with permission.

History

Meadowbrook Garden Center's roots go back to the 1960s when its founder, Bill Ward, built his first small greenhouse. Although growing plants was only a hobby to him, neighbors came to regard him as an expert in plants. More and more, they solicited Bill to start flower and vegetable plants for their gardens.

The early to mid-1970s was a peak period for the floriculture industry. Consumers became very interested in using plants and flowers in the home, and items such as foliage plants and terrariums became quite popular. Inspired by local demand for plants and expertise, Bill resigned his position in a related field to establish Meadowbrook Garden Center.

During the initial years, Meadowbrook Garden Center literally operated as a "mom and pop" operation. Both Bill and his wife, Janet, operated Meadowbrook Garden Center solely with the assistance of their children, Jack and Rachel. Continually increasing demand necessitated the hiring of additional personnel, even more so as Jack and Rachel left for college and found other jobs.

In 1992, Bill "retired" from the business, relinquishing control to his son Jack and Jack's wife, Rebekah. Together, the two run the operation as its general and retail managers. Jack, following in his father's footsteps, is now well respected for his expertise. He is a specialist in a related field of the physical sciences and alone has nearly twenty years of experience in plant cultivation and pathology. Additionally, his wife Rebekah has just under ten years of experience in the industry.

Mission and Objectives

Despite Jack's statement that Meadowbrook Garden Center's "mission" is to provide the highest quality and variety of floriculture products possible to its diverse clientele and to support that quality with expertise in both plant pathology and cultivation, the company has neither a formally documented mission nor objectives.

As objectives, Jack notes that Meadowbrook Garden Center strives to:

- Use only high-quality floriculture inputs in the growing process. Meadowbrook Garden Center obtains its growing stock (bulbs, cuttings, seeds) either from producers with a reputation for quality or by raising stock plants itself.

- Properly execute each task involved in the growing process. Jack personally supervises each worker in each step of the growing process, including planting, transplanting, handling, and the regulation of environmental variables.

- Provide expertise in plant pathology, maintenance, and care for their customers. Meadowbrook Garden Center's employees and management collectively possess over forty years of experience in the floriculture industry.

Jack also has three personal goals that could strongly impact the goals of the organization: (1) to spend more time with his family, (2) to devote more time to the pursuit of his own personal interests, and (3) to devote more time to business interests of a more strategic nature.

All of these are important considerations for Jack. While Jack's official role is general manager, he currently devotes the vast majority of his time to operational activities, most of which involve supervising the greenhouse. Jack says he wishes employees were more willing and capable of performing responsible tasks on their own. And, while saying that he does not desire expansion, he adds, "Everything should run correctly. There is no use expanding your business if you've got problems."

Figure 1
Meadowbrook Garden Center - Organizational Chart

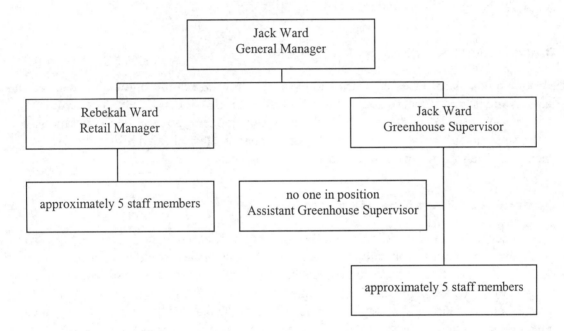

Target Market

Meadowbrook Garden Center services two customer groups: wholesale customers are served directly through the greenhouse; the retail center services retail customers. These groups are described below.

- Wholesalers: Contractor and reseller classes comprise the wholesale category. Contractors include landscapers and grounds maintenance organizations. These entities rely primarily on grower expertise, product availability, and quality. Price is not heavily emphasized by landscapers, because costs are passed on to their customers.

- Retail Consumers: Four classes of consumers comprise the retail consumer category. New homeowners comprise the first class—foundation planters. These are consumers who have recently constructed new homes and require first plantings ("foundation plantings") to place at the foundations.

The second class of retail consumers, "fixer-uppers," is comprised of established homeowners/apartment dwellers who want to spruce up the grounds surrounding their homes. They want to be able to select from an assortment of healthy plants; they de-emphasize price. Their purchases serve more as a "little luxury" to which they are treating themselves than as a budgeted expense.

Enthusiasts comprise the third retail class. These are hobbyists who not only want a geranium, they want "that one that was featured in Southern Living" last month.

The final retail class, "browsers," are consumers who enter a greenhouse/nursery "just looking." As these customers appear undirected, growers may "make the sale" either by price ("what a bargain!"), uniqueness ("I've never before seen one like this!"), specialization ("This is an unusual color!"), superior quality ("This is the nicest one I've ever seen!"), or simply by being available and informative.

Organizational Structure

Meadowbrook Garden Center is structurally flat (Figure 1), exhibits a low degree of formalization, and is highly centralized. Although Meadowbrook Garden Center is departmentalized into two broad departments—greenhouse/growing operations and retail operations—with respect to authority relationships, Jack is in charge. He makes all hiring and firing decisions. The staff ranges from ten to fifteen employees.

Operations and Personnel Management

Jack closely inspects plants throughout the growing cycle and maintains strict control over greenhouse operations. Ironically, there are few published rules, guidelines, or procedures in this area. All direction and training comes directly from Jack. Because most staff members are part-time, Jack explains that he must manage the growing operation in this manner to assure that procedures are properly executed. Further, Jack states that employees are incapable of assuming greater responsibility. Once employees complete a task, they must return to Jack to obtain the next task assignment.

Conflict Management

Although employee conflicts rarely come to his attention, when one does, Jack's solution is either to ignore it and let the employees settle the matter or to suspend the employees for a day, sending them home to think about it. On some occasions, for repeat offenders, he has terminated the employees. Similarly, when an employee comes into conflict with Jack, Jack generally ignores it.

Employee Facilities

The employee lunchroom is located in the area where Meadowbrook Garden Center places its supplies, maintenance tools, overstock seed and chemicals, obsolete inventory, and anything else for which it can find no other suitable storage space. Employees entering this room must pass by a hazardous chemical storage cabinet located immediately beside the doorway of the room. Once inside, the room appears temporary, dirty, and crowded.

Meadowbrook Garden Center provides a microwave oven and small cube refrigerator for employees to use. The table in the room is functional, yet the chairs are uncomfortable, mismatched, and obviously corporate outcasts from days gone by. The room has running water, yet employees are warned about drinking it. In the retail area, however, there is a soda machine and a water fountain with clean water.

Recruiting

Meadowbrook Garden Center does not actively seek candidates on the basis of their qualifications to perform the jobs of agricultural worker, grower, or any variation thereof. Elements such as formal job descriptions, titles, and specifications are absent. Meadowbrook Garden Center's only recruiting device is a "Now Hiring" sign placed at the entrance to the business. Jack places all applications he does not weed out in an applications-on-hand file. He considers the applicants who filed them to be viable job candidates, and he conducts applicant interviews on an as-needed basis. When an employee either quits or is terminated, he reviews the file of applications-on-hand and invites a candidate in for a brief interview. Previous related experience is not required. If mutual interest still exists after the interview, Jack takes the candidate on a brief tour of the operation. If the candidate still shows an interest after the tour, Jack offers him or her a position.

Training

All training at Meadowbrook Garden Center is informal and on-the-job.

Evaluation and Promotion

Meadowbrook Garden Center does not conduct formal evaluations of its employees. Rather, most feedback comes in the form of verbal comments from Jack. Employees normally receive no written feedback on their performance. Jack conveys dissatisfaction with an employee's performance by giving no raise or a minimal one.

No promotions are available to employees in Meadowbrook Garden Center's retail operation, for no higher position exists than that of retail manager. Employees may qualify for a position as assistant greenhouse manager by remaining with Meadowbrook Garden Center for six months. This signals to Jack that they are serious about the job—essentially that they are not going to leave. Additionally, Jack determines whether an employee demonstrates technical competence by assessing his or her ability to complete assigned tasks correctly and in an efficient manner.

Turnover

In the first ten months of 1996, Meadowbrook Garden Center's payroll "turned over" five times (staff typically consists of ten to fifteen members). Of the fifty-three employees that left, thirty-nine were fired. The vast majority of these separations were in the form of terminations for insubordination, poor performance, or non-performance.

Questions for Discussion

1. What are the key problems facing Jack and the Meadowbrook Garden Center?

2. How would you classify Jack's leadership style? Which leadership theory might be useful for Jack as he works towards solving Meadowbrook's problems? Explain how.

3. Using job design characteristics and Herzberg's Two Factor Theory, explain the possible causes of dissatisfaction and turnover and how turnover could be reduced. Why and how do you think employees could be prepared to handle more responsibility?

4. How can Jack eliminate the problem of "unable" employees in future hiring practices?.

43

LEADERSHIP AT PRODIGY ELECTRONICS*

Dennis Jackson couldn't understand what had gone wrong. Jackson, vice-president of marketing for Prodigy Electronics, had recently hired Tony Cafasso as marketing manager for the Robotic Controls Division. This division was responsible for developing road-show presentations and marketing plans tailored to a great variety of world markets. The marketing team members needed to have considerable creativity, as well as sensitivity and awareness of cultural differences and global issues, to do their jobs well. Accordingly, there was substantial ethnic diversity in the department: Seven of the marketing representatives were white, five were Asian, three were African-American, and two were Hispanic. Along with being specialists on the cultural differences of specific markets, most of the marketing representatives were fluent in at least two languages.

Jackson had hired Cafasso because of his impressive track record as a manager. Jackson often played tennis with Cafasso's former boss, who described Cafasso with glowing praise and as a nice guy who got results.

At his former job, Cafasso had managed an assembly line at a watch factory and had been charged with carrying out regular performance appraisals and making salary and promotion decisions. Faced with a team of veteran employees who had apparently lost the desire to work, Cafasso had turned them around by letting them make changes to the assembly line and giving them a say in how things were done. He also joined the group's softball team and was often invited to their regular parties after work and on weekends. Under Cafasso's management, productivity on Cafasso's line at the watch factory had increased dramatically.

Jackson was sure he had hired a great leader, but he couldn't understand why the performance of Tony Cafasso's marketing team wasn't better. The team members were working, but their ideas lacked the kind of creative spark that Jackson had sought. He decided to speak with some of Cafasso's subordinates individually to get their perspective on Cafasso's management style.

Jackson decided that he should speak to the more experienced employees first. He called Chuck Pritchard, a white, 49-year-old man who had worked for Prodigy for seventeen years.

"Tony is a great guy and a super manager," Pritchard assured Jackson. "Whenever I go to him for advice, he always turns my questions around and asks me what I would do. When something major is happening in my area, we work as a team to figure out what we should do. You can't argue with the results. Sales in my area have gone up 20 percent since Tony joined the team."

When Jackson spoke to Nancy Bartels, another white employee who had been with Prodigy for thirteen years, she was just as enthusiastic.

* This case was written by Scott Weighart.

"Last month my region had the highest sales in the office, and Tony made a point of singling me out in our monthly strategy session. He told me he wished he had the authority to give me a raise or promotion. It made me feel really proud. I have more enthusiasm for my job than I've had in quite a while."

Next, Jackson decided to speak to Amanda Chan, a 35-year-old Chinese-American woman who had been with Prodigy for just over seven years.

"I think Tony's very nice and everything, and I really don't have any problems with him, personally. I like the fact that I have a say in how things are done. But, sometimes Tony doesn't think. Last month he praised SooAe at the strategy meeting. She was so embarrassed that she didn't come to work for over a week, and I got stuck covering both of our territories. Plus, he keeps telling her that he wants her to make important decisions. She lacks the experience needed to make the best decisions, and she's terrified of making a mistake. I try to help, but I can't afford to let my area slip, too."

Jackson called SooAe Kim into his office. A 26-year-old Korean woman, SooAe had joined Prodigy less than a year earlier. Jackson found himself more confused than ever as SooAe told him that she thought Mr. Cafasso was a very good manager. Jackson pressed her with questions, but she had absolutely nothing negative to say about her boss. When asked about her absence earlier in the month, Ms. Kim lowered her head, apologized, and said it wouldn't happen again. Finally, Jackson shrugged his shoulders and said she could leave.

Alone in his office, Jackson tried to make sense of what he had heard. He was sure Cafasso wasn't a racist. After all, he had praised SooAe, given her encouragement in a time when she was struggling, and was even giving her a chance to control her own destiny. He decided he had better speak with some of the other employees.

"Do you think Tony is fair to everyone, regardless of race?" Jackson asked Lou Andrews, a 38-year-old African-American man who had been at Prodigy as long as he could remember.

"Of course he is!" Andrews replied. "Tony treats everybody the same. Race doesn't make any difference to him. The guy goes out of his way to make sure that everyone makes decisions. If something does go wrong, he never gives anyone a hard time about it. He usually doesn't even mention it. Tony's a positive thinker. The best thing this company could do would be to give Tony a raise, or at least give him the authority to hire and fire people. Otherwise, things are great."

Jackson was starting to think that there wasn't a problem. He wondered if it was just a slowdown in the marketplace. However, he knew that other divisions were soaring along. It didn't add up. He decided to speak to some of the younger workers, starting with Katie Langston, a 27-year-old African-American woman who had joined the company after getting her BSBA six months earlier.

"I think Tony means well," she said. "But I hope he knows what he's doing. I'm still learning the ropes around here. It's exciting to be given so much responsibility so early in my career, but I'm really not sure if I'm doing a good job. With this kind of work, rules and methods seem kind of vague. It's an art, trying to match robotic controls with the needs of customers in some specific part of the world. I like the work, but I'm always worried that I might be making some kind of huge mistake."

Juan Delgado, a recent MBA who had just joined the company as the coordinator for the South American marketing strategy, had somewhat similar concerns.

"Sometimes I just wish somebody would tell me what to do," he said. "In business school, we learned how great it can be to let workers make decisions for themselves. Now that I'm in the real world, I don't think it's so great! Tony is always pushing me to make my own decisions. Maybe if I had more experience, I would like it. Right now, it's driving me crazy. Sometimes I think I'd be better off making my strategy decisions by throwing darts at a dart board. I just hope I'm doing a good job. I'll never find out from Tony. He's always chatting with the guys who have been around here for a while—brainstorming, he calls it. Anyway, I never get invited to join in. He must have something against me."

Again, Jackson was confused. Perhaps Cafasso had trouble dealing with Hispanics? Next, he invited Pedro Mantilla, a Mexican-American, into his office.

"I've been with this company for sixteen years," Mantilla began, looking Jackson straight in the eyes. "And I tell you, Tony Cafasso is the best manager I've ever had."

"Now what?" Jackson thought to himself after Mantilla left his office. He decided he had better interview the new marketing representatives, almost all of whom had been hired within the previous six months. Jackson was dumbfounded as one after the other the employees stated that they found Tony Cafasso to be a poor manager. They all mentioned that he pushed them to make their own decisions in spite of their inexperience, and most said they felt unsure about the level of their own performance.

"Tony likes to pretend that mistakes don't exist," one worker said. "He seems to think that if you don't talk about them, mistakes will just go away."

Most of the other recently hired employees seemed to share this view as well.

Dennis Jackson thanked the last worker for coming to his office, closed the door, and tried to make sense out of everything he had heard.

"It seems like the older workers—the few that we have—think that Tony is great," Jackson said to himself. "Meanwhile, the young people think he's terrible. I wonder why that's the case?"

"And what about the question of racial and ethnic differences?" Jackson thought. "What's going on here?"

Questions for Discussion

1. Are there problems with the kinds of leadership being displayed in this case? What? Why?

2. Compare what appears to have been Tony's success in his previous job with what you believe his level of success is at Prodigy. If you see a difference, what do you believe the basis of that difference to be?

3. If you were Jackson, what would you do?

44

TWO SUPERVISORS—A STUDY IN STYLE*

Floor One and Floor Two are located in the same building and are very similar in physical features and workforce size. Employees on both floors make pacemakers, highly technical and delicate devices that are surgically implanted in a user's chest. Reliable performance of the device is often a life-and-death matter for the user.

Floor One

Conversation is minimal on Floor One. Mr. Martin, the supervisor, sits at his desk in a glass-front office where he is able to see much of the rest of the floor. A sign on Mr. Martin's wall reads: "There is too much at stake for mistakes."

Mr. Martin runs a tight ship on Floor One. He is known throughout the company as an organized and systematic manager: strict, but fair; courteous, but not exceptionally warm. He takes his work very seriously, telling new employees that they "each play a small role in the large endeavor of saving lives."

No one doubts Mr. Martin's commitment to his work. On his walks around the floor his manner is formal and detached, but keenly observant. When asked a question or for directions, his responses are always crisp, concise, and unambiguous. His technical knowledge of the work is highly regarded by all.

Mr. Martin is extremely thorough in doing everything possible to ensure that nothing leaves his shop with any defects. Whenever possible, he personally oversees the end-line inspection of the product—what he calls "the last and by far most important step in the process."

Asked once about why he doesn't loosen up the reins, Martin responded: "We're in the business of making devices that keep people alive. There can be no question about final quality of product—every defect that leaves here is a potential killer. There will always be human error, and no matter how good these folks may be, I can't let their mistakes endanger our customers. My job is to make sure that everyone follows procedure to the letter, and that if mistakes are made they are caught before they go out the door."

Martin delegates almost no authority to his assistant, Mr. Smith. When Martin is away and Smith is in charge, the atmosphere on the floor changes. There is a good deal of chatting and gossiping, and at times even some horseplay. Some of the older workers are concerned that the lack of tight discipline when Smith is in charge might lead to mistakes.

* Copyright 1992 by Organizational Dynamics, Inc. (ODI), 25 Mall Road, Burlington, MA 01803. Special thanks to George H. Labovitz, Ph.D., President and CEO, ODI, for permission to reprint this training exercise.

The attitude among the younger workers toward Martin's supervision is expressed in the following statements:

"Martin runs a very strict floor, and the workers resent him because he treats them like trainees."

"When I came here, Martin checked up on everything I did, and that was hard to adjust to. I felt like a rookie all over again."

"I've had what I thought were some pretty good ideas of how we might improve what we do around here and maybe even do some things differently that would save a few bucks. But I guess Martin feels that he's the only one who should be thinking about how we might make things better."

"When Martin is off, the workers are in a more sociable frame of mind. The whole atmosphere seems more relaxed."

"I was hired as a quality inspector and am more than adequately trained for my job. But I feel here that I'm the one being inspected."

Martin keeps the younger workers on Floor One under rigid discipline, and they complain to their supervisor that they are not being given responsibility. They are being asked to do only routine work. This makes them feel that they are not learning as much as they might in other places. Younger workers ask few questions of either Martin or the older workers; they rarely talk to anyone.

The older workers' attitude is different, as the following statements show:

"I like working with Mr. Martin. I know a lot of the workers complain about him because he's particular and checks on them. Personally, I'd rather work on this floor than anywhere else for exactly that reason. Everything here is done properly."

"I picked this floor because I liked the supervision here. I worked with Mr. Martin while I was a trainee and I knew what to expect. I honestly feel I still need a responsible person nearby to supervise me. I need guidance, and therefore I prefer to work on a floor where there is a fairly strict supervisor. On some of the other floors things are too slipshod."

"I like things done in an orderly fashion. I prefer to work hard and get it done with, and then relax. Mr. Martin doesn't believe in relaxation at all, but I can see his point. After all, you have these orders that have to be taken care of as quickly as possible. He's got to lay down the law to us to a certain extent. I keep telling my wife how lucky she is to be in her line of work. Everything in her place is buddy-buddy. But I guess with this work it just can't be that way. The head man has to be strict in order to get the work done. Isn't that right?"

"Some of the supervisors are great to work with, but others just aren't good at supervising. They don't know how to communicate. Now when Martin is on, it is altogether different. He knows how to get things done right the first time."

The relationships on Floor One tend to be formal and impersonal. There is very little give-and-take or camaraderie. Martin equitably divides and clearly assigns the work, and no one complains that his workers are slack in carrying out their tasks. Yet when Martin is off the floor, there is evidence of antagonism between the older workers and the younger workers.

Floor Two

The atmosphere on Floor Two is informal and friendly. Workers discuss their problems with one another, and there is a good deal of talk and good-natured horseplay.

Mr. Franklin, the shop manager, spends much of his time on the floor helping with problems and informally chatting with workers. He often consults with workers about quality problems and changes in procedures.

Franklin expresses his attitude about supervision as follows: "The shop has changed since I was a trainee. At that time, it was just losing the old military discipline and becoming more reasonable in its approach. Nowadays you've got to trust that your employees can and will accept responsibility for the quality of their own work. If I was always looking over their shoulders, I'd go nuts, and they'd rebel."

Franklin encourages interaction among the workers and a group approach to problem solving. He set up a task team to study the process of end-line inspection and rubber-stamped their recommendations to cut back resources at that point. He also set up a system in which quality control responsibility is rotated to the various members within each work group. The system seems to work well, because the workers are happy with it. There is some concern, however, that more supervision and tracking of the system may be necessary.

Franklin deliberately shares authority with his assistant, allowing him to order supplies and supervise certain tasks. He consults with him when making decisions. When Franklin is absent, the assistant supervises much as Franklin does. There is little difference in the atmosphere on the floor whether Franklin or his assistant is in charge.

One of the younger workers on Franklin's floor describes the situation as follows: "I like it here. On this floor we can all speak up whenever we feel like it, and we get along fine. The workers on this floor are very good to work with. Mr. Franklin is an excellent manager, and there is good spirit."

The older workers feel somewhat differently:

"Franklin is a very nice person, and everyone has been great to me, but I don't think the organization is as strict as it used to be. I get nervous about mistakes being made. It's very easy to forget something. It happened to me once."

"I don't know whether I'm doing a good job or not. Maybe there are complaints about my work. If so, I never hear about it. I just have to assume that I'm doing all right. Sometimes I wish that somebody would come along to check up and let me know when I do things wrong and how I can improve. I must have plenty of room for improvement."

Franklin says that he enjoys training new workers but has some problems in maintaining discipline. Trainees seem to be accepted as an integral part of the social group. They take part in informal discussions and are free to ask questions.

The relationships among the different groups of workers on Franklin's floor are easy and informal, and there is a strong spirit of camaraderie. On the other hand, there is some confusion as to who is accountable for what. One worker explains it as follows: "Franklin believes we should all be responsible for our own work and making sure that we don't pass mistakes on to the next guy. Personally, I'm glad I'm not policed, but I wonder how many folks out there aren't just sliding by, figuring no one's looking that closely and that whatever happens 'the group' will take care of its own anyway. I don't know; seems to me someone's gotta be the one to take the fall if something's not right. Right?"

The workers do say that if they had a problem they would feel comfortable taking it straight to Franklin.

Questions for Discussion

1. What are the major characteristics of the two floors? What are the major differences in management styles between Floor One and Floor Two?

2. If you were purchasing a pacemaker, would you prefer one made on Floor One or Floor Two? Why?

3. Assuming you could design a new floor—Floor Three—what attributes of Floors One and Two would you use? Why?

45

THE FIRST FEDERAL BANK*

After graduating from Boston University's MBA program three years ago, 27-year-old Susan Pasqualari accepted a job in the marketing department of The First Federal Bank in Des Moines, Iowa. While her salary level and title have not changed in more than a year, her work environment has. From a reasonably pleasant though intense situation, Susan now finds herself dreading to go to work in what has become an atmosphere filled with stress and insecurity. She has become increasingly unhappy, and she is concerned because she knows that her unhappiness shows in the quality of her work.

Last Wednesday, Susan's immediate supervisor, Liz Dickey, called her into her office and gave her a verbal warning.

"Look," Liz had said, "you've missed two deadlines recently. I was told that I had to talk to you about it. We both know that things aren't easy around here, but I'm under a lot of pressure, and if I didn't say anything to you, it wouldn't do either of us any good." Despite Liz's assurances that she was only passing along what she was told to and that she knew that Susan had always done outstanding work before, Susan had walked out of the meeting shaken. In the past, Liz had seemed to know innately how to motivate Susan, inspiring her to give every project a 110 percent effort. If Susan needed help or advice, she had always found Liz's door open. Now something had changed.

Background

During the first two years after she had been hired, Susan had been promoted a number of times. For the last year and a half she has been the product manager for personal account credit services for the bank's major depositors of $25,000 and up. Since starting that position, she and Liz, who was the product management coordinator, have had a great working relationship. In Susan's eyes, her slightly older boss was "God's gift to marketing." In turn, Liz had faith in Susan's work and helped her make and meet goals and deadlines.

Each day at around 4:30, Liz would check in with each of her four product managers to get an update on the day's activities, work out the next day's priorities, and get an overall progress report. When Susan was the last in Liz's round of check-ins, the two would go up to Jay Anderson's office to chat. Jay was the director of private bank marketing and was someone Susan always enjoyed. In fact, she loved this part of the day. The few minutes of transition between work and her half-hour trip home allowed her to relax, plan her evening, and discuss work problems or questions in a comfortable and informal setting. Liz, believing that a friendly environment and flexible management style were best for productivity, encouraged Susan to ask Jay marketing-related questions directly rather than go through her.

* Copyright 1993 by Fred P. Roe. Used with permission.

Nine months ago, Susan had returned refreshed from a week's vacation on a Caribbean island. She had received a generous year-end raise, despite a sour year for the bank, and she was optimistic that the coming year would be successful. Liz had written rave reviews about her in her annual evaluation, and the marketing program that Susan had been working on was soon to be completed. However, Susan's expectations of the new year turned out to be anything but accurate.

Within the first week after Susan's return, Liz announced the dates of her maternity leave. To Susan's surprise, instead of taking the usual six weeks, Liz planned to take six months and said she would then be returning on a part-time basis only. Although Jay knew that Susan, or one of several other product managers could temporarily fill Liz's position, he decided that the job would remain unfilled for the length of Liz's maternity leave. He asked the product managers to report to him directly and to take over the paperwork and some other duties for which Liz had been responsible. Having established a strong relationship with Jay, Susan took the transition well. As much as she was sad to see Liz go, Susan was sure that this would be a good opportunity to expand her understanding of the work.

This arrangement worked well for almost five months until one Friday afternoon when Jay dropped the proverbial "bomb." Walking into Jay's comfortable office, Susan was greeted abruptly with, "We have to talk."

Looking out at the nearby skyscrapers, Jay began in a slow and controlled voice. "You and I have had a great relationship since you came to the bank," he said. "So, I wanted you to hear this from me rather than through the grapevine or some silly memo a few weeks from now."

Susan tensed, sensing from Jay's tone and what he had said thus far that she wasn't going to like what she was about to hear.

"I've been offered a job at another company," he told her. "I'll be a senior partner at a marketing firm in Sioux City. The firm is fairly small, but they have plans for expansion, and there's a merger in their near future. I'm not at liberty to talk about it right now," he continued, "but in eighteen months, if you're interested, I think there might be a job there for you. I've told the bank's president about my new position, and he agreed to let me resign immediately. He says they'll probably replace me with someone from the outside."

"I'm happy for you," Susan told him, feeling a lump starting in her throat. "It sounds like a great opportunity."

After a long hug, Susan left Jay's office and started home.

"This just can't be good," she thought to herself as she got into her new V.W. Jetta. "I've lost two bosses and good friends in less than six months."

Change Comes Rapidly

Over the next few weeks, Susan found herself constantly on the elevator to go up to the executive suite to get the necessary approvals and directions for her current projects from the bank's vice president for marketing, Stefan Smith. Stefan always seemed pleased to see her and often complimented her on the thorough quality of her work. On more than one occasion he invited her to sit down and talk about her views on the bank's overall marketing strategies and her suggestions for improvements and innovations.

Susan liked working at the top. Not only was she working on her own project, but Stefan increasingly asked her to take on projects left behind by Liz and Jay. Because of her hard work and her open and friendly demeanor, Susan was well liked by the other top executives and by the various clerks and secretaries.

Six weeks after Jay had left, Liz returned from maternity leave, having made the decision to return full-time after all. Instead of Liz taking over on the trips upstairs, she and Susan now went together. For Susan, it was terrific. She had more responsibility, more challenge, and she also had Liz back. Unfortunately, the fun did not last long.

Karina Bulle

Several weeks later, Karina Bulle, middle-aged and with strong credentials in both the marketing and financial fields, was hired to fill Jay's position. She had come from another bank, and using their contacts, Liz and Susan "checked her out" before she started. At first all they heard was that she was "very good at getting things done." But the weekend before Karina was to move into Jay's office, Susan ran into an old friend. Telling her about her new boss, her friend chuckled.

"She sure gets around," Susan's friend said. "In the last twenty years, she's worked for about twelve different organizations. Good luck!"

Susan asked her friend to explain, but her friend declined, merely adding, "You'll see. She's really efficient!"

On her first day, Karina circulated a printed schedule of thirty-minute meetings with each of the product managers and Liz. The note at the bottom of the schedule read, "Be prompt. Time is money."

A few minutes before Susan's appointment, Liz stopped by her desk.

"Well, I've had my appointment," Liz groaned. "It started and ended exactly according to schedule. Maybe I ought to work part-time after all. Good luck. She's no Jay."

It didn't take long for Susan to realize this for herself. Jay's comfortable couch and small desk had been replaced with small wooden chairs and a mammoth desk adorned with only a clock and a single pad of paper. There were no family pictures, no plants, and no other signs of life.

Karina started almost before Susan sat down.

"Here is what I expect from you, Susanne."

Susan was about to correct Karina's pronunciation, but she was prevented from doing so as Karina continued without pause.

"Do your work, do it right, and do it by my deadlines. When you are finished, you will give it to Ms. Dickey, and she will give it to me. If you have a problem, see Ms. Dickey. I don't want to hear about it unless it's from her," Karina told her. "As part of my responsibilities here, the bank has put me in charge of purchasing a new computer system for the marketing department. We will be replacing the personal computers with a mainframe. When it goes online, I will measure your productivity from my terminal. Your project is scheduled to be finished next Monday. It will be done by then, won't it?"

Susan started to answer but was immediately interrupted by Karina's droning voice.

"Good," she said flatly. "And one more thing, anything that leaves this office will do so through channels. I have heard that you often visit upstairs. That will be unnecessary from now on. Now I have another appointment."

Karina stopped talking and began to write notes on the pad of paper on her desk.

Realizing that she had been dismissed, Susan nodded and quickly left the office. She felt frustrated, tense, and like she wanted to cry. Slowly, she wandered back to her desk. She couldn't think right. The rest of the day she spent staring at her computer. It was no great machine, but Susan liked it, and she knew how to use it. The very next day it was replaced by an alien monitor and keyboard. The thick manual provided little information besides instructions on how to sign on.

Despite her personal goal of trying to finish her project a week early, Susan missed her deadline and only finished the morning after it was due. To manage even that, Susan had had to get a secretary from the executive pool to do her a favor and type the first fifty or so pages into the new computer system. Because neither Susan nor the secretary knew how to use the new spell-checker or the graphics component, the report still contained a few typos and missing graphs when she handed it to Liz. Both Liz and Susan knew she was capable of better quality work, but because the report was overdue, Liz presented it to Karina with the errors left in.

The next morning, Susan came in late. On her desk was a terse memo from Karina clipped to the cover page of her report. The memo was addressed to "All Personal Banking Marketing Employees."

"Recent work produced by a member of this department is very disappointing. Let me make clear that quality and timeliness are critical to your continued employment."

"I need this job," Susan thought to herself. "But this is impossible. I don't know whether I can hold on until Jay needs me, if he ever does. He says it might still be months before the merger is complete and the job he has in mind for me is available. I can't afford to be out of work that long, and there aren't many options open right now."

"Liz is right," she announced out loud to no one in particular. "Karina's no Jay. But as far as those people who claimed that Karina's good at getting things done, I have some real questions about that!"

Questions for Discussion

1. Using French and Raven's analysis of the bases of power in organizational settings, identify and describe the sources of power that Susan, Liz, Jay, Stefan, and Karina have and how they use them.

2. Using a leadership theory, compare and contrast Karina's and Liz's leadership styles.

3. What effect is Karina's leadership style likely to have on Susan and the other employees? Why?

4. If you were Liz, what would you do to help Susan keep her job?.

46

THE ELEVENTH HOUR: A FISH BOWL ROLE PLAY

Objectives

- To explore the dynamics that make groups effective or ineffective
- To practice methods for dealing with various group dynamics

Background

You have been assigned to a group in a class that requires a group project. The grade you receive for the project will be the same as every other member of your group.

You took the course partly because you had heard it was a terrific opportunity to learn about effective groups. From your own work experience, and from reading articles in business publications like *The Wall Street Journal* and *Forbes*, you know that the current business climate absolutely requires workers to be able to function effectively in groups.

As part of the project, you are required to keep a budget and make regular reports to the professor. If the financial reports have mistakes, you will be assessed fines. At the end of the project, your group has to be solvent in order to get a grade above a 'C.'

The members of your group, including yourself, are Pat, Chris, Lee, and Billy. (You will be assigned one of these four roles.) Pat and Chris met in a class a year ago and are good friends. Before you started the project, Lee and Billy did not know either Pat or Chris, nor did they know each other.

Pat

Pat's family has always stressed the importance of good grades. Pat has a 3.8 grade point average.

Chris

Chris is taking a full course load and is also working almost forty hours a week. Chris has always gotten good job performance reviews at work and is considered to be an excellent and dedicated worker. Chris has vowed to do everything possible to be a good group member and to attend the group meetings regularly. However, Chris has often made vague excuses for why a particular meeting time is not acceptable.

Lee

Lee is intelligent and very creative but really does not like things that have to do with math. In addition, when the group conversation is not related specifically to Lee's part in the group project, Lee seems distracted. Lee also seems to agree to things without really thinking about them.

Billy

Billy seems to work hard but also seems to take a long time to understand what's going on in the project. It's often difficult to understand Billy's ideas and comments.

Meeting #1

Your group had a great beginning. First you set a number of dates and times for group meetings, and you found it relatively easy to do this. Of course, everyone was busy. Pat, for example, mentioned a chess club meeting that was on Thursday nights, but the group managed to work around it.

Next, you got down to assigning roles for the project. You discussed whether or not your group should have a leader. Pat, particularly, argued in favor of having a leader. Finally, after a long discussion, you all agreed that everyone should be equal and that you would operate without a leader.

You then decided what other roles needed to be assigned. Chris volunteered to be the marketing director, Pat agreed to be the campaign manager, and Billy volunteered to be the secretary. Lee didn't express a preference. The remaining role that needed to be filled was that of finance manager. Lee said, "Well, I suppose I can do it if that's what we need." You all questioned Lee to make sure it was really acceptable, and Lee assured you that it was.

The project was on its way.

Meeting #3

The day before the third meeting, Billy found out that a relative needed to be picked up at the airport the next day. Unfortunately, the plane was due to arrive at the exact same time that the group meeting was to start. Billy called each of you, and the meeting was moved back three hours. Everyone was willing to change the meeting time.

Meeting #4

The fourth meeting was scheduled for Friday at 6 p.m. Everyone was supposed to come with a written list of ideas for organizing the project. Pat showed up at 5:50, and Lee was there by 6:00. Billy arrived at 6:10 and began talking with Pat and Lee. A few minutes later, a friend of Lee's walked by the meeting room. Lee got up and talked to the friend for the next fifteen minutes. Just as they were finishing their conversation, Chris rushed in and apologized for being late. Pat said, "Don't worry about it."

Pat started the meeting by suggesting that everyone share their list of suggestions. Chris had forgotten to bring it. Billy claimed that you had all agreed to develop the list at this meeting.

Pat laughed it off and suggested taking what you had and begin to develop the plan together. This was successful.

You scheduled the next meeting and decided to use it to begin some of the technical aspects of the project.

Meeting #5

Billy was in a car accident and couldn't make the meeting. You understood and, with some difficulty, found another time to meet.

Meeting #6

Pat showed up early as usual. Chris came on time, and Lee was ten minutes late. Billy came twenty-five minutes late and told you about how emotionally draining the accident had been.

After a few minutes, Chris suggested that you get started. Pat had sketched out many of the technical details but said that this was just a starting point and that you should work together to make the necessary modifications.

As Pat was explaining the details, a friend of Lee's walked by. Lee hadn't seen this friend in a while and jumped up to chat. After fifteen minutes, Lee returned to the group.

As Pat was explaining the ideas, Lee seemed distracted and was doodling. Then, Chris got up and said, apologetically, "I didn't think this meeting would last so long. I have another commitment. I'm already late, and I have to go."

Lee and Billy agreed with most of Pat's ideas and provided very little additional input. The meeting ended.

Meeting #8

At the eighth meeting, you got a letter from the professor. Because of some financial miscalculations, you had been assessed a fine. Lee had made a major mistake, and it was going to cost.

You spent about ten minutes discussing your feelings about the fine and then went on to discuss the project. Pat presented several ideas for discussion. Lee seemed distracted and was doodling. Billy was quiet and didn't contribute anything.

After a few minutes, Billy and Lee got into a side conversation about Lee's friend. Pat and Chris continued to work on the details of the group project.

At the end of the meeting, since Billy was an expert on the computer, Pat assigned Billy to create a graphic that would be used for the project. Billy said it would be done by Saturday.

After scheduling the next meeting, you all left at 10:00 p.m.

Meeting #11

It is now Saturday morning. You are about to begin the eleventh meeting.

Instructions

Step 1 (15 minutes)

Read the background information on the group and its members. You will also be given a role description. Read this carefully as well. Do not share the details of your role with others in the class, especially your other group members. Decide what you will say to your other group members and how you will behave at the eleventh meeting.

Step 2 (10 minutes)

One group will be selected to role play the eleventh meeting while the rest of the class observes. Observers should look for both effective and ineffective behaviors and for strategies for dealing with the situation.

As a role player, the more real you can make the situation, the more effective the learning will be. Get into your role. Be the person. Remember, this is your group, and you want it to be successful.

Step 3 (full class: open-ended)

Explore the effective and ineffective behaviors, and make recommendations for improvement.

Step 4 (10 minutes for the role play and open-ended discussion)

Repeat Steps 2 and 3. Each round should have a different group in the fish bowl.

Step 5 (open-ended)

General class discussion.

Questions for Discussion

1. What assumptions did each of the role players appear to be making about one another? What was the result of these assumptions?

2. Were the groups able to resolve their conflicts? Why or why not?

3. In what ways could group members have been more supportive of one another? If they had been more supportive, how do you feel the outcomes would have differed?

4. Did all of the role players accept responsibility for the current problem? If some did not, what was the impact of this on the group and its process?

5. What could this group have done differently that might have resulted in a healthier process and better resolution?

6. In what ways did the process change and improve with successive role plays? To what do you attribute this improvement?

47

THE TROUBLEMAKER*

Background

In 1981, Derek Hornfeldt became engineering manager for Belle Technologies' Robotics Division. He was hired at a time when the division was facing severe managerial shortages caused by rapid growth and a poor labor market. Since that time, Derek's division has had a slow but steady improvement in market share. Today, Belle Technologies is one of the five largest organizations in Brockton, Massachusetts, employing 600 workers locally and 1,000 more at other plants and offices in New York, Rhode Island, and Connecticut. The annual revenues of Belle are approximately $200 million.

Industry experts claim that Belle's ongoing success has been due to numerous innovations by a staff of experienced engineers. The Belle engineers work as individual contributors rather than as team members, although they occasionally provide each other with advice and support.

By 1990, Derek supervised fifteen robotics engineers in two divisions. Five veteran engineers work in Process Engineering, which focuses on finding the best ways to assemble new products. The rest work in Product Engineering. The senior engineers are responsible for new products, primarily SACRA robots. These are complex and sophisticated machines capable of three-dimensional movement. Custom-designed for industrial users, the high-quality SACRA robots are subject to frequent design revisions as the engineers attempt to keep up with fast-changing technology. Many of the products are purchased for $100,000 to $500,000 by motor vehicle manufacturers. Despite their high price, the robots were designed to make assembly procedures more efficient, thereby reducing personnel and labor costs.

The remaining engineers work with Cartesian robots that sell for $30,000 to $120,000. These devices can only move on an X and Y axis and are limited to such simple and straightforward tasks as inserting electronic components into printed circuit boards. Derek assigns newly hired college recruits to work with these robots. Cartesian robots are a "cash cow" for Belle Technologies: they make decent profits on a predictable basis without anything but word-of-mouth advertising. The engineers assigned to work on them are expected to do simple "fire-fighting"—solving production bottlenecks and making sure everything matches the design engineers' specifications.

Derek has a B.S. in Electronic Engineering for a New York college, and an MBA from a small school in Rhode Island. Over the years, he hasn't kept up with the electrical engineering technology, preferring to focus on being a manager and a "people person." No one who has worked for him could deny that he is a nice guy—good humored, personable, and friendly. If someone came in with a $20 expense report that needed his signature, Derek

---

* Copyright 1994 by Scott Weighart. Used with permission.

would joke, "Spending my money again, huh?" When he returned from taking his wife and children to Europe, he showed his vacation pictures to every engineer in the group, not wanting anyone to feel excluded. Derek never yelled at his workers, and he avoided giving feedback that could possibly hurt anyone's feelings.

Derek had several responsibilities as the supervisor of fifteen engineers. First, he had to approve every EEJ (Equipment Expenditure Justification). Any capital equipment costing more than $20,000 had to go through this proposal process. If Derek approved the EEJ, he would forward it to his boss, Bob Spiers, who would give it a quick look before initialing it and sending it to Belle's finance department along with an authorization form. No one outside the organization ever saw this paperwork.

Derek had a keen eye when editing the proposals, and he insisted on professional work. Before he approved any EEJ, he would carefully proofread it, circling any typos or sentences in which the diction was lacking or the sentence structure was awkward. If the document wasn't printed in an attractive typeface—Derek felt that Times and Palatino were the best fonts—he would send it back to be redone. Almost all the EEJs were submitted by the process and product engineers working on the new SACRA robots; these engineers often claimed they needed newer, better, and—inevitably—more expensive machines for manufacturing. While they grumbled about Derek's editing, he would remind them politely that quality was the top priority.

In terms of watching costs, Derek was a hawk. He demanded accountability on even the smallest purchases. "I still remember the look on Jaime Polatin's face when I told him to report to my office immediately so I could ask him why he needed to buy four plastic bushings for twelve cents each," Derek recalls smiling. "It seemed like he couldn't believe how on top of the details I was. He was just speechless."

When asked how he motivated workers, Derek said, "Workers are different; they need to be managed in different ways. I treat my experienced guys one way and the college kids another way.

"My philosophy is to throw the recruits into the water to teach them how to swim," Derek said. "But keep in mind that I would never have them do anything that could make the division look bad if they screwed up. Basically, I tell them that their job is to solve any problems that come up. I purposely try to have as little contact with them as possible." Although the inexperienced workers got anxious about their new assignments—"I never see my boss" and "I hope I'm doing a good job" were typical comments—Derek believed this was the best way for them to learn.

"Just about everything I know about engineering," Derek said, "I learned from my own mistakes. About all I ever did was remind them that I expected greatness from them, and there's no limit to how high they can go if they put in the effort."

The young product engineers spend about 50 percent of each day in meetings where they are updated about product sales, production figures, and procedural difficulties. For the rest of the day, they take care of administrative details such as paperwork. Some will occasionally seek out the more experienced engineers in other groups for assistance.

Each year Derek had been manager, four new engineers were hired. Generally, just one of the four was still at Belle a year later.

"We hire the top students from WPI, MIT, BU," Derek said. "Unfortunately, they have no practical experience, so the learning curve is pretty long. Some are just talented but impatient kids who want it all yesterday. Other companies try to scoop them up with all kinds of smooth talk, and some take the bait. That's life."

Derek Hornfeldt treated his experienced engineers very differently. "These guys are working on crucial projects that are worth a fortune to the company, so I make sure to walk through every step with them," he said. "I check in with each of them as much as six times a day, asking if all the basic specs are right, making sure the blueprints are neatly drawn, finding out if they followed procedure when checking prices on parts—everything."

"I ask them if they want to bounce ideas off me or even if they have any personal problems," Derek added. "Sometimes they call me a mother hen or say that I am their personal problem. I don't take it personally. This is stressful work. Things get tense. Somebody might blow up and tell me to get out of their hair, but nobody stays mad. I buy doughnuts for everyone, and they're all happy again."

The Troublemaker

"I had a real troublemaker in my department," Derek said, "an experienced engineer named Ted Olin. He's an extremely bright guy, but he seemed to think he knew everything about my job.

Last April, Ted showed up in Derek's office after hearing rumors that the division might be split up. "I'm telling you, there are some problems here that have to be dealt with, for your own good as well as for the good of the department," Ted had told Derek. "For one thing, our department has a 50 percent turnover rate. Eight out of fifteen engineers have been replaced in the last year."

"Ted, you're overreacting," Derek had responded. "Three of those eight were just college kids. In this job market, they're not hard to replace."

Ted rolled his eyes. "Fine. Then what about the rest? What about Jamie Polatin? He was one of our top engineers, and he left. Do you really think it was the money? The word from the guys is that he felt suffocated here."

"Listen, Ted," Derek said. "My style is to groom people for bigger and better things. As a result, sometimes we have to lose good people. If I'm developing people for better opportunities, then I'm doing a good job."

"Well, people are certainly moving on to bigger and better things—I'll agree with you there," Ted had said, walking out of Derek's office. For the next month, Ted didn't say much of anything to his boss. Derek was glad that he hadn't heard anything more from him, figuring the matter had been forgotten.

In late June, however, Ted walked into Derek's office and tossed a completed EEJ for a wave-soldering machine on the desk.

"Yesterday," Ted fumed, "I showed this to a senior engineer in the Industrial Controls Division. Do you know what he said to me when he saw the length and detail of it? He said 'What the hell are you trying to do? Write a Russian novel? In his division, they don't have to waste time making a simple EEJ look like a literary masterpiece.'"

Derek cleared his throat, but Ted kept talking.

"Anyway, we really need this machine, and when I asked you about it in March, you kept insisting that I get one for less than $28,000. So I put in all kinds of hours and finally found a used one that could do the basic functions for a lower price. So today—and I want you to hear this from me first—I showed this to your boss, and he said, 'Let's not buy a Hyundai if we can afford a Cadillac.'"

Derek was uneasy; he hated confrontations. "Now Ted," he started, "hear me out: Why buy a Mercedes when a Toyota will get you from one place to the next just as well?"

Ted sneered. "Well, let me ask you this then, Derek, why do you own a BMW when you could have bought yourself a nice used Ford Taurus?"

Derek thought for a moment about his beloved BMW.

"Bob really said we could spend more?"

"He said we could easily justify $65,000."

"Well, I guess it's okay then."

Ted shook his head. "You really stand up for what you believe in, don't you?" he said sarcastically.

After Ted left, Derek took four antacid tablets and popped them into his mouth. It seemed as if there was no pleasing Ted Olin, and they got along best when Derek didn't talk to him at all.

The Bonus

At the end of August, Bob Spiers reported to Derek that he had been hearing complaints from some senior engineers about Derek "breathing down their necks."

"It's Ted," Derek thought. No one else had made a similar complaint to him recently.

"Another thing," Bob told him, "performance review is coming up. We have enough money in the budget to justify a five percent increase in your department's payroll. Split it up as you see fit, but be careful: I don't want to hear an avalanche of new complaints from your engineers."

For the next three nights Derek could barely sleep. He was worried about how to divide up the bonus money without getting anyone angry. Finally, he thought he had a really good solution: He would treat everyone the same—no favorites. Even Ted would get as much as anyone else.

On the following Friday, Derek met with each of the fifteen engineers privately. He gave each a five percent pay increase and told them they were all outstanding performers. He directly quoted the definition of "outstanding work" from Belle Technologies' Performance Appraisal Manual. Everyone, including Ted Olin, seemed happy or pleasantly surprised, and Derek assumed when he overheard several engineers making plans to go out together after work that it was to celebrate. Derek was pleased with himself.

The Climate Grows Cold

The following Monday, Derek was surprised that several of his top performers seemed unhappy and reluctant to talk to him. One even pointedly walked away when Derek stopped to chat.

When he walked back to his office late in the morning, there was a voice-mail message from Bob Spiers. Bob had decided to split up the division; Derek would now manage three employees in the packaging and shipping department. Indranil Sinha, one of the senior engineers, was put in charge of the college recruits working on the Cartesian robots. The final insult was that Ted Olin, the "troublemaker" who had given Derek so many headaches, had been named to manage the other eleven engineers.

Questions for Discussion

1. What went wrong and why?

2. Using a situational leadership theory, analyze Derek Hornfeldt's leadership style with his various workers as well as the situational needs of these workers.

3. What sources of power does Derek have available to him? Analyze whether he uses these sources effectively and what the outcomes are.

4. What recommendations would you make to the new managers for leading their respective workers? How can they best use the sources of power?

48

THE OUTSPOKEN EMPLOYEE*

You work for a prominent management consulting firm where your job is to serve as a coach to middle and upper managers for a variety of your firm's clients. Jayne Graham, the director of human resources at a firm of 78 employees, has just told you the following story:

"Several months ago, we started having monthly meetings at which employees were encouraged to bring up any issue of concern to them. Generally, we go around the room, and each employee has a turn to talk.

At today's meeting, one employee started off by telling us that he had many issues to discuss and that he didn't want to be interrupted.

Almost every issue he brought up was degrading to our company president. He said it was the president's fault if we failed, the president didn't know how to run the business, and that the president should resign. He also claimed that we offered an employee a lot of money to stay.

At one point, the president asked the employee if he was finished with his comments. The employee pretty much barked at him, saying, 'No, I'm not finished, and don't interrupt me until I am finished.'

We let him finish, and then the president told him he wasn't going to comment since most of the things that were said were untrue.

The employee said, 'Tell me just one of the issues that is untrue.'

The president told him that we didn't offer money to any employee to stay. The response from the employee was, 'I don't believe you, because you're a liar.'

The president looked at me and told me to tell him how much we offered the employee in question to stay. I answered without thinking, and then I also told him that the money issue is none of his business and what we say to other employees is none of his business.

He told me I was a liar, too, and no one in the room should believe me. After the meeting, I told the president and vice president that we should terminate this employee immediately. The vice president says that since we told the employees that the meeting was an open forum where anyone could bring up any issues of importance to them, they should be able to speak their minds. I disagree, but I don't want to send the wrong message to the rest of the employees.

What do you think we should do?"

* Copyright 2000 by Paul Lyons, Frostburg State University. Used with permission.

Questions for Discussion

1. What would you advise Jayne to do next? Why?

2. What do you think the company should do about what took place? Now? In the future? Why?

3. What do you think of the advisability of this kind of meeting? Why?

49

THE X-Y SCALE*

Objectives

- To examine beliefs about employee motivation as it applies to Theory X and Theory Y
- To explore the likely outcomes of both Theory X and Theory Y leadership

Instructions

For each of the following statements, circle the answer that best completes it for you:

1. When a person is not working up to capacity, I am likely to assume that
   A. it is because she or he is inherently lazy.
   B. the lack of productivity is a result of the person's experience and that the situation can be changed.

2. I believe that the best way to motivate employees is to
   A. tell them what to do and how and when to do it.
   B. provide them with objectives to which they can be committed.

3. I believe that most people work because
   A. they are seeking security.
   B. they are attempting to fulfill ego/esteem or self-actualization needs.

4. When delegating work, I am likely to
   A. assume that some of the work will need to be redone.
   B. do so with confidence, assuming that the work will be done correctly.

5. In searching for a creative solution to an organizational problem, I would be likely to ask for input
   A. only from a select few.
   B. from all levels of the organization.

6. I believe that most people
   A. actively avoid taking on responsibilities in the workplace.
   B. actively seek taking on responsibilities in the workplace.

* This exercise was written by Gail E. Gilmore.

7. When a manager goes on vacation, I believe that employees are likely to
   A. use the absence as an opportunity to slack off.
   B. keep up their usual level of productivity.

8. I believe that employees will
   A. use up all their sick time, even when they're not sick, simply because they are entitled to do so.
   B. usually take sick time only when they are sick.

9. I believe that most employees want to
   A. have decisions in the workplace made for them.
   B. be a part of the decision-making process.

10. I believe that most employees consider work to be
    A. a necessary evil.
    B. an opportunity to contribute to society.

Scoring

Assign 1 point for each "A" answer, 2 points for each "B" answer, and total the points.

If your score falls between 16–20, you probably adhere to Theory Y principles.

If your score falls between 10–14, you most likely adhere to Theory X principles.

If your score is 15, you probably adhere to some of the principles of both theories.

Questions for Discussion

1. Under what circumstances would a Theory X leadership style be more appropriate than Theory Y leadership? Under what circumstances would a Theory Y leadership style be more appropriate?

2. Discuss the relationship between Theory X and Theory Y and the concept of self-fulfilling prophecy. How do they interact?

3. What are some of the possible positive and negative outcomes using Theory X leadership or Theory Y leadership for an organization?

50

DANGER: RADIO ACTIVITY HITS COUNTRY IN LONG ISLAND*

Barbara Lankford and Max Vaughn looked at each other uneasily as they walked through the hallways of the radio station where they worked. They were about to meet Rex Honeycutt, the new owner of WPOP Radio, 98.6 FM on your dial, in Smithtown, Long Island. Although she didn't look forward to it, Barbara figured she'd find a way to handle the new boss; Max was more apprehensive, wondering what his fate would be.

Many rumors had been going around the office; some said that Honeycutt planned radical changes for the station. When they sat down in Honeycutt's office, Barbara and Max's worst fears were confirmed. Honeycutt greeted them, giving Max a handshake and a hard slap on the back. Barbara noticed a brass spittoon on the floor alongside Honeycutt's desk. As he laid out his plans for the future of the radio station, he paused occasionally to spit out a mouthful of juice from the wad of tobacco he had stored in his cheek.

"Well, boys and girls," Honeycutt said, "I reckon you're mighty curious about how things are gonna be with a new cowboy leading the herd down here in Smithtown. So here's the big news: This here station is about to be turned upside down. I got an idea that's hotter than Alabama asphalt."

Barbara and Max glanced at each other in despair.

"First off, as of next week," Honeycutt said, "we are gonna have the first all-country music station in all of Long Island! From now on our official call letters are gonna be WAOK. Has a nice ring, don't you think?"

Honeycutt explained that he had done a great deal of industry and demographic research about making such a move. WPOP's ratings—and advertising revenue—had reached an all-time low. Until just over a year ago, WPOP-FM had been a big hit. More recently, ratings had sagged as listeners began to tune into a more powerful, all-mix station from New York City.

DJ "Mad Max" Vaughn had been an extremely popular local celebrity for quite a number of years. Lately, though, fewer fans had been asking for his autograph when he walked through the Smithtown Mall. Hospitalized teenagers no longer requested his autographs, and one sponsor had recently canceled Max's on-air endorsements of their products. Still, Vaughn liked to think that there was a "silent majority" of Long Islanders who loved him.

As for Barbara Lankford, advertising sales manager, she was horrified to think about what the change would mean for her. She had built up great relationships with the advertising executives of local companies; now it seemed as if all her hard work would be wasted.

After meeting with Rex Honeycutt, first together and then separately, Max and Barbara went out for a long lunch to discuss the situation.

* This case was written by Scott Weighart

"This guy's going to make me pull all my hair out within two weeks. I can't believe I'm saying this, but already I miss Craig," Barbara said, referring to the station's previous owner.

Max nodded. "Yeah, I know," he said sadly. "Craig didn't treat us like we were in some kind of radio kindergarten."

Max and Barbara had both been offended by Honeycutt's order-giving style during their first meeting. Handing a pen and a pad to Barbara—which made her feel like a secretary—Honeycutt had named a long list of companies and had told her to call their advertising managers immediately.

"I used to work at a country station in Virginia," she said. "You wouldn't believe the kind of 'folksy-folks' you have to deal with."

Barbara pulled a paper out of her purse and read Honeycutt's list of potential advertisers: Red Snake Chewing Tobacco, Real-Valu Hardware, QTP and Puritan Motor Oil, the Crawfish County Tourist Bureau, and John Foxe Tractors.

"I'm surprised he didn't name any chain saw companies," she said.

"You're still better off than I am," Max responded. "He told me he was changing the name of my show. Instead of hosting 'The Mad Max Hit Parade,' I now get to be DJ for 'The MAXimum Country Hour.' He also said that I had to start my next show with that song 'I Don't Care if It Rains or Freezes, as Long as I Got My . . . .' well, you know. Plus he's going to decide my whole play list—every song—every day—for our first week of playing country."

"Ridiculous," Barbara said. "The guy's been in Long Island for two weeks, and he acts like we're the ones who are clueless about local radio."

Craig Sugerman had taken a very different approach to running the business. At first, Barbara had found him to be frustrating. He had constantly given them extremely vague memos. "Sell a few ads this morning" was the memo he sent to Barb on her first morning at the job. She walked to his office, hoping he would give her some idea of exactly how she was supposed to go about doing this, but his secretary had told her that he was meditating and couldn't be disturbed. When Barbara tried again in the early afternoon, she was told that Craig had invited some electronic engineers over for a "power lunch."

This lack of interaction was especially frustrating, since Craig's memos generally ended on some inspirational note: "I expect you to do everything possible to make us the best radio station west of Syosset."

Eventually, Barb realized she would have to do as well as she could by learning from her mistakes. She stopped seeking advice or attempting to confront her boss with complaints. After six months on the job, she was no longer bothered by his lack of specific instructions, and until just about a year ago, she had been the top-grossing radio time salesperson on Long Island. Several competing stations had tried to woo her away, but she realized that she appreciated the autonomy of her job at WPOP, and she knew she could handle it.

Still, Barb often had wished that Craig would meet with her occasionally, give her some feedback, or work together with her to brainstorm about new ad possibilities. She felt somewhat unappreciated, and sometimes she had trouble getting out of bed to go to work.

As for Max, he thought Craig had been the perfect boss; as long as you didn't interrupt him or waste his time with idle chitchat, he had no problem with you. Max had devoted his life to radio. In seventh grade he had built a small radio for a science fair. Max had been a DJ for almost twenty years and took great pride in his ability to predict the songs that would top the pop charts. He was rarely wrong and loved to introduce a song by reminding the listeners about his predictions: "This is Mad Max, the Radio Warrior, playing this week's number one song. Remember, you heard it here first!"

The thing Max liked most about being a DJ was that his days were pleasantly predictable. He had regular hours, and his play list was largely structured by the songs he liked that were popular at the time.

As for country music, Max didn't mind listening to it while sitting alone in a bar, drinking martinis, and brooding about his three failed marriages; but, he didn't follow the Nashville scene and couldn't tell if he was listening to the Judds, Dolly Parton, or Tammy Faye Bakker. Being a country music DJ would be like starting a whole new job.

On the other hand, Barbara had worked for three different radio stations and sold ads for five different formats: all-news, Top 40, classic rock, classical music, and country. Her days were unpredictable. She would make numerous phone calls to advertisers, visit local businesses, and try to come up with new ideas for attracting clients, sometimes taking them out to dinner and then taking time off the following morning. She felt humiliated by the way Honeycutt had ignored her considerable experience. He acted as if she were a college intern with no mind of her own.

Despite her strong negative feelings, Barb was afraid to openly complain about the way he treated her. After all, Honeycutt was now responsible for any raises she might or might not receive in the future and, in fact, he controlled her job. If she complained about the new format and the amount of work needed to reestablish contacts with the appropriate advertisers, he could certainly just fire her.

Honeycutt had told Max and Barbara that he had an "open barn door" policy as a manager.

"If any of you farm hands find yourselves gettin' in deep manure on the job, you just make sure to stop by for a good heart-to-heart so we can pull out the weeds before they smother the vegetables. And if you've got some fine ideas, well, we can just put 'em out on the porch and see if the cat licks 'em up."

From Honeycutt's point of view, the first few weeks of the job had gone quite well. He had enjoyed meeting Barbara and Max, and he was glad when they told him they thought a country format would be just fine. Now, however, he felt that there were some problems with the pair of veteran employees.

During the first week of the job, Barbara barely talked to him and seemed moody. He asked her if anything was wrong, and she hesitated before saying no. What was eating her?

Max was even more of a mystery. During the first week, he had done a terrific job. He had followed Honeycutt's play list and had acted like a real professional all week. Rex figured that Max was a pretty sharp DJ and told him he could make up his own play list for the second week. On that Monday, Max had seemed tense on the air and had fumbled lines repeatedly. His choices of music were sometimes good, sometimes strange.

While driving his 4WD to work one morning that week, Rex had turned on the radio and had been surprised to hear an obscure country song called "Pa's Got Cancer, Ma's Got the Flu, and Me I'm Just Plain Missin' You." It turned out that Max had accidentally cued up the flip side of a new 45. How could such an experienced guy make such a bonehead mistake? Rex had crunched the numbers and knew that switching to the country format was a good idea. Still, he noticed that Barbara was not working as well as she had under the previous owner, and her sales attempts were yielding only mediocre results.

Rex had offered both workers many chances to talk, but they never took advantage of the opportunity. Still, he could spot a problem that stuck out like a ten-gallon hat. Things could be better between himself and his employees, but how could he go about turning around a situation that appeared to be headed for disaster?

Questions for Discussion

1. Using one or two situational leadership theories, analyze the main characters of the case and explain, in theoretical terms, just what has happened to them since WPOP became WAOK.

2. Using the same theory or theories, compare the present situation with the situation that appeared to have existed when Craig Sugerman was the boss.

3. What sources of power have an impact on the present situation, and how are they being used?

4. Develop a comprehensive and specific set of recommendations for what you believe Rex should do as the new leader of WAOK based on the theories of leadership and power that apply.

PART IV

ENHANCING INDIVIDUAL AND INTERPERSONAL PROCESSES

Overview

This section demonstrates ways in which managers can use their human resources to make both dollars and sense. We will examine how managers use goal-setting and managing by objectives (MBO).[1] Additionally the section deals with managing group performance, group decision making and how it affects the speed and quality of decisions, and brainstorming and its relationship to creative problem solving. We hope this section will also help you learn about performance appraisal as a motivational tool and as an equity issue, and about stress as something that can inhibit managers as they try to get the most out of their human resources.

Goal-Setting and Reward Systems

How should companies go about setting goals? In your experience, have your employers effectively communicated the company's objectives to you? Or have they told you what to do without specifically saying what you should strive to achieve?

Research done by Edwin Locke in the 1960s led to his development of the Goal-Setting Theory. Locke believed that establishing specific, difficult goals—but ones that are achievable—leads to better performance. In other words, a manager would be smarter to tell assembly workers to try to have fewer than one percent defects than just telling them to give it a good try. All the evidence indicates this is true, but only, Locke concludes, when employees have accepted the goals because they have been involved in helping to set them or have some other good reasons for goal acceptance.[2]

Imagine that you have an uncomplicated job working at a Detroit automobile factory. Each time a car comes down the assembly line and stops at your station, you screw four bolts into each of the two axles on the passenger side of the car. Then the next car comes along, and you screw four more bolts into each axle. This is all that you do—eight hours a day, forty hours a week, fifty weeks per year.

Let's say you've had this job for twelve years. You just might have mastered the fine art of screwing bolts into axles. Then your hotshot MBA manager comes along and tells you that he or she has a new and challenging goal for you: he or she wants to speed up the assembly line. Now, you have to screw in 20 percent more bolts each day—at your present salary, of course.

Clearly, there has to be an incentive to make you want to reach goals and objectives. This is why many American companies have begun to use goal-setting methods such as participative management and MBO. Surprisingly, even though these concepts originated in this country, they have been more widely used in Japan.

Participative Management and MBO

The key component of participative management is that workers are much more likely to reach a goal—even a difficult one—if they have a say in what kind of goal should be set. MBO, the mutual setting of goals by employees and their supervisors, is a specific kind of participative management that takes place at both the macro and micro levels of the organization. At the macro level, managers, working with one another, attempt to set organizational goals. If a company is suffering from excessive turnover, for example, the management team might set a new quantifiable, specific, and time-bounded goal (for example, "let's reduce turnover by 9 percent within the next six months"). Ongoing feedback will be sought from all involved in implementing the goal, and adjustments will be made along the way. This ensures that there will be no unpleasant surprises at the end of the target period.

When MBO is used to help an individual focus on achieving specific and quantifiable goals, this is referred to as the micro level of MBO. How is this implemented? A manager meets with his or her employees individually, and the manager and employee set goals together. First, they define the employee's job. Second, they set priorities and determine new performance expectations. Then they compare current performance with expected performance. If there is a large gap between these two performance levels, they discuss performance obstacles and what can be done about them. Then, over time, continuous feedback is given so that the individual knows if he or she is making appropriate progress toward the desired objectives.

Job Design

For a moment, reconsider life on the automobile assembly line. Frederick Taylor, the father of scientific management in the early 1900s, devoted himself to the notion that there are specific and scientific ways to maximize performance.[3] His approach was to break complicated tasks into a series of small, simple ones. He found that such specialization could dramatically increase productivity. As a result, many organizations adopted assembly line tactics in manufacturing.

Regrettably, the principles of scientific management have also resulted in jobs such as "Axle Bolt Installation Specialist." As you might expect, many workers find such jobs dull and uninteresting. Accordingly, researchers have sought alternatives to job simplification or specialization.

In the 1950s, job enlargement was a new approach toward delegating work.[4] This widened the range of tasks for which employees were responsible. While increasing task variety can be helpful, there are limitations to such an approach. If you're a custodian whose job has been to mop floors, it is unlikely that you will enjoy your job more if your duties are expanded to clean the company's restrooms. Most likely, you might start thinking that there is something to be said for monotony.

246

Job enrichment has proven to be a more effective solution to the problems created by job specialization.[5] In contrast to job enlargement, job enrichment gives an employee significantly more control over how his or her work is to be done. Some large manufacturers have used this concept to radically alter job design. Let's say that a novelty products factory has an enormous problem; production workers consistently make too many defective Halloween masks. Under the old system, the defective likenesses of politicians and other monsters were carted over to the repair department where three repair people worked full-time correcting the masks.

To the astonishment of the workers, management decides to eliminate the repair department. Instead, the three repair people become production workers. If they and the other workers make defective products—if the gash on Frankenstein's forehead isn't quite gory enough—they have to correct their own errors. Additionally, pay and bonuses are closely linked to the quantity and quality of output. As a result, the workers have a greater sense of ownership and responsibility, and this makes them better at their jobs.

Hackman and Oldham's Job Characteristics Model (JCM) suggests that any job can be described in terms of five basic job dimensions: skill variety, task identity, task significance, autonomy, and feedback.[6]

Reconsider the Halloween mask example in terms of the JCM: under the new system, the workers have much higher *skill variety* since they both produce and repair the masks. *Task identity* has also been improved considerably. Since workers now own the responsibility of the whole process and are held accountable for their performance, making the best rubber masks is more important to them.

Since making masks may not seem quite as purposeful as seeking a cure for cancer, flying a jet, or teaching sign language, the *task significance* of this job may be relatively low regardless of management's changes. Nonetheless, *autonomy* has been improved by the change. Workers now have more control over how work is done but, because the masks are produced by following a highly standardized series of steps, autonomy is still not incredibly high. However, *feedback* increases significantly because workers are now being judged on the quality and quantity of the masks produced.

Performance Appraisal

We live in an era in which employees are increasingly likely to sue employers because of unfair pay. Many organizations are recognizing that to protect themselves and to be sure that employees are being treated fairly, they must have structured performance appraisal systems.

Performance appraisals can have dramatic impact on employee productivity and job satisfaction. Some interesting examples are evident in the sports world. When baseball players negotiate contracts with the general managers of their teams, they frequently disagree about how to determine a fair salary. Let's say the general manager gives the highest pay raises to those players with the highest number of home runs and stolen bases.

During the following season, a player's teammates and manager complain that the player is striking out too often because he "swings for the fences"[7] every time, and he tries to steal bases even when he has a pulled hamstring muscle. The team is behind 11–0, and he should be running the bases conservatively. Can we really blame the player for trying to do what will be rewarded by the performance appraisal system?

A major performance appraisal issue is equity, which we have already discussed as a motivation issue. When a fairly average free-agent pitcher signed a $3 million per year contract before the 1991 season, better pitchers started demanding that they receive similar or better contracts. Some claimed that they were "insulted" by being offered a mere $2 million per year, and sports fans across America began wishing that their bosses would offer them a similar insult.

Organizations have to carefully consider many questions when it comes to performance appraisal systems: Who should perform them? Should there be more than one evaluator? Can the appraisers be objective and fair? How often should the evaluations take place? How much input should employees have in determining performance appraisal measures? There is no simple "right" answer to these questions; the "best" performance appraisal system appears to be one that is customized to the company's objectives and human resources.

Stress

Stress occurs when we are unable to adequately confront demands due to various limitations. It would be extremely difficult to put a precise dollar figure on how much stress costs companies today. Stress can be reflected by low productivity, high absenteeism, low quality of work, and high turnover. For the employee, stress on the job has been found to be directly related to high blood pressure. Researchers have found that the amount of stress experienced by employees can be controlled or reduced by giving workers greater control over their jobs.[8]

There are two primary types of stressors: organizational stressors and life stressors. How would you like to be an air traffic controller at a busy metropolitan airport? You have dozens of planes flying in various directions at various speeds and altitudes. You know that their fate depends on your skill and alertness, but you never have contact with the people in the planes. All you see are blips on a screen. It's like a video game, except for the fact that you have thousands of lives at stake instead of twenty-five cents. As you might imagine, turnover among air traffic controllers is quite high; people get burned out quickly. This is an example of an organizational stressor.

Although life stressors happen outside the workplace, their presence can strongly affect employee performance. Divorce, the death of a loved one, marriage, injury or illness, problems with children, and many other personal factors can have a strong impact on a worker. Life stressors may also be more difficult problems for supervisors who may want to be supportive and understanding but must also respect the individual's privacy and not try to be the employee's psychotherapist.

To prevent the problem of managers inappropriately crossing boundaries to address their workers' personal problems, many companies now rely on Employee Assistance Programs (EAPs). EAPs are outside agencies that provide confidential counseling for employees with problems; employers pay for these treatment services.

Decision Making and Creativity

Although group decisions are usually better than individual ones, managers should hesitate before involving a group in the decision-making process, first considering the importance of decision quality and employee acceptance. If both of these are of low concern, a manager might as well flip a coin instead of wasting company time on small matters.[9]

When a manager is looking for a creative solution, a heterogeneous group can be an excellent resource. Brainstorming is one decision-making technique that creates synergy. A leader throws out a problem, and individuals throw back ideas that are recorded without being praised or criticized. Eventually, individuals begin to build on each other's ideas, and the power of putting so many heads together is reflected in an imaginative solution.

Group decision making can have drawbacks in addition to being time-consuming. A phenomenon called groupthink may occur if no individuals in the group are willing to criticize a group decision.[10] This may happen for a number of reasons—for example, too much emphasis is placed on group harmony; the group allows itself to become insulated from outside opinions; or individuals fear that their status in the group will be diminished if they are the lone voice of disapproval.

Conflict[11]

Conflict can be beneficial. Although conflict may be disruptive, it is an important part of human interaction and has certain benefits. Dr. Robert Bolton quotes Gibson Winter (p. 207), a sociologist who says: "No one benefits from the random expression of hostile feelings. There are, however, occasions when these need to emerge…. We cannot find personal intimacy without conflict…. Love and conflict are inseparable." Bolton references two studies that provide evidence of the potential value of conflict: in the first, it was found that "animals that did not hold back their aggression became 'the staunchest friends'"; the second showed that "some types of dissension in the home is healthy for children…. Families that tend to express open dissent and disagreement tend to raise children who have that priceless quality-high self-esteem." Finally, Bolton states, "Another value of conflict is that it can prevent stagnation, stimulate interest and curiosity, and foster creativity."

Constructive controversy has also been found to be beneficial in teams. Teams that create an atmosphere where differences can be openly aired and fully discussed have been found to be more effective than teams that strive to maintain harmony. Tjosvold[12] has shown that cooperative goals serve to promote constructive controversy. When team members have competitive goals, they tend to avoid conflict. The tension, however, does not go away. It builds until it is released in catastrophic fights. On the other hand, when teams engage in constructive controversy, they respect each other, explore opposing views without being judgmental, focus on integrating perspectives to achieve mutual goals, explain the reasoning behind their views, and in the process strengthen the team and generate creative solutions. Thus, appropriate forms of conflict serve as a positive force to promote effective teams.

Sources of Conflict

What then is the difference between productive and nonproductive conflict? Conflict can be thought of as being one of two fundamental types—*realistic conflict* and *nonrealistic conflict*.

Realistic conflict stems from having opposed needs, goals, means, values, or interests. This type of conflict can be addressed using problem-solving and negotiation techniques.

Nonrealistic conflict stems from improper handling of differences in perceptions, lack of communication, ignorance of important information, errors, and any other causes that are the result of misunderstanding rather than a genuine opposition of needs. Nonrealistic conflict can be reduced through improved interpersonal skills.

Resolving Realistic Conflict

There are six methods that people use to resolve conflicts; some are more effective than others. The most effective method is collaborative problem solving. Other methods can be used occasionally under certain circumstances, but repeated use will generally have some negative consequences.

Collaboration. The needs of both parties are taken into consideration. The two parties work to find a solution acceptable to both. Often the problem will be redefined and a novel solution found which results in a win/win situation. This method works most of the time but may be ineffective in time-critical situations. Use this when you want to come up with a solution that integrates concerns and has the commitment of all.

Denial. Conflict is put out of consciousness, and one pretends that everything is fine. Repeated use of this method will lead to severe distress.

Avoidance. While there is an awareness of the problem, it is avoided. Continued use eventually leads to distance and missing of opportunities, and can lead to denial. Groups that use this style favor the status quo, withhold critical comments, express criticism privately, and feel a sense of frustration. This method may be effective if the issue is trivial, tensions are too high and people need to cool down, or when you need to gather more information.

Capitulation or Accommodation. One person gives in without a struggle to have their needs considered. This can lead to resentment. Capitulation can be used if you find out you were wrong or the issue is much less important to you than others.

Domination or Competition. One person attempts to impose a solution on others without consideration of their needs. Prolonged use of this method can lead to resentment, sabotage, passive resistance, emotional distance, and the need to constantly monitor the implementation of the solution. This can be used when quick action is required.

Compromise. Concessions are made by both parties. It may not lead to new and innovative win/win solutions, as does collaboration. Too much compromise can inhibit creativity and stifle people. This method can be used to achieve temporary settlements to complex issues, to arrive at expedient solutions under time pressure, or when equally powerful parties are committed to mutually exclusive goals.

Controlling Nonrealistic Conflict

Controlling nonrealistic conflict is accomplished by improving communication and interpersonal skills and paying careful attention to the organizational environment. Practicing good listening skills and being able to assert one's own position will help avoid two major sources of conflict: errors in perception and lack of information. It is important to be tolerant of others, understand their perspectives, and accept them for who they are. In other words, create an environment where it is safe to be open and honest. Being argumentative, disagreeing, becoming defensive, or raising other barriers to communication will tend to cause others to close down.

The manner in which an organization is structured, and its climate, will affect the degree to which nonrealistic conflicts arise. Organizations that are flexible are less likely to have nonrealistic conflicts. Collaborating to achieve goals, while raising realistic conflicts, will reduce nonrealistic conflicts. It is also important to have a well-defined mission, clearly stated policies and procedures, and a clear understanding of roles.

An organization undergoing rapid changes with inadequate communication is likely to exhibit a high degree of unnecessary conflict. Finally, there must be agreed-upon ways of handling grievances and mechanisms for resolving conflict. Needless to say, training in conflict management and interpersonal skills is important.

Barriers to Communication[13]

Bolton defines twelve major barriers to communication. These barriers result from the content of a communication from one person to another. Some of these may seem obvious, e.g., name-calling. Others may seem a little more puzzling, e.g., advising. It must be remembered that the context in which the barrier occurs is important. For example, advising may be appropriate under some situations but will cut off communication in others, e.g., when not asked for or wanted. The twelve barriers listed below can be grouped into three major categories: judging (1–4), sending solutions (5–8), and avoiding the other's concerns (9–12).

1. *Criticizing.* Judging a person, his or her attitudes, or actions negatively. "You don't understand what you are talking about."
2. *Name-calling.* Categorizing or demeaning another. "You're just lazy."
3. *Diagnosing.* Playing detective to explain another's actions. "You must be having a bad day." "I must have done something to irritate you."
4. *Praising Evaluatively.* Praising someone with the intent of altering behavior. "You are my most talented and dedicated employee. You're the only one I can trust to get this report done. Will you agree to do it?"
5. *Ordering.* Telling a person to do something. "I want this done tomorrow."
6. *Threatening.* Trying to influence another by reminding them of negative consequences. "I'll be very upset unless you do this."
7. *Moralizing.* Preaching to another about what he or she should be doing. "You ought to explain exactly how you are feeling."

8. *Excessive/Inappropriate Questioning.* Closed-ended questions inhibit dialogue. "Were you trying to humiliate him?" "Do you regret what you said?"

9. *Advising.* Giving advice or providing solutions to a person's problems. "That happened to me, here's what you can do…." "What I would do if I were you is…."

10. *Diverting.* Diminishing the problem or changing the subject "Don't worry about that, it's nothing." "That's too depressing; let's focus on more positive things."

11. *Logical Argument.* Making a rational argument based on facts and avoiding the emotional side. "You couldn't have known about that ahead of time, so it doesn't make sense to worry about what happened as a result. You'll learn and do better next time."

12. *Reassuring.* Trying to make the other person feel good without acknowledging the negative emotions. "Don't feel bad, everyone goes through this at one time or another." "Trust me, it is for the best."

What should you do?

Treat the other person with respect. Listen until you "experience the other side." State your views, needs, and feelings.

Sources

1. For additional information on MBO, see P. F. Drucker, *The Practice of Management* (New York: Harper & Row, 1954) and P. F. Drucker, *The New Realities* (New York: Harper & Row, 1989). Mr. Drucker is generally credited with having developed the concept of MBO.
2. Locke, E., Shaw, K. N., Saari, L. and Latham, G., "Goal Setting and Task Performance, 1969–1980," *Psychological Bulletin* 90(1), pp. 125–152.
3. Taylor, F., *Principles of Scientific Management*, New York: Harper and Row, 1911.
4. See also J. Carlzon, *Moments of Truth* , Cambridge, Mass: Ballinger, 1987, p. 60.
5. See F. Herzberg, "One More Time: How Do You Motivate Employees?" *Harvard Business Review*, January–February 1968, p. 59.
6. Hackman, J.R. and Oldham, G.R., "Development of the Job Diagnostic Survey," *Journal of Applied Psychology* 60, 1975, pp. 159–170.
7. Tries to hit home runs.
8. Winslow, R., "Study Uncovers New Evidence Linking Strain on Job and High Blood Pressure," *The Wall Street Journal*, April 11, 1990, p. B8.
9. Frohman, M.A. and Frohman, S.W., "When Are More Heads Really Better than One?" *Training* , September 1988, pp. 65–68.
10. Janis, I. L., "Group Think," *Psychology Today*, November 1971, pp. 43–46, and I. L. Janis, *Victims of Groupthink*, Boston: Houghton Mifflin, 1972.
11. Bolton, Robert, *People Skills: How to Assert Yourself, Listen to Others, and Resolve Conflicts*, New York: Simon & Schuster, 1979.
12. Tjosvold, Dean, "Cooperation Theory, Constructive Controversy, and Effectiveness: Learning from Crisis," In Guzzo, Salas, and Associates (Eds.), *Team Effectiveness and Decision Making in Organizations*. San Francisco: Jossey Bass, 1995, pp. 79–112.
13. Bolton, Robert, *People Skills: How to Assert Yourself, Listen to Others, and Resolve Conflicts*, New York: Simon & Schuster, 1979.

51

THE CODFISH COMPANY*

Part I (45–60 minutes)

You and four of your classmates have been assigned a team project that requires each of you to carry out at least one face-to-face interview with a manager at a company of the team's choosing. After you have completed these interviews, you and your teammates must then get together, compare interview results, and compose a single fifteen- to twenty-page paper on the job of a manager—for which you will all get the same grade. You must also do a twenty-minute presentation to your other classmates on your findings.

Your team has decided to interview managers at the Codfish Company, producers of high-quality marine hardware. All of your team's members agree that the product area is one that interests them. The project must be completed and turned in exactly six weeks from today; the oral presentation is to be delivered exactly one week later.

You realize that the best way to avoid last-minute chaos is to do some planning now. This will include selecting a leader, dividing the task into manageable pieces, and establishing a schedule. This will provide a structure or framework within which to accomplish your task. The following must be completed; they need not be done in order.

A. Working together, choose a name for your team that you feel best describes its organizational culture. Team name:_____

B. It is important that the team and the team's leader have clear and consistent expectations about the leader's role and responsibilities. As a team, discuss your expectations for the leadership role. List at least six to ten below:

1. _____	6. _____
2. _____	7. _____
3. _____	8. _____
4. _____	9. _____
5. _____	10. _____

* Copyright 1992 by Bruce Leblang. Used with permission.

Next, decide on the specific duties you would like your leader to perform. List at least six to ten below:

1. _____	6. _____
2. _____	7. _____
3. _____	8. _____
4. _____	9. _____
5. _____	10. _____

Now that you have defined the leadership role and the leader's expected duties, select a leader. The leader should be a person you feel is best qualified and is willing to meet the expectations listed above. Enter that individual's name below.

Leader's Name:_____

C. Discuss what you believe the central (superordinate) goal of your team should be. Briefly and clearly state it below:

_____

_____

_____

_____

D. Discuss the other goals and values shared by the team (e.g., making the most out of a learning experience, doing the least amount of work possible, being professional, etc.), and list at least three to five below:

_____

_____

_____

_____

E. Divide the required project into at least six to eight component parts or jobs, and list them on the following grid. Be sure to include such jobs as typing the paper, proofreading, data gathering, organizing the oral presentation, and so forth. Assign each part or job to one or more person(s) on your team. List that person's name next to the job.

Part/Job   Assigned to

1. _____

2. _____

3. _____

4. _____

5. _____

6. _____

7. _____

8. _____

F. Develop a timeline or schedule to indicate by what date each component of your project should be complete. Draw the time line below.

G. Assume that you have been given the right to fire a fellow student; under what circumstances would you do so? List the reasons.

_____

_____

_____

_____

H. Next, on a separate piece of paper, develop a firing policy that is agreed to and signed by all members of the team. The policy should include provisions for serving notice on the individual to be fired and a list of the circumstances under which that individual can make amends and preserve his or her position in the team.

Part II (20-30 minutes)

By your set due-date for completion of all interviews, two of the members have not yet held them.

A. Knowing what you do about motivation, briefly describe below how you can convince the two who haven't completed their interviews to do so.

_____

_____

_____

_____

_____

B. What should you do if you are unable to persuade the others to complete their interviews? Briefly describe below what the role of your leader should be in dealing with this problem.

_____

_____

_____

_____

_____

C. The two members who had not done their interviews on time finally hand them in. You realize that the two have made the interviews up and haven't actually done them. The paper is due in two days. Briefly describe below what you believe you should do.

_____

_____

_____

_____

_____

D. In what ways is your method for dealing with this problem consistent or inconsistent with your team's stated goals and values? Are you comfortable or uncomfortable with your goals and policies and the way in which they address your team's needs in dealing with a problem such as this? Why or why not?

Describe below any changes you would like to make to your statements of goals and policies to better meet such problems.

_____

_____

_____

_____

_____

E. Your team finished the project and got an A– (with two faked interviews). Briefly describe below in what ways you believe your team was or was not successful.

_____

_____

_____

_____

_____

52

ASSIGNING THE TEAM PROJECT TASKS

Objectives

- To examine the strengths and weaknesses that each individual member brings to a team

- To explore ways in which to capitalize on the collective strength of the group

- To enable students to assign team project tasks in a way that utilizes each member's individual strengths

Background

One of the primary reasons that teams are an integral part of most of today's organizations is the recognition that individuals bring to assignments or projects a variety of both strengths and weaknesses. When the strengths and talents of team members are appropriately harnessed, invariably the final product is superior to that which any individual member could have accomplished alone. However, teamwork only produces superior results when tasks are assigned according to each individual's strengths and talents. Assigning a given task to the team member who is least able to successfully perform that task will almost inevitably diminish the team's effectiveness.

As you work through this exercise, carefully consider where your strengths lie and what your most significant contributions to a team would be.

The Team Project

You have been assigned to a team with which you will be working for the entire semester in your management course. Although you will be completing many small assignments together throughout the semester, they all seem fairly manageable. Your teammates appear to be serious about the course, and you don't generally anticipate any problems.

You are worried, however, about the final team project. To complete this project, your team has to select an organization, interview five to six managers in that organization, write a twelve-to-fifteen page paper, and give a professional presentation of your findings to the class. It's obvious to you that a significant amount of planning needs to take place in order to complete the project successfully. In fact, the more you think about it, the more the various tasks begin to "boggle your mind!" You decide to have a discussion with your team about assigning tasks for the team project. You believe that this needs to be done soon and that it needs to be done with care.

As a team, you decide that each member will make a list of her or his strengths and how she or he will best be able to contribute to the team project. You will then meet, make a list of the tasks that need to be completed, and assign each task to the person whose strengths and talents best match the task.

Instructions

1. Identifying strengths and talents (individually: 10 minutes)

Working individually, identify the strengths and talents you feel you could bring to your team as you proceed with the project described. List these below:

_____
_____
_____
_____

Next complete the sentence:

I will best be able to contribute to the success of the team project by . . .

_____
_____
_____
_____

2. Identifying project steps and tasks (teams: 20-25 minutes)

As a team, make a list of each step required for the team project and of the task(s) necessary to complete that step. [Do not fill in the name of the individual(s) who will complete the task—this will take place during the next phase of the exercise.]

Example

Step: Find an organization to interview

Task(s): Research area companies
Make telephone calls to any contacts we may have at area companies
Make telephone calls to companies at which we have no contacts

Individuals who will complete task(s):

3. *Assigning tasks (teams: 30 minutes)*

Working as a team, compare the lists of strengths and talents and the contributions each member feels she or he is best able to make to the team project.

Based on this information, assign members to appropriate tasks.

4. *Report out and discussion (full class: 30 minutes)*

Questions for Discussion

1. In what ways did the assignment of tasks for this team project differ from what you have experienced in the past? What do you see as the advantages or disadvantages of this method? Why?

2. Were you able to utilize effectively all members' strengths and talents in assigning the team project tasks?

3. Were there any tasks that you identified for which no team member had the requisite strengths or talents? How did you deal with these? Similarly, were there any tasks for which all members were qualified? How did you deal with these?

4. What do you see as the benefits or drawbacks of using this methodology in the workplace?

5. As a manager, would you participate in a team's use of this method? How? Why?

53

MANAGING GROUP PERFORMANCE*

There are five critical components of this exercise: To be effective, they should be used in the order in which they are presented.

Introduction

Good groups are not an accident: A group member's participation, attitude, and understanding of how groups function can make a difference in whether the group is effective and productive.

"Managing Group Performance" is designed to help your group manage its performance. The components take you from the forming stage of your group through a face-to-face developmental feedback session for each group member.

"Managing Group Performance" has been used by thousands of graduate and undergraduate student groups. The overwhelmingly positive results have been documented by V. U. Druskat and S. B. Wolff in a paper entitled "Effects and timing of developmental peer appraisals in self-managing work groups" which appeared in *The Journal of Applied Psychology*, 84(1), 58–74 in 1999. Their findings are that although some students initially feel anxiety about doing parts of the exercise, those who take the exercise seriously almost always recognize its benefits. The majority of students who have completed this exercise have suggested that all groups do it and that the feedback session be done more than once. While feedback may be given as often as group members wish, face-to-face performance feedback is only done once in class due to time limitations.

To help you understand the importance of each exercise component and how they build on each other, an explanation of the rationales for the exercises are provided on the following pages. You should read these as a group before proceeding with the exercises beginning on page 267. Whether your group turns out to be a nightmare or a terrific experience is in your hands and depends on the choices you make. To help you make effective choices, we have also included in the following introductory material a discussion of the factors that we have observed to make a difference in how effective each exercise component is for any particular group. We hope this will help you avoid common pitfalls and make the most of this exercise to create a high-performance team.

* Copyright 1994 and 2001 by The Rappay Group. The five exercises under this heading were written by Steven B. Wolff. Used with permission.

Component One: Group Formation / Psychological Contract

Each group has a unique combination of people. For your group to be successful you must understand the needs, preferences, styles, strengths, and weaknesses of each member. Some group members may be pressed for time, while others may need to socialize. Some group members may work best under pressure and wait to the last minute to complete an assignment, while others may be stressed by this and prefer to follow a methodical plan.

Some group members may find the project worthwhile and a good learning opportunity; others may just want to get it over with. You need to understand and accept each member and be flexible enough to accommodate their needs, use their strengths, and compensate for their weaknesses. When group members do not take the time to understand each other, differences may be evaluated negatively, resulting in tension. The people in your group are who they are; it may not be your preference, but you can't change them. It is your responsibility to accept them and make the differences and similarities work to the group's advantage. The forming portion of the assignment helps the group to understand the differences and similarities and to develop a plan to make them work for you. Getting to know one another has the added benefit of developing cohesiveness.

When a group starts, members have different expectations of how the group should operate. These expectations are referred to as a psychological contract. Some may expect the group to reach decisions by consensus; others may expect a vote to be taken. Some may prefer to have a leader, others may not. Some may expect their ideas to be respected and listened to, others may prefer a free-for-all. Some members may expect everyone to put in maximum effort and be available all the time; others may expect to do only what is necessary to pass the course. For your group to work together harmoniously, you need to agree on how the group will operate. You need to negotiate expectations and make them explicit. The psychological contract portion of this exercise asks you to do just that. This process is sometimes referred to as setting ground rules.

Developing a Culture

The initial interaction in your group has a significant impact on the culture that develops. Thus, doing this exercise is only half the battle. How you go about doing the exercise will also impact the development of your group. What people actually do sends a more powerful message than what they say they will do. How group members act as you go about completing this exercise will form the basis upon which members make impressions about how the group is "really" going to work. Group members will be observing to determine whether it is OK to be late to meetings, to sit quietly and not contribute ideas, or to do a superficial job. People will be forming impressions about whether group members can be trusted, whether the group a safe place, and how much commitment is expected. Your behavior will affect your group and send a message to your teammates. Think about the culture you desire, and act accordingly.

Success Factors

- All group members are present.

- A few hours are devoted to the assignment.

- Members are focused on getting to know one another not just completing the assignment.

- The group recognizes the importance of the exercise to its future success.

- Group members act responsibility and with respect.

One of the most frequent comments by groups that had difficulty managing performance is that they wish they had taken this exercise more seriously.

Component Two: Developing a Performance Plan

The performance plan is an official agreement that spells out what constitutes acceptable performance and what will be done when performance is either above or below the standard. This is an important tool often used in organizations to manage performance. It also serves as the basis for providing performance feedback. The official agreement means that everyone knows what is expected and what the consequences of their actions will be. Each group member is responsible for choosing his or her own behaviors. The group as a whole is responsible for carrying through on the agreement should performance be above or below what has been agreed to be acceptable, i.e., ensure consequences of behavior are as agreed to.

Group members sometimes find it distasteful to formally discuss acceptable performance and consequences for performance above or below what is acceptable. They would rather trust that everyone will perform acceptably and not think about the unpleasant potentiality that the group might have problems. If you are lucky, everything will work out fine. If you are like most groups, counting on luck alone is a mistake that eliminates a useful tool for managing performance. Good managers and groups set themselves up for success—they don't just hope for it.

Success Factors

- All group members are present.

- Thought is given to developing a comprehensive set of performance objectives.

- Performance objectives are set that are important and meaningful to the group. If you list an objective, you should feel strongly enough about it to take action if it is not met. If the objective is not meaningful to the group, leave it out.

- Objectives are specific and measurable. "Doing quality work," is subjective, while "Work should be free from spelling and grammatical errors," is specific and measurable.

- A set of policies and procedures that you feel comfortable using when performance is above or below what is acceptable is developed. If you aren't going to use it, don't include it.

- Policies and procedures are very specific. The more explicitly you define how the procedure will be initiated, who will be responsible for carrying out the policy, and what exactly are the steps to be taken, the more likely it will be a useful tool.

- A good set of rewards is developed. It is more effective and easier to recognize positive behavior.

The main reasons groups develop ineffective performance plans are: 1) they never anticipated having to use them, 2) they did not define the details clearly enough, 3) they defined policies they did not feel comfortable using, 4) all members were not present when the plan was created, 5) they did not feel comfortable following through on the consequences as agreed to, and 6) the consequences they did develop were either too weak to be effective for managing performance or so harsh they did not feel comfortable using them.

Component Three: Observing Peer Performance

This and the remaining two components in this exercise are directly related to the face-to-face performance review that your team will conduct for each member. This review is based on the performance plan developed in the previous component. To be the most helpful when providing developmental feedback, you need to have good information.

You will be most successful when you can describe specific behaviors and their effects. Taking notes on performance allows you to provide the information needed to conduct a successful feedback session. As you take notes, remember that you should observe both positive and negative performance.

Students sometimes feel that taking notes on a teammate's performance is like spying. However, you are not spying. Instead, you are setting yourself up to provide the most helpful feedback possible. You are showing respect for your teammate by taking the time necessary to provide examples of behavior and explain their effect. In an ideal world, you should be providing feedback immediately when a behavior warrants it. If your group is able to provide feedback on a continuous basis, you will be far ahead of the game. Unfortunately, this does not always happen. In that case, you will need the information for the formal performance review.

It is also important that you observe your own performance. This information allows the person providing you with feedback to know what you are already aware of and what information will be new to you. This allows them to prepare a performance review that will be most helpful to you.

Success Factors

- Keeping notes regularly
- Making notes as soon after your observations as possible
- Writing down specific behaviors and their effects
- Being honest and thorough with your self-observation

264

The most common factors that cause problems are 1) waiting until the last minute to write down your thoughts; 2) being evaluative rather than noting specific behaviors and their effects; and 3) being unbalanced, i.e., not providing both positive and negative observations.

Component Four: Peer Evaluation

Before you can successfully conduct a performance review, you must thoroughly prepare. Providing positive feedback is often easy; however, many people feel somewhat uncomfortable providing developmental feedback. This is often because of the way they frame what they are doing. If you are upset with certain behaviors, you may see providing feedback as a way to express your displeasure and change the person's behavior. Even if you are not upset, you may see providing feedback as criticizing a person or telling them they are inferior in some way. Such frames of mind are likely to make the recipient defensive and make you feel uncomfortable. A better way to approach providing feedback is to see yourself as being helpful and supportive. No one is perfect, and it is an act of caring to help a person understand how he or she can improve his or her performance. Think about someone criticizing you and telling you that you were doing a horrible job and needed to improve; how would you feel? On the other hand, if someone showed respect for you, didn't evaluate you but explained how you could be more effective, and then provided support to help you improve, how would you react?

To provide feedback from a supportive and caring frame of mind requires extensive preparation. You must first be in touch with your motives for providing feedback. Often, when you are upset with something it has as much to do with you as the person you are upset with. If you are angry and want to express it, you need to acknowledge this, understand why you are angry, and practice a more supportive approach. If you think the person is inferior, you need to acknowledge this, understand why you think so, and practice being non-evaluative.

If you are timid about providing developmental feedback, you need to acknowledge this and practice getting your message across clearly and in a way that avoids diminishing the message. Practicing giving feedback out loud and critiquing yourself will help you approach the process in a caring, nonjudgmental way. Also remember that no matter how caring your intentions are, in some situations the recipient will still react defensively. Anticipate this possibility, and practice your response. This will help you remain composed and in control of the situation. You deserve the most thoughtful and helpful feedback possible, and so do your teammates. Failure to practice thoroughly shows a lack of caring, diminishes your ability to help your teammate become more effective, and ultimately hurts the performance of the team.

Success Factors

- Self-reflect to recognize your motives in providing the feedback.
- Think of providing feedback as being caring, supportive, and helpful.
- Practice, practice, practice. Choose your words carefully. Watch your tone.
- Anticipate possible reactions and practice your response.

Component Five: Performance Review / Feedback

This exercise component is the face-to-face performance review that will be conducted by your team. In most organizations, employees receive an annual performance review. Performance reviews are typically done by a manager; however, in an increasing number of organizations, self-managed teams conduct peer evaluations. The previous four exercise components set the groundwork for providing feedback. You will have gotten to know one another, developed a performance plan, observed performance, and prepared for your feedback session.

Giving and receiving feedback are important skills in today's organizations. In a fast-changing business environment, employees and organizations must continuously learn and improve. Doing so requires information about performance. When conducted in a respectful, caring, and supportive manner, the process creates stronger bonds among team members and improves the performance of the team as a whole.

The reviews are not intended to be the only time that peers provide feedback to each other. This should be an ongoing process. Whenever someone shows either positive or negative performance, she or he should be given feedback. The longer the time interval between the behavior and the feedback, the less effective the feedback. If timely feedback has been given, there should be no surprises during the formal review process.

Success Factors

- Excellent preparation

- A caring, supportive, and helpful frame of mind. If what you are saying is not intended to be helpful, don't say it.

- Balanced positive and developmental feedback

- Use of specific examples of behaviors and their effects

- Developmental feedback is not diminished, e.g., "It's really not a big problem but. . ."

- Mutual problem-solving approach is used

- A conversational approach, i.e., review is not read or given as a prepared speech.

MANAGING GROUP PERFORMANCE

This exercise, and the four that follow, are meant to be used as a series.

GROUP FORMATION / PSYCHOLOGICAL CONTRACT

Objectives

- To manage the forming stage of group development by getting to know one another

- To acquaint participants with the concept of the psychological contract

- To give participants experience in managing psychological contracts by negotiating expectations

Background

Good groups are not an accident; you *can* make a difference. In this exercise you will learn what you can do to get your group off to a good start. The work of developing an effective group begins from the first minute you are together. The way that your group handles the forming stage and group member's expectations, impacts whether your group is going to be a pleasure, a nightmare, or somewhere between. What you do at this point will affect your group's culture, your ability to work together effectively, and ultimately the group's product. The purpose of this exercise is to help your group manage the forming stage and psychological contract in a way that will develop a positive and effective culture.

As you can imagine, in almost any group, members will have different needs and expectations based on their personalities and individual styles. Members will also have different strengths and weaknesses. One advantage of a team is that one person's strength can compensate for another's weakness. One disadvantage is that differences among members must be addressed, which takes time and energy. To avoid clashes due to differing expectations and to take advantage of different strengths and weaknesses, a team in the forming stage needs to do three things: 1) group members need to get to know each other, 2) you need to understand similarities and differences in the strengths, weaknesses, styles, and needs of group members, and 3) members need to come to an agreement as to what is to be expected of team members and how the group will operate. This exercise asks you to do these three things so you can get your group off to a good start.

As you do this exercise, it is important to realize that your group culture is beginning to form. The way the group operates, the behaviors that are acceptable, and what group members think of each other are all beginning to take shape. Thus, how you go about this exercise is just as important as doing the task. The culture that begins to develop is not cast in stone. It will change as time goes on, however, starting on a positive note will make your work together more enjoyable and effective in the future. It will also be less likely that you will need to expend time and energy to modify an ineffective culture.

Instructions

1. Review the material on this exercise in the introduction to the series of exercises.

2. As a group, share information about:

   - Personal backgrounds.

   - Work history.

   - Current time constraints.

   - What you like and dislike about groups.

   - Strengths and weaknesses of working in a group.

   - Learning goals for the project/class.

   - Hopes and fears about the group.

   - How you work best.

   - If your instructor asked you to do self-assessments, share your results.

   - Please add other information you feel would be useful to know about one another.

3. You are likely to be similar in many ways and different in many ways. Similarity can make it easier to work together, but it can also reduce creativity and lower the quality of decisions. Diversity can make it difficult to come to agreement and can cause tension, but it can also lead to greater creativity and higher quality decisions. Discuss a strategy for using your similarities and differences. For example, discuss how you can use strengths to complement weaknesses; accommodate each member's style and needs; help each other meet learning goals; and avoid lack of creativity. For example, you might find one member likes to wait to the last minute to complete assignments while another member gets very anxious when things are left to the end. How will your group work together so the needs of both members are met? You might have found that some members are working full time while others are not. How will you take this into consideration when organizing your work? You might find that you think alike about certain issues. How can ensure that your group will remain creative? Write down your strategy.

4. Discuss your expectations of each other and how the group should operate.

   - How committed do you expect people to be?

- How much socialization do you expect?

- How much do you expect all ideas to be explored?

- Do you expect people to be prompt to meetings?

- How prepared for meetings should people be?

- How timely do you expect work to be done?

- How much should team members support each other?

- How do you expect team members to treat each other?

- Please add other relevant expectations not listed above.

5. You will likely have different expectations of each other and different ideas about how the group should operate. Come to a consensus on a set of expectations that you all agree on. Write these down, being sure that each expectation is explicit, clearly explained, and agreed to by all.

6. The group should hand in one paper that discusses:

- The strategy you agreed to for using the similarities and differences within your group. As you discuss the strategy, provide enough information about the characteristics of members to illustrate why you have chosen your strategy. Do not list each member and their characteristics.

- The agreed upon expectations of group members and how the team should work.

- An assessment of the impact of this exercise on the team.

Completion Checklist

☐ Spent time getting to know one another.

☐ Discussed expectations.

☐ Discussed a strategy for using the diversity in the group.

☐ Developed a document that discusses your strategy for working with the team's similarities and differences, your shared expectations, and the impact of this exercise on the group.

DEVELOPING A PERFORMANCE PLAN

Objectives

- To develop a performance plan to use as a tool to manage group performance
- To give participants practice in developing a performance plan

Background

As your group begins work on your task, you may be optimistic that everyone will perform as expected. Organizations cannot rely on hope that people will perform as required, and neither can your group. To manage employee performance, organizations often develop specific objectives that define acceptable performance. They also have a set of policies and procedures that define what will be done if performance either exceeds or falls below the acceptable standard. In this exercise, your group will develop performance objectives along with policies and procedures.

As you develop your policies and procedures, keep in mind that they will only be helpful if, when it comes time for you to carry them out, the group feels comfortable following through. When you agree to a set of policies and procedures, you need to be willing to follow them or they become hollow words written on a piece of paper that have no meaning. One common set of policies and procedures used in organizations is called *progressive discipline*. Each time performance falls below expectations, the disciplinary action becomes more severe. The first instance might be a verbal warning and progress through termination. At each step, the employee is told why the performance is below expectations and how to bring it up to an acceptable level. In this way the employee is responsible for making the choice about whether he or she will meet expectations, knowing full well the consequences for failure to do so. The organization is responsible for carrying out the agreed-to consequences for failure to meet expectations.

Many groups find it difficult to discipline a peer. Keep in mind two things: first, if you have carefully developed and agreed to a set of objectives along with policies and procedures for addressing unacceptable performance, then discipline is simply implementing what the group has agreed to. Everyone knows and understands the consequences of their behavior and it is not uncommon for people to test the boundaries. If there are no consequences for inappropriate action, then your group's agreement is meaningless and you will not be able to successfully manage your performance—a position that a good manager or group member does not want to be in. When a boundary is tested, failure to act means the boundary will be pushed ever further. Second, it is much easier to address an issue the first time it comes up than to wait until it has become such a bad problem it can no longer be ignored. Remember, helping your teammate meet expectations is an act of respect and caring. You should try to find out what he or she needs to meet expectations and provide any support that is reasonable. If you think of addressing performance issues as scolding or demeaning your teammate, you are less likely to carry through because your gut feeling is telling you doing so is inappropriate and potentially harmful, and your gut is correct.

In addition to helping the group manage its performance, in many organizations a set of performance objectives forms the basis of the annual employee review. The employee sits down with his or her manager and reviews how well his or her performance met the objectives. This process generally uses a performance appraisal form that summarizes the objectives and provides a place for the manager to offer feedback and suggestions on each objective. The final portion of this exercise asks you to create a performance appraisal form that you will use as a basis for conducting a performance review at a later date (see the last exercise in this series). Your form should summarize the group's objectives and provide room for written feedback and suggestions.

Instructions

1. Review the material on this exercise in the introduction to the series of exercises.

2. Working as a group, agree to a set of performance objectives for all members. You should develop your own set of objectives; however, to get you started you might want to think about the following issues common in groups:

   - What do you expect concerning meeting attendance?

   - What do you expect concerning timeliness of task performance?

   - What do you expect concerning quality of task performance?

   - What ethical standards do you expect?

   - What do you expect concerning participation at meetings?

   - What do you expect concerning returning messages?

   - What do you expect concerning flexibility, e.g., meeting times?

   - Please add other objectives as you feel appropriate.

   Describe your objectives in behavioral terms that are measurable. For example, it is better to include an objective that says, "We expect members to have their work ready on schedule," than to say, "We expect members to do their work." In the first case, you can measure whether the work was received on time. In the second case, the person may be doing her or his work but may not have it ready when needed. Another example might be "We expect members to correct spelling and grammar in their written work," as opposed to "We expect members to write well." In the first case, there is something you can measure. In the second case, writing well is subjective and can mean different things to different people.

3. As a group, agree to the procedures you will use if a team member's performance falls outside the agreed-upon norms. A typical system of progressive discipline might include

procedures for giving rewards (don't forget the positive side), giving oral feedback, giving a written warning, placing someone on probation, and termination. Define the set of procedures that you feel will work best for your group.

Be as specific as possible when you write your procedures. Think about how the procedure will be initiated. Who is going to be responsible for carrying through on the procedure? Exactly what steps should be taken? The more specific you are, the more likely you will use your procedures.

4. You now need to develop a set of policies that define the specific behaviors that will cause each procedure to be invoked. For example, you may decide coming to one meeting late is grounds for giving oral feedback; being late to two meetings is grounds for placing a person on probation; and being late to three meetings is grounds for dismissal. You may also decide that not finishing an assignment on time is immediate grounds for dismissal.

5. Based on the agreed-upon objectives, develop a performance appraisal form on which to summarize each team member's performance. This form will serve as a guide for giving feedback during a formal performance review conducted in class or elsewhere. Include space on your performance appraisal form to:

- Evaluate strengths.

- Evaluate areas for improvement.

- Provide suggestions and comments for each objective.

- Provide comments for each item that is scored by a scale (e.g., excellent to poor, or 1 to 5. Scalar ratings alone are not helpful unless explained).

- Include the name of the person being reviewed.

- Include the name of the reviewer.

6. Put together enough copies of the written performance expectations, policies and procedures, and performance appraisal forms to supply a complete packet to each team member and your instructor.

Completion Checklist

☐ Developed performance expectations.

☐ Developed policies and procedures for managing performance.

☐ Policies and procedures are specific.

☐ Developed performance appraisal form.

☐ Left adequate space on performance appraisal form for extensive comments.

☐ Put together and signed a copy of the complete performance plan for each team member and the instructor.

OBSERVING PEER PERFORMANCE

Objectives

- To provide experience observing and documenting performance
- To prepare for a peer performance evaluation

Background

To successfully manage performance, every team member must be prepared to provide helpful and accurate feedback to other team members. It is important to keep regular notes on the performance of peers to refer to when providing feedback. Relying on memory does not work. Notes should include examples of actual behaviors, positive as well as negative, and the effects the behaviors have on you and the group. The more specific you are, the better.

The purpose of keeping notes is not to create a secret log to spring on a teammate during a performance evaluation but rather to use as an aid to providing accurate and constructive feedback. The quality of your notes will have a direct impact on the effectiveness of the feedback you are able to give. In business, notes are useful in determining appropriate rewards for jobs well done and can also mean the difference between winning or losing costly wrongful dismissal lawsuits.

Instructions

1. Review the material on this exercise in the introduction to the series of exercises.

2. Read the "Guide for Giving and Receiving Effective Feedback" beginning on Page 275.

3. Using a separate "Performance Observation Sheet" for each team member, record observations immediately following every group meeting. To be sure that these sheets will be useful to your teammates when they see them, include specific examples, and document any behaviors and their effects. Your entries should be honest, constructive, balanced (i.e., both helpful and unhelpful behaviors are noted), and meant to be helpful.

4. Because it is helpful to have a person's self-evaluation when providing feedback, you should also fill out a "Performance Observation Sheet" for yourself. This will be given to the person providing your feedback.

Completion Checklist

☐ Understand guidelines for providing constructive and helpful feedback.

☐ Added notes to each teammate's "Performance Observation Sheet" after each meeting.

☐ Used a "Performance Observation Sheet" after each meeting to provide a self-evaluation.

GUIDE FOR GIVING AND RECEIVING EFFECTIVE FEEDBACK

Giving feedback, either positive or negative, can be difficult; but, if you respect the person, sincerely intend to be helpful, and understand a few simple guidelines, it can work out well. Receiving feedback will allow you to see things about yourself that you could not see in any other way. By illuminating your blind spots, you will be able to correct behaviors that are inhibiting your growth. Constructive feedback is an important gift. Every time you are able to use it wisely, you will have taken another step in your own development.

The following are some guidelines for giving and receiving feedback.

Giving Feedback

1. Feedback must be intended to be helpful.

2. Do not evaluate. Instead, describe behaviors and their effects. Use "I" or "we" messages. For example say "When you do this, I feel …" or "When you do this, we fall behind schedule because…." Do not say things like "You have a bad attitude" or "You're lazy." Such phrases are evaluative and most likely will produce defensive reactions.

3. Provide specific examples. The more recent the examples, and the more clearly they illustrate the behaviors and their effects, the better.

4. Be tentative. You are presenting your perceptions, not absolute truth.

5. Keep in mind that the receiver must be able to take concrete action based on the feedback.

6. Try to understand how you or the group may be contributing to the behavior of the person to whom you are providing feedback. For example, someone may not be contributing because they feel the group does not value their inputs. Ask the person to help you understand the factors that are contributing to their behavior.

7. Indicate a sincere willingness to help. It is difficult to change behaviors. As a manager, you must be willing to work with a person and make him/her immediately aware of behaviors that require change. In this way, you will help him/her develop. Be tolerant of recurrent behavior, but expect it to decrease in frequency. Also, if you or the group are contributing to the behavior, accept your responsibility and ask the person to help you be more effective in bringing about the desired behavior.

Receiving Feedback

1. Try to understand the feedback. Listen to the person giving you feedback, and try not to interrupt.

2. Try to avoid becoming defensive. This can be difficult, especially if the person giving the feedback is not highly skilled. You may have different perceptions of yourself, but it is important that you understand the perceptions of others.

3. You will gain more from feedback if you assume the feedback giver is trying to be helpful.

4. If the feedback is not clear, ask for clarification and examples.

5. Summarize by rephrasing the feedback. Ask the feedback giver to confirm that you have heard correctly.

6. Take responsibility for any behaviors that you agree might have been unhelpful and show a sincere willingness to modify these behaviors.

7. Avoid justifying your behavior unless asked to do so.

8. Remember, you are taking in information about how others are affected by your behavior. The information says something about this group at this time. It does not mean what you are doing is good or bad, so don't take it personally. Different people will be affected differently by the same behavior. Although you may not like your group's reaction to your behavior, it is an important skill to be flexible enough to adjust your behavior to the needs of this particular situation.

Performance Observation Sheet (POS)

Person you are observing: _____

Your name: _____

Record the positive and negative behaviors you observe and their effect on you and the group. Be specific. While you should use your performance plan as a guide, you may see behaviors that are particularly helpful or detrimental that are not specifically defined in your plan. Record these as well. If you need more space, use additional paper.

Keep a separate form for each member of your group (including yourself), and make notes each time your group meets. Include the dates and circumstances under which the behavior occurred.

These forms may be removed and freely copied for use with this exercise.

Helpful behaviors	Effects on you and the group

(over)

Unhelpful behaviors	Effects on you and the group

PEER EVALUATION

Objectives

- To provide experience conducting a peer evaluation
- To provide experience in preparing for an actual performance review

Background

Providing feedback requires careful preparation. This exercise is preparation for an actual performance review in which each person on your team will give feedback to one member and receive feedback from one member.

The exercise has two parts: first, your group must decide the logistics of who will provide feedback to whom. The second part, done individually, asks you to thoroughly prepare the feedback you will give to one of your teammates.

In the actual performance review, oral feedback will be given one-on-one; however, it must reflect the views of all team members. Thus, when you prepare your feedback, you must incorporate the perspectives of all of your teammates. Your goal is to provide an accurate picture of the team's feelings, not just your own. As you prepare for the peer review session you should use your team's "Performance Appraisal Form" to summarize the feedback you will give. You will work from this form when you deliver the feedback, and it will be given to the recipient, so make it helpful and complete.

Instructions

PART 1

1. Distribute blank copies of your team's "Performance Appraisal Form" to each member.

2. Decide who will provide feedback to whom. Do not give feedback to the person who gives you feedback. A simple way to meet this requirement is to sit in a circle and each person is designated to give feedback to the person on his or her left. If you know someone is going to be absent during the formal reviews, do not include her or him. However, provide that person with feedback from the entire team at another time.

3. Collect the "Performance Observation Sheets" that each group member has filled out for the person to whom you will be giving feedback, including the person's self-assessment.

4. Look over the sheets, and make sure you understand them. Ask questions if necessary. Be sure you are able to illustrate performance with specific behaviors and their effects.

PART 2

5. Review the material on this exercise in the introduction to the series of exercises.

6. Working individually, thoroughly examine the information on the "Performance Observation Sheets" and summarize the data on your team's "Performance Appraisal Form." If there are differences in your teammates' observations, note in the comments that some people felt one way and others felt another way. Everyone's view must be represented, but you do not need to discuss this with your teammates. Also, take into consideration the person's self-evaluation. This will help you understand what points require more explanation because the person is not aware of them. Your team's "Performance Appraisal Form" should have a space to provide a general comment on strengths and opportunities for improvement; be sure to include at least one strength and one opportunity for improvement.

7. Put together a package that includes the completed "Performance Appraisal Form" and all "Performance Observation Sheets." You will give this packet to the reviewee after the in-class feedback session.

8. Read the "Guide for Giving and Receiving Effective Feedback," and practice the review session. Examine your motives and frame of reference. Practice giving the feedback out loud. Revise your feedback until you are being respectful, caring, supportive, and non-judgmental. Be sure you have specific examples of behaviors and that you explain the effects of the behavior. As you practice, remember that a person's behavior is often influenced by the context: Ask the person if the group has contributed to his or her behavior in any way. For example, has the group made the person feel unvalued? Practice being supportive and working with the person to develop a plan that takes into consideration both an attempt on the group's part to provide a more supportive context and an attempt on the recipient's part to modify his or her behavior. Anticipate reactions and practice a response that conveys you are trying to be helpful. Your feedback should be balanced. It is just as important to explain the positive behaviors and their effects as it is to discuss unhelpful behaviors. As you practice make sure you convey the positive without diminishing the message you are trying to convey when delivering the developmental feedback. Be sure that you have practiced enough to provide the feedback without reading it from the performance appraisal form.

Completion Checklist

☐ You have carefully read the instructions.

☐ You have been assigned a person to review other than the person reviewing you.

☐ Members who will be absent from the actual review are not included in the assignment.

☐ A time for the entire team to review members who will be absent has been arranged.

☐ All POS's have been exchanged.

☐ All information on the POS's has been summarized on the "Performance Appraisal Form."

☐ You have included extensive comments for each item evaluated.

☐ You have all forms to bring to the actual peer review.

☐ You have rehearsed for the review and are able to represent the team's perspective.

PERFORMANCE REVIEW / FEEDBACK

Objectives

- To provide practice using a performance plan to evaluate performance
- To provide practice giving constructive feedback
- To provide practice receiving feedback

Background

This exercise provides an opportunity to practice both giving and receiving feedback and will also provide a structured opportunity to address any performance issues that may exist within your project group. As you provide feedback, you should remember that your intent is to be helpful. If a person is performing well, you should let them know. Often, people are not aware of the positive ways that they affect the group. If a person's performance needs improvement, you should provide feedback in a developmental way. Help the person understand the behaviors that need improvement and their effects. Provide specific examples.

Behavior is partly driven by the person and partly by the situation the person is in, thus, to be truly helpful, you must understand the ways in which you and the group have contributed to the behavior.

You will be much more successful in improving the person's performance as well as the group's performance if you accept responsibility for the ways in which you and the group have brought about the person's behavior. This does not imply that the person is not fully responsible for their behavior, they are. It recognizes the reality that the recipient will often perceive the situation differently than you and that he or she is likely to partially attribute his or her behavior as being a reaction to the group. For example, a person may justify not having work done on time because another group member always criticizes it and eventually does it over. Whether the person's perception is accurate is not important, what matters is that performance improves. This is more likely if you treat developmental feedback as a problem-solving session. It is a two-way communication process where you work on the issues together and develop a mutual plan of action. For example, if a person shoots down ideas too quickly, get an agreement that the group will politely point this out when it happens and that the person will try to catch him or herself. If the person feels he or she must shoot down ideas because the group often gets off track and he or she is pressed for time, then ask the person to let the group know when it is off track. This will likely help the group remain focused and will also reduce the need the person feels to shoot down ideas—a win-win situation. Remember, behavior is hard to change and reoccurrence does not mean the person is not trying.

Instructions

1. *Do the following (5 minutes):*

   - Review the material on this exercise in the introduction to the series of exercises.

   - Review the "Guide for Giving and Receiving Effective Feedback."

   - Review what you are going to say.

   - Anticipate possible reactions.

   - Consider how you can be the most helpful.

2. *Conduct a performance review for each member (10 minutes for each review).*

   The two members conducting the review should sit facing each other, with the rest of the team observing. Do not rush through the process. Use your full 10 minutes as instructed below.

   The reviewer should:

   - Refer to the composite "Performance Appraisal Form" and POS's.

   - Provide specific examples of behaviors and their effects.

   - Explain any numeric ratings.

   - Include at least one strength and one opportunity for improvement.

   - Ask how the team may be contributing to the person's behavior.

   - Discuss how the team can help.

   - Develop a mutual plan for improving performance.

   - Give the reviewee a copy of the "Performance Appraisal Form" and all POS's.

   The observers should:

   - Look for behaviors that either help or hinder the feedback process.

   - Take careful notes.

   - Be sure that the reviewer has completed all that is required as indicated above.

   - Provide feedback to the giver and recipient of feedback after each session.

   After each review:

   Remember that you are practicing the skills of giving and receiving feedback, so use the remaining allotted time for each review to process what happened. Observers should provide immediate feedback. What did they do well? What could they have improved? The observers can use the "Guide to Giving and Receiving Feedback" as a guide to answering these questions. The reviewer and reviewee should talk about what they were feeling as the review was taking place, what worked well for them, what felt uncomfortable, and what might be done differently to make the process more effective. Giving and receiving feedback are important skills so try to help each other learn as much as you can about the process and how to do it effectively.

When time is up, go on to the next performance review. Adjust your chairs so the next reviewer and reviewee are facing each other. Repeat Step 2 until everyone has been reviewed.

3. *After all reviews are completed, use any remaining time to discuss the team as a whole.*

Examine what is going well and what could be improved to make the team more effective? What are the strengths of your group? What are the weaknesses? If there are any issues that you feel are important but were not raised in any review session, this is a good time to discuss them.

Completion Checklist

☐　　All members were reviewed.

☐　　Plans to review absent members have been made.

☐　　Every session has been critiqued.

☐　　Observers have given their feedback.

☐　　Original Performance Appraisal Form and all POS's have been given to reviewee.

☐　　Remaining time has been used to discuss the team as a whole.

54

CALENDARS AND CLIPS

Objectives

- To examine the role of feedback in employer-employee relations
- To practice the skills of active listening and two-way communication
- To practice dealing with problems in stressful situations
- To practice giving feedback and setting goals

Background

The setting is an independent business, Calendars and Clips, that deals in retail and quantity discount office and stationery items. It is wholly owned by Role Player 1, who employs five part-time clerks; a full-time assistant who handles stock, makes deliveries, and does odd jobs; and a full-time outside salesperson who receives a base salary and commissions.

The outside salesperson, Role Player 2, has been with the company for three years—since graduating from college. During this time, the personal-service aspect of the company, selling to small local professional offices and businesses that have the products delivered, has grown from practically nothing to over $500,000 in gross receipts per year.

The owner and the salesperson have had a reasonably good working relationship. Today, the salesperson returns midway through the afternoon and announces across a store full of people that the store's biggest customer, a first cousin of the owner's spouse, has switched to the competition. The salesperson then walks into the owner's office and slams the door.

Instructions

Step 1 (5 minutes)

Read the brief background of the situation at Calendars and Clips, and consider what you would do if you were the manager or the salesperson. In addition, familiarize yourself with the areas for consideration in the Part I Observer Sheet.

Step 2 (10 minutes)

The facilitator will distribute Part I, Role 1 to half of the class and Part I, Role 2 to the other half of the class. Read the role to which you have been assigned.

Step 3 (20-30 minutes)

Perform the role play. While doing so, stick to the facts that have been given, and stick closely to the role in an attempt to make the experience as realistic as possible. Try to reach a point at which there is mutual understanding of one another's position and further dialogue is possible. This exercise does not present a specific problem with a specific answer; rather, it requires the sharing of feelings in such a way that it is possible to preserve the relationship and to move ahead.

Step 4 (30 minutes)

Class discussion.

Step 5 (60-90 minutes)

Repeat the above steps with Part II of the exercise.

Note: The roles for the owner and salesperson are in the Instructor's Manual.

Part I Observer Sheet

1. Did the owner allow the salesperson to take the lead in the discussion, listen, and make an effort to understand what the salesperson's concerns were? What clues did you have that this was or was not happening?

   _____

   _____

   _____

2. Did the owner encourage the salesperson to talk about the issue? How?

   _____

   _____

   _____

3. Did the owner focus on the issue to resolve it, or did the owner become sidetracked by personality or behavior issues? Why or why not?

   _____

   _____

   _____

4. Were there ideas and attitudes of the owner and the salesperson that got in the way of their ability to communicate? Describe them.

   _____

   _____

   _____

5. Did the owner make a timely effort to discuss solutions for the problem and plan for a future opportunity to get together and explore ideas generated by this meeting? How was this done?

   _____

   _____

   _____

Part II Observer Sheet

1. In what ways did the owner try to set a relaxed and cooperative tone for the meeting?

   _____

   _____

   _____

2. In what way did the owner involve or fail to involve the salesperson in the performance appraisal process?

   _____

   _____

   _____

3. In areas in which there were problems, did the owner involve the salesperson in generating solutions? How?

   _____

   _____

4. Was the owner able to give negative as well as positive feedback in a way that the salesperson could understand?

   _____

   _____

5. Did the owner and the salesperson agree on an action plan? Was it realistic? Why or why not?

   _____

   _____

   _____

6. Did they set a date for a future meeting? _____

7. If you were the owner, what would you have done differently?

   _____

   _____

   _____

55

NO FOLLOWERS? NO LEADERS!
THE LANGUAGE OF EMPOWERMENT*

Objectives

- To help participants explore the decision making and action options of followers

- To develop skills for fostering a knowledgeable and responsible followership

- To practice the leadership and followership skills necessary for communicating empowerment

- To practice the skills of giving helpful and supportive feedback

- To practice the skills of making one's needs understood

Background

Empowering employees is the means for ensuring their maximum involvement and contribution. Without such empowerment, there is little chance of achieving total quality.

For leaders, empowering followers means avoiding being a highly directive "micromanager" who constantly looks over shoulders and is ready to jump when a subordinate errs. Instead, the empowering leader takes the role of a coach. The leader as coach supports the efforts of subordinates to take responsibility and works collaboratively with them to resolve problems. Empowered followers also have responsibilities. They can no longer rely on the hierarchy and rule book to dictate every decision and action.

Empowered followers have a responsibility to make their needs known and understood and to participate actively in organizational activities. They must make carefully thought-through decisions, take responsible actions, and be open to admitting mistakes when they occur.

The following exercise will give you an opportunity to practice and better understand the language of empowerment from the vantage points of follower, leader, and observer. The exercise was developed as a training exercise for middle managers, and each role scenario is based on an actual experience of a middle manager in a large company.

When you play the role of a leader or a follower in this exercise, you will be given frank and honest feedback from your teammates on how well you used the language of empowerment.

* Copyright 1993 by Janet W. Wohlberg and The Center for Executive Development, Inc. Used with permission.

When your role is that of observer, your responsibility is to take careful notes, using the observation sheets as a guide, and actively participate in the debriefing that follows the role play. If your team does more than one role play, use additional paper for your notes.

Instructions

1. (10 minutes)

Working in your small team, decide who will play the leader and who will play the follower in each of the role plays. Over the course of the exercise, each team member will play either a follower or a leader at least once. Therefore, for a team of eight, select four leaders and four followers.

While there is only one leader role, there are several follower roles. If you are a follower, briefly scan the roles and select one. Negotiate with the other followers over who will play which roles so that each follower's role is played only once.

Hint: If you're uncomfortable with being a leader, play the leader's role. If you have problems making your needs known, elect to play a follower's role.

If you are a leader, try to avoid the temptation to read the roles of the followers.

All team members should read the "Leader's Role" and the "Questions for Observers."

2. (10 minutes)

Begin each role play by having the follower explain why she or he has asked for the meeting and what his or her needs are. Continue until a resolution has been reached or time is up, whichever comes first.

3. (10 minutes)

After the role play, discuss the effectiveness of each of the role players in dealing with the situation presented. Use the "Questions for Observers" as a guide.

While observing and during the debriefing, keep in mind that giving feedback is meant to be a helpful process. Give *specific* examples that illustrate your points, and concentrate on things over which the role players have some control, for example, "Your voice is irritating" probably is not helpful; "You spoke too fast" is something that can be changed with thought and practice.

During the debriefing, be sure to elicit from the role players their reflections on how they thought things went, why they did what they did, and what they might want to do differently in the future.

It is important for *all* team members to give input during the debriefing.

4. (30 minutes per round)

Repeat Steps 1 to 3. However, change to the following timing:

- 5 minutes to prepare by reviewing roles and questions
- 10 minutes for the role play
- 15 minutes to debrief

Continue to repeat the exercise until all team members have had the experience of playing either a leader or a follower.

5. (Open-ended)

Select a reporter for your team to describe what happened in your team to the class.

Questions for Observers

1. In what ways did the leader set the stage for an open and honest dialogue with the follower?

2. What evidence did you see of the role players' making sure they understood one another's needs and concerns as they went along?

3. In what ways did the role players come to an understanding of their common interests, for example, meeting customer needs, making one another's lives easier, finding a mutually acceptable solution to the problem, etc.?

4. In what ways did the leader try to empower the employee to make decisions and take action to solve the problem presented?

5. What would you have liked the leader to have done differently? Why?

6. Do you think it is likely, given what you observed, that the follower will feel empowered to make decisions and take action in the future? Why or why not?

Leader's Role

You recently took a management course in which you learned about leadership skills and how to develop a followership that is able to make well-thought-out decisions and take effective actions. You were told that when employees aren't encouraged or allowed to use common sense and judgment, they may be unable to take action on customers' requests, frustrating the customer and making themselves appear foolish.

Now you're ready to try out what you have learned. It looks as if you're going to have a chance sooner than you had planned. One of your subordinates is on his or her way into your office. Recognizing some anxiety in your employee's voice when you spoke on the phone a few minutes ago, you agreed to meet right away, even though it's already after 5 p.m., and you're eager to go home.

Today has been about as hectic as possible, and the thought of having to deal with one more problem is not a happy one. You're not sure why your employees just don't go ahead and resolve problems instead of running to you with them all the time, but given what you learned in your course, you think this might be a good opportunity to find out. You think you would like to work cooperatively with the employee to understand and find some guidelines for solving the problem you are about to discuss. You would like to empower him or her to take the necessary action. You are also determined to convey to him or her your new belief that more decision making should be done by people closer to the problem.

Follower's Role 1

You have just realized that some of the information in the report you gave to your boss last week was plainly wrong. You're pretty sure that the report has already been passed along to your boss's boss and that it is being used as the basis for some talks with a customer. If action is taken on the basis of this information, it will be costly to the company.

You actually recognized the mistake two days ago, but it's only today that you've gotten up enough courage to admit your mistake. You could blame the mistake on the people who supplied the information to you, but it was really your responsibility to have double-checked before passing it along.

It occurs to you that your boss also should have checked the information before passing it along—but you sigh, recognize that the boss is always the boss, and you think that sooner or later you would have gotten blamed. You have finally decided to try to cut your losses and admit to the mistake sooner rather than later.

Your boss has always had a tendency to "go ballistic" when mistakes are discovered.

At the start of the exercise, be sure to tell your boss why you have come and what your needs are.

Follower's Role 2

Two weeks ago your boss delegated an important job to you that was supposed to have been completed by today. At first you felt a bit overwhelmed by the size and importance of the project, so you procrastinated on getting going.

When you finally did start the project, you realized it wasn't as bad as you had thought-or at least it wouldn't have been had you not waited so long, not had a full desk, and not had some distracting issues going on in your personal life.

It's now late in the day, and not only have you not delivered the project, you are still at least a couple of days from completing it if you do nothing else but work on it. In fact, even this is dependent on getting some information from someone who was really annoyed when you requested it on such short notice.

You know you need some help in figuring out how to fit the work for the project into your otherwise busy schedule. (As you talk to the leader, include information on the things you might actually do on a typical day.)

Your boss has a tendency to "go ballistic" when deadlines aren't met.

At the start of the exercise, be sure to tell your boss why you have come and what your needs are.

Follower's Role 3

For the past several weeks the people in your work unit have been angry with one another. You have overheard whispers in the hallways and restrooms, and it seems that everyone has something nasty to say about someone else behind his or her back.

It all started, you think, with a misunderstanding between two people. Now, however, it seems to have spread. As far as you can tell, everyone is lined up on sides.

As the leader of your team, you have made a real effort to stay out of the battle and let your employees work it out among themselves. You thought it would blow over quickly, as these things have in the past. Now you recognize that it isn't going to go away so soon. Not only is productivity being severely and negatively impacted, you're also seeing some real undermining of individuals. You realize that things are either not getting done or not getting done well, and your own work is starting to suffer.

You need some help to figure out how to handle the problem, what to say, how to say it, and to whom to speak. You realize there could be repercussions for either taking or not taking action when it comes time for your performance evaluation, and your boss might blame you for letting the fight get so out of hand.

You hate to admit what is going on to your boss, but frankly you're not sure where else to turn. It's late in the day, but you've finally decided to ask for some help.

At the start of the exercise, be sure to tell your boss why you have come and what your needs are.

Follower's Role 4

Seven months ago you asked for and got a lateral transfer because you were interested in learning some new skills and getting a broader understanding of the business. Your new unit has a reputation for being a great training ground and for being efficient and well run. This, you thought, would be the right way to learn what you had to learn and prove yourself in order to get ahead.

The first five or so months were terrific. Your boss told you exactly what to do and how to do it. If decisions had to be made, your boss was there to make them. You asked a steady stream of questions, and your boss always gave you clear and precise answers.

Now you really understand your job and can do it easily and well. While you appreciate your boss's availability, you think it is about time to start using your judgment and making some decisions on your own. Despite your competence, you have recently gone through a string of situations in which you took actions that your boss said were wrong even though the results were fine. When you pointed this out, your boss became visibly annoyed.

The relationship between you and your boss, which had been very good, now seems to be strained. You know it would be a mistake to ask for another transfer so soon and, besides, you like the work and the people in this unit.

You have decided that you're going to have to talk to your boss about your concerns and hope for the best.

At the start of the exercise, be sure to tell your boss why you have come and what your needs are.

Follower's Role 5

Seven months ago, one of your peers in your team was promoted to supervisor. You were all pretty happy because the new supervisor is someone who works hard, is well liked, and gets along with virtually everyone.

Since then, your supervisor has never once said "good job" or even "bad job." When it was time for your annual review, you wrote up your accomplishments, but you never got a chance to sit down with your supervisor and discuss them. All you got were some numbers on a standard appraisal form.

Once or twice you have asked for comments on particular projects, but your supervisor has just changed the subject. Instead, the discussion has ended up being more of a friendly chat about things that have nothing to do with work.

This morning you learned that your supervisor, without ever saying anything to you, almost completely rewrote a report that you had prepared. You wonder whether this has happened before. You have another report due tomorrow at noon for which your supervisor has given you little guidance.

You realize that the lack of feedback and interaction around job issues is keeping both of you from growing and moving ahead.

You have decided to talk to your supervisor about your concerns and hope that your comments will be taken in the spirit in which they are being offered.

At the start of the exercise, be sure to tell your boss why you have come and what your needs are.

Follower's Role 6

Six months ago you were promoted to a manager's position. In this short time, you have been able to pull your people together into a hard-working, cohesive, and productive team by supporting and coaching them to make decisions and take actions.

When your people bring you bad news, you thank them, take responsibility, and work with them to resolve the problems. When they bring you good news, you thank them and make sure they get credit for their accomplishments.

Two of your best people had applied for transfers just before you arrived. Now they have made it clear they want to stay.

It's important to you to encourage your people to grow and move ahead, and you have made a point of giving each of your team members special opportunities to do so. For example, last week, when your team was to meet with upper management, you asked one of your people to run the meeting. You also asked several team members to give various parts of the report that had to do directly with their jobs, even though you know that giving the entire report was something the manager before you always did herself. An hour ago you read your annual performance appraisal. It says that you're not doing your job and that the only reason your team is succeeding is that you have good people working for you. Despite your team's efficiency and productivity, your boss has given you C/C+ rating at best.

You have decided that you have to talk to your boss about your concerns.

At the start of the exercise, be sure to tell your boss why you have come and what your needs are.

56

EARTHQUAKE
A TEAM BUILDING SIMULATION*

The Situation

Monday, July 27, 7:12 p.m.

You and five coworkers are finishing a presentation for tomorrow's early-morning meeting. You are in the basement library of your ten-story downtown office building.

"Oh my gosh, what is happening?" "I can't stand up."

"I think it's an earthquake! Watch out for those books, take cover, and get under the table!"

"Oh no, there go the lights!"

The building shakes violently and then stops. There is a deathly silence except for the slow groan of the building settling. You begin to pick yourselves up and assess the damage.

"Is everyone OK?"

"I think so, but my arm hurts."

"I've got a cut on my leg. One of those huge reference books hit me."

"Hey, does it look like the column in the corner came up over there?"

"It sure does. I wonder how badly the rest of the building was damaged?"

"How can you see anything in the dark?"

"There is some light coming in from the crack in the wall over there near the water heater. I'll go over and take a closer look."

"Forget about the damage, let's get out of here before the rest of the building gives way!"

"I think I smell gas. Does anyone else?"

"Do you hear a hissing sound?"

"I'm not sure if that is hissing or the building moving."

"Hey everyone, we aren't going anywhere. The stairs to the basement are completely blocked. There must be a ton of concrete here."

---

* Copyright 1992. Aviat, a subsidiary of Orion International, Ltd., 555 Briarwood Circle Drive, Suite 140, Ann Arbor, MI 48108. Used with permission.

"We have to get out of here. The whole building could cave in!"

"Everyone needs to calm down. We need to start looking for another way out. What about the elevator?"

"Nope, the shaft is jammed with rubble. I can feel a draft coming down, but I can't see through all the debris."

"Can we climb up on the water heater, and get out of the crack you found in the wall? The water heater seems to be OK."

"Forget that idea. Only a small animal could fit through here."

"I'll check the phone. Maybe we can call for help. The telephone lines are not always damaged in these things—forget it, the lines are dead."

"You obviously haven't experienced a bad one yet. A great deal more than telephone lines are usually damaged."

"How do you know it was a bad one?"

"It lasted longer and shook us around a lot more than most of them do."

"Oh, so that makes you an authority on earthquakes?"

"Would you two stop arguing and come over here with the rest of us?! I found a radio by the janitor's work bench. The news report will be a far more reliable source of information than you two."

We interrupt this broadcast to bring you an Action One special report . . .

There has been a major earthquake. At 7:12 p.m. this evening, San Francisco and the surrounding areas were rocked by an earthquake that experts say may have measured as high as 7.5 on the Richter Scale. It is believed to be one of the worst earthquakes to hit this area in decades. Initial estimates say that the quake lasted for approximately forty seconds and that the danger from the earthquake may not be over. There could be more shaking. The city's telephone network is paralyzed. Electrical wires are down and a number of fires are burning throughout San Francisco. Gas explosions and water main ruptures are occurring throughout the city. Many buildings in the downtown area appear to be severely damaged. City officials say they may be forced to shut down all utility services to prevent fire outbreaks. Many freeway overpasses have collapsed and most of the San Francisco surface streets are clogged with debris and abandoned cars. Air traffic does not appear to be coming in or out of the San Francisco International Airport. Unofficially, the mayor was reported as saying that it could be seventy-two hours or more before city repair crews are able to restore communications and utilities. The mayor also requested that city residents stay off the streets, except for emergencies, until further notice and be prepared to be on their own for at least three days. Stay tuned for more updates . . .

"It really does sound bad."

"I wonder how long it will take someone to find us? Oh no!! The aftershocks are starting already."

Within ten minutes of the quake, a violent aftershock occurs and stirs up more dust and debris in the basement.

"How are we ever going to survive this? Being stuck in this basement during these after-shocks isn't very comforting."

"At least they know there is damage to buildings in our area. Maybe they will look for us right away."

"I don't know. With all these aftershocks, it may be a while before they are able to dig us out."

"You can never tell with these things. We might be here for a while, or someone may find us right away, so we need to make the best of it. Anyone find something we can use to look around a bit?"

"I found a flashlight. Let's do an inventory of what we have to work with."

After searching through the rubble you find:

- a working, battery-operated radio
- two candles
- cleaning supplies: mop, bucket, bleach, window cleaner, screwdriver, wrench, and work gloves
- a first-aid kit: bandages, antiseptic, gauze, and aspirin
- a package of matches
- a coffee machine, half pot of coffee, and three packages of coffee
- a flashlight with extra batteries
- four leftover chicken salad sandwiches in the refrigerator and two bags of chips (from the lunch meeting earlier in the day)
- three full ice-cube trays in the freezer
- six cans of cola

Action Steps

There are **seven action steps you should take** to ensure your survival and rescue and **five action steps that you should not take** because they are either unnecessary or may harm you. Decide which **seven** of the action steps listed **you would take**, assigning a "1" to what you would do first, a "2" to your second step, etc. (1-7). Then continue the ranking with the remaining **five** steps **you would not take** numbering them 8-12, twelfth being reserved for the most dangerous or least helpful step, eleventh, the next less dangerous step, etc.

Complete the individual ranking without discussing the situation with anyone else. Place your answers in column **A**.

Next, repeat the process in teams. Select, by consensus, the sequence that the team thinks makes the most sense. Put the team answers in column **D**.

Your Rank	*Expert Rank*	*Difference A to B*		*Team Rank*	*Expert Rank*	*Difference D to E*
A	**B**	**C**		**D**	**E**	**F**
			Attempt to remove rubble from the entrance to the first floor			
			Divide the sandwiches and ration them over the next few days			
			Light the candles so you can see and rescuers will be able to locate you			
			Locate and secure a water supply			
			Divide the sandwiches and eat them this evening			
			Discuss long-term survival strategies as a group			
			Pound on the pipes with the steel wrench			
			Assign someone to monitor the radio and listen for updates			
			Check for injuries and administer first-aid			
			Shut off all utilities			
			Develop day & night signaling techniques: begin signaling immediately			
			Purify the water source			

Individual Score: ☐

Team Score: ☐

Team-Effectiveness Scores

STEP G   Average Individual Score

Add up each Individual Score (the total of column C) in the group and divide by the number of people in the group.

STEP H   Team Score

The total of column F.

STEP I   Synergy Score

The difference between the TEAM SCORE and the AVERAGE INDIVIDUAL SCORE. If the TEAM SCORE is lower, then the "+" is indicated, signifying that the team achieved some degree of synergy. If the TEAM SCORE is higher, then a "–" is indicated, signifying the group did not work together effectively.

STEP J   Percent Change

The SYNERGY SCORE divided by the AVERAGE INDIVIDUAL SCORE.

STEP K   Lowest Individual Score on the Team

STEP L   Number of Individual Scores Lower Than the Team Score

57

THREE BRAINSTORMING EXERCISES

Objectives

- To practice the problem-solving technique of brainstorming
- To examine the impact of discounting on the creative process

Background

Following are three problems for which brainstorming is a particularly useful technique. The first, "Flying Down to Rio," is based on a mythical situation, while the two following, "Preschool Television" and "Cop Out," are based on actual problems for which brainstorming proved useful.

Use the following instructions and discussion questions for all three problems:

Instructions

Step 1 (5 minutes)

Read the problem to be sure that you understand the issues and limitations of the possibilities.

Step 2 (40 minutes)

Using the six steps in brainstorming (see the "Methodologies and Skills" section at the beginning of this text), solve the problem presented.

Either the instructor or a class member should serve as facilitator.

Be sure that the ideas generated are recorded in a visible place.

Questions for Discussion

1. Was the process successful? By what means did you measure its success?

2. Did ideas emerge that you hadn't considered? Were you able to keep an open mind to the ideas of others?

3. To what degree did you use the ideas of others as sparks to your own creativity?

4. In what ways do you think brainstorming helped with problem solving?

Flying Down to Rio[1]

Today is Thursday: You have just learned that there is a school trip leaving first thing Monday morning for Brazil's famous coastal city, Rio de Janeiro, where the beaches are white, the sea is clear blue, and the night spots are jumping. The trip is being sponsored as a field trip by your school's sociology department. Over the ten days in Rio, you will have to attend a couple of lectures—although you've heard from friends who have been on this trip before that no one really pays much attention to whether you're at the lectures or not. Best of all, the trip is subsidized by a grant, so that for a mere $450, you'll get everything—transportation, meals, and deluxe hotel accommodations (four to a room) at a hotel on the beach.

The problem is that you don't have $450. You have already spent your entire year's allowance, and your parents say "not one penny more." Your grandparents are living on their social security, and while they really love you, there isn't much they can do. You really want to go on that trip! Use the brainstorming technique to find a way to raise the needed money.

Preschool Television

You are part of a team that has been asked to design a new television show for preschool children, ages two and a half to five and a half. The show will run on PST (Preschool Television), a new cable channel, from noon until 2:00 p.m. PST executives would like the show to be focused on a central character that can also be used as a logo for the entire cable channel.

Use the brainstorming technique to develop the appearance and personality of the character, and/or

Use the brainstorming technique to select a name for the character.

Cop Out[2]

You have been hired as consultants to a rural community of eight thousand year-round residents. From approximately June 20 through Labor Day, the town has an additional two thousand summer residents, mainly retirees and families with young children. During ski season, mid-November through late March, two to three thousand skiers arrive each weekend.

The town employs six full-time police officers and five full-time firefighters. There is no more money in the budget for additional hires. There is, however, a $72,000 budget line item to cover overtime hours worked by police and firefighters at peak times. At time and a half, this averages $20.10 per overtime hour. The members of the town board that hired you would like to cut the overtime budget by at least 15 percent, but they're also worried about safety and law enforcement.

1. Special thanks to Professor Kent Seibert, Wheaton College, Wheaton, Illinois for this idea.

2. Special thanks to criminalologist Roni Mayzer, Michigan State University, for her help with this exercise.

During the summer months and over the Christmas holidays, when fire risk is high, the fire department often becomes severely stressed. Up to three more firefighters may be needed on any given day. During this time, sick days for firefighters increase due to fatigue.

Should a major fire break out, at least twice the force size could be required. Between fires, and during most of the rest of the year—when fire risk is low—the firefighters often sit around doing little. Demand for police time is at its peak during the winter months when domestic violence increases. Demand also increases on the evenings of ski weekends due to a fair amount of hard drinking. During these periods, up to 10 percent of the emergency calls have a greater than 20 minutes response time. Some general calls, such as for traffic snarls, get no response at all.

The town's contract with the police department mandates that all members of the force be graduates of the police academy or trained by the department. The contract with the firefighters mandates that all firefighters be employed full-time. Volunteer firefighters may be used so long as they have completed the four-week certification program run by the state. The contract also specifies that at no time is there to be more than one volunteer for every two full-time firefighters.

First define the parameters of the town's problem. Then, use the brainstorming method to find a solution.

58

WHAT DO YOU MAKE OUT OF THIS JUNK?

Objectives

- To practice the technique of brainstorming

- To give participants a chance to examine and practice the facilitator's role in brainstorming

Background

You are an executive management team of Old News, Inc. Until recently, your company has been able to generate a substantial profit by producing and selling cellulose insulation for buildings. Your primary production materials have been old newspapers, purchased at low rates from recycling programs, and lock-top-style plastic bags. Recently, however, a new form of insulation has been sweeping the market, and you see your market share steadily decreasing.

You have several warehouses full of your basic materials and an ample and inexpensive supply of more of the same readily available. Your job is to come up with (1) a new product for your company to produce that uses both of these available materials, and (2) a name for your product.

Several management teams from Old News, Inc. have been assigned to brainstorm and come up with suggestions for the most marketable and most profitable product. There will be a large financial bonus for the group that comes up with the idea that is ultimately adopted.

Instructions

Step 1 (40–60 minutes)

Working with three to five of your classmates, assign a facilitator, and go through the six steps of the brainstorming process (see the "Methodologies and Skills" section at the beginning of this book) to find a product and then to decide on a name.

If you finish early, use the time to generate a backup concept in case your primary product proves to be impractical.

Step 2 (10–15 minutes)

Report your decision to the class, and discuss the merits of each of the suggestions.

Step 3 (open–ended)

Class discussion.

Questions for Discussion

1. What were the strengths and weaknesses of the brainstorming method?

2. In what kinds of situations would you use this method? In what kinds of situations would this method be inappropriate?

3. How did you feel during the process? Were you encouraged to participate? If not, what got in the way, and why? At any time, did you feel discounted? Why?

4. In what ways would you alter this process to make it more effective?

59

DOING THE IMPOSSIBLE*

Objectives

- To explore ways to challenge and move beyond personal assumptions

- To better understand individual and organizational resistances to thinking about and doing things differently

- To explore the ways that individuals and groups can be powerful forces for creativity in the change process from old ways of thinking and doing to new

Background

How can you stretch your imagination beyond its current limits, overcome what appear to be barriers, and do what seems to be impossible? This is often the predicament faced by organizations as competition and the need for rapid technological advances demand innovation and change.

This exercise requires you to move beyond your usual ways of thinking about and doing things to do something which, on its face, seems to be, if not impossible, at least something you cannot now do. Moving beyond traditional ways of thinking is a process that requires work and change for most people. The difficulties presented when innovation is required suggest some of the reasons that individuals and organizations resist doing it and therefore resist change.

It is clear that when new ways of thinking about and doing things are called for, working in groups is almost always more effective than working individually. Using techniques such as active listening and brainstorming, a group is usually able to generate more ideas than an individual, but only if the members are willing to let go of their individual biases and listen to one another with openness and respect. If not, groups and individuals in groups can create barriers to creativity and change.

The Leader

In "Doing the Impossible," each group member has a responsibility to support the efforts of the leader and fellow group members, as well as to make his or her own significant contributions.

* Copyright 1993 by Janet W. Wohlberg and The Center for Executive Development, Inc. Adapted for classroom use, 1997. Used with permission.

The group leader has the potential to positively impact the group's process—but also the potential to interfere. It is the leader's task to provide a clear vision of the project, to help develop a well thought-through plan of action, to actively involve the participants, and to be sure that the ideas of group members are given appropriate support and validation.

The Task

Your task is to come up with a safe way to read while jogging. Before proceeding, briefly review the "Questions for Discussion" below.

Part 1 (small groups: 40-45 minutes) In completing the five steps below, be sure to budget your time.

1. As a way to assess the resources and expertise in your group, spend a few minutes finding out about one another.

2. Select a leader and a spokesperson for your group.

3. As a group, come up with an agreed-upon design for a safe way to read while jogging. This will require you individually and collectively to think about the task, interpret what is meant by "a safe way to read while jogging," communicate your ideas for a solution clearly to your group mates, and listen for the value in your group mates' ideas.

4. When you have agreed upon a design or concept, use the poster board and markers supplied to you to illustrate your solution.

5. Reflect individually and as a group on the process your group followed and your personal role in coming up with the solution. Write some brief answers to each of the Questions for Discussion, below. Then discuss your answers with your group.

Part 2 (5 minutes per group and open-ended discussion)

Present your solution, using the graphic you have developed on the poster board, to the larger group. The spokesperson should briefly describe the barriers to developing a solution to the problem that your group met and how you overcame those barriers. Particularly consider the role your group leader played in facilitating the solution.

Questions for Discussion

1. What traditional ways of thinking did you and your group mates have to overcome in order to complete this task?

2. How did your group overcome the barriers to solving the problem and executing the task?

3. In what ways did your group leader facilitate solving the problem? What should the leader have done differently?

5. How can you apply what you have just learned to the workplace?

60

CYRIL AND EDNA: THE MANAGER AS MEDIATOR

Objectives

- To develop skills for managing and mediating conflict in the work place

- To practice the skills of active listening

- To practice the skills of making one's needs understood

- To help parties to a conflict recognize their common superordinate goals

Background

"Cyril and Edna" presents a case of interpersonal conflict in the work place in which many behaviors continue without comment (avoidance) despite their irritating nature. In an attempt to keep peace, coworkers often let their feelings fester and build, finally reaching a boiling point. When this happens, it is generally the role of the manager to surface the issues and mediate the dispute in a helpful manner. When the manager fails to do this, the frequent result is employee turnover, diminished productivity, and loss of morale.

Before beginning this role play, be sure to review tips for handling conflict in the work place and active listening skills in the "Methodologies and Skills" section at the front of this book.

If you are the manager, decide which of your two employees you will have speak first and how you will explain that choice to them. Hint: If you decide that one employee has more invested in the dispute than the other and should therefore begin the discussion, you are going to have to make that clear without minimizing the other's concerns. Other possibilities are to flip a coin or explain that you have made an arbitrary decision to start with the employee, e.g., sitting to your right.

Be sure you have given each employee ample opportunity to say what is on his or her mind before moving to the other. This will require you to listen actively and ask probing but non-threatening and open-ended questions to elicit the necessary information. Remember that some material may be difficult for your employees to talk about, and some may be difficult for you to hear. In this case in particular, there are issues of race and racism that are likely to emerge and with which you must deal.

As manager, be sure to set some basic ground rules at the outset, most importantly that only one employee may speak at a time. Avoid making decisions for or imposing solutions on the participants.

If you play the role of either Cyril or Edna, feel free to add any details to your story that suit your purpose. Think about how you would react if you were actually in your character's position, and bring that to the conversation. You do not need to reveal all of your feelings and issues about the events in the office immediately if your own personal style is to leak out a little at a time.

When your role is that of observer, your responsibility is to take careful notes, using the "Questions for Observers" as a guide, and to give the role players explicit feedback.

Instructions

Step 1 (10 minutes)

You will be working in groups of three or more. Decide who will be the manager, Edna, Cyril, and the observers (if there are to be any). *Everyone should read the manager's role and the "Questions for Observers,"* both of which are found on the following pages. The roles of Edna and Cyril will be distributed to you.

If you are Cyril, do not read Edna's role, and vice versa. In addition, the manager should not read Cyril's or Edna's roles.

Think carefully about your role and how you wish to play it. Make margin notes on the role description to help yourself along. Before beginning, be sure you are clear on what your issues are.

Step 2 (20–30 minutes)

Begin by having the manager explain why the meeting has been called and what the ground-rules are to be. Continue until you have reached a resolution that is agreeable to both Edna and Cyril and that is realistic, or until the time is up.

Step 3 (15 minutes)

Using "Work Sheet 1" as a guide, describe to your group what you felt as you played your role. Be honest and open, for example, if you felt your manager wasn't listening to you, say so, and explain why.

Step 4 (10 minutes)

Using "Work Sheet 2" as a guide, record your group's resolution and some general observations about your group's methods, successes, and areas for improvement. Discuss.

Step 5 (open- ended)

Report your outcome to the class. Discuss.

Questions for Observers

1. What mutual interests do Cyril and Edna have? Did these become clear during the mediation? How?

2. What was the resolution? Was it satisfactory to both parties? Why or why not?

3. What did the manager do well?

    a. Did the manager set out clear reasons for meeting?

    b. Did the manager clarify the process and the guidelines?

    c. Did the manager listen to each party without being judgmental?

    d. Did the manager rephrase and clarify the issues raised?

    e. Did the manager ask open-ended questions to elicit information?

    f. Was the manager able to control repetitious arguing?

4. What would you have liked the manager to do differently?

Note: The roles for Cyril and Edna are in the Instructor's Manual.

Role: Manager

You are the manager of the technical support division of a medium-sized software development firm. Your job is to manage fifteen technical support representatives, eight of whom are regularly on the road visiting customers. The other seven take phone calls from often frustrated and sometimes abusive customers.

Generally morale has been high in your unit, despite the intensity of your employees' jobs. You've tried to create an atmosphere of having fun, and you have fostered cooperative decision making and problem solving.

Each representative sits in a cubicle; the seven cubicles are separated by partitions that are approximately five feet high. There is considerable visiting from cubicle to cubicle and a fair amount of conversation over the partitions.

Yesterday, Cyril and Edna, two of the telephone representatives, came to you independently complaining of one another's behavior. You do not yet know the details of their complaints, and you were surprised because in the past they seemed to have gotten along. Each has been in your division for a little over two years, and both have demonstrated a high degree of competence in their jobs. Customers seem to like them.

Cyril is a 25-year-old black man with an engineering degree. Edna, 48 years old, returned to the workforce after raising her children. This is her first job since going back to work. Both Cyril and Edna have been with the company for between two and two and a half years.

You have decided that the best way to deal with the conflict is to bring Cyril and Edna together in your office to find out what is on their minds and to work out a resolution. Your job is to mediate the dispute, being sure that each of the disputants is heard, that the resolution comes from them, and that it is agreed to by both.

Work Sheet 1

1. Briefly describe at least five feelings you had as you played your role. Begin each description with the words "I felt . . ." and then describe why you think you felt the way you did. For example, you might note, "I felt frustrated because my manager kept interrupting me," or "I felt Edna wasn't really listening to me because she was always looking in the other direction."

   _____

   _____

   _____

   _____

   _____

   _____

   _____

   _____

2. Briefly describe why you believe the resolution, if you were able to reach one, will or will not satisfy your needs and the needs of your organization.

   _____

   _____

   _____

   _____

   _____

   _____

   _____

Work Sheet 2

1. Briefly describe the mediation process and its results.

_____

_____

_____

_____

2. Were all issues dealt with appropriately? Why or why not?

_____

_____

_____

_____

3. In what ways did you feel the process was successful?

_____

_____

_____

_____

4. In what ways do you feel the process could have been better?

_____

_____

_____

_____

61

CONFRONTATION AT CAPTAIN COOK'S*
PART 1

Objectives

- To examine the origins of conflict

- To examine personal styles in reacting to conflict

- To practice the skills of managing conflict through confrontation

Background

When people live together, work together, and even play together, a certain amount of conflict is inevitable and actually even healthy and useful when managed effectively. Ineffective management of conflict most often results in strained and sometimes broken relationships and a stressful environment in which far more than just the direct parties to the dispute become involved. As conflict continues unresolved, stress builds, and morale and productivity generally go down.

Effective conflict management allows the parties to the conflict to learn and grow from the experience, develop a more open and cooperative relationship, and build skills for handling future conflict. It can also result in creative solutions to difficult problems.

"Confrontation at Captain Cook's" presents conflict between two individuals, supervisor and subordinate, who have different needs and for each of whom the path to fulfilling those needs seems to be contrary to the other.

Before performing this role play, be sure you are familiar with the skills of managing confrontation and of active listening, described in the Methodologies and Skills section of this book. Be sure also to read the Observer Sheet that appears just after the roles. Since the roles of both the manager and the waitperson are in the book, try to limit yourself to reading only the one to which you have been assigned.

When you play the role of the manager or the waitperson in this exercise, you will be given frank and honest feedback from one or more observers on how well you managed the confrontation.

Diligent observers are critical to this exercise. Since managing conflict by confrontation requires a structured set of skills, observers must take careful notes and be prepared to explain to the role players what they did well and what they will need to work on in their conflict management styles. Use the Observer Sheet as a guide.

* Copyright 1993 by Sandra L. Deacon. Used with permission.

Instructions

1. *(small groups:10 minutes)*

Working in your group of three to six participants, decide, without looking at the roles, who will play the manager and who will play the waitperson. All others will be observers. Also, select a spokesperson for the group who will report to the rest of the class.

If you are to play either the manager or the waitperson, read your role carefully (at least twice) and make notes as to how you will present your side of the conflict. Be sure also to read the Observer Sheet.

If you are an observer, review the skills of active listening, the tips for managing confrontation, and the Observer Sheet. It is not necessary for you to read the roles.

2. *(small groups: 15 minutes)*

Begin the role play by having the manager explain why the meeting has been requested. Continue until a resolution has been reached or time is up, whichever comes first.

3. *(small groups: 15 minutes)*

After the role play, the manager and the waitperson should describe how they felt during the role play and in what ways they acted differently from their usual behavior in the face of conflict.

Next, have each of the observers report what they observed, using specific information, and make suggestions for what could be improved. It is important for all members of the group to give input at this stage.

4. *(open-ended)*

Have your spokesperson report your findings to the rest of the class. Discuss.

Role 1: Manager

You are the new manager of Captain Cook's, a small seasonal restaurant on the southern coast of Maine. You got the job after having been a line cook in the restaurant last summer, when you received the Captain Cook Award for excellent work. You also gained some experience as a waiter at a five-star resort hotel in Colorado over the winter.

You have heard through the grapevine that some of the waiters and waitresses who worked at Captain Cook's during the previous summer are wary of your new position and skeptical of the new policies and procedures for servicing customers. In discussing your concern about this with the owner, he said that he would support you 100 percent in enforcing the new policies. "If anyone gives you a hard time," the Captain told you, "you let me know, and they're history."

During the first couple of weeks of the summer season, some of the waitstaff complained about the lack of customers during the lunch shift. In response, two days ago you sent two of your employees out to distribute menus to the various hotels, cabins, and bed and breakfasts in the area. Yesterday, you overheard Mickey, one of the waitstaff, talking about having difficulty making enough money during the lunch shift to cover the cost of a baby-sitter and wondering whether it's worth working at all. Hearing this, you offered to have Mickey become the host-cashier for today's lunch shift, a position that insures a reasonable hourly wage rather than having to depend largely on tips. After a few moments of thinking about it, Mickey took your offer.

Last evening, when the restaurant was busy, you pitched in to help some of the waitstaff in addition to performing your duties as host-cashier. You left last night feeling satisfied that you are doing your best to support your employees and keep them happy. You are particularly pleased that your goal of having an "open-door relationship" with your employees seems to be working.

Today, after your meeting with the Captain, you stopped into the restaurant during the lunch shift. The outside deck was filled with customers, and the waitstaff was busy. At the host-cashier desk, however, you were confronted by an angry customer.

"What do I have to do to pay my bill around here?" he demanded. "I've been standing here for twenty minutes waiting to pay. You're lucky I'm honest, or I just would have left without paying. Two people ahead of me just gave up and took off."

After apologizing to the customer and handling his payment, you discovered that Mickey was outside on the deck taking an order from a table. It was at least five minutes before Mickey returned to the host-cashier desk, during which time you took payments and showed parties to their tables. "Mickey," you hissed through gritted teeth. "Be in my office right after your shift, or else."

You're angry, and you want to know why Mickey was waiting on tables instead of tending to the hosting duties. You're also upset that you're going to be called to account for the checks that went unpaid.

Lunch shift is over, and Mickey is now in your office. Confront Mickey with the problem.

Role 2: Mickey

For the fourth summer in a row, you were hired as a member of the waitstaff at Captain Cook's, a small seasonal restaurant on the southern coast of Maine. You were surprised to discover that the new manager is much younger than you, was only one of the line cooks last summer, and is someone who never particularly impressed you. In addition, this manager has introduced a lot of new policies and procedures that make you uncomfortable, like greeting repeat customers by name and making specific menu recommendations.

The first few weeks of the season had been extremely slow, and you were not even able to make enough money to cover the cost of the baby-sitter you hire to watch your young child. When the manager asked if you would prefer to work as the host-cashier during the usually slow lunch shift, you accepted, figuring that the hourly wage would be a safer bet than relying on tips. As the host, you would be responsible for seating customers, and as the cashier, you would take credit-card and cash payments and make change.

Today, on your first day as host-cashier, you quickly realized that the lunch shift was much busier than yesterday or anytime since the restaurant opened for the season. As you seated more and more customers, it became obvious that the waitstaff was making a lot in tips—more than you would make for your four-hour shift. Because you really need the money, you decided that you would wait on a couple of tables on the outside deck along with doing the host-cashier job. One of your friends who works the dinner shift told you that the manager had done the same thing last night when things got busy.

After serving one table and taking an order from another, you came in off the deck to find your manager, who wasn't scheduled to start working for another three hours, at the cashier desk taking a payment from a customer. About five other customers were waiting to pay. You're sure they hadn't been waiting very long, because you had checked the desk just a few minutes earlier.

You don't think anyone heard the manager angrily telling you to report to the office immediately after your shift. You're not sure what this is all about, and as far as you're concerned, you were doing your job and doing it well. You're also feeling rushed, since you have to get home in time for your baby-sitter to leave for football practice. You realize that you'll have to find a way to defend yourself if you're going to keep your job. Lunch shift is over, and you are now in your manager's office.

Observer Sheet: Part 1

	Yes	No
1. Did the manager listen to the employee?		
2. Did the manager focus on the behaviors rather than the person?		
3. Did the manager show emotions?		
4. Was the manager's show of emotions appropriate?		
5. Was the manager direct and assertive?		
6. Did the manager ask for specific behavioral changes?		
7. Did the manager discuss the consequences should the behavior occur again?		
8. Did the manager check to see that the employee understood the message?		

9. What emotions did the manager display, and how?

_____

_____

_____

10. What specific behavioral changes did the manager request? In what ways was the request appropriate or not?

_____

_____

_____

11. What did the manager do particularly well in managing this conflict by confrontation?

_____

_____

_____

12. In what ways does the manager need to improve?

_____

_____

_____

CONFRONTATION AT CAPTAIN COOK'S
PART 2—TWO DAYS LATER

Instructions

1. (5 minutes)

Assign the Part 2 roles of manager and waitperson to two new role players. Repeat the process as in Instruction #1 of Part 1.

If you are the manager, consider how you feel about what your employee has done (as described in Part 2) and what you believe motivated her or him. Based on this, make some notes about how you will continue.

If you are the waitperson, consider what your manager is likely to feel about what you have done (as described in Part 2) and whether you feel you handled the situation appropriately.

If you are an observer, review the questions on the Observer Sheet that follows the roles.

2. (15 minutes)

Begin the role play by having the manager explain why the meeting has been requested. Continue until a resolution has been reached or time is up, whichever comes first.

3. (15 minutes)

After the role play, the manager and the waitperson should describe how they felt during the role play and in what ways they acted differently from their usual behavior in the face of conflict.

Next, have each of the observers report what they observed, using specific information, and make suggestions for what could be improved. It is important for all members of the group to give input at this stage.

4. (open ended)

Have your spokesperson report your findings to the rest of the class.

Role 1: Manager
Two Days Later

Although you feel you might have done a few things differently in your confrontation with Mickey two days ago, you feel that you got your message across and that the matter was settled.

This morning, at your meeting with the Captain, you were surprised to hear that Mickey had gone to him to complain that you have been "taking tables away from the waitstaff when you were supposed to be the host-cashier." After you told the Captain about what had happened and how you handled it, he tells you, "I don't care what you do over there because I trust that you are doing a good job. But I don't need any employees who are going to be back-stabbing the people they work with. It's up to you how you handle this."

When you got to the restaurant, you asked Mickey to meet you in your office immediately after the lunch shift. Mickey has just walked into your office. Begin by telling Mickey why you have requested the meeting.

Role 2: Mickey
Two Days Later

Your meeting with your manager two days ago left you with some unresolved feelings about what happened. In particular, you felt that your manager was being pretty hypocritical about not wanting you to be both host-cashier and a waitperson when things got busy. After all, this is exactly what the manager has been doing; so why shouldn't you?

Since this is your fourth summer at Captain Cook's, and you feel you know the Captain pretty well, you decided to go to him and tell him about the manager taking tables away from the waitstaff. After all, you think, if you can't make extra money by waiting on tables while being host-cashier, why should the manager?

Yesterday afternoon, you dropped by and had a chat with the Captain. The two of you had coffee and an amiable conversation about the town, the tourist season, and events at the restaurant. When you told him of your concerns, he said he would speak to the manager about your complaint. Now the manager has requested another meeting with you, and you have just walked into the office.

Observer Sheet: Part 2

	Yes	No
1. Did the manager listen to the employee?		
2. Did the manager focus on the behaviors rather than the person?		
3. Did the manager show emotions?		
4. Was the manager's show of emotions appropriate?		
5. Was the manager direct and assertive?		
6. Did the manager ask for specific behavioral changes?		
7. Did the manager discuss the consequences should the behavior occur again?		
8. Did the manager check to see that the employee understood the message?		

9. If you were Mickey, what would you have done differently?

_____

_____

_____

_____

10. In what ways did the manager handle this second confrontation appropriately?

_____

_____

_____

_____

11. What would you have liked the manager to have done differently? Why?

_____

_____

_____

_____

62

FIVE CONFLICT MANAGEMENT ROLE PLAYS

Objectives

- To consider the components of conflict

- To examine personal styles of reacting to conflict

- To explore ways of finding mutual interests in conflict situations

- To practice the skills of conflict resolution

Background

The following five role plays offer scenarios of conflict that are either vertical (between two persons of differing positions and power) or horizontal (between peers with roughly equal power). They are based on typical conflicts that most people encounter many times in their lives. Characters in these conflicts confront one another over differences of opinion, needs and concerns, and objectives.

Before trying this exercise, be sure you are familiar with role plays, the skills of managing confrontations, and the skills of active listening, described in the "Methodologies and Skills" section of this book.

The emotions of the role players are not clear in the role descriptions. Role players should project their own feelings and emotions into the situations presented in the role descriptions. For example, if you are a role player and find yourself in a situation in which you believe you would feel angry or frustrated, convey those feelings through your role.

Each role play should be repeated at least twice (for a total of three times) with different players. Discussion should follow each round and should explore what the role players did well and what they might have done differently.

Instructions

1. (individually: 10–15 minutes)

Read both roles of the role play assigned. In the margins, make some notes about where you see the areas of disagreement and how you might feel about your situation should you be in one of the roles. For example, in the role play between parent and teen, think about how you would feel if you were the parent and how you might feel if you were the teen. Use the "Questions for Discussion" as a guide.

2. Role play (10 minutes)

Two people will be selected at random to play the given roles in front of the entire group. After 10 minutes, the role play should stop whether or not a resolution has been reached.

During the role plays, observers should make notes as to what the role players are doing well and what they might have done differently.

3. Debrief (whole group: open-ended)

Using the "Questions for Discussion" as a guide, explore what the role players did well and what they might have done differently to bring about a different resolution.

4. Repeat the role play with new players, as above.

Questions for Discussion

1. Were the role players able to state their interests clearly? What else might they have said, and how might they have said it?

2. Did the role players listen to one another? If not, what kinds of static got in the way? Include in this a discussion of the emotions that were displayed and how the display of those emotions impacted the ability of the role players to reach resolution.

3. What did the role players do well in bringing about a meaningful resolution? What might they have done differently? If no resolution was reached, what might the role players have done to come to an agreement?

4. In the repetition of the role play, what traps did role players appear to have avoided by having seen the previous role play(s)?

Role Play 1—The Photography Store

Manager

You are the manager of a branch store of The Colorworks, a company that processes and prints still film and sells photography supplies. Some of the processing is done in-house on a Fuji Minilab 23MII. Black-and-white developing and unusual format printing, such as posters, are sent to your central processing plant. Your store is one of the busiest in the region. Salaries are low throughout The Colorworks network, and turnover is high. Most employees are unskillled and learn on the job.

This morning, just as the shop was getting busy, your two employees got into an argument with one another, blamed it on you, quit, and walked out. This has left you alone to complete the in-house processing and wait on customers.

Customer

You arrived at The Colorworks about 15 minutes ago to pick up the black-and-white prints that you dropped off for processing about a week ago. You're parked at a meter that is about to run out, and you had expected much faster service.

When you finally get the prints—photographs of family members, some quite elderly, taken at a once-in-a-lifetime family event—you notice that the envelope in which the prints are packed is stamped "received damaged."

Checking through, indeed you find that about 1/3 of the prints are badly spotted and scratched. In addition, all but a couple are poorly printed, and detail is washed out.

You are a fairly experienced amateur photographer and don't believe that the fault is either with your photography or your brand new, $3000 Leica camera. You also don't believe that you delivered the film damaged, as you actually had taken the film out of the camera at the shop.

Role Play 2—The Party

Parent

You are the parent of an 18-year-old who is home for the first time since leaving for college this past September. Tonight, your college student wants to take the car to go to a party at the apartment of a high school friend, Pat.

Pat, also 18, did not go to college after high school and, from what you know, has done little other than hang out and get drunk at local bars. Pat lives alone.

Twice over the past several months you have read in the local paper about parties at Pat's being busted up by the police. Pat has been accused of serving alcohol to minors and disturbing the peace, and is currently out on bail on a drug charge.

The drinking age in your state is 18.

College Student

Since going off to college this past fall, you have worked and studied hard to keep up a 3.7 grade point average. Nights and weekends, when your classmates have been partying, you have limited your drinking to a single beer and have generally returned to your dorm room early to get your work done. You have also considered it important to get enough sleep to be alert for your 8 a.m. classes. This is a change from some of the things you did during your high school years.

While you were in high school, you, Pat, and some other friends were caught by the police having a drinking party in the school's football field. Your parents had to come to the police station to bail you out. After that, you moved your parties to the houses of friends whose parents weren't home. Pat was always the one who brought the beer and pot. A couple of times you left your car at the friend's house and walked home because you were too drunk to drive.

You haven't seen your high school friends since you left for college. All of your closest friends will be at tonight's party.

Role Play 3—The Last Will and Testament

Sibling #1

Your grandmother has asked you to get together with your sibling and come up with an agreed-upon list of what, besides money, you would like her to leave each of you at her death. There aren't a lot of her things about which you have strong feelings, but there are three 18th century oil paintings and your grandfather's pocket watch that you want. At his 75th birthday party, your grandfather told you that these would someday be yours.

Sibling #2

You have walked through your grandmother's house and have carefully selected the things you would like her to leave you. There are a few pieces of furniture that you don't really care that much about, although they would be useful to furnish your rather sparse living quarters. What you do want, however, are her three 18th century oil paintings and an antique chair. While on his death bed at age 79, your grandfather told you that these would someday be yours.

Role Play 4—The Commission

Car Salesperson #1

You are a salesperson at Sheldon Volkswagen/Audi. This past Saturday, you spent almost two hours with a couple who said they were trying to decide between the Audi A8 and a BMW 740. You took them for a test drive and worked out a price with all the options they wanted. After they left, you located the exact car they were looking for at another dealer and called them with the news. They said they still hadn't made up their minds but would get back to you. This is one commission for which you have really worked.

Car Salesperson #2

Today a couple walked into your dealership and asked for Salesperson #1, who was taking a vacation day. You offered to help them, and they accepted. They told you that they had located a BMW dealer who had offered them a great deal, that they were definitely going to buy a car today, and that it would be the Audi A8 if you could meet their price. Otherwise, they made clear, they would be buying the BMW. After a lengthy negotiation, a number of private conversations with your boss, and decision to substantially cut your own commission, you closed the deal. Your name is on the order form: The commission is yours.

Role Play 5—Music, Music, Music

Coworker #1

You work for a major diamond importer and are often asked to deliver orders to jewelry outlets within a 500 mile district. Today your boss has asked you and a coworker to deliver an order to a city just over four hours away. You have been assigned a company car, and you and your coworker will take turns driving.

You found out in advance that the car is equipped with a brand-new CD player. In anticipation of the long trip, you went out and bought a number of CDs of your favorite music, i.e., Mozart piano concertos, a Rachmaninoff symphony, and a great new recording of the opera Cosi fan Tutte. Rock music makes you itchy and nervous. You have no intention of allowing your coworker to play that junk while you're in the car.

Coworker #2

In anticipation of the long driving trip you're making today, you went out and bought a bunch of CDs of your favorite music, including Lucas Santtana, Toad the Wet Sprocket, and Pearl Jam. You also researched which radio stations along the way play the best pop rock. You like your music wild and loud, and you're looking forward to hearing your new CDs. Classical music gives you nightmares about the piano lessons your parents made you take as a small child. You have no intention of allowing your coworker to play boring classical music while you're in the car.

63

A PLACE OF YOUR OWN: A NEGOTIATION ROLE PLAY

Objectives

- To give participants practice in negotiation skills
- To give participants practice in making their needs and desires understood
- To give participants practice in active listening

Background

Negotiation is an integral part of daily life. Even simple decisions among coworkers, such as who will go out to get the coffee, or among friends, such as what movie to see, involve negotiation. When emotional needs or interests are minimal on the part of one or more parties to the negotiation, agreement or compromise may be easy and swift. If two friends want to go to the movies and one doesn't care what movie they see, while the other has a very specific preference, the resolution is simple. But if each of the two friends has a different preference, they will have to find a creative solution if they are going to enjoy the night out. The two friends may decide that one friend will pick the movie while the other will pick the restaurant for dinner after the movie.

One principle of negotiation is that by increasing the number of items over which the negotiation is taking place, in this case negotiating over not just the movie but also the restaurant, opportunities are provided for a more satisfactory solution.

The following role play, which involves two parents and a college age son/daughter, will give you an opportunity to practice your negotiation skills in the face of potentially high emotional interests. The roles have been left purposely vague so that you may fill in what you believe your underlying interests would be. If you play one of the parents, you should decide whether what your child is proposing is a good, bad, or neutral idea. In playing these roles, try to consider what your own parents' underlying interests might be if they were in the position described. Be sure you have a clear idea of the assurances you would want from your son/daughter before agreeing to the proposal. Use the questions that appear with the role to guide you to think about and plan what you will say. If you play the college student, project yourself into the role, and use the arguments you would make to your own parents. Here again, it will be necessary to ascertain just what you believe your underlying interests would be and what alternatives exist for meeting those interests. Use the questions that appear with the role to guide you to think about and plan what you will say.

There is also a role for one or more observers. As an observer, your responsibility is to take careful notes, using the observation sheet as a guide, and actively participate in the debriefing that follows the role play.

Before proceeding with the role play, be sure you have read the overview to this section.

Instructions

1. (10 minutes)

Working in a small group, determine who will play each of the roles—Student, Parent 1, Parent 2, Observer(s).

Read the background information and your role carefully. Determine what your underlying interests are in moving off campus if you are the son or daughter or what your underlying interests are for your son or daughter if you are a parent. As a guide, use the questions that appear with your role. Develop a strategy that will help you achieve your underlying interests. You may read the other roles, although they are not likely to be of much help. If you are an observer, read the questions on the "Observation Sheet" and all roles.

2. (20 minutes)

Begin the role play by having the student explain his or her interests. One or both of the parents should then respond. Continue until you have reached an agreement or time is up, whichever comes first.

As a parent, you do not have to agree to having your son or daughter live off campus, you need not agree with your spouse, and you may make any demands you wish.

3. (10 minutes)

Working in the role play groups, the observers should report what they saw and why they believe the negotiation was successful or not. The role players should also report how they felt during the role play and describe the various points they were trying to make, what they saw as their strategies, what they thought they did well, and what they might have done differently.

4. (20 minutes)

Select a spokesperson from your role play group to report to the class what happened in your role play, the outcome, and whether and why the role play succeeded or failed.

Role 1: Student

You are currently completing your sophomore year in college. This year and last, you have lived in the dorms. Recently, four of your friends, male and female, suggested that you move off-campus together for your junior and senior years. They have found a great three-bedroom house near fraternity row that is just a short bus ride from campus. In nice weather, you can walk, roller blade, or bike to classes. Your rent at the house will run about 20 percent less than the room-and-meal plan costs in the dorm.

You think it's a great idea, but you're not sure how your parents are going to feel. Since they're going to be paying for most, if not all, of your living expenses, you'll need to get their agreement. You'll be getting together with them to talk it over shortly. Before you get together, answer the questions below.

1. What do you see as the benefits and drawbacks to living off campus? Why?

_____

_____

_____

_____

2. What do you believe your parents will see as benefits to your living off campus? Why?

_____

_____

_____

_____

3. What do you believe your parents' objections are likely to be? Why?

_____

_____

_____

_____

4. What are you willing to do that you think will make your parents more comfortable with your plan?

_____

_____

_____

_____

Role 2: Parent 1

Your son or daughter has expressed an interest in living off campus beginning this fall for his or her junior and senior years. You understand that the plan is to live in a three-bedroom house with four friends, male and female, near fraternity row. You have quite a few concerns about such an arrangement, and you're not sure whether this is in his or her best interest. You lived off campus during your senior year in college, so you have some sense of what it's like.

You and your spouse will be getting together with your son or daughter to talk things over shortly. Before you get together, answer the questions below.

1. What are your concerns about your son or daughter living off campus? Why?

_____

_____

_____

_____

2. What do you see as the benefits of your son or daughter living off campus? For him or her? For you? Why?

_____

_____

_____

_____

3. What do you want from your son or daughter in return for your consideration of his or her request? (Be specific.)

_____

_____

_____

_____

4. What assurances from your son or daughter do you want to make you feel comfortable with this plan?

_____

_____

_____

_____

Role 3: Parent 2

Your son or daughter has expressed an interest in living off campus beginning this fall for his/her junior and senior years. You understand that the plan is to live in a three-bedroom house with four friends, male and female, near fraternity row. You have quite a few concerns about such an arrangement, and you're not sure whether this is in his or her best interest. You never went to college, so you really don't know much about what it's like to live in a dorm or off-campus with friends.

You and your spouse will be getting together with your son or daughter to talk things over shortly. Before you get together, answer the questions below.

1. What are your concerns about your son or daughter living off campus? Why?

   _____

   _____

   _____

   _____

2. What do you see as the benefits of your son or daughter living off campus? For him or her? For you? Why?

   _____

   _____

   _____

   _____

3. What do you want from your son or daughter in return for your consideration of his or her request? (Be specific.)

   _____

   _____

   _____

   _____

4. What assurances from your son or daughter do you want to help you feel comfortable with this plan?

   _____

   _____

   _____

   _____

Observer

Before beginning, read each of the roles. Familiarize yourself with the questions below. Take notes during the exercise in response to each of the questions below.

1. In what ways did the role players make clear or fail to make clear their underlying interests?

   _____

   _____

   _____

2. In what ways did the role players focus on interests rather than demands?

   _____

   _____

   _____

3. In what ways were the role players able to focus on issues rather than personalities?

   _____

   _____

   _____

4. In what ways did the role players reflect or fail to reflect a willingness to address one another's needs?

   _____

   _____

   _____

5. In what ways did the role players show creativity and flexibility in resolving the issues?

   _____

   _____

   _____

6. What do you think each of the role players could have done differently that might have brought about better results?

   _____

   _____

   _____

64

RABBIT FEVER*

Objectives

- To practice the skills of negotiation
- To examine the meaning and purpose of the reservation price
- To examine the meaning and purpose of the no-agreement price
- To practice planning a negotiation strategy

Instructions

Step 1 (20 minutes)

Read both the "General Information" and either the buyer's or seller's "Confidential Information," depending on which role you have been assigned. Identify your no-agreement alternative (your best other possibility should you not be able to reach an agreement on this negotiation), and determine both your reservation price (for the buyer—the absolute most you would be willing to pay; for the seller—the absolute least you would be willing to take) and your target price (the amount you would like to spend or realize). Prepare your negotiating strategy which should include, if you are the buyer, your opening counter to the seller's advertised asking price.

Step 2 (30–40 minutes)

Meet with the other party in an attempt to negotiate a mutually acceptable price for the used Rabbit convertible described below. By the end of the time period, you should have reached an agreement on a price or concluded that it is not possible for the two of you to agree on a price.

Step 3 (open-ended).

Participate in class discussion regarding the negotiation. Topics for discussion may include the specifics of any agreement reached; your reservation price and the basis on which it was determined; your negotiating strategy and why it was or wasn't successful; whether you or the other party departed from the facts contained in the confidential instructions; whether you are happy with the process; and whether you are happy with the substantive outcome of the negotiation.

* Copyright 1992 by Morris Raker. Used with permission.

General Information

You and another individual will negotiate concerning the purchase and sale of a used car. The locale is Minneapolis, during the second week of December 1999.

The vehicle in question is a 1991 VW Rabbit convertible with the following features:

- The body is yellow and in excellent condition. The vehicle had been rust-proofed when new. The seller is the original owner, and the car appears to have been well-maintained and garaged overnight.

- The fully-lined, black canvas top is in excellent condition. The boot (a separate lined, black canvas piece used to cover the top when it is down) is missing.

- The interior is clean. The fabric-covered sports seats show only modest wear.

- The odometer reads 53,783 miles.

- Replacement radial tires are in good condition, with about 15,000 miles of wear.

- The AM/FM radio works fine; however, the tape player is not functioning.

- The vehicle has been advertised for sale in the newspaper at $5,900.

In addition to these general instructions, you will also receive confidential, personal instructions.

You will have fifteen minutes to develop your strategy and tactics. Make some notes below on your ideas and plans about how to bargain:

1. What is your goal?_____

2. What is your reservation price?_____

3. What are your opponent's likely goal and reservation price, and how will you attempt to learn more about them?_____

4. Strategically, how will you seek to persuade your opponent? _____

   _____

   _____

   _____

5. What will be your tactical moves? _____

   _____

   _____

   _____

   _____

   _____

   _____

Negotiator's Worksheet and Checklist

The following worksheet sets out the critical areas for planning for and carrying out a negotiation.

1. Describe your best no-agreement alternative, and set your reservation price.

   _____

   _____

   _____

   _____

2. Describe the actions that you think you can take to improve your no-agreement alternative.

   _____

   _____

   _____

   _____

3. List what you know about your opponent that could possibly be helpful in your negotiation, including possible interests and available alternatives. Describe what you believe his or her negotiating style is like.

   _____

   _____

   _____

   _____

4. List ways and sources for learning more about your opponent.

   _____

   _____

   _____

   _____

5. Briefly describe what you believe your opponent's best no-agreement alternative is. Estimate what you believe his or her reservation price is.

_____

_____

_____

_____

6. Identify ways in which you can worsen your opponent's no-agreement alternative.

_____

_____

_____

_____

7. Describe your underlying interests.

_____

_____

_____

_____

8. Describe what you believe are your opponent's underlying interests.

_____

_____

_____

_____

9. In integrative bargaining situations, identify areas of potential joint gain. This includes identifying and analyzing the differences between you and your opponent (in relative valuation, forecasts, risk aversion, time preferences, etc.), the possibility that you share certain interests, and the potential for using economies of scale.

_____

_____

_____

_____

10. Identify ways you believe would make it possible to satisfy the interests of both parties.

_____

_____

_____

_____

_____

11. Identify the various arguments that you or your opponent might use to support the fairness of your respective bargaining positions. Prepare to use the ones that best support your position. Prepare arguments against those you think your opponent will use.

_____

_____

_____

_____

_____

12. Use the early stages of the negotiation to learn more about your opponent's interests and style, and to set a favorable tone. The object is to cultivate opportunities for cooperation and creativity, and to reduce the potential for conflict. Focus on a joint effort to find a solution to what is seen as a common problem. Avoid using threats and otherwise personalizing the problem. Make it possible for your opponent to accept your position without loss of face.

_____

_____

_____

_____

_____

PART V

ORGANIZATIONAL PROCESSES AND CHARACTERISTICS

Overview

This section deals with organizational structure—that is, the ways in which organizations set up chains of command; the impact of the external environment on internal operations; the climate of internal operations, generally referred to as the corporate culture; and issues related to managing change.

Organizational Structure

Typically, the word *bureaucracy* is used negatively. Aspiring politicians attack "fat-cat bureaucrats" in federal government, many people complain about having to "cut through the bureaucracy" at work, and students often feel frustrated when, because of the bureaucratic structures of their colleges, they are sent from department to department to achieve what should be simple tasks, such as getting a student ID card or a transcript.

A university graduate got a word-processing job at a European company that manufactured large commercial boilers. Besides typing his manager's correspondence, the grad's responsibility was to take the huge pile of mail and faxes that arrived each day and stamp each document with the date and a list of twelve sets of officials. His boss would then go through the pile and put checkmarks next to some or all the officials' names. The people whose names had been checked were to get copies of that piece of correspondence.

From what the grad could tell, the job was taking mounds of paper, making them into bigger mounds of paper, and delivering them so everyone could have a bigger mound of paper. A cynical veteran employee explained the system to him: "When the amount of paperwork is equal to the number of tons of water the boiler can hold, then that job is finished."

Chances are we have all had negative experiences with large, impersonal bureaucracies; then why are they created? Instead, why don't companies separate themselves into small independent units in the name of efficiency? Because often, large corporations are more efficient than smaller ones. As frustrating as it is to follow the endless rules and procedures of a formalized, mechanistic bureaucracy, large corporations generally are able to provide goods and services more cheaply than their smaller counterparts.

Unfortunately, the rigidity of bureaucracy may undermine creativity. Over the last decade, for example, we have watched as IBM, once the world leader in computers, became increasingly water-logged by bureaucracy. Innovation, necessary for survival in today's technological environment, simply did not happen, and the smaller, sleeker companies pushed "Big Blue" aside.

Less formal, more organic structures—sometimes called adhocracies—may not be able to match the cost-efficient bureaucratic machine, but this looser structure encourages creativity and innovation. When people are not tightly bound by a set of rules, the possibilities are numerous.

Today, many companies are moving in the direction of adhocracy by decentralizing, getting rid of cumbersome management layers, and *empowering employees* by giving them more decision-making responsibility. In addition, many companies are encouraging cross-functional collaboration to give employees a greater sense of connection to the processes. Self-driven or self-managed teams responsible for complete products are increasingly replacing assembly lines and bureaucratic hierarchies.

The External Environment

Forces outside of an organization can have dramatic impact on the success of a company's operations. Assume you want to start a business training dogs to be guides for the hearing impaired.

Numerous sectors of the external environment can have a substantial impact on such a venture.[1] Zoning laws may require you to own a specific amount of land. The Board of Health may have laws that limit the number of dogs you may have on your property at one time. Labor laws will dictate the minimum wage you must pay your employees, which in turn will determine the number of employees you can afford to hire.

Chances are that other companies offer the same service. You will need to convince your target market that your service or product is superior. You will also need to be aware of the advertising efforts of your competition.

Clearly, there are many external forces that can affect your venture. The main point, however, is that organizations cannot control everything that helps or hinders their business success. Accordingly, good managers have to effectively monitor the external environment to determine how best to use the resources that are within their control.

Corporate Culture

Corporate culture refers to the values, habits, and attitudes that are commonplace in an organization, attributes that can be positive, negative, or both. Whether managers consciously attempt to establish a particular organizational culture, one always develops.

Imagine working for a company at which everyone is obsessed with developing a revolutionary new machine. For twelve months straight, the engineering team works roughly sixty hours a week on the project. In the summer, everyone comes to work in shorts and T-shirts, and pranks are pulled all the time. Upper management understands that this is a good release from the pressures of completing the machine; they encourage the workers to have as much fun as they can.

Toward the end of the project, most group members are working seventy to eighty hours a week. They bring in sleeping bags and nap under their desks. When the project is completed, the whole team goes out to celebrate—and then comes to work the next day, completely depressed. No more pranks are played; the workers start wearing ties again and working conventional hours. To a casual observer, everything appears to be functioning smoothly but, in actuality, the engineers are nowhere near as productive as they had been during the project. Before, they had agreed-upon norms, high cohesion, and a common goal. Now, the goal no longer is clear; there is no focal point for efforts or relationships.

Not all cultures are this strong. Have you ever had a job in which a powerful culture made you do things you wouldn't ordinarily do? When you think about a job you had, what kinds of cultural values, habits, and attitudes come to mind?

Culture can also be revealed if you study symbolic gestures, official company functions and rituals, or the physical setting of a company. Lush furniture and elaborate marble entrances may suggest that a company is concerned with money, prestige, and image. Conversely, some companies may intentionally opt for nondescript offices to show stakeholders that they are interested in value and conservation of resources.

Organizational Change

In preparing to write this book, we asked more than a dozen managers and executives what they consider the key issues facing organizations today. Without exception, they cited the need for change and the ability to manage it. Human resource professionals told us they often refuse to consider otherwise highly qualified candidates for positions if they feel the candidates are rigid and unable to make necessary changes on a personal level. Older workers, for example, who have not become seriously computer literate, are often placed in this category. Daniel J. Wrenn, a principal of the Eagle Elevator Company in Boston, notes, "Some managers become so complacent in their jobs that if they had been in charge back in the days of cavemen, we'd all still be living in caves."

Many forces drive the need for change. These include the evolving needs and habits of an increasingly diverse population; products or services becoming obsolete because the competition is making them faster, better, and cheaper; and rapid innovation in technology that introduces more and better possibilities.

Just as people tend to avoid conflict, few people really enjoy the idea of change. Their reasons are not necessarily irrational; often change does hurt. In terms of economic factors, for example, changing from manual systems to automated ones can make some jobs obsolete. Realistic as the fear of change may be, refusal to change may hold out even more severe consequences, particularly in making not just jobs but whole companies obsolete.

Nonetheless, change is inevitable. A few tools are available to assist managers with the implementation of change. Force field analysis, for example, is used to disaggregate problems of change into driving forces—things that push toward a needed change, and restraining forces—things that push back and create a stalemate.[2]

Let's say that the TNT Dynamite Factory is having a problem with defects. Twelve percent of the dynamite produced is defective and frequently explodes during shipment. Generally this means one of the eight TNT trucks explodes each month.

The ideal situation for TNT would be zero defects; a number of factors drive the need to work toward that change. Certainly the loss of trucks and products are factors, as are concerns about product safety after delivery. The customer base is shrinking as TNT is less able to meet orders, and the high level of defects is driving up the cost of production, which in turn pushes up the cost to the customer.

Some restraining forces make the necessary changes difficult. The plant is located in New Mexico, where temperatures often top ninety degrees. If the dynamite sits in the loading dock too long, it warms up and is more likely to explode when the trucks go over bumps or come to sudden stops. The cash bonus for defect-free work for employees is only $5; management claims it is meant to be a symbolic show of recognition. Given the amount of money TNT has had to spend on repairing trucks, bigger incentive bonuses for defect-free work are unlikely. Also, there is a high turnover among shipping clerks, and the new, inexperienced clerks often toss the dynamite into the boxes, which loosens the caps.

With a force field analysis, it is possible to isolate those restraining forces that can be eliminated or diminished. Once a manager understands the forces involved, she or he can plan the change process. This can be done by finding ways to increase the driving forces and/or reduce the restraining forces. It is generally a good idea to thoroughly consider ways of reducing resistance. TNT may not be able to give the workers bigger bonuses, but perhaps it can educate the new shipping clerks. It is unlikely that the plant can be easily moved, but better shipping controls can be instituted to avoid having the dynamite sit in the sun for extended periods of time.

Kurt Lewin's Process Model of Change

Lewin's perspective on change makes a number of assumptions: 1) organizations achieve an equilibrium between forces that drive for and restrain change; 2) people are inclined to resist change; 3) we can know the desired future state of an organization; and 4) once we know the future state, we can develop a strategy for getting there. Each of these assumptions can be questioned.

Unfreezing

The first step in the change process is unfreezing. During the unfreezing stage, a manager must focus on reducing resistance to change. A manager must unfreeze perceptions, attitudes, and old habits. People resist change because they want to hold on to something they value.

Sources of Resistance

Habit. It is easier to do something in the same way. Learning something new takes effort.

Security. There is comfort in doing things the same old way. People feel comfortable knowing some things stay the same even though change is going on around them.

Economic factors. Change may threaten employees' steady pay, or they may fear that change will make their jobs obsolete. People are afraid of losing things of value.

347

Fear of the unknown. Some people fear anything unfamiliar. People become familiar with their current situation. They build a set of relationships and expertise, which helps them do their jobs. Disrupting these may create fear that the job may be made more difficult.

Lack of awareness. A person may not recognize a change and thus not change their behavior. People may only pay attention to those things that support their point of view.

Social factors. People may worry what others may think. People may think change will hurt their image.

Techniques for Overcoming Resistance to Change (Kotter and Schlesinger[3])

Education and communication. Use to help participants see the logic for the change or when they have inaccurate information. People must recognize the need for change.

Participation and involvement. Use when you need participants to feel ownership for the change. If they can resist the change or impede implementation you need their buy-in.

Facilitation and support. Use to help participants adjust to the changes.

Negotiation and agreement. Use when the change results in loss to the participants.

Implement the Change

This is the second step in the change process. An organization is a set of interdependent elements. Making a change in one area often requires supporting changes in other areas. Nadler and Tushman[4] define one framework that includes tasks (complexity, interdependence, etc.), individuals (intelligence, skills, attitudes, etc.), organizational arrangements (structure, reward systems, goals, etc.), and the informal organization (norms, intergroup relations, power distribution, etc.).

Refreeze

This is the third step in the change process. People are likely to revert to old habits unless the change is reinforced by management. People need to practice and repeat new procedures. The change is also more likely to take hold if people have positive experiences as a result of the change. Managers are often advised to plan the change such that there are repeated small successes.

Reevaluate

Although this stage is not part of Lewin's original model, it is part of Organizational Development. Change is a continuous process. You need to constantly evaluate the changes you have made and make adjustments. When you plan the change, this step should be an integral part of your plans.

Other Perspectives on Change

Some theorists argue that organizations are constantly changing. Change is the normal state of affairs, and equilibrium is an indication that the organization is stagnating. In today's complex and changing business environment, an organization must be continually improving and learning if it is to remain competitive. Maintaining the status quo means that the organization is not generating new ideas and more effective ways of operating.

People can also be seen as generally embracing change rather than resisting it. We make changes in our lives all the time. We decide to go to college, buy a house, get married, find a new job, etc. When change agents assume people will resist change, they create a self-fulfilling prophecy. Instead of finding ways to reduce resistance, change agents could concentrate on ways of attracting people to the change. This will focus the change agent on understanding those affected by the change and taking their needs and goals into consideration when planning the change. Instead of viewing those affected by the change as obstacles, they become partners.

Planning change assumes that we can somehow determine the ideal future state. Although this may be realistic for some planned change, it is often difficult for organizations in a complex and rapidly changing business environment to predict very far into the future. If we cannot know the future, we cannot know what future state will be best. Organizations must remain flexible so that they can take advantage of opportunities as they arise. This requires constant learning. When an organization builds its capabilities and knowledge, it is more likely to be able to quickly take advantage of opportunities.

Although managers may not be able to predict optimal future states, they must still attempt to lead the organization in a direction that reflects their best judgment. As they attempt to attain this future state, they should not be surprised that their plans need to be changed. An effective implementation plan is viewed as a series of experiments and will involve frequent measurement and adjustments. Failures in the plan are opportunities for learning and reassessment. In this way the organization constantly moves forward although it may end up in a very different place than it intended.

Sources

1. For additional information, see R. L. Daft, *Organization Theory and Design*, St. Paul, Minn: West Publishing,1983, p. 55 ff.

2. Lewin, K. and Cartwright, D., eds., *Field Theory in Social Science*, New York: Harper & Row, 1951.

3. Kotter, J. P., and Schlesinger, L. A., "Choosing Strategies for Change," *Harvard Business Review*, March–April 1979, pp. 109–112.

4. Nadler, D.A., and Tushman, M., "Organizational Frame Bending," *Academy of Management Executive*, 3(3), 1989, pp. 194–204.

65

THE CRAIG MIDDLE SCHOOL*

Part A

Two years ago you completed your graduate program and took a job with an educational consulting firm that specializes in helping public and private schools shift from traditionally centralized, top-down management to school-based management (SBM). Under this new system, principals and teachers, often working with parents, community leaders, and even students, make most of the critical decisions on how a school should be run. You have been assigned to consult to two elementary and six middle schools in three school districts. One is the Craig Middle School.

The Craig Middle School, an old brick building in dire need of repair, is located on a residential street of single- and two-family homes. The custodian can no longer cover the years of graffiti and abuse to which the school has been subjected, and major renovation is not scheduled for at least another two years due to fiscal constraints. Many of the lockers that line the hallways have broken hinges that can no longer be closed tightly, and the paint is chipped, showing the multi-colored layers underneath. Children's art and classroom projects adorn much of the available wall space, placed there in an attempt to brighten the inside of the building and make it a more inviting place for students, staff, and visitors.

"The Craig," as it is affectionately called, has a reputation as a traditional school with an emphasis on basic, general education. It has a stable, experienced teaching staff of twenty-four. About 80 percent of the school's five hundred multi-ethnic sixth to eighth graders live in two of the most crime-ridden neighborhoods and housing projects in the city. Some of them have seen family members and relatives shot, beaten, and even killed. Many come from single-parent families, and the vast majority qualify for free or reduced-cost lunches. Until recently, the school was known for having the lowest standardized test scores of any middle school in the city.

In the last decade, there have been five principals. The current principal, Ms. Smith, who arrived two and a half years ago, is liked and respected by virtually everyone. She knew that to bring about changes in the school, she would need the involvement of the teachers. She has an open-door policy, actively listens to the needs and concerns of her staff, and has been able to get even the most reluctant teachers to participate in curriculum and instructional innovations. She has encouraged teachers to become involved, and for the first time, most are participating in everyday and long-range decision making and planning. As a result, many new programs are being researched or have already been implemented.

One recent innovation involves the fairly large number of special needs (SPED) students who had previously been in substantially separate or resource rooms for most of the day.

* Copyright 1994 by Steve B. Wolff and Maida Broadbent Williams. Used with permission.

They are now being included in regular classrooms. Although teachers were initially hesitant to have these SPED students in their classrooms, Ms. Smith has worked with them to rearrange schedules and provide additional support, opportunities for team teaching, and slightly reduced class sizes. Teachers seem to appreciate this support.

Another recently implemented idea is the addition of an after-school enrichment program. This came about when, at the suggestion of several parents, Ms. Smith called a meeting of parents and teachers to explain and discuss the need for the program. Begun at the end of last year, it requires the participation of all teachers on a rotating basis. After the meeting and some additional work by the teachers on the fine points of implementation, it was put to a vote, passed with a majority of 80 percent of school staff, and has been enthusiastically received by the children and their parents. Many classroom teachers have noted that the children who use the program seem to be learning at a quicker rate than those who are not involved; they also see an improvement in self-esteem and a decrease in behavioral problems.

The program is coordinated by Ms. Carole, an energetic teacher who devotes her entire life to teaching. Although Ms. Carole is very efficient and task-oriented, she tends to dominate teacher meetings, take control, and tell people what to do. She remains in the after-school program even on days when she is not scheduled to be there, frequently interrupting teachers as they are working with children. Several teachers have quietly mentioned that they wish Ms. Carole was less bossy and disruptive.

As Ms. Smith was reviewing teacher attendance figures recently, she discovered that over the last two years there had been a slight increase in the number of teacher absences. She also sensed that within the last few months these rates have increased. Ms. Smith told you about her findings. Expressing concerns that maybe not all the teachers accept the changes that have been made, Ms. Smith asked you to collect some data for the first eight months of this school year, which you did.

You found the following pattern that indeed reflects a significant increase in teacher absenteeism over Ms. Smith's earlier figures:

Average Days Absent by Grade

	This Year	*Previous Year's Average*
Grade 6	7 days/teacher	6.4 days/teacher
Grade 7	6 days/teacher	5.6 days/teacher
Grade 8	11 days/teacher	9 days/teacher
School Average	8 days/teacher	7 days/teacher

Average Days Absent by Day of Week

	This Year	*Previous Year's Average*
Monday	1.7 days/teacher	1.5 days/teacher
Tuesday	1.6 days/teacher	1.5 days/teacher
Wednesday	1.2 days/teacher	1.2 days/teacher
Thursday	1.3 days/teacher	1.2 days/teacher
Friday	2.2 days/teacher	1.6 days/teacher

As you were collecting the data, Mrs. Apple, a reading teacher in the eighth grade, walked into the room, saw you looking through the records, and left without even saying hello. Through the office window, you saw her get into her car and drive away. Later you learned that a student teacher was covering her class that afternoon.

You probably wouldn't have paid much attention to Mrs. Apple's swift entry and exit, but collecting data on teacher absences made you more aware of when teachers were not in their classes. When you casually mentioned what you had observed to a seventh grade science teacher who happened to stop by the office, he said he didn't know why Mrs. Apple had left. He did mention, however, that he had heard her in the faculty room talking about how tired she felt from the longer days required by the after-school program and the research she was doing for a new reading program.

Questions for Discussion

1. How would you define the problem at "The Craig"?

2. What do you think is causing the problem?

3. As a consultant, what are your next steps?

DISABILITY SERVICES DISABLED*

Clara Suarez, coordinator of disability services for MBA students at a large university in Arizona, checked her outline and overhead graphics, made a few last-minute margin notations, stuffed the papers into her briefcase, and headed down the hall. She was to make a presentation at the disability services coordinators' meeting that afternoon on the issues faced by disabled students who return to school after having had successful careers, and she had spent considerable time and energy interviewing students and gathering facts in preparation.

Clara had been in her job for five years, and she loved it as much now as she had on the first day. She had graduated with a Master of Education in Educational Administration from one of the top five programs in the country and had written her thesis on the administration of disability services. With now over ten years of work experience in the field of disability services, she was exceptionally well qualified for her job and was considered by others in the field to be an expert.

Prior to her current position, Clara had held a similar position at another university, but there she had been miserable. Rarely, if ever, had her previous boss bothered to take into account the needs or opinions of those working directly with service recipients, and policy decisions were merely handed down from above. Frustrated with having to implement programs that did not meet the needs of the population for which they were intended, Clara quit and took a position at a nearby university, Turnerville, where teamwork and consensus in decision making were emphasized. As far as Clara was concerned, this was one of the best decisions she had ever made.

The Meeting

Today's meeting was being run by Ethel Sherman. A paraplegic with a slight hearing impairment, Ethel was the university-wide director of disability services.

"Good afternoon, everyone," Ethel said. "Before we go on, I want to ask if it's possible to modify the agenda; I have some changes I'd like to discuss. Clara, would you mind saving your presentation for the next meeting? I think that should leave enough time for what I have to say." Startled, but trusting Ethel's judgment, Clara agreed.

"That's fine," she replied, nodding to Ethel, with whom she had always had an amiable relationship. "I don't have anything that can't wait until our next meeting."

Ethel straightened up and smiled at Clara and then looked around at the others in the room.

* This case was written by Gail E. Gilmore.

"As most of you know," she began, "I've been more than a little overextended during the past six months. I don't feel that this is productive, either for me or for our program. Therefore, Theodore Slater, who you all know, will be taking over my liaison duties. All coordinators will now deal directly with him. Theodore and I have spent a great deal of time together working out just what his responsibilities will be. I'm pleased, as was the provost, that we have someone of Theodore's outstanding qualifications willing and able to take over this position. He has devised a set of plans for the delivery of various services, and he'll be sending copies of them to all of you shortly. Theodore and I have gone over the plans from every possible angle, and I'm confident that they're ready for immediate implementation."

"I've also asked Theodore to present these final plans to the provost at their meeting this afternoon. The provost was very excited with the preliminary report on this that we showed him ten days ago, and he was very pleased that we're all thinking along such creative and productive lines."

"Unfortunately," Ethel added, glancing in Theodore's direction, "Theodore has to leave the meeting early, so he won't be able to answer any of your questions, but he would like to take a few minutes to discuss some other changes which he and I will be implementing over the coming months. Theodore?"

"Thanks, Ethel. Sorry I'm going to have to run right after I finish. As it is, I'm going to be late for my meeting with the provost, but I at least wanted to let you all know that starting next month there will be two major changes in the delivery of services. One is that we will be offering a set of standardized programs to all the schools within the university, and the other is that we will now be requiring all schools to contribute equally for the operating costs of these programs. I really think this will make a big difference in the quality of our services. Again, I'm sorry I can't stay to discuss this further, but if you have any questions, you know where to reach me. See you all at the next meeting."

With that, Theodore quickly gathered his things and left the room.

Once the door had closed, Clara turned to Ethel.

"Look Ethel," she said, "we've all had sympathy for how hard you've been working, and while I think it's really good that you know how important it is to make some changes, I don't know about the others, but I do know that I really object to the way you've gone about making them."

"I don't understand what you mean," Ethel replied with an incredulous note in her voice. "There's no secret to what needs to be done. All I'm doing is moving things along."

Clara was suddenly conscious of the need to control the tone and level of her voice. "Well first of all," she said, "I have some real problems with your choice of Theodore as coordinator liaison, and it's not just because you didn't consult us first. I'm sure I'm not the only one in this room who has found him inflexible and difficult to talk to, and he has only been in his current position for a year. Laurinda has been there for three years, is easier to work with, and would have been a much better choice. Why did you choose him?"

"I chose him because he has some really good ideas about what kinds of changes should be made."

Ethel's reply was terse, and it was clear that this conversation was becoming less than cordial. Several of the others in the room began showing their discomfort at what they were witnessing by shifting in their seats or suddenly finding fascination with small specks of dust on their clothing.

"But that's just the problem, Ethel," Clara challenged. "His ideas aren't good; they're completely unrealistic. First of all, these plans. Granted, I haven't seen them yet, but the fact that we were never asked for input as to whether they'd be appropriate to each of our programs makes me very nervous. I'm also upset that you would even support something like this; it's not the way things are done here at Turnerville. Decisions have always been made by consensus, and you know that as well as I do. And this idea of standardized programs— how could you possibly think that something like this will work? Students have different needs; you can't standardize everything and expect it to work. The needs of an adult student returning to school are totally different from the needs of an undergraduate student. And I'm sure that if we went around the table and each of us described what our students need, we'd all come up with something different."

Clara paused and looked around at her colleagues, many of whom nodded in agreement. Knowing she had support, Clara went on. "In addition, how can you require all schools to contribute equally to the operating costs of these programs? For some students they may be totally inappropriate. Come on, Ethel, you know and I know that this is ridiculous!"

"Clara, you're overreacting; you don't even know what you're talking about," Ethel retorted angrily. "These changes will work. I'm disabled, and I have a much clearer sense than you do of what is and is not appropriate in terms of service planning and implementation."

"I completely disagree with you, Ethel," Clara replied quietly, making a real effort to bring the level of the conversation to a less explosive level while at the same time not wanting to lose ground. "And I resent your assumption that you can speak for everyone and anyone who has a disability. I'm certainly not egotistical enough to presume to know what's appropriate for everyone from my background.

"Look," she went on, "I don't mean to make you feel defensive. All I want is to have this group sit down together and come to a consensus on the types of changes that need to be made and the best way to implement them. With the way you've gone about this, I feel like we're all being forced to accept something we had no part in deciding, and that goes against everything this university stands for."

"I understand what you're saying, Clara, and I can't think of any reason why we can't do that. But, in the meantime," Ethel continued, "Theodore and I will keep working on some of the changes we're planning, and we'll open them for discussion at the next meeting."

Clara felt her body get cold and her face get hot. She couldn't believe what she had just heard Ethel say.

"Obviously, Ethel, you haven't heard or understood one word of what I've said. I have to tell you that under these circumstances, you will get no support from the Business School, financial or otherwise, for these programs. And I assure you, I will see to it that none of the other schools support you either. You've basically just derailed the entire disabilities services program, and you're not going to get it back on track until you're willing to work with us."

With that, Clara got up and left, slamming the door behind her. After a brief and awkward moment, the other committee members got up and left as well, but not before letting Ethel know that they agreed with Clara. Alone in the empty room, Ethel pondered what had just happened and wondered exactly what had gone wrong. What else could she do, she wondered half aloud, to regain the support of the coordinators? She'd agreed to discuss the changes once they'd been made; what more did they want?

Questions for Discussion

1. From what you know about managing change, explain why Clara reacted the way she did.

2. What else do you think is going on in this case that might account for the various reactions? Why?

3. How would you suggest Ethel go about regaining the support of the coordinators? What should Theodore's role be?

THE BUREAUCRACY GAME*

Objectives

- To examine the effects of bureaucracy on productivity, morale, and decision quality
- To explore the limitations on innovation imposed by bureaucracies
- To explore methods for overcoming the limitations of bureaucracies

Background

The Wildcat Compact Disc Company has just started operations, but upper management is already thinking big. They have discovered a new music group called Nuclear Lunchbox, who, they believe, will become the hottest group of the decade. The Nuclear Lunchbox sound combines elements of punk rock and rap music, but the band members play nothing but classical instruments.

You work for the Wildcat Compact Disc Company where a task team has been formed to consult with all departments to work out the many specific details for the forthcoming Nuclear Lunchbox CD. Decisions will have to be made regarding each of the following:

- *Color of compact disc label*: Some companies produce nothing but the basic silver CDs, while others use various colors. What will Wildcat do?

- *Production cost*: Most CDs retail from $11.99 to $14.99. Obviously, production cost must be much less than that to make a profit, but the costs of ensuring a top-quality product are generally high.

- *Packaging*: Some CDs are boxed in cardboard, while others are packaged in inexpensive polymerized plastic. Still others are wrapped in more expensive but recyclable fritillated plastic. Which of these three options should the company choose?

- *Running time of CD*: Since all of Nuclear Lunchbox's songs are equally good (or equally bad, depending on how you look at it), the band's manager has stated that they have as much material as you want to use. The average CD runs about forty minutes, although seventy-five to eighty minutes is possible with the latest technology. How long should this compact disc be?

Each of the various departments at the Wildcat Compact Disc Company has strong opinions regarding the issues raised above. Wildcat's president hopes that the appointed task team will be effective as a liaison that can, after gathering all the vital input, make the best decisions.

---

* This exercise was written by Scott Weighart.

At times there may be unsolvable conflicts between departments. If this occurs, the task team is allowed to submit a written memo to the executive board. If the board's members decide a rule change should take place, they will send a memo notifying all department heads. This memo must then be initialed by two members of each department.

Important Note: Regardless of what any task-team member may say, all rules must be followed unless countermanded by a duly signed written memo from the executive board.

Instructions

Step 1 (20–30 minutes)

You will be assigned to one of the following: Research and Development (up to six people); Production (up to six people); Marketing (up to six people); Finance (up to six people); Task Team (three to six people); Executive Board (two to three people).

After receiving your assignment, read the background sheet, which also gives the rules of the game. You will receive a sheet with job descriptions for the people in your department. Assign the roles, and discuss both the roles and the background information to be sure there is mutual understanding of the assigned tasks.

Step 2 (45–60 minutes)

Following the directions given on the background and role sheets, and any oral instructions that may be given, develop a project proposal that is acceptable to everyone involved. If no agreement is reached, the game will be stopped at the end of one hour, and the participants will be debriefed. No proposal will be considered to be acceptable until it has been signed (use the "Proposal Sheet") by the managers of every department as well as by the Executive Board.

Be sure that all rules are followed—for example, everything should be in writing—unless rule changes are agreed to according to the protocol given. During the game, observe the following:

- What effects does bureaucracy have on productivity, morale, and decision quality?

- What tactics did the task team attempt to use to get the proposal approved (i.e., persuasion, logic, threats, compliance with rules—no matter how absurd)? What tactics worked best?

Step 3 (open-ended)

Class discussion

Product Proposal

We, the Task Team, hereby submit our product proposals to gain the approval of all concerned parties. We wish to produce a CD that has the following characteristics:

Color of CD label: _____

Production cost: _____

Packaging material: _____

Running time of CD: _____

Approved by Research & Development: _____

Approved by Finance Department: _____

Approved by Marketing Department: _____

Approved by Production Department: _____

Approved by Executive Board: _____

68

THE DAY CARE RESOURCE AND REFERRAL AGENCY–PART A

Background

The Day Care Resource and Referral Agency (DERRY) was founded in 1985 in Brighthaven in response to an increased workforce demand, particularly for factory workers, clerks, warehouse and utility workers, and a variety of other unskilled and semi-skilled positions. Facing labor-pool problems, high turnover, and costly absenteeism, a local utility company executive, Clark Donovan, recognized the need to reach out to a group of potential and current employees, namely women with young children, to make it possible for them to obtain and keep steady work. "Find day care for the children," thought Donovan, "and women will be available to work at the relatively low-paying jobs that need to be filled. Women with working husbands," he further believed, "will be happy with the second income."

It hadn't occurred to Donovan that his ideas about finding day care providers might also generate opportunities for some women, particularly single mothers, to get off welfare and begin career paths. Donovan wasn't at all concerned with welfare problems or the local economy; his interests were purely self-serving. In his company, as in most companies, every position that went unfilled for a week, a month, or even a day was expensive in lost productivity. Every time an employee left, the cost of recruiting, hiring, and training a replacement was staggering. It wasn't until his own secretary left because she couldn't find day care for her two young children that it hit Donovan that his problems with absenteeism and turnover might be connected to the lack of available and affordable day care. An hour on the floor chatting with his people confirmed it.

Donovan raised the initial funding for DERRY by selling the idea to or pressuring a number of his golf buddies, all of whom were local executives and who faced the same labor problems. With a number of small ($5,000–$10,000) contributions from area businesses, DERRY was set up with a director and a secretary working in a converted closet in the corridor outside Donovan's office. The first director was Donovan's wife who had trained as a social worker but never practiced, having gotten married right after receiving her MSW degree. With her children now in their teens, Connie Donovan had grown bored with the round of ladies' lunches and volunteer projects with which she occupied her time.

It was the job of Connie and her secretary to get on the telephone and call every possible day care provider within a twenty-five mile radius to locate slots and get pricing and other pertinent information, such as hours of operation. In less than six months, while many slots were located and filled, it became clear that far too few day care providers were available to fill the demand, and even the high-cost day care programs lacked space. In addition, without subsidy, it made more sense for many of the mothers, particularly those on welfare, to stay home rather than work low-paying jobs and hassle with commuting and bosses who turned on them when they had to miss days because of child-care problems. Thus the demand for steady, reliable, semi- and unskilled labor was still greater than the supply.

Recognizing this, Connie Donovan proposed that DERRY conduct training programs for potential day care providers and help them get certified through the state office for children. This meant hiring someone to oversee the training as well as hiring one or two recruiters who could find, interview, and establish the suitability of potential providers. This also meant a larger budget and a necessity for more space.

Once more, Clark Donovan approached his friends for funding, but this time they insisted that if they were to shell out the dollars, they wanted their contributions to be tax deductible, and they wanted some say in how the organization was run. In compliance with their wishes, Clark called on his lawyer to draw up some by-laws and articles of incorporation for DERRY that would allow him and his friends to serve as officers and a board of directors. They also applied for and got a tax-exempt status and registered as a social service agency with the state's attorney general.

This having been completed, Clark, as the new president of DERRY, called a board meeting at which decisions were officially made to expand the organization by three people and to move its offices to a building at the edge of the city near where they hoped to recruit both potential providers and potential users of their day care services. To support this, the board members each pledged an annual contribution for a minimum of five years in return for which it was agreed that their companies would receive preferential treatment for day care slots. Some of the members with political connections also agreed to approach the governor for state support.

Within two years of their expansion, DERRY had become swamped with requests to provide day care support to area businesses, hospitals, law firms, and the local university. To meet the need, Connie hired, over the next year, three new recruiters, a head of training, a bookkeeper, a business liaison administrator to secure and service day care contracts with local businesses, a full-time fund raiser, a part-time fund raiser, and three secretaries. In addition, they recruited interns from the university; within a short time, this necessitated the hiring of a full-time supervisor to oversee the internship program.

What had begun as a small, two-person operation now employed more than two dozen people, eight of whom were from the communities in the area in which the offices were located and only three of whom were men. Most of the jobs in the agency were low paying, with the exceptions of the director, the fund raiser, and the business liaison, the latter two being men, each of whom made roughly twice what the highest pay was for any of the other employees.

Overseeing DERRY had become more than a full-time job for Connie Donovan and substantially more than she wanted to handle. In April, she informed the board that she would be resigning, effective June 15, but that she would like to continue her involvement as a board member. Hearing that Connie was leaving, DERRY's bookkeeper, Bertha Mendez expressed an interest in the position. When Bertha approached her about it, Connie smiled and told her that a search was underway. Nothing more was said.

After deciding that there was no one within DERRY with the necessary background to do Connie's job, an outsider, Tom Lichtenberg, was hired by Connie and approved by the board. Tom was single, thirty-six years old, had an undergraduate degree in psychology, an MBA, and thirteen years of social-service agency experience.

When Tom was appointed, Bertha was furious. She immediately rounded up her friends at the agency, told them of the skewed salary structure, and got them to agree to undermine Tom at any chance they could get.

"Every one of us has worked hard to get where we are," she told the other women. "They treat us like dirt, pay us next to nothing, and expect us to bow down to them. Like most of you, I lived in welfare housing and went to school nights to get my high school degree and get me and my kids off welfare."

"Let's face it," she said angrily, "without us, they wouldn't have an agency. We know the work, and we have the connections. This is our community, and we should be the ones in charge."

With nods all around, the women agreed that Tom had to go.

The Sad, Short Reign of Tom Lichtenberg

One of the first things Tom noticed on taking over as executive director was the dismal state of the financial records. With his business background, he was quick to recognize that no standard bookkeeping system had been used. As a result, it appeared that some providers had been paid more than once for the same services, and some of the companies that had contracts with DERRY hadn't been billed in as much as two and a half years. In addition, the payroll system was indecipherable. Tom also observed a great number of other inefficiencies throughout the agency.

After six weeks on the job, Tom made a complete report to the board with a number of recommendations including that Bertha be replaced by a computer and someone with a college accounting degree and some experience. "You can't do that," Connie argued. "Bertha has been with us for a long time, and she's got the ear and respect of the other workers. We'd have a revolution, and some of them might walk out."

"That's exactly what needs to happen," Tom responded. "As is, this agency is unmanageable, and it's being run in an unbusiness-like fashion. It's headed for financial disaster. I don't want to be at the helm of a sinking ship, so you decide—it's either them or me."

"We'll think about it," was the board's response.

Two weeks later, Tom quit in disgust.

Andrea Chierico

Andrea Chierico was the daughter of one of the CEO's of a company that supported and used DERRY's services. After completing her undergraduate degree in sociology, Andrea had gone into the Peace Corps for two years and then had been a supervisor in VISTA (Volunteers in Service to America). Tired of traveling, and wanting to return home, Andrea got her father to ask his friends about job possibilities in Brighthaven. When he mentioned Andrea to Clark Donovan during a golf game, Clark's response was "when can she start?" Ten days later, Andrea was the executive director of DERRY. Andrea's first move was to call the entire staff together.

"You're the people who'll be doing the work," Andrea told them, "So you're the people who'll be making the decisions. I'll be here to help if you need me, but I'm going to trust you to do the right thing. We're all here for the same reason. We all want to help poor women and children get off welfare and into the workplace where they can have some dignity. Please be sure you report to me regularly, and let me know if you need anything."

Bertha Mendez chuckled to herself as she walked out the door. "Who does this kid think she is?" Bertha asked her friends. "What a joke! But at least now we can run this place the way we want. I think I'll start by getting her to hire a friend of mine to be my assistant. My friend doesn't have much experience, but she is on welfare, and you heard the girl say we're here to get her 'off welfare and into the workplace' where she can 'have some dignity.'" Bertha snickered as she thought of the possibilities Andrea's appointment opened up.

Within a few months, at the instigation of Bertha and her friends, twelve new employees were hired to work at DERRY, all of them women from the local community. Bertha also convinced Andrea to promote her to the newly created position of chief financial officer and to give her a substantial raise. While the board of directors expressed concern over the increased financial burdens imposed by the rapid expansion, they felt they had to support Andrea in her attempts to build the agency. By this time, too, state grants and contracts were coming through, and managing these required yet another increase in personnel.

The Meeting

Less than two years after Andrea's arrival, the fund raiser and the business liaison asked her to meet with them outside the office.

"I've been telling you for a long time that this place is going to 'hell in a hand basket,'" the fund raiser, Jim Teicholz, began the meeting. "Our corporate sponsors are complaining that their contributions are not only going unacknowledged but also that their checks aren't being deposited for months on end. I'm also hearing that they're not getting the preferential treatment they were promised, and several have told me that unless we can get our business in order, they're not going to continue to give. Worse still, someone called me from the attorney general's office the other day to say that we haven't filed the paperwork necessary to keep our charitable and tax-exempt status, and we're in danger of losing it if we don't file soon!"

"I'm having the same problem with our provider contracts," the business liaison, Al Hawkes, added. "Contracts aren't being processed efficiently or in order. One of our top business partners found out that he got his contract to us more than six weeks before someone else and that the other person got serviced first. When he called to ask what was going on, he was told that there weren't enough spaces to fill his employees' needs even though the other person got a full quota of slots. He's furious, and I don't blame him. Bertha and her friends are running this place into the ground."

"Look," Andrea told them. "We're a social service agency, and we're committed to diversity and to serving our area. Every organization has some slip ups. I'm sure you can work this out with the people directly responsible for doing the work."

"That's a joke," Al snorted. "Bertha talks to me like I'm a little boy, and when I ask her for anything, she tells me how busy she is. Busy, my eye. Every time I see her she's talking on the phone with her friends or gossiping with some of the other lazy people around here. She's nothing but a troublemaker. Open your eyes; she's even making a fool of you. I'm convinced that the financials Bertha gives you for the board meetings every month are phonies. Jim and I have been comparing notes, and nothing adds up. Bertha has even put off that audit that the board ordered over a year ago, always saying that she's still getting the information together. I wouldn't be surprised to find out that she and her friends are having a good time with the agency's money."

"That's a pretty serious accusation," Andrea started.

"Anyway," Jim broke in, "we're here to tell you that unless you get things under control, we're leaving, and we all know that without us and our contacts, you might as well kiss DERRY goodbye!"

"Okay, I'll talk to Bertha," Andrea sighed. While she didn't believe that Bertha was diverting agency funds, she did know that because of Bertha's foot dragging she had been unable to produce the audited financials for which the board had been hounding her. She also knew that virtually everything else that Jim and Al had said was true. In her heart, she knew it was probably time to start looking around for another job.

Bertha Goes Ballistic

It took Andrea until the end of the week to get Bertha into her office. Every time Andrea tried to suggest that they meet, Bertha said she was just too busy and would get there as soon as she could free up some time.

"They're nothing but a couple of male chauvinist pigs," Bertha had screamed when she and Andrea had finally started to talk. "And this is nothing more than discrimination. We work hard. They think because we're women, because some of us are minorities, and because we've been on welfare that we don't have any brains; and they think they're so great because they belong to the country club. Let them go. We can move Ella and Josie into their jobs."

Andrea tried to hide her astonishment. Neither Ella, who was Bertha's niece, nor Josie, had high school diplomas, and she couldn't imagine them at meetings with high-power business people.

"Do you really think that would work?" Andrea asked her.

"You don't think so because you're not one of us either," Bertha shot back. "This agency is for people like us, and we should be running it."

Bertha stalked out, slamming the door behind her.

Andrea made a few phone calls, updated her résumé, put on her coat, and left. Within two weeks she had landed another job and had given the board her two week notice. In the meantime, Al and Jim had given their notice as well.

Questions for Consideration

1. DERRY has undergone innumerable changes since its inception. Analyze these changes, and describe how each of DERRY's leaders, formal and informal, have participated in or driven those changes.

2. Based on what you know of DERRY, what changes do you believe now need to take place? Why?

3. Using any theory of managing change, develop a plan for carrying out your proposed changes. Include a time frame, and describe the order in which you will carry out the various elements of the change.

THE DAY CARE RESOURCE AND REFERRAL AGENCY–PART B

The members of DERRY's board of directors were collectively stunned by the mass exodus from the agency. "This time," Clark Donovan told the somber group, "we need to have a clear game plan for who to hire for the executive director's position. I guess we never expected DERRY to get this huge, so we haven't done the kind of planning we would have done in our companies. When I hired Andrea, I don't think I took DERRY seriously as anything other than a vehicle for getting what we all needed—a steady employee pool. Now we're finding ourselves running a million dollar business—but I guess we've been running it like a hobby."

"What about the business-liaison and fund-raising jobs?" one of the board members asked.

"Maybe we should wait to get a new executive director in place before we rush to fill Al's and Jim's jobs," Donovan replied. "That way, we can work with the new executive director to get someone all of us like. In the meantime, I think we can convince both Al and Jim to come on as part-time consultants at least to keep the critical bases covered."

"At this point," he continued, "I'd like to set up a board committee to develop a job description for the next executive director. Then, we'll write an ad for the position in the local newspapers, *The Wall Street Journal*, and some trade publications like *The Chronicle of Higher Education.*"

Step 1

You have been appointed to the special board committee. What traits and characteristics do you believe the next executive director should have? Why?

_____

_____

_____

_____

_____

_____

_____

_____

Write a job description to use as a guide when hiring the next executive director:

_____

_____

_____

_____

_____

_____

_____

Write the copy for an ad for the executive director's job:

_____

_____

_____

_____

_____

_____

_____

Over the next several weeks, the board committee developed the job description and ran the ad in a number of publications. They received more than three dozen résumés. From this, they selected six possible candidates who they then interviewed. Two of the interviewed candidates were deemed inappropriate for the position. On the following pages, you will find the résumés of each of the remaining four, along with the interviewers' notes.

Step 2

Read the résumés and interviewers' notes that follow, and analyze the strengths and weaknesses of each candidate.

MELVIN BAKER

297 Marlborough Avenue   **Smith and Mullins**
Brighthaven   **One Fire House Square**
262-4841   **Brighthaven**
                                                                    338-2897; FAX 338-2880

Education:

Harvard University, Law School   **J.D.**   **1964**
    Emphasis on business and administrative law

Yale University   **B.S.**   **1961**
    Chemistry

Professional experience:

1992 Spring   **Adjunct Faculty, Brighthaven University, Graduate School of Management**, teaching courses in negotiation

1992–   **Adjunct Faculty, Brighthaven Institute of Technology, Management Program for Corporate Counsel**, teaching senior attorneys from corporations around the world how to manage litigation more efficiently

1990–   **Consultant, Litigation Cost Containment**, advising companies on how to apply decision analysis to reduce the transaction costs of litigation

1968–   **Partner, Smith and Mullins**, with expertise in complex financial transactions, regulated industries, administrative law, negotiation, and computer modeling in the settlement of complex disputes; admitted to practice before the Supreme Court of the United States, the U.S. Courts of Appeals for the First, Second, Third, Fifth and District of Columbia Circuits; the U.S. District Courts for Massachusetts, Connecticut, Florida, Virginia, Texas, Utah, and the Eastern District of Pennsylvania; and the Supreme Judicial Court of seven states

1964–1968   **Associate, Smith and Mullins**

Professional memberships:

    American Bar Association
    American Arbitration Association
    Economics Club of America

Publications:

Baker, M. (1992), "Modelling the Uncertainties in Litigation," Trial Practice in the 21st Century, Chicago: The American Bar Association.

Baker, M. (November 23, 1987), "Settlement of Complex Litigation." Presented at the ILP Symposium on Computer Models and Modeling for Negotiation Management, Massachusetts Institute of Technology.

Baker, M. (April 14, 1986), "Litigation Prospects," The National Law Journal, New York: The New York Law Publishing Company.

368

Sarah L. Penniman
5 Tremont Street
Boston, Massachusetts 02115
(617) 262-1396

Education

Stanford University, School of Education   Stanford, CA
Masters in Language, Literacy and Culture   1991
Research areas included bilingual education, bilingualism, biculturalism, tracking, and issues in comparative international education.

Stanford University   Stanford, CA
Bachelor of Arts in Linguistics   1990
Emphasis on sociolinguistics

Stanford University Center 1988 Summer Focus Program Oxford, England
Britain in the Third World: The Third World in Britain

Professional Experience

Development Director   Boston, MA
Day Care Concepts   1991–
Develops outreach and training programs for day care providers from throughout the New England area. Consults to government agencies, businesses and professional organiza-tions on in-house day care programs, contract, and voucher system programs. Also develops community-based training programs for providers.

Instructor, Stanford University, Weekend Workshops Program 1990–1991
Taught workshops in self defense for women.

ESL Teacher   Boston, MA
Asian Senior Citizen Society   Summer 1990
Developed English and community resources for Chinese senior citizens.

International Experience

Masaryk Fellow   Prague, Czechoslovakia
Students for East European Democracy   Northern Bohemia
Charter Seventy-Seven Foundation   Summer 1991
Designed and implemented original curricula for teaching English as a foreign language.

English Teacher   Hamamatsu, Japan
Volunteers in Asia   1988–1989
Edited medical papers for publication and presentation at international conferences. Instructed researchers, surgeons, and other members of the university educational community in English conversation, writing, and grammar.

Linda P. Spiers
135 Wright Avenue, #5
Iselin, New Jersey 08830
(908) 205-4881

Professional Experience:

1986– *Instructor, Coolidge University, College of Management*
Teach graduate and undergraduate courses in Public Policy, Organizational Behavior and Leadership. Instructor in the International Student Orientation Program, MBA Program, MBA and Doctoral Programs. Responsible for recruiting, hiring, training, and supervising 8 to 12 instructors per semester and overseeing program that served 700 to 800 students per year.

1982–85 *Public Relations Professional, LPS & Associates, Newark, N.J.*
Responsible for overseeing all agency work for clients in non-profit and charitable areas, including hospitals, colleges, and community organizations. Included prime responsibility for fund raising and charitable events.

1985 *Guest lecturer: Boston University School of Management*
Fund raising and development, three-week capsule course.

Community Activities:

1987–90 *Member, Police Training Commission, Iselin, N.J.*

1970– *Member, League of Women Voters*

Education:

Coolidge University, School of Education *EDD* *1994*
Human Development

Richardson University, School of Management *MBA* *1985*
Public Policy and Management

Boston University, College of Liberal Arts *BA* *1964*
Philosophy and Government

Additional Relevant Programs:

American Hospital Association, Management Development *1979*
University of Detroit, Grantsmanship *1979*
University of Detroit, Successful Public Relations Techniques *1982*
Education Technology Consortium, Dealing with the Angry Public *1987*
Promotional Perspectives, Getting into Print *1988*

Professional Memberships:

Association of Management
Associated Grantmakers
Pi Lambda Theta (National Honor and Professional Association in Education)
Phi Delta Kappa (National Honorary Society for Educators)

Awards:

Outstanding Thesis: Corporate Responses to Social Needs and Welfare: Employer-Supported Child Care—A Recent Corporate Response, Coolidge University, School of Education, 1994

Rosa Gonzalez-Bueno

34 Bridge Road

Brighthaven

262-8199

Education:

Brighthaven High School	1977-79
G.E.D.	1989
Somerville College, B.A. (honors), History	1993

Work Experience:

State Office for Children, director, voucher system program
1991-

State Office for Children, clerk-secretary
1988-91

State Welfare Office, clerk   1984-88

Woolworths - Brighthaven Center, sales   1978-84

Other Experience:

Elected member, Brighthaven School Board	1990-
Brighthaven Youth Commission	1991-
Brighthaven Community Council	1989-
Learning Haven Elementary School P.T.O., president	1989-1990

Other Information:

Speaks fluent Spanish.

Interviewers' Comments on: Melvin Baker

Mel is a friend and the personal lawyer of Clark Donovan. He set up the original by-laws, etc., and has handled a number of legal issues for DERRY on a pro bono basis since its inception. He's a high-energy individual who says he's fed up with his law practice and wants to make a more significant social contribution at this point in his life. He told us that DERRY represents a chance to help people, particularly women, who are caught in the system and won't be able to get off welfare and into productive lives unless affordable day care is available. He says he's felt that the agency has needed some serious reorganization for some time now, and he's been aware of a number of the problems. He says he has already told his partners that he's leaving the firm by the end of this month and says this is his plan whether or not we hire him. (Checked with Clark who would like us to give Mel some additional consideration but not at the expense of a more highly qualified candidate.)

Interviewers' Comments on: Sarah Penniman

She's a very animated young woman who makes an excellent appearance. She says she really likes her current job, but she wants to return to Brighthaven where she was born and grew up—she still has most of her family here. She thinks her interest in multiculturalism along with her background in a day care consulting agency make her a good candidate for this job. Since she hasn't really been back here to live for quite a few years, some of her knowledge of the community may be based on old stereotypes, but she struck us a being very gregarious and thorough. She had done quite a bit of research into what DERRY is all about and had even sniffed around enough to know about some of the problems. She has told her current employer that she is actively looking for a job closer to home, and she gave us permission to contact her boss for references. We spoke to two people at Day Care Concepts, and both gave her outstanding recommendations. She has also been taking night courses in management (accounting, marketing, etc.) for three semesters because she feels this is her weak area.

Interviewers' Comments on: Linda Spiers

Linda struck us as a powerhouse. While she hasn't had any direct agency experience, she has done some consulting to agencies, and she has had some real responsibility for human resources in her current position at the university. While it doesn't show up on her résumé, apparently she was very involved with the League of Women Voters to get legislation passed to regulate the day care industry and also to push through the state voucher system. Apparently this was what ultimately led to her doctoral work. She has also lectured to civic groups in New Jersey on the importance of day care to the economic health of communities. We think that her fund raising experience is a plus. She says she wants to get out of higher education where she feels she's behind most of the others in her department because of her late entry into the workforce. She also says she thinks she probably wouldn't get tenure, and therefore her prospects are limited at Coolidge. Linda says she would be able to leave at the end of the current semester, about seven weeks from now, and is completely open to moving to Brighthaven. She has not yet let her colleagues know that she's looking elsewhere for a position.

Interviewers' Comments on: Rosa Gonzalez-Bueno

Rosa is well known to all of us because of her activism in Brighthaven, and two of us supported her in her run for school board. She's no-nonsense, all business, and has never been known to back away from conflict. She has pushed a number of minority issues, and she has the political savvy and connections to get things done. Before getting on the school board, she was an activist for better funding and school-based management for the schools in her district. She also successfully backed a plan for stricter guidelines for student conduct, including the right to expel and/or suspend students who carry weapons, smoke, or use drugs on school grounds. Rosa's also about one of the most aggressive fund raisers we've ever seen—last year we figured out that she hit us up for a collective contribution of five full college scholarships for deserving minority students from Brighthaven High. Somerville College, where she went, is a new school for non-traditional students, e.g., older students, people without traditional high school degrees, etc. It isn't accredited yet, but it has a pretty good reputation.

Questions for Discussion

1. Based on what you believe must take place at DERRY if it is to succeed, which of the candidates for the position of executive director do you believe will be best able to carry out the necessary changes? Why?

2. What potential problems do you believe the new executive director is likely to encounter in carrying out the necessary changes? What advice do you have for him or her?

Part C of this case appears in the Instructor's Resource Manual.

69

PLAYING FOOTSY WITH THE FAMILY BUSINESS

Background

In 1990, Joseph Savenor, founder of a small shoe manufacturing company in North Deighton, Massachusetts, died at the age of ninety-six. Although he had turned the day-to-day management of his business over to his son-in-law, Abe Seiler, ten years earlier, Joseph Savenor had continued to go to his office daily until just two weeks before his death. Savenor's strong hand and Old World management style were very much a part of the company culture. He knew all the workers, some of whom represented second and third generations in the company; they considered him to be the grand old man and, indeed, Joseph had treated them with a firm hand but well. More than one told stories of his coming to their aid in times of sickness, helping them to educate their children, and supporting them as if they were family. The company had never had a strike and, notwithstanding attempts by the Shoe and Boot Workers Union to organize them, the Savenor employees had shown no interest. The company had always been profitable, and the Savenors had become one of the wealthiest families in the North Deighton area.

Beginning in 1980, Joseph had begun to gift shares of stock in the company to workers on the twentieth anniversary of their employment. By the time he died, this amounted to about 20 percent of outstanding stock, largely held by employees who had retired or were nearing retirement. In his will, the old man left his remaining 80 percent stock interest in the company, as well as the other assets of his considerable estate, to his two daughters and two sons in equal shares.

One daughter, Eleanore, in her sixties and never married, worked for the company as head of sales. She managed seven people, who had been with the company an average of twenty-seven years. Their sales routes were well established and changed little. It had been more than five years since there had been any growth in the customer list, and sales were sluggish. The market for shoes had shifted largely to discounting, with domestic shoemakers having an increasingly hard time competing against foreign manufacturers.

Joseph's eldest son, Malcolm, was a busy and successful ophthalmologist in Manhattan. Malcolm had never had much interest in his father's business, considering it a "trade" that was far beneath him both socially and intellectually. Malcolm's wife, Anne, however, saw the words "my son the executive" written all over the inheritance. Here was a perfect opportunity to install Jeffrey, a thirty-year-old college dropout with a spotty work record, in an "appropriate" position.

Harold, the "baby" in the family, was a professor of sociology at Simmons College in Boston. Like his brother, he had little interest in the business. To him, the best thing he could do with his stock would be to sell it and use the proceeds to finance his studies of primitive tribes on remote Indonesian islands. Nonetheless, he had some sentimental feelings toward

374

his father's company and especially toward the cutters and stitchers, who, when he was a small child, used to fashion playthings for him out of leather scraps and often sat him in their laps and let him pretend to run the huge machines.

The other daughter, Susanne, was married to Abe Seiler. She shared her father's loyalty to the family and had grown up with the feeling that the employees at Savenors were an extension of that family. Susanne and Abe had two sons and a daughter, all of whom had worked for the company for a number of summers, each coming on full-time after graduation from college.

The Plan

Abe Seiler had, for a long time, wanted to make radical changes in the company, moving it primarily into retail operations with a series of outlet stores. This would mean phasing out manufacturing and wholesale sales and purchasing leather goods—shoes, belts, purses, and so forth—from abroad. He believed that the long-term future of the company depended on taking it in new directions, but he was also aware that this was not feasible during Joseph's lifetime. Quietly, and without discussion, Abe researched the possibilities, worked out a plan, and became increasingly convinced that the retail store concept would be enormously profitable and considerably enhance the value of the company's stock. He knew that he would have to get rid of the "dead wood" and bring in new, young, and dynamic leadership to execute the plan.

After Joseph's will had been probated, Abe moved quickly to try to buy out the others' shares. He had the business appraised and offered Harold just slightly more than the appraised value of his 20 percent. Harold gladly took the money. Eleanore and Malcolm weren't so easy. Indeed, Eleanore was adamant about retaining her stock, and Malcolm offered Abe a true Hobson's choice—either he would sell his shares to an outsider, or he would turn them over to Jeffrey—Abe could decide. Malcolm and Anne also wanted Abe to agree to make Jeffrey a vice president. Personally, Abe believed he would have fewer problems with an outsider, but Susanne was uncompromising about wanting to keep her father's company within the family. For the sake of his marriage, and because his wife was both a stockholder and a director, Abe grudgingly agreed. Malcolm and Anne turned their stock interest over to Jeffrey, who also became vice president for manufacturing. "At least," Abe thought to himself, "if all goes as planned, manufacturing and wholesale sales will be a thing of the past within two to four years, and this kid will have to find something else to do."

Board of Directors

Prior to Joseph's death, the company's board of directors consisted of Joseph, who was chairman and CEO; Abe, who was president and chief operating officer; and each of the four children. The board met four times a year, received a brief report on operations and the latest company financial statement, and voted a dividend. Once a year, they went through the formality of reelecting the officers. Joseph used these meetings as opportunities to gather his family around him, and it was understood that the meetings were essentially ceremonial. No other meaningful business was transacted, as there was a tacit understanding and agreement that Joseph was in charge. Therefore, the board meetings, often scheduled around holidays, served as little more than joyous reunions for this close-knit family. Joseph had always been generous in gifting a portion of the dividends to his children; in the years following his wife's death in 1978, this portion had steadily increased.

After Joseph's death, Malcolm, Susanne, Harold, and Eleanore remained directors. Abe became CEO, the board was reduced in size to five, and the position of chairman went unfilled.

Abe

Abe Seiler was a high school physics teacher when he met and married Susanne Savenor. Susanne's father was openly critical of both his daughter's choice of spouse and Abe's choice of career. "He'll never be anything," Joseph had told his daughter on many occasions, "and just how happy are you going to be living on his salary when your hormones stop running your life?" Susanne knew that Abe was happy in his job, but after their second child was born, Susanne too began to worry about how they were going to survive.

After seven years of marriage, Abe went to work for his father-in-law in the purchasing department. Abe's style was abrasive, and it was only because of his concern for his daughter that Joseph intervened when Abe offended the workers by making what they considered to be unrealistic demands. After a while, the workers began to joke about Abe and essentially ignored him. Joseph, aware of the problems, nonetheless was insistent that Abe remain a part of the business. While it took pretty close to ten years, Abe finally began to like the business and actually got quite good at handling purchasing and finance, areas that did not bring him into close contact with the employees in manufacturing and sales. Later, despite his being second in command, he remained largely shielded from employee contact, those relationships being maintained by Joseph and Eleanore.

Eleanore

Eleanore Savenor had gone to work for her father immediately after graduating from Katherine Gibbs Secretarial School. Her whole life revolved around her family and, like her sister, she saw the employees at Savenors as family. Once a month, Eleanore and her sales staff would get together at Leonard's, a local restaurant, for lunch, and the group often entertained one another in their homes. Retired members remained very much a part of this network.

The Workers

Virtually all the workers at Savenors lived in North Deighton, within a mile or two of the plant—it was rare, even for a retiree, to move away—and most of them belonged to a local Portuguese church. Turnover at the company was virtually nonexistent. Employees tended to join the company after high school, a few completed college, and most stayed until retirement. In many cases, husbands, wives, and children of the same family all worked at Savenors at the same time.

376

The company had been late in instituting a retirement plan; thus most of the retirees lived on their Social Security and welcomed the small dividends they received from their Savenor stock. When one of them ran into trouble, he or she would go to Joseph Savenor, who invariably reached into his own pocket to help them.

Abe's Problem

Eight months have passed since Joseph's death, and Abe Seiler wants to move ahead with his plan to change the direction of the company. Deep down inside, Abe has a feeling that getting some of the members of the family and many of the employees to accept what he has to propose will not be easy. Not being a "people person," however, he really isn't sure why. He knows that his plan will make money and possibly even save the company from a severe downslide. But Abe has never taken courses on management, and he needs help to figure out how to get his plan accepted.

Does Abe Seiler have the power, insight, and ability to change radically his late father-in-law's company from a stagnating manufacturing operation to what he believes will be a more viable import and retail outlet operation with the potential for growth and expansion? Abe has limited power, as an outsider in a family-held business, and his credibility with at least some of the stakeholders is in question. To effect the change, Abe is going to have to do a meaningful stakeholder analysis and gain an understanding of how to convince at least some of those stakeholders that the move will benefit them without seriously damaging existing norms and interests.

Which of his interests can Abe realistically meet to achieve his ultimate goal, and how can he best go about meeting them?

Questions for Discussion

1. Analyze the group dynamics at Savenor Shoe Company and the roles of the members within the various groups, being sure to identify and discuss the areas of group cohesion, norms, stages of group development, uses/abuses of power, potential for intergroup conflict, ethics, and leadership.

2. Identify the resistances to change that Abe is likely to encounter, and suggest some ways in which Abe can reduce these resistances to introduce and manage the change that he is proposing. A graphic depiction of a force field analysis might help Abe understand your suggestions.

Procedure

Step 1   Draw a chronology of the events.

Step 2   Draw organizational charts of the board prior to 1990 and after 1990. It might also help to draw a chart of what is known of the present organizational chart at Savenor Shoe.

Step 3   Identify and analyze the relevant individuals and groups that are stakeholders who are likely to have an interest in the issue at hand. Explain why each of these stakeholders would resist and/or support the proposed changes.

Step 4   Do a force field analysis.

Step 5   Identify the macro and micro problems presented by the case.

Step 6   Give five to six recommendations for Abe to use in effecting the change.

70

THE PROVIDENCE PRIVATEERS*

Objectives

- To examine the impact of change on various stakeholders
- To understand how to analyze change management concerns
- To consider ethical and social implications of change

Background

The Providence Privateers is a major league baseball team located in Providence, Rhode Island. Like most small-market teams, the Privateers is plagued by numerous financial woes and is struggling for existence. Because of low television exposure, revenues are modest. In addition, the team just finished its fourth losing season in a row. The decreased attendance that has come with losing seasons has also caused a decline in other stadium revenues including parking, souvenirs, and food and beverage sales. Even in winning years, the Boston Red Sox, New York Yankees, and New York Mets cut deeply into the Privateers' market share, and with escalating player salaries, the situation is now a crisis.

The city fathers of Jacksonville, Florida, have approached the owner of the Privateers about moving the franchise to their city. If they become the Jacksonville Privateers, the city will build the team a state-of-the-art stadium and grant lease concessions in the early years. Additionally, favorable provisions in the deal would greatly enhance revenues from stadium-related parking, and food and beverage, merchandise, and luxury sky-box sales. It seems a deal too good to pass up.

The owner is convinced it is the right move for the team but is worried about how to announce the move and see it through. The Privateers have been playing major league baseball in Providence for over 100 years, and the community deeply identifies with the team. Small businesses around the stadium receive considerable income from fans attending the games, and it is clear that the impact on the community of the team leaving will be deep and far-reaching.

Your group is one of several consulting teams the owner has brought in to analyze the situation. The team that produces the most thorough analysis and set of proposals will ultimately be hired to help manage the move.

Instructions

1. *(30–60 minutes)*

Divide into teams of 3 to 5. Read the case, and prepare an analysis and five to seven minute presentation on the issues and problems of the case (see "Questions for Discussion" that follow). Prepare your presentation as if you would be making it to the team owner.

2. *(5–7 minutes each group)*

Present your analysis to the class.

3. *Discussion (open-ended)*

Discuss the merits of each analysis either immediately after each presentation or after all presentations have been made.

Questions for Discussion

1. Knowing what you do about managing change, what do you see as the situation and the relevant change management concerns?

2. What are some of the methods and actions you believe will be successful in managing the change? Why? What tactics are sure-fire losers and should be avoided? Why?

3. What are the strategic issues in the case in the political, economic, sociocultural, and technological domains?

4. Who are the primary, secondary, and tertiary stakeholders in Jacksonville? In Providence?

5. What are the key steps management should take to address stakeholder and strategic issues?

6. Are there ethical and social responsibility issues in the case? If so, what are they and what actions should management take to address them?

7. From a marketing perspective, should the team change its name, team colors, and logo? How would this help or hinder the change management effort?

THE SEATTLE FERRY COMPANY*

Klaus Wade worked as a deckhand on his stepfather's passenger and car ferry during the summer between his sophomore and junior years at Boston University's School of Management. Arriving at the loading ramp one morning, Klaus found the Coast Guard turning customers away as they attempted to board the ferry. Allegations had been made, a Coast Guard Officer told Klaus, that the ferry's engineer, Henrique Valdez, had been illegally dumping raw sewage and plastic bags of trash into the Sound. The Coast Guard continued to delay the ferry's departure for a number of hours until various crew members and the company's officers had been interviewed.

In addition to the problems with the Coast Guard, Klaus also learned that one of his fellow deckhands, a seventeen-year-old high school student from a nearby town, was in critical condition in a local hospital. Klaus learned that the deckhand had left work at 8 p.m. the night before, had driven his car along a country road at speeds estimated to have been up to eighty miles per hour, and had failed to make it around a particularly bad curve. He had been charged with "driving under the influence," and it was clear that, at the very least, he would not be back to work before summer's end. An investigation by the police revealed that the company not only had failed to prohibit on-the-job drinking, but that beer was actually available to the mostly-underage deckhands in large and unrestricted quantities.

Fortunately for the crew and the owners, the ferry continued to run despite the wide range of allegations that had been levied against it. These included not just the dumping and the accident, but also stories that the parents of several previous deckhands had filed complaints with the wage control board for unfair compensation practices by the company. The company, the parents alleged, coerced their underage children into working twelve-hour days without remuneration at even minimum-wage levels, not to mention overtime. The length of the day and the failure to compensate violated both state and Federal laws.

Public outrage and articles and editorials in area newspapers cast the owners, Klaus's stepfather, Dick Ahab, and his stepfather's brother, as evil villains. Demands for change followed public revelation of the events and the charges. The Seattle Ferry Company was ordered to change its practices. Klaus and the other deckhands wondered how severe the changes would be and whether some of the unpleasant parts of their jobs would still be worth doing without the fun and relaxed atmosphere that had attracted them to the jobs in the first place.

Background

The previous February, Klaus had called Dick Ahab to ask if he could work as a deckhand for the ferry company the following summer. Klaus didn't know his stepfather very well,

* Copyright 1992 by F.P. Roe. Used with permission.

since he and Klaus's mother had gotten married just shortly before Klaus had left for college. He knew that Dick was only minimally involved with the ferry company's operations and that Dick's brother had assigned day-to-day management of the ferry line to his son, Robert. He didn't learn until he was on the job that Robert showed up only a few hours a day, chatted briefly with the seasoned captains, and then took off in his little sports car, his golf clubs or tennis racquet propped obviously in the back seat.

Klaus liked the idea of a summer outdoors and had heard from a friend that the work atmosphere on the ferry was like a daily party. In addition, he knew that the money was good. Other than that, before showing up for work on the first day, Klaus had little idea of what to expect. He had spoken to Dick on the phone only briefly, although he had been puzzled as to why Dick had asked him to please not tell the others what their relationship was and to keep his eyes open.

"I'm not sure just what's going on up there," Dick had said cryptically. "This is really my brother's business that he wants to keep going for his son, but I have a financial investment in it, and as a co-owner, I also have legal responsibility."

"Anyway," Dick had said, "I'll sign you on as a deckhand. Show up at 7 a.m. on June 1st. You'll like the people. Most of the senior crew members have been with us for a long time, and we really depend on them to run the show and do the hiring. The deckhands are all high school and college kids like yourself. A lot come back year after year."

June 1

When Klaus reported, the captain "oriented" the newcomers with a whirlwind tour of the boat, explaining safety features, duties, and responsibilities. It was then that Klaus met the crew: a mate, an engineer, a bartender, a purser (to sell tickets), and six other deckhands. He was told that the captain was in charge of the ship and the safety of the passengers; the mate had sole responsibility for the deckhands; and the engineer maintained and oiled the engines and serviced the ship.

Tersely, the captain described what was to be the daily routine, barking it out like a drill sergeant: the entire crew would arrive by 7 a.m., the boat would be checked for cleanliness, and the freight would be loaded. At 8 a.m., passengers could board, and at 8:30, the cars were to be loaded. At 9 a.m., the two-hour trip would begin. Each crew member was to stay on his[1] assigned deck unless he had "wheel watch." This meant he was to stay in the pilot house and either steer a course assigned by the captain or point out buoys. When the boat docked on the island, the deckhands were to secure the boat, direct cars off, and help unload passengers and freight. Each deck was then to be thoroughly cleaned for the trip home. As soon as this was done, usually by 11:30, the crew was free until 4 p.m. at which time they were to report back to the boat to load it for the trip home. At exactly 5 p.m., the boat would leave, and another crew member would have a wheel watch. At 7 p.m., back on the mainland, the decks had to be swept and mopped. The bathrooms had to be cleaned and restocked.

Klaus began to have a shaky feeling in his stomach. Suddenly his ideal summer sounded like it was going to be a nightmare. "If I had wanted this kind of summer, I could have joined

---

1. All crew members were male.

the Marines," he thought to himself. "This is going to be hell." Klaus turned out to be right, but not for the reasons he expected.

The Ship Sails

For the first week, Klaus was assigned a deck on the boat that he and his partner were to monitor and clean. It didn't take him long to notice that the other deckhands spent most of each run sleeping, playing cards, and eating in the crew's quarters. Stefan, a college student returning for his second summer as a deckhand, explained, "They don't pay me enough to stay up there and answer passengers' dumb questions all day. It is so boring; nothing ever happens. And we all know that Jack, our fearless mate, never comes out of the pilot house anyway."

"Frankly, it's better that way," Stefan told Klaus. "When he's on deck, all he does is give orders and complain about how lazy we are. He thinks the only way to get us to work is to yell and order us around, but he's the lazy one. He never does anything but cause trouble."

"When he retired from the Coast Guard," Stefan continued, "they should have cut him loose at sea."

Klaus had noticed that once the boat pulled away from the ramp, the mate, Jack Daniels, sat in the pilot house drinking coffee and talking with the captain. He seemed to leave his duties up to Derek, a deckhand who had returned for his third summer. Derek checked the decks at the end of the day, assigned wheel watches, and made the "days-off" schedule. He wasn't particularly thorough, and he took good care of his friends. When a few of the deckhands showed up late and hung over, it was Derek who had to warn them, half jokingly, not to do it again. Jack didn't seem to notice.

A couple of times a week, during the layover on the island, Jack actually took charge. According to company policy, the boat had to be washed down twice a week. Jack's policy was to announce a wash day and prohibit anyone from leaving after the boat had been unloaded at 11:30. He seemed to do this entirely on whimsy, without any sort of advance warning to the crew. Instead of going to the beach or a restaurant, the deckhands scrubbed the boat. Since each deckhand was paid $50 a day, as opposed to an hourly wage, each received the same pay for going to the beach as for scrubbing the decks.

On wash days, Jack would watch the deckhands work and slowly check their progress. Rather than help, he yelled and screamed to prevent anyone from slowing down. Regardless of the finishing time, the deckhands stayed until Jack had meticulously inspected and approved the boat. Jack never helped clean; he simply searched for missed spots and insisted they be cleaned immediately.

An Ill Wind

One morning, a few weeks before Paul's car accident, Klaus had noticed a pattern of Paul volunteering to collect tickets. This miserable job required the unlucky deckhand to separate the different tickets—round trips, one-ways, adults, seniors, and children—as well as fielding questions. One windy day, a few tickets blew out of Paul's hand onto the ramp. In a scramble, Paul tried to pick them up. Leaning over to help, Klaus noticed that the tickets had no register printing on them. The purser had simply cut tickets the same shape as the receipts from the register and initialed them. This way the purser sold tickets that looked as if they had come out of the register. Paul collected the fake tickets with the legitimate ones, and at the end of the day, he sorted out the fake tickets and threw them overboard. Klaus suspected that by keeping the money from every fifth or sixth ticket, the two were stealing hundreds of dollars a day, with little chance of getting caught.

This was not the only way Paul had been stealing from the company. Every night, he and Stefan cleaned the main deck, which housed the bar. Each night, Liz, the bartender, gave them a case of beer in exchange for cleaning her bar. She alone was responsible for ordering and inventorying the supplies, food, beer, and hard liquor, so Liz knew that the beer would not be missed. Nobody else knew what she was buying, selling, giving away, or bringing home. At the end of the day, the receipts from the cash register only had to equal the cash on hand, so it was not until the end of the summer that it would likely become clear to anyone that something was wrong.

Klaus Wades In

Despite all of the problems, the crew continued to act as if nothing had happened. Jack spent every trip drinking coffee in the pilot house, beer continued to disappear from the bar, and the deckhands went right on sleeping or fooling around during working hours. When a new valve needed for pumping sewage into the proper holding tanks arrived, Valdez casually tossed it overboard and continued to dump sewage into the Sound. "They got the wrong size," he joked to Klaus. The company was clearly in danger of losing its license if changes weren't made.

About ten days after the problems at the ferry had been made public, Klaus was asked to meet with Dick over dinner. Arriving at his mother's house, Klaus saw Dick, his brother, Robert, and you (a management consultant), sitting around the table. After dinner, Dick asked Klaus to tell them what he knew. Carefully avoiding any mention of Robert, Klaus went into some detail about the beer, the thefts, the dumping, and a number of other problems that he had observed. When he was finished, Dick's brother and Robert became defensive.

"I suppose you think we ought to just fire everyone," Dick's brother challenged. "Well, I'm not going to. Those people have been loyal employees, and besides, there's no way we would be able to replace them fast enough to keep the ferry going for the rest of the summer. We'd just have to shut down."

"My interest in that ferry company is going to Robert in a couple of years, so we had better get this all straightened out," he added.

"I work hard at keeping that company going," Robert piped in. "But with all the paperwork that needs to be done every day, I can't watch over anyone once they leave the dock."

"Nevertheless," Dick told them. "Some changes need to be made or we're going to lose our license, so let's concentrate on what needs to be done and how we're going to do it."

Questions for Discussion

1. What sources of social power did Jack Daniels, Derek, the owners, and Robert have and use? How? Do you consider their uses of social power to have been appropriate? In what way(s) did their uses and/or abuses of social power contribute to, positively or negatively, the problems at the Seattle Ferry Company?

2. This case involves managing change. As a management consultant, what changes do you believe ought to be made and how? Set out for the owners what you believe the problems are and the resistances you expect them to encounter. Use of a force field analysis that identifies the driving and resisting forces might be helpful here. Be sure to use at least one of the models of change set out in the text.

3. Klaus has become a whistle-blower. Do you believe he did the right thing by telling Dick about events on the boat? Why? Why not? Was he correct to omit information about Robert? Why? Explain your answer in full.

HEALTHY SNACKS: A CASE OF FOOD FOR THOUGHT*

...rs a Sermon

...ph began, standing up and waving his arms dramatically. "I just want to deliver
...at's what I was hired for—that's what I'm going to do. I don't know why they
... do all this other stuff. We hardly have time to get the deliveries to the stores accu-
... on time as it is. What makes them think I can provide all these additional
...

... of the older route service representatives (RSRs) around the table nodded their
... agreement, while some of the newer reps just sat quietly. The rumors about the
...s in distribution were coming true, and the more vocal members of the group were
...ly voicing their displeasure. Ralph was one of these vocal RSRs—and he didn't care
...was listening. He was going to get his point across to anyone within earshot.

...Dale's is trying to do too much too quickly," he went on. "I don't know about you guys,
... I'm not going to 'sell' anything while I'm out delivering. I'm not going to change what I
... because some honcho in the head office thinks I should!"

The Dale's Heritage

Dale's Healthy Snacks, the market leader in healthy snack specialties, had come a long way
in the past twenty-five years. Dale's had been born through the vision of Dr. Dale
Wasserman, a pediatrician, and Dr. Yetta Robinson, a food engineer, in Boulder, Colorado.

Over the years of his practice, Dr. Wasserman had spoken with literally hundreds of
mothers who complained of having to wage constant war against their children's demands for
high-calorie, low-nutrition snacks. To meet this problem, he devised a health bar made of
ground fruits and nuts bound together with whole wheat flour, rolled oats, and fruit juice. For
the first six months, he kept a canister of the bars on his desk, using them as rewards for his
young patients. The children loved these healthy treats, and many mothers requested the recipe for home use. However, one mother, Dr. Robinson, saw the bars for a different kind of
potential.

"I have a number of contacts in the food processing industry," she told Dr. Wasserman.
"Let me work on the recipe, add some basic vitamins and minerals, and let's go into the
healthy snack food business. We can add other products as we go along."

Over the next twenty-five years, Dale's Healthy Snacks added more than two dozen products which they sold mainly in Colorado, Utah, and Wyoming. Deliveries were made by

* Copyright 1997 by Scott R. Handler. Used with permission.

a cadre of route service representatives who also stocked the racks in the small, independent shops that made up the bulk of the company's customers.

The Changing Healthy Snack Food Environment

In 1986, Dale's Healthy Snacks was sold to a large Dutch conglomerate. Since then, annual sales for Dale's products have increased almost three hundred fold. The products are now available in virtually every major grocery and pharmacy chain throughout the United States, Canada, and much of Europe. Today, the healthy snack food industry results in over four billion dollars of sales. For Dale's, the addition of Large Format Retailers (LFR), such as United Foods, has resulted in a dramatic increase in the public's awareness of healthy snacks and a huge increase in the percentage of such snacks sold outside of grocery stores in venues such as fitness gyms and school vending machines. A low-calorie line is also sold through diet and weight-loss centers.

However, with success had come competition, with many of the competitors offering larger profit margins and some retailers switching their allegiances to these newer brands. With these events, Dale's has begun to suffer a significant loss in market share.

Distribution: Changing with a Changing Environment

Under the new parent company, Dale's had handled its U.S. distribution through a combination of independent distributors and direct shipment through its own distribution services. The two systems, together, operated in forty-five locations throughout the country with many instances of two or three distribution networks servicing the same geographic area. The independent distributors promoted Dale's products with their own sales forces and were responsible for the entire sales process, from order-taking to delivery and from credit issues to returns. All of the other major health snack food manufacturers distribute their products exclusively through independent distributors.

Recently, Dale's changed its distribution structure for the continental United States and Canada. When Dale's executives reviewed their statistics, they recognized that the existing RSRs had over a half million contacts with retail outlets. Through a series of distributor non-renewals, Dale's completed a change to an entirely internal distribution system with twenty-five locations across the continent. Now, all aspects of distribution are handled by Dale's own RSRs.

Says Dale's manager of special projects, Walter Sheldon, "To take advantage of these numerous contacts, we need to insure that we can control the level of service that we provide to our customers. No other company in this industry will be able to match the service that we can provide. Even if they were to start today, it would take them at least five years to get 'on line.' This puts Dale's in a great position to fully utilize our competitive advantage of value-added service."

With the distribution system changes has come a restructuring of the jobs of the RSRs. Previously, they had been responsible only for insuring that deliveries to health clubs and nutrition centers occurred accurately and on time. Under the new system, the RSR position

account manager (RAM) position. A RAM will now be required to
ct but also to merchandise, rotate inventory, deliver and build displays,
d educate customers. To support this added responsibility, RAMs are to
nd-held computers that will allow them to process orders, credits, and
ot. Each RAM will service only ten to twelve customers per day, rather
twenty that an RSR currently visits.

an into Action

is change, Dale's has created the new job position of district manager (DM)
to train, motivate, manage, and evaluate the RAMs. Along with key account
e DMs and RAMs will work in teams and be given authority to "run their busi-
geographic region assigned to them.

positions have been filled by a combination of internal promotions and outside
ny of those who were hired from outside the company have a background in con-
ods distribution with companies such as Pepsi or Frito Lay. Those promoted from
ere exclusively from the sales force.

es has set up four pilot locations throughout the country in order to test various ways
viding this "value-added" service. Although Arizona has only been up and running for
onths, there has already been a ten percent increase in same-location sales. In addition,
ncreased service has caused some customers, particularly those with limited shelf space,
iscontinue competing products.

Under the current plan, all of North American distribution will switch from an RSR to a
AM based delivery system within the next five years. Over the next year, each RSR will be
given the opportunity to become a RAM. Meanwhile, district managers in the test markets
are to begin the process of training RSRs to take on RAM responsibilities.

Chicago's Pat Withers sums up his view as follows: "These guys are either going to shape
up or ship out. Sure, there may be some areas where RAMs aren't needed because of geographic constraints, and we may be able to keep a few of these guys in their current positions,
but that will be the exception. They need to realize that RAMs are the future. If they don't
want to take on the responsibilities of the position, then the 'out' door is right over there.
Hey, I've got enough to do just making sure this whole thing goes right. This is the new
Dale's. If they don't have the job skills to handle the position, I'll teach them—if they want
to take on the challenge. For those who don't, it's easier for me to hire somebody who
already has the skills and is willing. And I'm sure I'm not the only DM with this view."

Martine Chavez, the newly appointed DM for Florida, has a different view: "I believe that
most of the RSRs will be able to perform the functions of a RAM. They just haven't had the
proper training in order to fully use their skills. Once they see how easy it will be to fully
service our customers via merchandising, education, and informing customers of special
programs, they'll be champing at the bit to expand their responsibilities."

"In fact," she adds, "I'm more concerned that some of them will start to go too far too
quickly, and I'll need to reign them back a little. Sure a few need some polish, but they all
can function as RAMs if we give them a chance."

Reactions to Ralph's Sermon

In an effort to start the transition, all RSRs throughout the company have been given preliminary skills training in merchandising and selling. At present, they are expected to sell in simple promotional programs and provide merchandising services for Dale's customers. Contests have been set up for the RSRs, with baseball tickets, gift certificates, or sports clothes awarded to the best performers, as a way of supplying some additional motivation. Some of the newer RSRs have been hired based upon having the qualifications needed to perform the job functions of a RAM.

When the group broke up after Ralph's sermon, Jim Rose, a new RSR, pulled his buddy Steve Stendahl aside.

"I didn't want to say anything in front of the other guys," Jim whispered, "but I'm looking forward to these new RAM positions. This delivery stuff can get pretty old pretty fast. I mean, I've only been on for six months, but once you have the system down, the biggest challenge of the day is finding a new store that you've never been to before. I think all I need is a little training to handle the RAM duties."

Steve wasn't so sure if he could say the same.

"Yeah, I guess so," he replied. "Hey, I gotta go."

As Steve headed for his truck, he began to think. He had been near the bottom in all of the contests. In talking with the other RSRs, he'd learned that those near the top really could sell in promotions, while the rest of the guys, like himself, just passed out a summary sheet and hoped for the best. He was wondering if he really had the skills for the RAM position or whether he should start looking for a new job. There wasn't a DM in position yet for this area, so the training had been disjointed at best. Even so, Steve wasn't sure if any amount of training would help. Maybe Ralph was right—he just didn't have the time for all these other responsibilities. Maybe there would still be some RSR positions that he could fill. That certainly would be easier than learning all this new stuff.

As Steve got into his truck, he heard Ralph yelling from across the loading dock, "Happy Selling—NOT!"

Questions for Discussion

1. What do you see as the strengths and weaknesses of the management approaches of Pat Withers and Martine Chavez? If you were a district manager for Dale's, what would you do to motivate the RSRs to take on the new responsibilities?

2. In what ways could Dale's use its heritage and/or the current environment in the industry as a tool for motivating the RSRs both now and as they assume greater responsibilities?

3. What motivational techniques would you specifically avoid using with Ralph and his co-workers? Why? Are Ralph and Steve lost causes? What would you do to bring them "into the fold"?

4. How might the district manager promote the idea of a learning organization in this situation?

THE DEEP-WATER HARBOR

the role of stakeholders in resisting and driving change

e identifying driving and resisting forces to change

ce using force field analysis to assess and plan change

und

mmunity of about 750,000 citizens has recently voted to deep-dredge the natural on which your town is located. Just under $1.2 million has been allocated for com-ʒ the project, which the town hopes to raise through a bond issue. Any need for addi-. funding would have to be brought back to the town government for approval.

he dredging is part of a plan to develop a deep-water shipping port to meet the needs of fish-packing plant at which many of your town's residents are employed. Without the lity to bring larger boats into the harbor, the owners of the plant say they will have to ove their operations to a more favorable location.

Loss of the fish-packing plant could be an economic disaster for your community, which is already in severe financial decline. At one time, the town was a center for the timber industry, but environmental concerns have brought that industry virtually to a halt, and the sawmills have all been shut down. The rail lines that were used by the timber industry are still accessible and make the proposed deep-water harbor extremely desirable. Container ships could be unloaded in the harbor and the containers then moved by rail across the country.

Your town is also a summer haven for vacationers, sailors, and tourists. The population very nearly doubles during July and August. Families come from surrounding states to enjoy the pristine beauty of the harbor, the surrounding mountains, and the woods.

You have been asked to serve on a special committee to plan and implement the deep-water harbor plan. You know there is a need for the dredging as well as considerable resis-tance to it—some of which may be yours—but there is now a mandate that must be carried out.

Instructions

Step 1 (5 minutes)

Read the role you have been given and consider what your position should be with regard to the proposed plan.

Step 2 (5–10 minutes)

Working in groups of six, introduce yourself (in your role) to the others. Consider that you and they are members of the committee. Explain what your position is with regard to the proposed plan.

Step 3 (15–20 minutes)

Identify the driving and restraining forces involved in making this change, and illustrate them in a graphic force field analysis. Propose a plan for implementing the required change, given what you have identified in your force field analysis. The fish-packing plant is also faced with a potential change—to move to a new location. You may want to do a force field analysis of the driving and restraining forces for the plant move as a way to clarify further where you can best place your efforts in managing the proposed change for your town.

Step 4 (open–ended)

When you have completed your force field analysis and your plan, present it to the members of your class. In class discussion, consider the ways in which your force field analysis helped you identify the resistances to the proposed change as well as the driving forces favoring it. In what ways did disaggregating this problem help you to develop solutions?

ISSUING A BLANKET STATEMENT*

The Fire

At 11 p.m. on a cold Saturday in February, fire engines screamed toward campus as frightened students fled, some clad only in nightclothes, from Thompson Hall. Gathering in the parking lot, the shocked students watched in horror and amazement as flames shot out of the third-floor windows.

The commotion drew students from all over the small midwestern college campus, and soon the residence hall staff, comprised mostly of doctoral students, had all they could do to keep the growing numbers of students calm and away from the burning building.

"That's my room, that's my stuff!" Mark, a senior hockey player, bellowed. "I have to get my stuff!"

As he ran toward the building, Mark was intercepted by the resident director of Thompson Hall, Rob Martin.

"You can't go in there," Rob told Mark, as he grabbed him by the arm. "Look at it—my stuff's in there, too. Come on."

The entire staff of resident directors (RDs) worked quickly and efficiently throughout the night to ensure that the distressed students were safe. They escorted some to temporary quarters at a nearby hotel; others went to join friends in other dorms.

By 5 a.m., the weary staff was able to get a glimpse of the extent of the damage—the roof on the east side of the building was gone, three rooms on the third floor were destroyed by the fire, and many others throughout the building had been badly damaged by the smoke and water. Firemen threw charred bed frames and water-soaked mattresses out of the windows.

By mid-morning, word had come from the fire chief that the fire, which had started in a third-floor room, had been caused by a faulty electric blanket that had been left turned on and crumpled at the end of a student's bed. The chief ordered the lower floors of the building closed until renovations and safety inspections, expected to take about a week, were complete. The upper floors were to be closed for much longer. That afternoon, the residents of Thompson Hall, escorted by an RD, were allowed to enter the building, one at a time, to collect what remained of their clothes and other "necessary" belongings. Some students were relieved to find only very minimal damage to their belongings; others weren't so lucky.

"My shirt, where's my hockey shirt? It was right there, on the wall . . .," whispered Mark, as he stared into the black hole that had been his room.

* Copyright 1992 by Sandra L. Deacon. Used with permission.

"It's gone, Mark," Rob told him. "I'm sorry, but everything is gone."

"But it can't be gone—it, it was my dad's—he played for the Northstars—he wore it in his last game. I have to find my shirt."

When the Smoke had Cleared

At 8 a.m. Monday morning, four exhausted RDs gathered for their weekly staff meeting with their supervisor, Susan Howell, Director of Residence Life.

"Where's Susan?" asked Lisa, the RD of Drake Hall, the only all-female residence hall on campus. "She's late. How are you doing this morning, Rob? Have you been able to get any sleep?"

"Not much, thanks, and you?"

"Sorry I'm late, guys," Susan said, as she entered the conference room. "How's everybody surviving? The first thing I want to say is that you all did an incredible job handling the crisis this weekend. I couldn't have asked for anything more—from any of you! None of us has gotten much, if any, sleep these past two days. I hope you're all holding up. You guys are great!"

"I was just in meeting with President Dickerson. He was not happy. It seems that he heard from the fire chief; according to the chief, that building was a fire waiting to happen. When the firemen investigated the building, they found candles stuck in beer bottles and tapestries hung on the ceilings to cover bare light bulbs. Not only that, but they also found microwaves, toaster ovens, mini-refrigerators, and coffeepots. The building isn't under code to allow appliances in students' rooms."

"President Dickerson," she continued, "is furious. He asked why we don't have a rule banning appliances. I explained that we do have one—it's in the student handbook—but it hasn't been enforced. I tried to tell him how hard it is to enforce the rule without turning the residence halls into police states, but he's insistent. He wants all appliances removed from every room in every residence hall within one week."

"You're kidding."

"But I thought we had agreed not to go looking for that stuff or even enforce the policy when we came across something. It's a privacy issue."

"Yeah, the students already feel that we're on their backs because they're not allowed to drink in their rooms—we can't go and tell them that they can't eat either. They already think we treat them like kids."

"It's not that they can't eat; they just can't cook."

"But the cafeteria is only open until 7:00 at night, and most of the athletes don't finish practice until 7:30 or 8:00. I have a lot of athletes in my building. How can they eat?"

"Besides, it was a blanket that caused the problem—not a microwave." Susan listened intently to the discussion. "I know," she said, "you have some good points, but President Dickerson gave the order—all appliances have to be out of the rooms in one week—they can either ship them home or take them home, but we have to do inspections in one week, and anything we find we have to confiscate."

"One week? This is incredible. The students don't like us much as it is. I can hardly wait to see what happens when we start taking away their toasters."

Rob had been sitting quietly throughout most of the discussion. "You know," he said at last, "I agree with what you're all saying. But maybe it won't be as bad as we think. Most of the students were on campus to see the fire—and those who didn't actually see it burning can see the damage. We were really lucky that it happened when it did. Someone might have gotten hurt if it had been at 4 a.m. on a weekday. I think we need to give the students some credit; seeing all the damage, they just might understand why we have to do this."

"Maybe Rob's right," Lisa responded. "I guess they would be crazy not to agree with the policy. It's for their own safety."

"And ours," added Rob. "I don't want to be in a situation like that again, or lose everything like Mark."

"Speaking of Mark, how is he doing?"

"He's still very upset. He lost some pretty important things in the fire. But I've been talking with him about it. He'll be all right."

"I think we'll need to meet again this week," Susan told the group, "just to check in to see how everyone is holding up. If you can all meet with your students before Wednesday, we'll have another staff meeting that day to talk about what we need to do next. Thanks."

The Winds of War

"By the looks on your faces," Susan began, "I'm not sure I want to know how things went with the students. Lisa, why don't you start?"

"Yeah, sure. My floor meeting was awful—all they did was complain. They brought up everything, 'What do you mean we can't even make coffee in the morning?' 'We're not two-year olds.' 'Why did you ever let us have the appliances in our rooms in the first place?' 'How can we eat? The cafeteria food is lousy!' Shall I go on?" asked Lisa, exasperated.

"My floor meeting wasn't much different," said Pat. "The athletes, in particular, are really upset. Even the snack bar is only open until 10:00. They can't afford to order pizza or take-out every night after practice. They wanted to know why they were being punished for someone else's stupidity."

"I thought the snack bar closed at one in the morning," Susan said.

"It used to, but the students responsible for the late shift hardly ever showed up, so the manager just decided to cut out that shift altogether and close at 10."

"Susan, I tried to reason with them," Lisa insisted. "I really did. I told them that the fire could have been in Drake Hall just as easily as Thompson, but they wouldn't listen. I told them that the rule hadn't changed; it was always there in the student handbook, but now it was going to have to be enforced."

"Ditto," said Eric. "I had the same reactions in my hall."

"Rob, you've been pretty quiet. What happened in your meeting?" asked Susan.

"I'm kind of surprised that you all had such a rough time," Rob told the group. "My meeting went pretty well in comparison. I got all the guys together at the hotel and told everyone about the change. A few people started to complain, but then Mark spoke up. He said that he agreed with the policy and that it might help prevent something like this from happening again. I think a lot of the guys look up to Mark, and they're pretty sympathetic toward him, too—his father having died and all—and toward some of the others who lost so much. They seemed to agree with him. At least no one said much of anything after that."

Epilogue

After spending a week trying to explain the reasons for the no-appliance mandate to the students, the RDs were thoroughly frustrated. On inspection day, they found themselves confiscating truckloads of toaster ovens, hot pots, and other appliances.

Even Rob, whose students had initially agreed to remove their appliances, found that they seemed to have changed their minds once they had moved back to Thompson Hall. He, too, had to confiscate his share of microwaves and mini-refrigerators.

Questions for Discussion

1. Why are the students resisting the change to enforcement of the no-appliance rule, despite the clear dangers of keeping appliances in their rooms?

2. Using a force field analysis, identify the forces driving and resisting the change. Which of the forces resisting the change do you believe could be reduced? How and why?

3. If you were a member of the residence staff and had this change to manage, what would you have done differently to reduce the resistance of the students? Why? Be specific.

INSUBORDINATION OR STRUCTURAL CONFUSION
AT OMEGA HOUSE?*

Ellen, the program director of Omega House, a hospice, didn't get much sleep. She was wondering how to deal with the new development officer, George. He reported to her and was also part of a cross-program task force on fundraising within the Social Action Consortium (SAC), the umbrella organization for a variety of service agencies which included Omega. When Ellen had been a full-time nurse, she would fall asleep immediately after an exhausting but satisfying shift; she could leave the problems at work. Now that she had become a manager, she found that things tended to nag at her and keep her awake. Like today, George seemed to be insubordinate. She would never have spoken to her superior in the way he had spoken to her. Did he think he could get away with it? Did she appear unsure of herself? Was George confused over where his loyalties should lie? Ellen was accustomed to working in a team and found George's non-communicative approach disconcerting. She was puzzled as to how to deal with the situation. George's job seemed unclear, with him reporting both to her and the SAC development office chief who headed the task force.

Background

Omega House is a sanctuary to those terminally ill patients who need to find peace and dignity as well as the best in hospice care for their remaining days. It is a place where grieving families and friends can be assured their loved ones are receiving the best possible care, and it is a retreat in which all involved can gather to gain strength and support one another. (Paraphrased from an Omega House brochure.)

Omega House was started by a group that was unable to sustain it financially. In the early 1990s, SAC assumed responsibility for it. It is one of many services provided by SAC, an umbrella organization that brings together 17 different groups, both small social service agencies and donor organizations that wish to be involved in more direct service than merely funding the United Way. For nearly 80 years it has provided service to the less fortunate and disenfranchised. It provides a wide range of services: In addition to Omega House, there are assorted special projects in the field of education, services to refugees, shelters and apartments for those with special needs, services for people with HIV, addictions counseling, an inner city health program and emergency food assistance, compulsive gambling seminars, and political advocacy for such issues as the minimum wage, abolition of the death penalty and others. SAC's expenditures and revenues in 1995 were roughly $6 million.

* Copyright © 2000 by Asbjorn Osland, George Fox University; and Shannon Gustafson Shoul, Pacificorp. This case was first published in a Nonprofit Management Case Collection of the University of San Francisco's Institute for Nonprofit Organization Management and has been revised for publication in this edition of *OB in Action*. Used with permission.

Ellen and George at Omega House

Ellen began working at Omega House as a registered nurse in patient care five years ago. Then, just over a year ago, she became the program director, assumed the managerial responsibilities for Omega House, and was responsible for clinical oversight of patient care. Ellen felt very comfortable dealing with clinical care and was fortunate to have a strong clinical staff, an excellent and devoted kitchen crew, and a dedicated volunteer coordinator who organized the extensive services provided by the volunteers. However, she was less comfortable with her managerial duties in relation to SAC. The SAC administration, in her experience, had proven both capricious and autocratic.

George, as the new development officer, had no history with Omega House and seemed to spend most of his time with the other development people at SAC, working on the cross-program task force on fundraising. Ellen understood that any grant given to SAC could help Omega House; however historically, she had had to fight hard for resources. Thus, when George was assigned to her, she thought he would focus most of his attention on Omega House and its financial needs.

What's George Up To?

Ellen entered the kitchen early Monday morning and said, "Hi, Dan. What's for breakfast today?"

Dan, with his back to her, was gyrating to the rhythm of a CD. His blaring boom box carried the sign "No Enya." Dan's wide-ranging preferences for music ran from the church hymns he played on Sunday evenings to punk. Ellen was not quite certain where this particular CD fit on the continuum but took the liberty of turning it down. Dan turned and noted her presence. "Oh, hi you old bitty—don't you like my music? I suppose you'd prefer Enya or Musak," he said, in a playfully scornful tone. Then he approached and hugged her, stating, "It's nice to see you. What's up?" Their relationship was typical of the friendliness existing throughout the Omega staff—approachable, playful, and comfortable. Ellen loved this about Omega House and encouraged this warm and supportive behavior by being a role model.

While giving Dan a hug, Ellen looked over his shoulder and noted a tray of long-stemmed glasses sitting on the counter in the dishwashing area and asked, "Who passed on?" The glasses were used by the staff to honor the departure of one of the patients. The average stay was only three weeks, as the patients were terminally ill upon entry. To avoid developing the lack of feeling that one can find in service settings where people routinely suffer tragedy, the staff engaged in this ceremony each time someone died; they left a light on outside the person's room and shared a toast of a non-alcoholic sparkling beverage.

"Theo. He had been active all weekend. Fortunately, his immediate family was with him last night," Dan responded soberly. "Active" meant Theo had been showing the physical motions that were symptomatic of impending death. They both paused a moment before continuing. The customary, "that's too bad," did not seem to fit, as it was a hospice designated for terminal cancer and AIDS patients.

Ellen continued, "Say, what time did George come in on Friday? I was at the SAC office for a meeting. He usually comes through the kitchen. Did you happen to notice?"

Dan looked out the window and thought aloud. "Let's see. I had finished breakfast and was outside having a cigarette. It must have been after nine. He seems to come at about that time except for a couple of times a week when he comes in while I'm doing the breakfast dishes, which would make it after 10:30."

Ellen thanked Dan and went to the portion of the old estate house where the patients were located. Her office was immediately behind the nursing station. She liked to be close to the action and sometimes wondered if she was cut out for chasing after administrative staff, like George, who weren't communicating regularly with her and whom she would sometimes go days without seeing.

That morning, she dealt with the customary managerial concerns for the first half-hour and spent the balance of the morning reviewing the financial statements in preparation for a budget meeting the next day. She noted that while SAC's development efforts had seemed to improve funding for Omega, Omega's own fundraising efforts had resulted in little change from the previous year when they hadn't had their own development officer. Now that they had George, she had expected Omega's contributions to increase. She also noticed that George's salary was charged to a grant assigned in its entirety to Omega's budget. She thought to herself, "If George is working for Omega, these numbers ought to be changing. Since he's charged to Omega, I really should be more aware of what he's up to." She resolved to speak with George that afternoon.

Confrontation

Ellen walked up the stairs of the main part of the house to George's office, and Dan's boom box and deep voice could be clearly heard from the kitchen downstairs. She found George at the photocopy machine. When he saw her, he looked somewhat sheepish. Ellen noted that the yellow copies looked like fliers. She caught a glimpse of the image of a backpack and the words "hiker's association" before he hastily scooped the copies up and put them in the opened briefcase positioned unsteadily on top of the photocopy machine.

"Just taking a few minutes to make some personal copies—I brought in my own ream of yellow paper. I hope you don't mind," said George, avoiding her gaze. He then cleared his throat and proceeded, "What can I do for you?"

"I don't want you making hundreds of copies on our machine," Ellen responded. The paper is a minor expense, but the copies are not. It's leased, and we pay several cents per copy," she went on, as forcefully as she could without shouting. She had not wanted their meeting to begin this way.

"Understood," responded George quickly. He continued, "I'd be happy to reimburse SAC for the copies. I've done 300."

"That would be fine," Ellen responded. She paused briefly while he closed his briefcase and went to his office. She followed him. After he seated himself, he gestured to her to sit in the chair customarily occupied by Lisa, the university intern.

Trying to change the mood from the disciplinary to the collaborative tone she had intended, Ellen continued, "I want to compliment you again on the 'jazz night' last week. It went well, and I've received several calls from people who attended." She was referring to a fundraising event they had held the previous week; it was an evening on the lawn listening to a jazz band. She wanted to begin with something positive, even though she had discovered that Lisa had had a larger role in the arrangements than she would have expected from an intern.

"Well, that's what I'm here for," George answered.

Fundraising

Fundraising was a big issue with Omega and SAC. Some of the low-profile SAC programs had been cut recently, but Ellen felt comfortable that her program would be okay. She was concerned, nonetheless, since she wanted to upgrade some of their equipment and complete the remodeling of the facility. To do so, she needed more money, and George had been recruited for that purpose. However, he seemed to spend a lot of time at the SAC office working for the benefit of the overall organization rather than focusing on Omega.

Some of Ellen's uncertainty also stemmed from the autocratic style the SAC director used to manage the various programs. Sometimes the director seemed capricious in how she would arbitrarily fire program directors. Ellen regarded her as insensitive; the director would come in from time-to-time, unannounced, leading a delegation of visitors through the facility. Since Omega was caring for terminally ill patients, some of whom had AIDS, Ellen felt that such visits should have been handled with greater awareness of the patient's privacy rights. The director also tried to micro-manage many of the programs. She would make decisions about minutiae, sometimes change programs without consulting the program director, and involve staff from the various programs in SAC issues such as the cross-program task force on fundraising.

Ellen understood that this was a large concern for SAC, and she knew that George, who was assigned to Omega, needed to participate in this fundraising task force at SAC. However, Ellen was concerned that Omega's internal fundraising efforts were not getting the attention they deserved. It was apparent to Ellen that Lisa, the student intern, had assumed a leadership role, filling the vacuum left by George. However, Lisa was a student, temporary, and not in a position to supplant George.

With this in mind, Ellen told George, "I was wondering how it was going with the Omega committee you're leading for fundraising." Ellen had formed an internal committee comprised of both staff and volunteers, some of whom were donors, to generate ideas for fundraising. She had heard from committee members that George was difficult to communicate with and frequently did not attend the meetings of the Omega staff; she related this to him.

George responded assertively, "Look, I can't get the job done if I have to work in committees all the time here and at SAC."

Ellen reacted quickly and decisively. "I asked you to be on that committee," she said, "and I expect you to participate. The people on the committee have been a part of Omega for years and give us important creative input. Those who are donors also provide a lot of financial support. They are the ones who keep us going. You can't ignore them. Furthermore, they need your fundraising expertise."

George responded more cautiously this time, noting Ellen's displeasure. "I had no intention of leaving anyone out of the loop or avoiding the committee," he said. "It's just that I'm part of SAC's cross-program task force. I've had a few conflicts where I had to decide where to focus my energies. I have to do what SAC wants."

Ellen was now walking around the room. She listened, thought for a moment, and then said, "I understand that you need to coordinate your Omega efforts with the SAC team's overall development plans and may be asked to do things with them. However, when I tell you specifically what to do, I expect you to do it."

"Maybe you should speak with the SAC development officer so that we can all understand our jobs better," George told her defensively.

Ellen felt she was not getting through to George. "You're assigned here," she told him. "You come out of my budget. I don't see the confusion. Yes, I'll speak with the SAC development officer to make clear what it is I told you to do and why I want you to do it. But that won't change that you're working here for me. So please do as I say." With that, she turned and walked away.

Ellen felt that she couldn't have been more explicit. Later, on her way home, she reflected on the problem. George reported to her and SAC's development chief. She recalled how SAC's development chief sat in on George's interview with her and lobbied for George because of his skills which, he said, would round out SAC's development team. She also thought about his irregular comings and goings, the problems she had with getting updates from him, his abdication of his responsibilities to a student intern, and his personal use of the copy machine.

"With all of this in the picture," she wondered, "is the problem George and what appears to be irresponsible and non-communicative behavior, is it confusion over who is to direct his efforts, or both?"

Questions for Discussion

1. What organizational factors appear to be influencing the relationship between Ellen and George? In responding to this question, consider organizational factors at both SAC and Omega.

2. In what ways do you believe the problems with George are personal and in what ways do they appear to be structural? Why?

3. If you were Ellen, what would you do next? Why?

4. If you were George, what would you do next? Why?

Exercise*

Write three brief job descriptions for George, one as you believe Ellen might write it, one as you believe George might write it, and one as SAC's development chief might write it. Include in the job description a short list of what you believe George's duties should be, a clear statement of who his employer is, how he should divide his time, and how often and in what format he should report his activities to his superior(s). Explore also what you believe his responsibilities should be with regard to attending meetings and developing relationships with donors.

Explore the differences among the three job descriptions, and consider how these differing perceptions might lead to the problems described in the case.

How might a coordinated job description help George do his job more effectively?

* This exercise was written by Janet W. Wohlberg.

401

76

THE JOB REFERENCE: AN ETHICAL DILEMMA

Objectives

- To help students recognize opinions about others' ethical behavior

- To recognize the possible lax awareness of one's own ethical behavior

- To encourage students to consider the implications of their behavior

- To provide an opportunity for discussing relationships between personal behavior and professional responsibility

- To provide a vehicle for discussing theories of ethical behavior

Background

Ethics is the study of what is "right" and "wrong" in decision making. It involves beliefs, morals, attitudes, and actions. The discussion of ethics is particularly germane to organizational behavior and management education, and the discussion of ethics is now commonplace. Stimulated by American Association of Collegiate Schools of Business (AACSB) requirements, increased emphasis has been placed on ethics in management education within business schools. Some colleges of business include an entire course devoted to the coverage of ethics in their curricula.

Instructions

Step 1 (10 minutes)

Read over the personal assessment test on the Page 404, and answer the questions truthfully. This short test is for your eyes only and will not be collected or shared in any way unless you so choose.

Step 2 (10 minutes)

Read the short case entitled "My Friend Pat" and the "Questions for Discussion." Make whatever short notes you would like concerning what you think of Pat and how you might answer the questions.

---

* Copyright 2000 by Nancy E. Landrum, New Mexico State University. Used with permission.

Step 3 (10 minutes)

A student will be selected to briefly present the case and suggest some of the key areas of concern.

Step 4 (open-ended)

Discuss in class how you would answer the various questions. From time to time, check back to your self assessment test to see in what ways your behavior is the same as or different from that of Pat's. Think about the implications of those similarities and differences in terms of the standards you are now setting for Pat.

My Friend Pat: The Self-Assessment Test

Please use a checkmark to indicate a "Yes" or "True" answer.

Please leave the line blank to signify a "No" or "False" answer.

Have you ever:	In the past year, have you:	
_____	_____	stolen something from work, a friend, a family member, etc?
_____	_____	shoplifted?
_____	_____	lied or not told the truth?
_____	_____	cheated on a spouse or significant other?
_____	_____	kept merchandise or money when the sales clerk or company made a mistake in your favor?
_____	_____	lied on an employment application?
_____	_____	used illegal drugs?
_____	_____	cheated on a test or exam?
_____	_____	broken the law or committed a crime not already mentioned in this survey (excluding speeding)?
_____	_____	plagiarized another person's work?
_____	_____	compromised your personal ethics to do something required for your job?
_____	_____	switched the price tag on merchandise?
_____	_____	knowingly bought merchandise (perhaps for a special event or occasion), used it, and then returned it?
_____	_____	unhooked or tampered with the car's odometer?
_____	_____	falsified work-related expense, travel, or time records?
_____	_____	charged personal items to the company (Xerox copies, etc.) and didn't pay for them?
_____	_____	falsified a subordinate's performance evaluation?

My Friend Pat: The Case

You have just hung up from speaking with your friend Pat, and your supervisor is due in your office any time now.

You have known Pat for many years. You attended the same high school and knew Pat as an acquaintance but wouldn't say that the two of you were friends during that time. While you both enjoyed academic and athletic pursuits, Pat was rebellious and often in trouble. During high school, it was well known that Pat had been caught shoplifting but didn't suffer any real consequences. You had seen Pat cheat on exams in high school on more than one occasion. You also know that Pat had confessed to stealing money from his/her parents regularly. Friends told you that Pat often arrived late and left early from a part-time job at the local McDonald's but would write in the full shift on timesheets.

You and Pat both attended the same college nearly 500 miles away. You each majored in business, had a couple of classes together, and began sharing rides home. You got to know Pat, and you were even glad to see a familiar face while you were so far from home. You were both accepted into the college's M.B.A. program and, over the course of these college years, the two of you became good friends; you were even in Pat's wedding following graduation. Coincidentally, you both received attractive job offers (in separate departments) from the major employer in your hometown. You both accepted the offers and returned home.

Pat and his/her spouse frequently socialize with you and your spouse. They often come over on weekends, and you usually meet for lunch at least once a week. While Pat has matured and "straightened out" for the most part, you believe that Pat's ethical and moral standards are still sometimes questionable. For example, this past Fall Pat was caught in an extra-marital relationship. Thankfully, Pat and his/her spouse were able to repair their marriage and, as far as you know, this has never happened again.

Pat recently confessed to you that he/she lied to a supervisor to gain additional time to finish an assignment. Pat often copies and mails personal items at the company's expense and occasionally fails to report to payroll that a personal expenditure has not been deducted from a paycheck. Pat cheated on income taxes a few years ago. Pat also continues to smoke marijuana on occasion.

You don't mean to be keeping an ethics balance sheet on Pat, but the two of you have had several discussions regarding the questionable nature of these types of behaviors. You believe that these conversations have helped Pat to see things in a new light and may have positively impacted his or her behavior.

You have recently been promoted to District 4 manager. Your regional manager is on her way to meet with you to get your recommendation for filling the District 3 manager position. Pat has just phoned to ask for your support and recommendation for this position. To Pat's benefit, he or she has been a hard worker for this company, has had consistently positive evaluations, and is well liked. While you feel loyalty to Pat and know that Pat is a good employee, you also want to make a good impression in your new position. You wonder if Pat is really the best (and safest) person to recommend for the job.

Your regional manager has just arrived at your office. She gets right to the point, asking if you have any recommendations for the District 3 manager's position. Do you recommend Pat?

Questions for Discussion

1. What responsibilities or obligations do you and Pat owe to yourselves, the organization, your profession, your peers, and the business community?

2. What are the implications of Pat's and your behavior and decisions?

3. Does a company have the right to be interested in employees' off-work behavior? At what point does personal life spill over into work life?

4. Would the type of job make a difference in your recommendation (i.e., an international assignment)?

5. Should those in leadership positions be role models for subordinates?

6. Should friendships in the workplace influence decision making? Should Pat have asked for the recommendation?

7. How is Pat any different from you or me or the person sitting next to you? What is the implication in judging others when we may be guilty, too?

8. Finally, would you or would you not recommend Pat? Why?

PRICE FIXING AT ADM*
Part I

"For the first few years, I loved working at the company. I was very proud of ADM and how it operated. I was very enthusiastic about my work, very excited. And I am still impressed with much of the way the company does business, especially with the speed at which it accomplishes things."

Mark Whitacre (Whitacre and Henkoff, 1995, p. 52)

Mark Whitacre began working at Archer-Daniels Midland (ADM) in 1989. Less than a year later, he was placed in charge of a new division, one that produced lysine, an amino acid derived from corn used in swine and poultry feed to promote lean muscle growth. Mark was excited to be working with the company, proud of its success, and pleased to be a part of the organization. Mark's responsibility was to make sure that the operation was up and running smoothly and on time. He was well qualified for the position, with a PhD in nutritional biochemistry from Cornell and both an MS and a BS in animal science from Ohio State.

Mark was attracted to the lack of bureaucratic structure at ADM, the freedom he was given to run his department, and the opportunity to build a new division into a successful operation. Starting from scratch, the company's goal, and Mark's, was to become a leader in the lysine market. Mark was excited about his career potential at ADM.

The first few years went well for Mark. By 1991, the lysine plant was operational. The company's first priority was to build market share; profitability would follow later. ADM invested $150 million in the business to ensure the division entered the worldwide lysine market from a position of strength. They gained market share quickly, but ADM's entry into the lysine market resulted in a price war. Prices dropped from $1.30 to less than $.60 a pound. Production costs for ADM remained high, and the lower price was unprofitable. Mark, however, wasn't particularly worried.

"We decided that our first priority had to be market share and that profitability would come in the second phase. That's the normal practice at ADM" (Whitacre and Henkoff, 1995, p. 53).

From time to time, Mark Whitacre had heard rumors that ADM had been involved in price-fixing schemes in other divisions. Price fixing involves competitors establishing an agreed-upon price for a product they both sell. It is a serious criminal offense, subject to heavy penalties. Even so, Mark did not feel it would affect him directly.

"It was during my first year or so at the company that I started hearing about price fixing at ADM—in four or five other divisions. People said it was fairly common. I didn't see it, but I heard about it from people who were involved with it either directly or indirectly. It wasn't

* Copyright 2000 by Ronda Roberts Callister, Utah State University, and Mary Sue Love, Maryville University. Used with permission.

an everyday topic. But it was stuff I would hear a couple of times a month. And one thing people would tell me when it came up was to beware of Terry Wilson, the president of the corn-processing division. But I didn't give it much thought" (Whitacre and Henkoff, 1995, p. 53).

After the plant had been up and running for about a year Mick Andreas, vice chairman and son of ADM chairman Dwayne Andreas, and Jim Randall, ADM's president, told Mark that they wanted him to work with Terry Wilson. It was suggested that Mark consider Terry his mentor, someone who could teach Mark "the way ADM does business."

"It was phrased just that way: How ADM does business" (Whitacre and Henkoff, 1995, p. 53). Considering the rumors about Terry Wilson, Mark was very uncomfortable with this situation. He took this change "as a slap in the face."

"When they told me that, I had a strong feeling about what they were getting at, about what was coming next. I was thinking that we were going to get into some of the price-fixing activities that people had been warning me of…. My philosophy was, let's get this plant going full ahead, become the low-cost producer, and kick butt. Don't make deals with competitors. Go out and earn the business, and then take the prices up when you run everyone else out of the market" (Whitacre and Henkoff, 1995, pp. 53–60).

Mark did not feel that he had been given adequate time for the market to stabilize and for his division to turn a profit. At the time, Mark briefly considered looking for another position, but there was tremendous potential in building the lysine plant. In addition, there had been some talk that he might be in line to be ADM's next president if he was successful with the lysine division.

"That was the deciding factor in my staying. The presidency of Archer-Daniels Midland Company was a very appealing carrot" (Whitacre and Henkoff, 1995, pp. 60–62).

So Mark met with Terry, although with some hesitation. He came to the meeting prepared to discuss operations, but Terry only asked about market share, total market size and the names of the main competitors in the market. Terry wanted to schedule a meeting with the competitors, stating: "We're not blaming the losses at the lysine plant on you. Obviously we needed to get market share first, and that's what we did. That was stage one. But now we need to take this business to a different tier" (Whitacre and Henkoff, 1995, p. 54).

Soon afterwards, in April 1992, another meeting was arranged. Mark and Terry flew to Japan to meet with each of the two main competitors in the lysine market, Kyowa Hakko and Ajinomoto. At the initial meeting the reception was cool. ADM had just captured a full third of the lysine market and, in the ensuing price war, all companies were now losing money. Terry wanted to form an amino acids association, a joint effort that would promote and expand the lysine business. There was some interest from the Japanese competitors, so they arranged to meet again in Mexico City. At this meeting, Terry asked about everyone's production capacity and the estimated size of the total world lysine market. When the participants agreed on these numbers, Terry summed up the situation by saying the problem was that there was about 20 to 25 percent more production capacity than demand for the product. He multiplied the current price ($.60) by the demand and compared that to the price prior to ADM's entry into the market ($1.30); the difference was about $200 million.

Terry pointed out how much the customer was benefiting, not the people who had invested the money in building the plants. Terry made a comment, one that was common among ADM executives: "The competitor is our friend, and the customer is our enemy" (Whitacre and Henkoff, 1995, p. 55). No deals were made at that meeting, but everyone left thinking about the $200 million. Back at the office, rumors had started to spread that Terry had been brought in to fix prices in the lysine market. As Terry had no background in lysine, people figured that was the reason he was involved. Mark's concerns began to grow. Even though no crime had been committed, he still felt that he was losing some control over the operations of the lysine plant. Mark was worried about what Terry would do next, but he was committed to making a success of the lysine division.

Meanwhile the plant was having major production problems. Bacteria used in the production of lysine were contaminated, and production costs were soaring. In fact, costs of production were twice the market price. Many solutions had been tried without success.

Eventually Mark Whitacre began to suspect that someone was intentionally contaminating the plant. In a conversation with an engineer at Ajinomoto in Japan about other matters, Mark asked about the possibility of sabotage. The Japanese engineer neither confirmed nor denied his suspicions. Mark was left wondering if someone was tampering with the bacteria.

Mick Andreas, the vice chairman, suggested Mark continue the conversations with the Japanese engineer, perhaps offering a finder's fee for information that could help them solve their contamination problem. Mick even suggested that Mark make an offer to purchase Ajinomoto's trade secrets from their engineer.

Mick said: "Just think what the lysine technology would be worth to us. Sure the mole too, if there's one out there. But maybe the contamination could be better solved by having a better organism" (Whitacre and Henkoff, 1995, p.56).

ADM knew that Ajinomoto had been in the business for 30 years and may have perfected the process. However, after several more calls, it became clear that the Japanese engineer was not interested in the offer.

Dwayne Andreas, the chairman of ADM, called a friend at the FBI to have it investigate whether sabotage had occurred. Mick Andreas became very concerned about the FBI's ensuing arrival and called Mark Whitacre in to discuss the situation. Mick was obviously worried that his father had not considered all of the ramifications of bringing in the FBI. Allowing the FBI access into ADM's operations could spawn an additional investigation that might implicate ADM in wrongdoing.

To try to ensure that the FBI had no reason to expand their investigation, Mick wanted Mark to be honest about the contamination problem but less than honest about two things: First, Mark should imply that Ajinomoto's engineer had contacted them about purchasing Ajinomoto's technology, not the other way around. Second, Mark should tell the FBI that he used a company phone line at home when he talked to the Japanese engineer, although he actually used his personal line.

Mark felt strongly that ADM was close to negotiating a lysine price with the Japanese firms and also knew that ADM had been implicated in an illegal technology purchase in the past. Mark suspected that Mick wanted to downplay any hint of wrongdoing on ADM's part. If Mark implied that Ajinomoto's engineer had contacted them about the technology purchase and indicated the conversations had taken place on a different line, ADM would almost certainly avoid a detailed investigation by the FBI. A meeting was arranged between Mark and FBI agent Brian Shepard.

Questions for Discussion

1. If you were Mark, would you follow Mick Andreas' directions exactly? If not, what would you tell the FBI? Why?

2. If you were Mark, would you go along with Mick's requests, tell the truth about the phone calls, or tell them everything including the rumors about price fixing? Why?

APPENDIX

CAREER DYNAMICS

MAKING THE IDEAL JOB COME TRUE*

Background

This exercise has been designed to help you better understand the concepts of career development. The first two parts of the exercise are meant to give you a chance to reflect on your own career aspirations. These can be done either in or before class. The third part of the exercise requires you to role play the part of a human resources manager helping an employee develop a plan for meeting his or her career goals.

The Task—Part A

Record detailed responses to the following:

1. Identify the ideal job for you when you graduate from college. What would your job title be? What, specifically, will your responsibilities be?

2. Draw a line down the middle of a piece of paper. Title the left column "skills" and the right column "where/how skill was learned." Use these columns to record your answers to the questions: What specific skills do you have that make you the right person for your ideal job? How did you acquire those skills?

The Task—Part B

Record detailed responses to the following:

1. Identify the ideal job for you *five years after the job* you wrote about in Part A. What will your job title be? What, specifically, will your responsibilities be?

2. What specific skills and experiences will you have that make you the right person for the job? How do you plan to acquire those skills?

3. What do you think is the responsibility of the company for which you work in helping you acquire those skills and experiences? What can your company do over the first five years of your employment with them to help you prepare for this new position?

4. What are the advantages and disadvantages for your company in helping you obtain new skills?

* Adapted from Wendell French, *Human Resources Management* (Boston: Houghton Mifflin Co. 1998). This exercise was prepared by Mia Louik, The Rappay Group, 1075 Main Street, Williamstown, MA 01267. Used with permission.

The Task—Part C

Working with a partner, do the following:

1. (20 minutes)

Have one of you take the role of a manager or human resources professional and the other the role of an employee. Based on the employee's responses to Part B of this exercise, develop a plan to help the employee realize his or her five-year career goal. Create a timeline that depicts the steps the employee will take over the next five years to achieve his or her goals.

2. (20 minutes)

Reverse roles, and proceed as in Question C1 above.

TED JOHNSON A*

Ted Johnson is a twenty-year-old sophomore at Hurry State, a large university in the Northeast. Since he had to declare a major by the middle of his junior year, Ted decided to take a "Self-Assessment and Career Planning" course as an elective. Through the course, Ted hoped to get more focused beyond his general interest in business.

Since Ted was halfway to graduation—and the dreaded "real world"—he decided to examine the self-assessment exercises he had recently completed with the hope that he could locate some trends or themes. Ted chose his interests survey, skills exercises, and his autobiography as starting points.

Ted's "story" showed a love of the outdoors. Having grown up in western Nebraska, Ted was used to a horizon that stretched as far as the eye could see—a view best appreciated from on top of a horse. On his family's thousand-acre cattle ranch and farm, Ted helped with odd jobs almost from the time he could walk. In addition to herding cattle, he loved to sit down with his father and go over the books. A farmer had to be an effective businessperson, and Ted seemed to have a natural talent for bookkeeping and finding "missing" entries. By age sixteen, Ted was handling the books and tracking the ranch's expenses. In high school, Ted excelled in his science and math courses, including biology, chemistry, and calculus. Although he had little time for extracurricular activities, Ted played on the soccer team and was the star of the chess club.

As Ted looked back on his life in Nebraska, which seemed awfully far away, his attention shifted to his interests survey. Many of Ted's experiences fell into the "realistic" area, but his highest scores were "investigative." His scores were supported by his behavior as a child; he was always asking "why?" Questions like why people ate cows when cows did not eat people always seemed to pop into his head. His problem-solving ability was very useful on the farm, but Ted wanted to experience life "back East" and get the broader perspective of a business education. On the interests survey, Ted scored fives on solving math problems, predicting what people would buy, solving a mystery, and organizing information.

Ted's key skills from his exercises included tending animals, planning and organizing, observing, initiating and changing, making decisions, analyzing problems, and generating ideas. Ted felt this information was accurate; he saw himself as a bit of a loner who was not afraid to take risks, such as coming east to go to school. Ted's parents were already pushing for his return after graduation, if not to the ranch, at least to their part of Nebraska. Ted had decided, however, that while visits to the farm were fine, he needed to work in a faster-paced environment. His mother suggested an accounting position in Scottsbluff, a town of 20,000 people near the ranch. He thought he might consider Omaha, a city of 500,000 people, about 400 miles from the ranch. An accounting position was not, however, attractive to Ted; he had no interest in sitting at a desk all day.

* Copyright 1992 by Bruce Leblang. Used with permission.

Now Ted was facing a number of major questions:

1. What subject areas within business might he study that would best fit his interests?

_____

_____

_____

_____

_____

2. How could he find a summer job or internship that would use his problem-solving skills but not chain him to a desk?

_____

_____

_____

_____

_____

3. What types of jobs would allow Ted to use the skills and interests he had identified?

_____

_____

_____

_____

_____

4. What do Ted's parents want him to do after graduation? Do you think this will pose a problem for Ted? Why or why not?

_____

_____

_____

_____

_____

TED JOHNSON B

Ted Johnson recently completed his junior year at Hurry State and now is enrolled as a first-semester senior. At this time, he is facing a number of major life decisions, including deciding the type of work to go into, where to locate, and how to balance personal and family commitments.

At his parents' urging, Ted returned to the family ranch this past summer. Through friends of his parents, he was able to land a job as an assistant to Dave Jackson, an insurance claims adjuster whose territory includes most of western Nebraska. During the previous year, Ted had done a lot of thinking about different jobs he might want to try; he also had talked to numerous alumni through his school's alumni advising network. Now, through a stroke of luck, he'd found a possible answer to his career questions. Working with Dave, figuring out how accidents really happened, and learning a lot about human nature, Ted felt he had discovered a job that wouldn't "chain him to a desk." At the end of the summer, Ted received an informal job offer from Dave, as well as an excellent letter of reference.

Although Ted wasn't planning to go back to Nebraska, he was very interested in becoming a claims adjuster. After getting back to Hurry State and talking to some friends, Ted began to question his plan. Denny, Ted's roommate and best friend, had a typical reaction. "Ted, insurance adjusters are the scum of the earth and, besides, you don't even need a degree to be one." Clearly, insurance adjusting was not a high-status profession, at least not among his friends back East. Ted felt that he could accept their comments as long as he was doing something he liked. Still, if Denny got a job with a company like P&G or in a major bank—well, he didn't really know how he'd react.

Ted was also dealing with the issue of where to live. After his "internship" with Dave Jackson, Ted felt he could learn how to be a claims adjuster and get a job in many areas of the country. Living on the ranch, or in the nearby town of Scottsbluff, seemed terribly boring after being in Boston, the home of Hurry State. After the summer, Ted realized he needed the excitement of living in a big city. Recently, he had visited friends in Chicago and had "fallen in love" with the city. Even though the city was huge, it still had a Midwestern down-to-earth feeling that made Ted feel at home.

Soon after his visit, Ted described his visit to Chicago to his parents during their weekly phone call. As soon as Ted had finished breathlessly describing his trip—"it was awesome"—Ted's father expressed his disappointment.

"Gee, son," he said, "we only want what's best for you. You know, Chicago is kind of far. What about Lincoln or even Omaha?"

Ted's mother followed with, "Ted, isn't Chicago a bit dangerous? What's wrong with Nebraska? Isn't Lincoln big enough for you?"

416

Now, with just a few months before graduation, Ted felt overwhelmed and confused. Didn't he owe something to his parents? As the only son, should he take over the ranch or at least live nearby? Finally, could he accept a job in a field with low status?

Ted wondered what his friends and family would say about his decisions and how much he might care about their reactions.

Questions for Discussion

1. What are the main decisions Ted is facing?

2. How would you resolve Ted's career dilemma?

3. How should Ted deal with his parents? What are his responsibilities toward them?

4. How should he decide where to live?